World War I in American Fiction

D1595619

World War I in American Fiction

An Anthology of Short Stories

Edited by

Scott D. Emmert

and

Steven Trout

THE KENT STATE UNIVERSITY PRESS

Kent, Ohio

© 2014 by The Kent State University Press, Kent, Ohio 44242
All rights reserved
Library of Congress Catalog Card Number 2013043043
ISBN 978-1-60635-196-3
Manufactured in the United States of America

LIBRARY OF CONGRESS CATALOGING-IN-PUBLICATION DATA
World War I in American fiction : an anthology of short stories /
edited by Scott D. Emmert and Steven Trout.
pages cm
Includes bibliographical references and index.
ISBN 978-1-60635-196-3 (pbk.) ∞
1. World War, 1914–1918—Fiction.
2. Short stories, American.
3. American fiction—20th century.
I. Emmert, Scott, D., editor of compilation.
II. Trout, Steven, 1963– editor of compilation.
PS648.W64W67 2014
813'.0108358403—dc23
2013043043

18 17 16 15 14   5 4 3 2 1

Contents

Acknowledgments

The twenty-six short stories included in this anthology (many never reprinted before) offer a window into a complex and pivotal moment in American history. Readers already familiar with First World War literature will note the omission of several works by well-known authors. Some of these carried prohibitive permission fees; the editors cleared others from the table of contents to make room for less familiar narratives. The literary quality of the selections varies tremendously, but each is absorbing in its own way.

The editors wish to acknowledge, with gratitude and sincere appreciation, all of the people who helped to make this book possible: Joyce Harrison at The Kent State University Press for her expert counsel and guidance; Michelle Webb for her painstaking efforts as copyeditor and manuscript formatter; Erin Holman, also a keen-eyed copyeditor, for improving the manuscript; Dr. Robert Winter and Dr. A. L. McLeod for permission to reprint Claude McKay's "The Soldier's Return"; Diana Lachatanere of the Schomburg Center for Research in Black Culture for information on Claude McKay's "The Soldier's Return"; Richard F. Allen, son of Hervey Allen, for permission to reprint "Bloodlust"; Brainerd F. Phillipson, grandson of Thomas Boyd, for permission to reprint "The Kentucky Boy"; Sally St. Leger Stallings, daughter of Laurence Stallings, for permission to reprint "The Big Parade"; Michael J. Frederick, grandson of *Midland* editor John T. Frederick, for assistance with stories from that magazine; Ann Y. Evans (White Homestead / Springs Close Family Archives) for her helpful responses to our inquiries regarding Elliot White Springs's "Big Eyes and Little Mouth"; Claggett Wilson Read, great nephew of Claggett Wilson, for his generous assistance with *Runner through the Barrage—Bois de Belleau;* Chris Chamness (retired) and Kelly Johnson, academic librarians extraordinaire at the University of Wisconsin–Fox Valley, for their diligence and success with numerous interlibrary loan requests; the University of Wisconsin–Fox Valley Professional Development Committee and Campus Dean and CEO Martin Rudd for subvention funds; the University of Wisconsin Colleges English Department Professional Development

Committee for subvention funds; Sarah White, coordinator of Facilities and Campus Services at University of Wisconsin–Fox Valley, for assistance with photocopying and mailing; Andrzej Wierzbicki, dean of the College of Arts and Sciences at the University of South Alabama, for his support of research on the part of department chairs; Jennifer Haytock, Jennifer Keene, Janis Stout, Edward G. Lengel, and Mark Whalen for their invaluable scholarly assistance and encouragement; Angela Williamson Emmert for, well, everything; and Maniphone Sengsamouth-Trout for, well, everything too.

Permission Acknowledgments

"*Among the Trumpets*" story © SEPS licensed by Curtis Licensing Indianapolis, IN. All rights reserved.

"Count Lothar's Heart" by Kay Boyle. Copyright 1936 © Kay Boyle. Reprinted by permission of the Estate of Kay Boyle.

"One Hundred Percent" by Leo V. Jacks. Reprinted with the permission of Scribner, a Division of Simon & Schuster, Inc. from SCRIBNER'S MAGAZINE, November 1928. Copyright ©1928 by Charles Scribner's Sons. All rights reserved.

"Pale Horse, Pale Rider" from PALE HORSE, PALE RIDER: THREE SHORT NOVELS by Katherine Anne Porter. Copyright 1937 by Katherine Ann Porter. Copyright © Renewed by 1965 by Katherine Anne Porter. Reprinted by permission of Houghton Mifflin Harcourt Publishing Company. All rights reserved.

"Pale Horse, Pale Rider" used by the permission of The Permissions Company, Inc., on behalf of the Katherine Anne Porter Literary Trust.

"Poor Little Black Fellow" from THE WAYS OF WHITE FOLKS by Langston Hughes, copyright © 1934 and renewed 1962 by Langston Hughes. Used by permission of Alfred A. Knopf, a division of Random House, Inc. Any third party use of this material, outside of this publication, is prohibited. Interested parties must apply directly to Random House, Inc. for permission.

"Private Walker Goes Patrolling" by Victor R. Daly. The Kent State University Press wishes to thank the Crisis Publishing Co., Inc., the publisher of the magazine of the National Association for the Advancement of Colored People, for the use of the material first published in the June 1930 issue of *The Crisis*.

Introduction

SCOTT D. EMMERT AND STEVEN TROUT

For nineteen months in 1917 and 1918, the United States experienced the upheaval of total war. In the blink of a proverbial eye, the nation's military grew from a few hundred thousand regulars to a force of more than 4 million citizen soldiers and sailors. Entire industries, including the country's railroads, fell under federal control; labor agitation and political dissent became felonies punishable with imprisonment; and ubiquitous war propaganda replaced rational public debate, causing German Americans to face widespread suspicion, abuse, and even lynching. Meanwhile, as women from coast to coast took up "men's work" (and found, in many cases, that they liked it), large numbers of African American workers left the Deep South for wartime industries in the North, where they met with a new wave of racial hostility. Americans of all descriptions on the home front did without, "Hooverizing" to save food for the troops. And in the inferno of the Western Front, approximately fifty thousand American soldiers were killed, more than four times that number wounded, on poison-gas-soaked, barbed-wire strewn battlefields of unimaginable devastation and gruesomeness. Half of these men died during less than two months of fighting in the fall of 1918, one of the deadliest periods in American military history. Unknowingly carried to Europe by the boys who were heading "over there," the Spanish flu claimed the lives of an additional fifty thousand American troops and simultaneously ravaged civilian populations throughout the United States, evoking comparisons with the medieval Black Death. In short, more than any other event during the Progressive Era, the Great War represented the signature of the twentieth century writ large—change, unstoppable and sweeping.

This turbulent historical period inspired more than two decades of intense examination by some of the nation's finest authors, a body of writing arguably unmatched in depth or complexity by the literary response to any other American conflict prior to Vietnam. Indeed, the literature of World War I bore little resemblance to that which shaped popular memory of the nation's original Great War—the Civil War. From a literary standpoint, the conflict of 1861–65 was an affair of generals, with Ulysses S. Grant's two-volume memoir as its standout masterpiece. Surprisingly, few accounts by enlisted men received much attention, and while fiction by former officers John W. De Forest and Ambrose Bierce evoked the war's terror, a young writer born six years after the war produced the most memorable account of combat as soldiers of the blue and the gray had actually experienced it. Published in 1895 and mistaken by many veterans as the work of an eyewitness, Stephen Crane's *The Red Badge of Courage* imagined the Civil War in a way that was far from standard in the literature of the time—namely, from the perspective of an ordinary soldier.

In contrast, books by top-level World War I commanders left little lasting impression with readers. Even John J. Pershing's memoir, *My Experiences in the World War* (1931), which won the Pulitzer Prize in 1932 (more in recognition of Pershing's military service than his writing ability), and Hunter Liggett's eagerly anticipated tell-all, *Personalities and Reminiscences of the War* (1925), never achieved the status of classics. Nor did works by foreign military leaders, including Germany's Eric Von Falkenhayn and France's Ferdinand Foch, find much lasting favor in America. Literacy rates among Americans in the 1910s, far higher than those of the mid-nineteenth century, combined with mass enlistments on the part of the nation's more educated citizens (male and female alike) to foster a literature that captured the Great War much closer to ground level—as experienced not by multiple-star generals but by lower-ranked soldiers and Marines, volunteer ambulance drivers, and nurses and relief workers.

American writers who approached the Great War via the novel did so at an especially exciting moment in the history of the genre. By the 1920s, novelists had at their disposal not only the conventions of literary realism and naturalism, both of which had dominated serious American fiction throughout the late nineteenth and early twentieth centuries, but also a host of new techniques for rendering consciousness and time—and for capturing that sense of disconnection from the past, that feeling of the *modern,* which the war had intensified. The list of significant American World War I novels is long and varied, and it includes contributions by nearly every major American modernist of the 1920s and 1930s. Among the titles: John Dos Passos's *Three Soldiers* (1921) and *1919* (1932), e. e. cummings's *The Enormous Room* (1922), Willa Cather's *One of Ours* (1922), Thomas Boyd's *Through the Wheat* (1923), Edith Wharton's *A Son at the Front* (1923), Laurence Stallings's *Plumes* (1925), Ernest Hemingway's *The Sun Also Rises* (1926) and *A Farewell to Arms* (1929), William Faulkner's *Sartoris* (1929) and *A Fable* (1954), Dorothy Canfield's *The Deepening Stream* (1930), William March's *Company K* (1933), F. Scott Fitzgerald's *Tender is the Night* (1934), Humphrey Cobb's *Paths of Glory* (1935), and Dalton Trumbo's *Johnny Got His Gun* (1939). Add to this list works in which the war is critical to the action, though not necessarily in the foreground, and the conflict's footprint on the American novel grows larger still. World War I, we recall, brings Fitzgerald's Jay Gatsby into tragic orbit around Daisy Buchanan. Returning doughboys parade down the Main Street of Sinclair Lewis's Gopher Prairie. And Cather's Professor St. Peter never recovers from his protégé Tom Outland's death on Flanders fields. Later in the twentieth century, World War I enters Ralph Ellison's *Invisible Man* (1952) through the mob of shell-shocked former soldiers featured early in the novel and serves as the inspiration for "National Suicide Day," a grotesque parody of military commemoration devised by a black World War I veteran in Toni Morrison's *Sula* (1973).

No less worthy of study, if less widely known today, are the literally thousands of American short stories that the war inspired both while it was underway and during the subsequent decades when Americans struggled, through competing cultural efforts, to define its memory. Indeed, war-related short stories became so numerous in 1917 and 1918 that they provoked a satirical response from Edith Wharton in a short story of her own (included in this collection). In Wharton's "Writing a War Story" (1919), "Miss Ivy Spang of Cornwall-on-Hudson," a volunteer nurse with nonexistent literary talent, becomes swept up in the writerly vogue for war fiction—until she learns the truth about her patently dreadful work from a hospitalized novelist. This anthology, the first of its kind, presents a sampling of American World War I short fiction in its full range, juxtaposing works of high modernism with those cast in earlier literary idioms, masterpieces by the likes of F. Scott Fitzgerald and Katherine Ann Porter with culturally revealing work by writers with more modest talents (though none, it is hoped, as modest as Ivy Spang's), and visions of war crafted by members of the nation's Anglo elite with counter-narratives offered by African American authors. Some of the latter, gleaned from the pages of African American periodicals such as the *Crusader* and *Crisis,* are reprinted here for the first time.

The reader will encounter many surprises. For example, much of the wartime writing included in this collection is artistically richer than one would expect, especially given the formidable reach of the federal propaganda effort led by public relations guru George Creel. Despite the best efforts of Creel's thoroughly Orwellian Committee for Public Information, which extended its influence into seemingly every corner of the mainstream publishing industry, ambiguity and dissonance never completely disappeared from 1917–18 vintage American writing. Stories created amid the feverish conditions of total war may have denounced the evil Hun (as expected), but often denunciation extended to war itself. And the line between the two becomes especially blurred in sophisticated stories like Dorothy Canfield's "The Permissionaire" (1918), a work of propaganda by a writer whose instincts led her away from the simplistic dichotomies and the absence of subtlety that propaganda demands. By the same token, stories that remember the war, as opposed to depicting it while it was underway, present conflicting memories.

Some of the post-Armistice pieces in this collection express the kind of pacifist sentiment, fueled by disgust with the conditions of modern warfare and contempt for Wilsonian idealism, that critics have long expected of American World War I literature. Others speak for what may have been (with apologies to Richard Nixon) the great silent majority of Americans in the 1920s and 1930s—those who feared further entanglements with Europe but who continued to honor American military service and wartime sacrifice. To read this collection is to see a memory landscape full of volcanic activity and fault lines, not the uniform wasteland that has served for so long as a backdrop for the so-called Lost Generation.

Published ten years before the United States entered the Great War, the opening story, Willa Cather's "The Namesake" (1907) is offered as a prelude, serving as a snapshot of the martial romanticism that lurked beneath the nation's fragile commitment to neutrality and that would run amok in 1917 and 1918. Recalled from his Paris studio to rural Pennsylvania to tend to his ailing aunt, the story's protagonist, Lyon Hartwell, is a sculptor who specializes, despite his expatriation, in American Civil War monuments. During the months in his aunt's home, Hartwell becomes fascinated by the personal effects of a long-dead uncle, a Union drummer boy killed literally at the mouth of a cannon during an attack on a Confederate fort. At the story's climax, the Frenchified aesthete gives way to American patriot as the story of Hartwell's heroic ancestor inspires the artist to feel for the first time "the pull of race and blood and kindred," a catharsis that ultimately inspires his best military statue. Among other things, this tale of war memory, identity, and art—a creative nexus Cather would later draw upon when writing *One of Ours* as a memorial to her cousin G. P. Cather, who died fighting in World War I—points to martial values deeply rooted in early-twentieth-century American culture. Though not entirely free of irony (the actual details of the drummer boy's death represent patriotic gore at its most grotesque), "The Namesake" enacts what historian George Mosse, in his study of twentieth-century nationalism, has called "the cult of the fallen soldier," a set of cultural practices that enlisted the war dead in continued service to the state.[1] Cather gives us a version of this cult tied to the Civil War. Through his death *for* the nation, Hartwell's uncle becomes a patriotic icon *of* the nation. And through his hero-worship of this icon, Hartwell becomes, for the first time, a true American.

Richard Harding Davis's story, "The Man Who Had Everything" (1916), evokes the frustrations and ambiguities of neutrality. Heavily influenced by Rudyard Kipling, as seen through its focus on a clublike group of male newspapermen, the story reminds us that Kipling was, for a time, the most popular writer in the English language. Indeed, his distinctive style, a combination of various professional discourses infused with proto-modernist ambiguity, can be heard throughout this anthology and was just as widely copied during the first two decades of the twentieth century as Hemingway's terse declarative sentences and lopped-off dialogue tags would be later. However, while evoking the stylistic and thematic territory of Kipling, "The Man Who Had Everything" focuses on a peculiarly American dilemma. Set in Salonika, the story examines the ethical issues that come into play when one "Mr. Hamlin," an American serving in the British army, decides to desert and approaches his fellow countrymen—the group of journalists—for assistance. Ironically, the would-be deserter, "the man who had everything" described in the title, joined the Allied cause primarily to amass material for future books, articles, and lectures about the greatest war of all time, and his tales of frontline violence and grotesquery are the envy of the American newspapermen. But after nearly two years at the front, this once-enthusiastic volunteer is on the verge of a breakdown.

The considerable tension in the story mounts as the journalists try to sort out their moral responsibilities. The questions they face speak to the problematic nature of American foreign policy from 1914 through the early months of 1917: Can someone who has broken neutrality in wartime reclaim it, as the would-be deserter hopes to do? And is it ethical, when one is neutral, to assist a sworn member of another nation's military in the commission of a crime (even when the criminal is a fellow American)? In the end, the journalists buy the soldier safe passage to Athens but then convince him that his dishonorable action will make his hard-earned experience impossible to share, either in writing or on the lecture circuit. Unless he remains at the front, the man with everything will have nothing. At the story's climax, the soldier angrily agrees to return to his unit, and the narrator reflects on the creature comforts that he enjoys along with the other reporters. His thoughts become an implicit critique of his homeland's refusal to fight:"[The soldier] was not a good loser. 'I hope you're satisfied,' he snarled. He pointed at the four beds in a row. I felt guiltily conscious of them. At the moment they appeared so unnecessarily clean and warm and soft. The silk coverlets at the foot of each struck me as being disgracefully effeminate. They made me ashamed." However, the strength of this story rests in its Kipling-like ambiguity, which returns to the narrative almost immediately after the narrator's seemingly pro-Allied musings. Have the narrator and his colleagues done the right thing or not? And is the war to which the soldier returns one that America should join? Despite the narrator's sense of shame, most of Hamlin's anecdotes describe a terrifying and meaningless conflict ("whole villages turned into a brickyard in twenty minutes . . . babies frozen to death"), and the story's closing image of "melted snow" and "stale blood," with which the soldier's filthy uniform stained the journalists' floor, leaves little question about his ultimate fate—a fate that his fellow Americans might have prevented.

Almost immediately after the declaration of war in April 1917, the U.S. government would do all that it could to suppress troubling, morally inconclusive war stories like "The Man Who Had Everything." A work of literature deemed seditious could land its author—and publisher—in a federal penitentiary. At the same time, Creel's Committee for Public Information, which its founder later described as having achieved the greatest advertising coup in American history, used all the tools of the dawning mass-media age to keep public discourse, of all varieties, on message. The film industry shifted into wartime mode right away, and many doughboys, like the impressionable enlisted men depicted in John Dos Passos's *Three Soldiers,* would arrive on the Western Front with celluloid images of exaggerated German brutality freshly planted in their minds. Plastered over every flat surface in sight, propaganda posters, often extorting viewers to dig deeper into their pockets for the sake of the war effort, became an inescapable feature of wartime visual culture. Americans desirous of information about the causes and history of the war to date could find the "truth" in a series of governmentally produced red-white-and-blue booklets, many of them authored by leading academics. Almost nothing in these publications was reliable. Indeed, even children's books became vehicles for propaganda—in ways that seem, in retrospect, especially disturbing. One such title from 1917, a British import aimed at kindergartners, presented German soldiers as cartoon sausages to be chopped up by Allied troops.[2]

Such a ferocious propaganda campaign, coupled with the wartime suppression of civil liberties, hardly created an environment conducive to great art. However, a surprising number of American stories published after April 1917 *do* comment on the conditions—and costs—of industrialized conflict in ways neither naïve nor uncomplicatedly jingoistic. For example, published months after the American declaration of war and later selected for the prestigious volume *The Best Short Stories of 1917* (1918), Fanny Kemble Johnson's "The Strange-Looking Man" offers the hellish vision of a country where men grotesquely wounded by war are so commonplace that a former soldier in good health is deemed "strange." Implicitly set in Germany, this grim tale might be taken for propaganda, as if imagining just retribution rained upon the Huns. However, the story's tragic tone and the absence of any overtly anti-German vitriol point to a different interpretation. Kemble's country of the maimed might just as easily be a postwar France or Great Britain—or even, it is implied, a nightmarish version of a future United States.

Though sentimental and predictably patriotic, Edna Ferber's "One Hundred Per Cent" (1918) offers surprises as well, registering the seismic shift that the Great War brought to American gender roles. A far cry from the neo-feminine matrons featured in conventional war propaganda, Ferber's protagonist, Emma McChesney Buck, is a successful New York businesswoman, now married to her former employer, who in the midst of her public war work becomes completely oblivious to her husband's— and her son's—desperate desire to serve overseas. In the end, she suddenly realizes her selfishness and ingeniously removes a number of obstacles so that the men in her life can join in the fray. In accordance with wartime ideology, "over there" operates in the story as a proper masculine domain, and by the story's conclusion Emma yields to its gravitational pull on the male members of her household. However, the skills she demonstrates throughout the story, whether leading in business or facilitating her husband's and son's enlistment, conform to definitions of masculinity operative at the time. The story also makes much of the various uniforms Emma dons while performing her patriotic tasks. Though sometimes comic and absurd, her quasi-military dress nevertheless blurs the line between the masculine and feminine (just as similar attire donned by wartime female truck drivers and switchboard operators did) and comes to signify her formidable generalship both at home and within the wartime economy.

Dorothy Canfield's "The Permissionaire" appeared in her 1918 collection *Home Fires in France,* one of the finest volumes of American short fiction published during the war. A devout Francophile (like her friend Willa Cather), Canfield wrote propaganda—but propaganda with a difference. The very title of her collection points to its complexity and sophistication in comparison with many wartime literary productions. The phrase "Home Fires in France" signifies, first of all, the intimate, domestic picture of the French people, of Gallic hearth and home, that Canfield offers—perhaps nowhere more effectively than in "The Permissionaire." Second, her title alludes to the destruction of war, to French domiciles incinerated and lost through German aggression. And finally, through her use of a phrase most Americans would identify with their own homes ("Keep the home fires burning," urged a wartime song popular in both Great Britain and the United States), Canfield suggests the deep historical and cultural bonds between France and America. *Our* home fires, she implies, are one and the same as those of France.

In "The Permissionaire," Canfield combines an account of a French soldier's leave (or *permission*), a familiar and often sentimentalized situation in wartime fiction, with a detailed description of conditions in areas of occupied France where the German military practiced a scorched-earth policy. Such areas, along with the swath of Belgium captured by the German army in 1914, offered irresistible material for Allied propagandists and became the focus of literally dozens of books and official reports, nearly all of them filled with exaggerated claims of Teutonic atavism and cruelty. Canfield's approach is more subtle—and ultimately more generous where the enemy is concerned. The Permissionaire of the story's title uses his twenty-one-day leave to return to his demolished home in formerly occupied territory, a once-beautiful farm all but flattened by German forces as they withdrew to the Hindenburg Line in 1918. There, miraculously, he is reunited with his wife and children. Canfield focuses the bulk of the story on the family's backbreaking effort to rebuild. Mindful that each passing minute brings him closer to the end of his furlough, the soldier works frantically, repairing the farmhouse's chimney, nearly the only thing left standing, and constructing a makeshift shelter. Joined by even his youngest children, he piles up debris, tills the family's land in preparation for planting, and struggles to save their fruit trees and vines, which the Germans have cunningly damaged, slicing them in such a way that they appear at first to have been spared. This attack on the soldier's fruit garden, apparently orchestrated by a sadistic horticulturalist, inspires the story's most indignant passage: "Everything, everything, peach-trees, apple-trees, grapevines, everything had been neatly and dexterously murdered, and their corpses left hanging on the wall as a practical joke."

Canfield does not, however, identify all Germans—or even all German soldiers—with such senseless and wanton destruction. Enemy officers, presumably Prussian, are her villains. Though terrified of their commanders, and thus helpless to prevent atrocities, the enlisted men receive a largely sympathetic portrayal—a significant departure from most Allied narratives focused on occupied territory. Moreover, the thematic emphasis in "The Permissionaire" ultimately falls not on German brutality but on more timeless concerns. The soldier's reunion with his family and their resuscitation of their apparently moribund farm come to symbolize the forces of life, growth, and renewal in the face of monstrous violence and devastation, the specific causes of which no longer matter. Though created in part to demonize Teutonic military leadership, their story could be that of any family caught in the path of an invading army during any period of history. This elemental quality comes across most forcefully in the story's closing image: as the Permissionaire leaves his farm for the front, his leave now at an end, he absentmindedly carries a garden rake instead of his rifle. This ending powerfully juxtaposes the urge to restore and to plant with the perverse delight in destruction experienced by so many combatants on the Western Front.

The absence of more aggressive propaganda in "The Permissionaire," a surprisingly tender and forgiving narrative, perhaps resulted from Canfield's realization that among middle- to high-brow American readers in 1918 (at least those of non-German ancestry) certain assumptions could be taken for granted. Her story proceeds confidently from three foundational notions—first, that Prussian militarism is an evil that must be eradicated (for the sakes both of the French and Belgians who suffer in the occupied territories *and* of Germany); second, that the French way of life, with its deep connection to the soil and its timeless cultural practices, represents the pinnacle of European civilization; and, third, that France and the United States share a deep and special understanding dating to the American Revolution. Other American Francophiles would cling to these assumptions well past the Armistice. Though laced with modernist irony, the final book of Willa Cather's *One of Ours* (1922) is an unabashed love song to France, as Nebraskan Claude Wheeler, the novel's long-frustrated protagonist, finally achieves self-actualization amid a culture whose aesthetic sensibility, traditions, and manners he finds instantly congenial. Edith Wharton's 1923 novel *A Son at the Front* might likewise have been published in 1917 or 1918. After agonizing self-examination, Wharton's American hero, an expatriate artist who seems to have stepped right out of Cather's "The Namesake," concludes that his son must serve in the French army. Wharton does not gloss over the brutality of war (nor, for that matter, does Cather), but when the son dies, the nobility of his sacrifice remains largely unquestioned.

For many Americans, however, the sense of moral certainty that undergirds books like *Home Fires in France* went to pieces within just a few months of the ceasefire on the Western Front. Indeed, as John Dos Passos understood when selecting the title for the second volume of his *USA Trilogy*, 1919 was an especially turbulent and in many respects ugly year in American history. None of the assumptions cherished by writers like Canfield and Wharton escaped a beating. For example, as hundreds of thousands of doughboys came home—to a country that had enacted Prohibition during their absence and to an economy that quickly slid into a recession—they frequently complained about the very people they had supposedly gone overseas to save. The French were dirty and rude, they reported, and their shopkeepers had openly fleeced Americans in uniform. Soldiers returning from occupation duty in the Rhineland often stated that they preferred the Germans. Diplomatic defeat at the Versailles Treaty negotiations also added to the atmosphere of letdown, as Woodrow Wilson's internationalist agenda, outlined in his overly optimistic Fourteen Points, disintegrated in the face of long-standing European ambitions and the desire for vengeance.

Along with this metaphorical violence to ideals and expectations, actual violence spread across the nation as well—as if the aggressiveness and bloodlust stoked by nineteen months of hatred-engendering propaganda demanded new outlets. Race relations, for instance, reached a new low. The year 1919 saw more lynchings than ever before, and many of the targets were recently discharged soldiers of color, some murdered while wearing their uniforms. Significantly, much of this violence occurred well outside the Deep South—in places that seemed unlikely, such as Omaha, Nebraska, where a group of smiling white veterans, one still wearing his overseas cap, were photographed next to the incinerated body of Will Brown, an African American accused of raping a Caucasian woman. In Washington, D.C., and on the south side of Chicago, where the Red Summer of 1919 earned its gory nickname, full-blown racial warfare erupted, leaving entire neighborhoods in flames and hundreds of citizens (mostly African Americans) dead or seriously wounded. At the same time, political radicalism—real or imagined—came under attack from federal authorities who extended the wartime suppression of civil liberties into the post-Armistice era. Under the supervision of Attorney General J. Mitchell Palmer and a young J. Edgar Hoover, head of the Justice Department's General Intelligence Department, government agents brushed aside search-and-seizure laws, arrested suspected anarchists on the basis of often flimsy evidence, and staged mass deportations. Not without reason, a later historian of the 1919–20 Red Scare called his seminal book on the subject *A Study in National Hysteria.*[3]

F. Scott Fitzgerald's "May Day" (1920) offers a vivid snapshot of this terrifying new America born from the violence of the Great War. Set in a sinister New York City that bears little resemblance to Ferber's sunlit version of the metropolis in "One Hundred Per Cent," published just two years earlier, the story focuses on the intersecting paths of several characters, including four recently discharged veterans. The first two, Carroll Key and Gus Rose, are buck privates, fresh off the troop ship, who drift aimlessly through the city in search of liquor; ultimately, they join a crazed mob as it storms the offices of a socialist newspaper. In the scuffle that ensues, Key falls to his death from an open window. Gordon Sterrett, the third veteran, has the right social connections and an Ivy League degree. However, he is too shell-shocked to hold down a job, and after his former friend and fellow Yale alumnus Philip Dean refuses to give him a loan, he hits rock bottom and blows his brains out. Dean likewise presumably served on the Western Front, and while apparently insulated from the recent past by money and comfort, his own life is spiraling out of control. Through his constant drunkenness and adolescent antics in restaurants, Dean behaves like a disruptive soldier on leave, thus relocating the relaxed social mores of wartime France to Jazz-Age Manhattan. With its cast of grotesques, its darkly comic violence, and its portrayal of post-Armistice New York as a modern-day City of Dreadful Night, "May Day"—named, ironically enough, after the day of international solidarity observed by radicals in Europe and the United States—looks nothing like the stories that precede it in this anthology. While Cather would famously argue that "in 1922 or thereabouts the world broke in two," Fitzgerald's edgy narrative presents the year 1919 as a moment of profound cultural rupture, and the very look and feel of his story—disjointed and surreal—reflects this central theme.[4]

Through its pledge of a "return to normalcy," the administration of Warren G. Harding, which took over the White House in 1921, promised an end to the turbulent modernity associated with the war and with the Red Summer and Red Scare that came immediately afterward. But even as the economy recovered and the violence of 1919 receded into the past, normalcy remained an illusion. Indeed, throughout the 1920s and 1930s America was a society haunted by—and continually struggling to understand—its experience of the Great War, a historical cataclysm that stubbornly refused to form a central body of myth or collective memory. In contrast, for the European nations that fought in World War I the conflict's meaning stabilized during the interwar period. Within ten years of the Armistice, Great Britain, for instance, saw the emergence of a nearly ubiquitous interpretation of the conflict—what cultural historian Samuel Hynes has called "The Myth of the War."[5] According to the myth, incompetent generals and politicians had sacrificed the nation's youth, a generation now missing, on the altar of their greed and ambition. In fascist countries, memory was mandated from on high and backed by force. Citizens of the Third Reich resisted the notion of the stab in the back—that is, the bogus memory of the German army's betrayal by Jews and communists—at their peril. Similarly pernicious representations of the war played a central role in Italian fascism. As described by Mussolini and his Black Shirts, the Italian war effort of 1915–18 had been a glorious affair, ushering in the final stages of the Risorgimento and the birth of a new Rome. This false memory conveniently ignored the chronic military incompetence that resulted in more than six hundred thousand Italian deaths and the lack of patriotic conviction among ordinary Italian soldiers, one-fifth of whom faced criminal charges.[6] In short, as raw material for fascist myth, the conflict served as an eminently malleable *mis*-usable past.

In America, however, collective memory of the Great War fractured, breaking into distinct and competing versions of the past, each upheld by its own committed constituency. One such constituency—and a force to be reckoned with throughout the interwar period—was the American Legion, the largest and most powerful veterans' organization in American history. Founded in 1919 and representing, at its peak, one-quarter of the country's 4 million veterans, the Legion celebrated the Great War as a time of beneficial "Americanization," during which citizens had shed their ethnic differences and united in a common cause. The Legion also stressed the manly virtues of military service—and continued to do so even after endorsing isolationism in the late 1930s.[7] When it came to war remembrance, the organization was ubiquitous. Indeed, most forms of American public commemoration devoted to the Great War resulted directly from Legion initiatives, including the Armistice Day holiday (now known as Veterans Day), the Tomb of the Unknown Soldier at Arlington National Cemetery (later retitled the Tomb of the Unknowns), and the scores of doughboy statues and memorial halls or stadiums erected in cities and towns from coast to coast. At the same time, however, there were signs, especially in the publishing industry, of ideological pushback from Americans who shared a very different memory of the so-called Great Adventure. As we have seen, Fitzgerald's biting "May Day" presented returning doughboys not as "Americanized" heroes or battle-hardened real men but as potential thugs dangerously susceptible to a mob mentality. One year later, in an even more devastating portrayal of the psychological damage inflicted by war experience,

Dos Passos's novel *Three Soldiers* turned American Legion ideology inside out, casting the American Expeditionary Forces (AEF) as a dehumanizing organization, within which citizen soldiers had suffered needlessly under the tyranny of sadistic officers. One of Dos Passos's central characters develops psychopathic tendencies as a result of this constant brutalization, and he murders a superior. Most Legionnaires hated *Three Soldiers,* but the book sold well, passing through multiple printings (even joining the prestigious Modern Library collection in 1932), and made Dos Passos an instant literary celebrity.

When Willa Cather's *One of Ours,* with its seemingly heroic story of an American soldier, appeared in 1922, it received an excoriating review from H. L. Mencken, who claimed that *Three Soldiers* had so definitively captured the truth about the war that any competing literary vision smacked of self-delusion.[8] The very intensity of Mencken's rhetoric points, of course, to the opposite conclusion—that no single book (or, for that matter, film, memorial, or veterans' organization) could express a version of memory shared by all or even most citizens. The war had left behind a memory vacuum that different Americans filled in different ways.

The stories that comprise the latter two-thirds of this anthology richly attest to this lack of consensus. Some—like Ema S. Hunting's "The Soul That Sinneth" (1920), George L. Stout's "Dust" (1924), and Mary Borden's "Rosa" (1929)—confront wartime separation and loss and express a sense of grief made even more painful by the many questions that the war inspired, questions that remain largely unanswered today: Was American involvement in the Great War avoidable? What did that involvement ultimately achieve? And why did more than a hundred thousand American soldiers (two times the number lost in Vietnam) have to die?

In Hunting's "The Soul That Sinneth," Henry Schultz, a German American farmer, receives word that his son Johnny has joined the "fallen" (to use the popular euphemism of the time) after just two weeks in the United States Army. Through the course of the story, Schultz expresses his grief through rage, berating his elderly mother-in-law for continuing to live when her grandson is dead, shredding the American flag that decorates his son's coffin, and terrifying the life insurance agent who arrives to pay off the soldier's $1,000 policy. Such violent behavior is not, of course, the way federal authorities expected parents of servicemen to respond to loss. Indeed, with characteristic sensitivity to the importance of visual branding (here identified with a less than pleasant product—namely, military fatalities) the Wilson administration discouraged traditional symbols of mourning, including black armbands for men and so-called widow's weeds for women, in favor of the newly introduced gold star. As upbeat as a symbol of death could be, the gold star appeared on window flags used to designate the homes of bereaved families and, along with the ubiquitous phrase "roll of honor," became an integral part of wartime rhetoric related to memory. Schultz, however, will have none of it. He completely rejects this commemorative apparatus, refusing even to have a military honor guard present at his son's funeral. Thus, although cruel and abusive in some respects, the protagonist carries out an ultimately successful rebellion against patriotic ritual and display. In this way, "The Soul That Sinneth," an obscure story never before reprinted, looks ahead to other, better-known attacks on state-sanctioned remembrance, such as "The Body of an American," Dos Passos's devastating treatment of the Tomb of the Unknown Soldier at the conclusion of *1919* (1932).

Stout's "Dust" focuses on tragedy of a different kind, as a sympathetic YMCA worker tries to help an elderly father, a Civil War veteran, locate his son amid the thousands of doughboys moving in and out of Camp Dodge, Iowa. Wrongly believing that his father would try to keep him on their Nebraska farm, the young man in question ran away and enlisted without providing any contact information. Thus, the father and son never said their goodbyes. After several battles with military bureaucracy, the YMCA representative finally convinces a colonel to look into the matter, and the soldier's whereabouts become sadly clear: he is already on his way to France. Along with the story's funereal title, its closing image suggests that the two will probably never be reunited: we last see the eighty-year-old veteran as he walks away from the camp, enveloped in an ominous "swirl of dust." Like "The Soul That Sinneth," this quietly moving story eschews any explicit commentary on the events of 1917 and 1918; however, it could hardly be read as a pro-war narrative.

Borden's "Rosa" carries the theme of loss beyond America's borders. Narrated by a nurse, the story presents a French soldier who slowly dies of a self-inflicted wound. And that is it. The narrator never learns the soldier's name, the cause of his suicide attempt, or the reason he speaks just one word—"Rosa"—over and over again. He is a cipher whose unexplained anguish comes to signify the inscrutability of the war itself.

Other selections in this anthology, such as Laurence Stallings's "The Big Parade" (1924) and Leonard Nason's "Among the Trumpets" (1929), view the war from the hard-boiled perspective of professional soldiers. The latter story, with its depiction of American cavalrymen performing scouting missions on the Western Front, seems at first sight as preposterous as any wartime propaganda narrative. As it turns out, however, at least one American cavalry unit *was* deployed in just such a manner. In addition, Nason avoids any hint of 1917–18–vintage propaganda by celebrating the American fighting man—seen here as tough, respectful of the enemy, and quick to adapt—without ever addressing the causes or outcomes of American intervention. His wisecracking, perpetually grousing doughboys are capable soldiers, not champions of democracy, and their goal is to kill the enemy and survive, not save the world. In this way, "Among the Trumpets" illustrates a formula that its author successfully followed in nearly a dozen war novels and short story collections published between 1926 and 1940. Not surprisingly, much of Nason's shorter fiction also appeared in American Legion magazines, where his emphasis on the war as a masculine proving ground (as opposed to a sacred crusade or a disillusioning debacle) found perfect ideological companionship.

Stallings, though, only sounded like a professional soldier (he enlisted in the Marine Corps in 1917 and was seriously wounded at Belleau Wood), and his vision of the Great War, violently unstable, embraced both sides of the memory debate. Indeed, Stallings was two writers at once—one thoroughly horrified by modern warfare, the other utterly enthralled by military life, especially as perfected by the Marine Corps' experienced regulars, its so-called Old Breed. In his hit play *What Price Glory,* cowritten with Maxwell Anderson and first performed in 1924, these incongruous responses stand side by side: the middle act, at the frontline, denounces the American war effort; the surrounding acts, full of service comedy and tribute to the Old Breed, focus on a love triangle involving two Marine Corps regulars (James Cagney would play one of these in a later film version) and a French barmaid. Ultimately, the humor in the play softens its antiheroic message.

This same dynamic operates in "The Big Parade," which provided the title (if nothing else) for King Vidor's silent film epic released in 1925. At the opening of the story, a lieutenant in the midst of the Aisne-Marne fighting receives orders to select eight enlisted men to accompany him to Paris, where he will lead them in a Fourth of July parade. The lieutenant assembles the nine most deserving soldiers in his unit, all survivors of multiple bloodbaths, and they draw lots. Of course, the loser turns out to be none other than the lieutenant's favorite—the company runner, Private Gianonni, formerly an undertaker's assistant in Brooklyn. Certain that Gianonni has received a death sentence, the lieutenant proceeds to Paris with his fortunate charges and unenthusiastically marches in the parade, an absurd public-relations spectacle staged primarily to reassure the French public that American combatants are just as grimy and sleep-deprived as their own troops. Afterward, while waiting on the train that will take them back to the front, the lieutenant seems to experience a moment of clairvoyance: an artillery shell, he is convinced, has just killed Gianonni. Just minutes later, however, the protagonist suddenly spots the undertaker's assistant in the flesh—dressed in a stolen officer's uniform, accompanied by a "piquante blond," and bound for a French resort. As it turns out, Gianonni has used the lieutenant's absence as an opportunity to go AWOL. Although it describes citizen soldiers, led by a hastily trained volunteer officer, the third-person voice in this seriocomic tale is that of an experienced regular. Stalling's playful, overly elaborate prose—"thunderous vapors turgid with mustard gas," "Moroccans who sometimes wore enemy eyes as bangles of prowess," et cetera—gives his persona an air of wide military experience and, like the surprise happy ending, blunts the story's effectiveness as a piece of satire and protest.

While Stallings ricocheted back and forth between denouncing the war as a tragic lottery (the metaphor that dominates the first half of "The Big Parade") and celebrating the high-spiritedness of its American participants, other writers offered far bleaker visions unrelieved by humor or admiration for the professional life of arms. In their short fiction, the war utterly debases its participants, transforming American soldiers (or their allies) into gangsters in uniform, psychopaths, or—worst of all—cowards who lie about their military prowess to others, thereby perpetuating the myth of combat as an ennobling experience. This anthology abounds with such characters. For instance, Private Hawthorne, the Kentucky boy presented in Thomas Boyd's story of that title (1925), is a homicidal maniac obsessed with murdering his mess sergeant. When we first meet Hawthorne, he comes across as a likable rogue (just as Stallings's Private Giannoni does), displaying a genius for insubordination that seems distinctly and attractively American. Indeed, it seems, at first sight, that Boyd has created a World War I version of Huck Finn. Fed up with the base hospital where he is recuperating from wounds, the rambunctious Hawthorne convinces another soldier, John Goodwin, to join him in an escape attempt. The two men manage to slip out of the hospital and begin the long journey back to their regiments, successfully eluding military police along the way. All goes well until Hawthorne's disturbing capacity for violence begins to show. When they encounter a soldier who insults Hawthorne's division, the Kentuckian calmly hurls an iron coffee stand at his head, nearly killing him. And when Goodwin questions his companion about his past, he learns that Hawthorne, upset over being served cold chow, once pummeled his mess sergeant until his "knuckles looked like raw meat" and later threw an ax at the same soldier. At the end of the story, utterly exhausted from their long trek, Goodwin realizes that Hawthorne's sole object in making the journey is to complete his unfinished business with the hated mess sergeant—to "carve [his] name" in the man's face.

The disturbing figure at the center of "The Kentucky Boy"—an exuberant American rebel who also harbors the capacity for murder—typified Boyd's antiheroic approach to characterization. In his first book, the novel *Through the Wheat* (1923), Boyd depicted a doughboy's harrowing descent from patriotic warrior to shell-shocked automaton. And in the short story collection *Points of Honor* (1925), which includes "The Kentucky Boy," he expanded his focus, creating an array of ironic situations that turn the propaganda version of the American war effort inside out. Boyd's vengeful Kentuckian is just one deviant figure among many in the book's gallery of grotesques, which include a war veteran who murders his adulterous wife and her lover, a once-compassionate officer who becomes a cruel martinet after overhearing some mild criticism from his men, and a thrifty French peasant who keeps the remains of several dead American soldiers—useful fertilizer—hidden in her garden. The latter character demonstrates, in particular, how far at least one variety of American war fiction had come since the days of *Home Fires in France*.

Through its presentation of a psychotic French aviator, James Warner Bellah's "The Great Tradition" (1928) takes aim at the popular notion of World War I fighter pilots as the Knights of the Air. The story focuses on the conflict between two airmen in the same squadron—Petitjean, an egomaniacal French ace (and media darling), and Comstock, a volunteer flyer from Texas. After the former's theatrics lead to the unnecessary death of Comstock's wingman, the grief-stricken Texan humiliates the celebrated French flyer by publicly insulting him and throwing him against the wall of their squadron headquarters. The next day, to Comstock's amazement, Petitjean opens fire on him in the midst of a dogfight. Some of Comstock's French comrades witness this event, and they subsequently cover for the Texan when he follows the ace to a local brothel and breaks his neck. Had Bellah ended the story here, with Petitjean's anything but heroic demise, his central theme would have been the same as Boyd's in "The Kentucky Boy"—namely, that war brings out violent proclivities in men that may just as easily find expression in crime as in acts of valor. But Bellah complicates the story through an unexpected denouement. Comstock's fellow aviators conclude that Petitjean must be given a hero's death; otherwise, "all history will be worthless." Aided by the Texan, they place the ace's body in the cockpit of a fighter plane, "with his feet on the rudder bar," and send the aircraft aloft. After the plane crashes near the front, the French press treats Petitjean's death as a tragic accident. By upholding the "great tradition" of martial heroism through a lie, Comstock and his companions reveal the hollowness of that very tradition. At the same time, however, the author suggests that the nihilistic truth about military glory may be more than Western civilization can handle. If war—even the supposedly romantic version of war waged in the air—is nothing more than released aggression and senseless injury, then how do nations cope with the suffering that this apparently inescapable human "tradition" produces?

The qualms that seem to shape the ending of Bellah's otherwise explicitly antiheroic narrative appear nowhere in William March's "To the Rear," an uncompromising study in callousness and dehumanization that ruthlessly explodes the notion of soldierly comradeship. Published two years before March's blockbuster novel *Company K* (1933), which depicts the American military experience of the Great War through the perspectives of 113 different soldiers in one unit, this bleak narrative focuses on a cadaverous doughboy, Private Ernest Lunham, who has inhaled poison gas while chopping some tree roots inside a shell hole. Though weak and nauseous, Lunham is accused by a medical officer of faking his condition, and so he must accompany his platoon on a grueling daylong march from the frontline trenches to the rear. During the march, his fellow enlisted men behave, at first, like the devoted comrades usually depicted in war fiction—one man carries Lunham's pack, another his bags of ammunition. But as the soldiers become increasingly fatigued and quarrelsome, they begin to harbor their own suspicions about his condition, and after an especially torturous section of road they refuse to carry his equipment any longer. Retching, Lunham collapses by the roadside. The platoon marches on. On the story's final page, a French farm girl happens by and gives the emaciated American some goat's milk, but it does no good. He continues to vomit. He is dying. Even the most experienced aficionado of war fiction will find "To the Rear" uncomfortable reading—both because of the physical misery that it depicts, in stomach-churning detail, and because of its none-too-gentle stab at the notion that the crucible of war forges military companions into a band of brothers. In short, March goes after the most untouchable (then as now) of the U.S. military's sacred myths.

Just as hard-hitting (if somewhat more predictable), Hervey Allen's "Blood Lust" (1940) depicts the atavistic transformation of an American innocent, Corporal Virgin, into a brute capable of lopping off a German's head with a sickle. Prior to 1940, Allen, a former AEF officer and the author of the runaway bestseller *Anthony Adverse* (1936), was known for having artfully sidestepped the ongoing controversy over the meaning of American participation in the Great War. In 1926, Allen had published *Toward the Flame*, a beautifully written account of his service in the Aisne-Marne fighting during the summer of 1918. As reviewers noted, Allen meticulously adhered to what he actually saw and experienced (or at least skillfully created that illusion) and avoided editorializing. Thus, his memoir steered clear of rhetoric identified with writers like Dos Passos, on the one side, and Nason, on the other. By 1940, however, with Nazi aggression reshaping Europe and American neutrality in the balance, Allen was ready to speak out about what American combatants had experienced in the previous world war and what soldiers in the latest conflict might expect. "Blood Lust" appeared that year in Allen's combatively titled collection of war stories, *It Was Like This*, and gave full expression to the disgust and indignation that the author had suppressed when writing *Toward the Flame*.

Indeed, by the end of this gruesome narrative, the reader suddenly realizes that the protagonist, a baby-faced adolescent turned stone-cold killer, has actually *become* the evil Hun of 1917–18–era propaganda. During the course of the Aisne-Marne fighting, Corporal Virgin casually murders two German prisoners, one of whom he bayonets, and after becoming a POW himself makes his escape by decapitating his guard, a mild-mannered "grocer's clerk" whose death seems completely unnecessary. In contrast, the Prussian officer who interrogates Virgin, employing a mixture of kindness and morphine, is a far cry from the jackbooted sadist routinely depicted on Liberty Loan posters, and the men under his command display none of the bestial qualities that become so prominent in the story's American protagonist. Allen ingeniously reverses wartime propaganda imagery, and he closes his story with a chilling reminder of war's transformative power for evil: after Virgin is discharged, his neo-patriotic mother comes to "realize that her son hadn't really come back. It was somebody else with the same name."

Leo Jacks's "One Hundred Per Cent" (1928) deals with violence of a very different kind—namely, the abuse of the past for political gain. This sardonic narrative demonstrates that false memories, cunningly manipulated, were not limited to totalitarian regimes in Europe. At the opening of the story, set in a small midwestern town, we meet an impressionable fourteen-year-old boy and his Uncle Jack, a veteran of the Great War. The two attend a Fourth of July celebration and hear their congressman, "the Honorable J. O. Coughlin," give the "French hell for not paying their war debt." Coughlin, likewise a former soldier, makes much of his wartime service and, like politicians then and now, skillfully wraps himself in the American flag. After the speech, Uncle Jack tells his nephew the story of a chronic straggler in his artillery unit, a man who always managed to disappear before each major battle. The final sentence of "One Hundred Per Cent" reveals, of course, that this cowardly doughboy was none other than the future congressman.

With its zinger ending and inset flashback, Jacks's narrative is a fairly typical—and fairly pedestrian—example of popular magazine fiction from the interwar period; however, the story's title deepens the satire. The phrase "one hundred per cent," never used in the narrative itself, comes, in this context, from the Preamble of the American Legion (written by future New York congressman Hamilton Fish Jr. in 1919), which pledged the organization to an agenda of "one hundred per cent Americanism." Among its critics, especially the American Civil Liberties Union, this murky formulation conveyed the Legion's almost fascist intolerance for open political dialogue, a charge not entirely unwarranted. Through its insistence upon loyalty oaths for schoolteachers, well-publicized clashes with Wobblies (members of the widely reviled International Workers of the World), and sundry forms of Red-baiting, the Legion made little secret of its desire to silence any and all radical speech. "One hundred percent Americanism" referred less to ethnic homogeneity—in fact, the Legion welcomed ethnic minorities of the right political persuasion—than to ideological purity.[9] As evoked in the title of Jacks's story, the phrase takes on a richly subversive and irreverent meaning. Coughlin, the right-wing patriot (or "one-hundred per-center," as Legion-affiliated politicians were known in the 1920s), has built his public persona upon a war record that is 100 percent fraudulent.

Elliot White Spring's "Big Eyes and Little Mouth" (1927) and Kay Boyle's "Count Lothar's Heart" (1936) explore the Great War's erotic dimensions, a significant feature of its memory. Indeed, sexuality played a larger and more open role in the historiography and literature of the Great War than in those of previous conflicts. There were even entire books on the subject, ranging from German researcher Magnus Hirschfield's *The Sexual History of the World War* (1930) to *Chicago Daily News* columnist Howard Vincent O'Brien's *Wine, Women, and War,* a memoir of amorous adventure published anonymously in 1926. Elliot White Springs, a textile magnate in South Carolina and ex–fighter pilot, repeatedly described the hothouse conditions of wartime Paris and London in a series of sometimes serious, sometimes dilettantish works of fiction. In novels such as *The Rise of Carol Banks* (1931), which Springs had printed on bed sheets taken from his own textile mill, and *Leave Me With a Smile* (1928), a title that illustrated his fondness for double entendres, the former ace presented aerial combat with chilling accuracy and with none of the heroics that characterized Hollywood aviation epics. At the same time, he looked back nostalgically on the sexual license enjoyed by aviators (and their partners) in wartime Europe.

The latter focus predominates in the story "Big Eyes and Little Mouth," which deals candidly with the war's liberating effect on male and female sexuality alike. When Jim Watson, a volunteer in the Royal Flying Corps and a notorious philanderer, is killed during a training flight, one of his fellow Americans, Tap Johnson, must write to the dead pilot's wife in the United States and carry the news to his mistress in London. Once Johnson meets the mistress, a ravishing beauty whose boldness anticipates that of the Jazz Age flapper, she aggressively pursues him, and the two enjoy a wild fling. Not all is as it seems, however. When Johnson returns to the United States following his own near deadly crash, he accidentally discovers that his lover was, in fact, Watson's widow, who had come all the way to London to be near her husband. The story concludes with the two Americans rekindling their romance. What stands out in "Big Eyes and Little Mouth" is its casual depiction of promiscuity and its uninhibited celebration of male *and* female desire, both signs of the war's devastating impact upon Victorian proprieties.

Originally published in Boyle's 1936 collection *White Horses of Vienna and Other Stories,* "Count Lothar's Heart" deals with homosexuality and war. Six years pass before Count Lothar, an Austrian officer taken prisoner by the Russians, returns to his family *Schloss* in the Alps. There he is reunited with his fiancée and childhood companion, Elsa, and with his elderly father. But the officer's homecoming is an empty one. Everything once magical about the Alpine setting has lost its charm for him—everything but the swans that he watches for hours on the lake. He responds listlessly when his father announces that he has found a banking position for him in Salzburg, and he shows little interest in the woman who has waited more than a half-decade for his return. At first, this paralyzing sense of ennui seems to result from the protagonist's combat experience and subsequent privations as a POW in Siberia. Then the story turns boldly in an unexpected direction. At the climax, Lothar reveals to Elsa that he slept with one or more Russian Cossacks, elegant young men in furs, with "eyes turned up like Oriental women's," who would periodically ride into the prison camp in search of male partners. While Lothar accounts for his behavior in biological terms—as the result of an overabundance of "female cells" in his body—Boyle treats same-sex desire as a mystery that transcends easy explanation. Lothar may have always been a homosexual (some details early on in the story suggest as much), or his years in the POW camp may have modified his original orientation. Either way, what matters is that in captivity Lothar finds erotic fulfillment. Once free, he feels only isolation and indifference. No less than "Big Eyes and Little Mouth," this poignant narrative of a soldier's return deals— albeit in its own way—with the theme of wartime sexual liberation; and through its sensitive, nonjudgmental treatment of homosexual passion, the story seems decades ahead of its time.

And then there are selections in this anthology that show how sickness—namely, the Spanish flu epidemic of 1918—worked alongside the metaphorical disease of racism to further complicate collective memory. Katherine Ann Porter's *Pale Horse, Pale Rider* (1939), which focuses on the romance between a journalist in Denver and an officer bound for France, presents an all-too-common tragedy that had little place in either the Legion-sanctioned view of the Great War as a test of American manhood or the antiheroic vision of senseless combat and brutality associated with writers like Boyd and March. Flu-induced pneumonia, not German machine-gun bullets or artillery fire, strikes down the sympathetic doughboy featured in this moving love story. Thus, Porter's narrative implicitly raises two questions: Where does a victim of bacteria figure in war remembrance? And how does one make sense of a conflict in which illness accounted for more than half of the military's total fatalities?

Throughout the interwar period, African American leaders like W. E. B. Du Bois, who had supported the war effort in hopes that blacks could leverage civil rights through patriotic service, raised an equally troubling question: how could a nation that had supposedly set forth to make the world safe for democracy continue to tolerate Jim Crow at home? Several stories in this anthology illuminate the intersection of race and memory. Caucasian author Hugh Wiley's "The Four-Leaved Wildcat" (1919) presents African American soldiers in the way that most whites cared to remember them during the postwar era—as clowns drawn from the minstrel tradition. Equally adept at perpetuating stereotypes of Asian Americans (as evidenced by his popular mystery series set in San Francisco's Chinatown), Wiley made a career out of racial caricature, and in the buffoonish figure of "Wildcat" Marsden he created what was for a time America's best known soldier of color. First introduced in "The Four-Leaved Wildcat," Wiley's protagonist went on to appear in dozens of short stories, many published in American Legion magazines, and several novels. Wildcat's debut offers a quick glimpse of his life as a semiprofessional lawn mower in the Deep South, before shifting the focus to wartime France, where he earns the Distinguished Service Cross and the Croix de Guerre entirely by accident. Throughout the story, Wildcat cares only about sleep, food, and dice; to make the caricature complete, Wiley arms him with an especially wicked-looking straight razor, which earns him the respect of his comrades—and a promotion.

The racism expressed in Wiley's story, and played upon for laughs, gives some indication of the obstacles facing African Americans as they attempted to barter loyal service in a time of national emergency for basic civil rights and increased socioeconomic mobility. So too does the rash of lynchings in 1919. Indeed, the widespread desire to keep blacks "in their place" after World War I, a desire shared by northern and southern whites alike, helps explain the popularity of Wiley's protagonist. Driven entirely by the desire for modest creature comforts and by his love of gambling, Wildcat is completely docile where whites are concerned, and his straight razor only comes out when fellow soldiers of color challenge him. He accepts the racial segregation of the AEF as a matter of course, navigating the U.S. military as if it were simply a larger version of his hometown, and never questions his assignment to a construction (or "Pioneer") regiment rather a combat unit. Published on the eve of the Red Summer of 1919, "The Four-Leaved Wildcat" offered a picture of twentieth-century African American manhood completely consistent with white America's most cherished and most belittling constructions of race—welcome reassurance, no doubt, for Caucasians who nervously watched armed black men returning from France.

In war-related short stories by African American writers, four of which appear in this anthology, we see the emergence of a counter-memory aimed squarely at the fictional world inhabited by Wildcat. Published in the *Crusader* magazine, the chief organ of the African Blood Brotherhood (a rival of the NAACP founded by civil rights leader Cyril Valentine Briggs in 1917), Carita Collins's "How Walter Regained His Manhood" (1919) deals with racial passing. The light-skinned pro-tagonist, Walter Cummings, renounces his racial heritage and hides his true identify from everyone—including, ironically enough, the African American woman with whom he falls in love. Thinking he is white, she rejects him, a turnabout he never expected. In response, he enlists in the United States Army, serves in a colored combat regiment (thereby openly acknowledging his mixed race), and distinguishes himself on the battlefield. At the end of the story, with Cummings's "manhood" now regained, the couple reunites. Claude McKay's "The Soldier's Return" offers no such happy ending. First published in Russian in 1925, this narrative focuses on a hapless African American veteran, Frederick Taylor, who is arrested for a cruelly ironic crime—frightening a white woman by wearing his uniform. In a lengthy prologue, McKay provides a rich sociological account of how the soldier's town—Great Neck, Georgia—welcomes its returning soldiers, white and black alike, while carefully preserving the color line. For example, in a series of patriotic speeches, the town mayor (naturally a member of the Caucasian elite) encourages white veterans to wear their uniforms, as symbols of service and victory, while insisting that black veterans change as quickly as possible into their civilian clothes "and return to the work which they had done before the war." Taylor fails to follow the mayor's orders, and on the story's final page he receives a sentence of several months on a chain gang. As the mayor explains, "We will take the uniform of a soldier of the U.S. off you and give you an outfit which is more appropriate for you."

While Collins treats white America as a source of demeaning racial lies, to which her protagonist falls prey (before learning to embrace his blackness), and McKay focuses on the efforts of the southern elite to contain the potential threat represented by African American veterans, Victor R. Daly's "Private Walker Goes Patrolling" (1930) treats black experience in isolation, without invoking white values or forms of oppression. Originally published in the NAACP's *Crisis* magazine, edited by W. E. B. Du Bois, this story emphasizes the sense of solidarity that many African Americans, of widely varying backgrounds, felt as a result of their overseas service. Daly introduces two soldiers who instinctively hate each another: Sergeant William Dade, an accomplished brawler from Memphis whose capacity for physical violence rivals that of Hervey Allen's Corporal Virgin, and Private Jerry Walker, a mild-mannered draftee from Arkansas who has no martial ambitions of any kind. However, when the two find themselves cut off from their unit in No-Man's Land, they work together and achieve a level of mutual respect. In this way, Daly suggests that racial advancement will only come when African Americans transcend the class distinctions and regional differences that divide them from within.

Perhaps the most powerful response to the racial ideology so painfully inscribed in "The Four-Leaved Wildcat" and other narratives like it came from Langston Hughes in "Poor Little Black Fellow." This remarkable story, set in New England and Paris, appeared in 1933 and was collected a year later in *The Ways of White Folks*. It demonstrates, through a pattern of grotesque irony, that white folks' ways are both cruel and deluded where racial difference is concerned—even when supposedly motivated by kindness. Hughes's African American protagonist, Arnie, is an orphan whose father has died fighting in the Argonne and whose mother succumbs to the

Spanish flu. As a patriotic gesture, the aristocratic Pemberton family, for which the protagonist's parents worked as domestics, decides to informally adopt this "poor little black fellow" and raise him as one of their own. Things go smoothly until Arnie enters adolescence. He cannot, of course, attend parties where white girls are present (too many parents object), and when sent to a summer camp for black children in Boston he discovers that he has nothing in common with the other campers. The Pembertons also limit his educational options (despite his high marks), enrolling him at Fisk, "one of the nicer Negro colleges," rather than Harvard.

When Arnie accompanies his patrons on a Paris vacation, things come to a head: he becomes friends with a scandalous African American dancer and vocalist (perhaps inspired by Josephine Baker) and amid her multiracial artistic circle finds a sense of belonging that has eluded him his entire life. He even has his first serious romance—with a girl from Romania. The Pembertons naturally object, and in desperation they cut short their vacation. But Arnie refuses to leave Paris, and the story reaches its explosive climax:

> "No," said Arnie. "I don't want to go. It'll be like that camp in Boston. Everything in America's like that camp in Boston." His eyes grew redder. "Separate, segregated, shut-off! Black people kept away from everyone else. I go to Fisk; my classmates, Harvard, Amherst, and Yale. . . . I sleep in the garage, you sleep in the house."
>
> "Oh," Grace Pemberton said, "We didn't mean it like that!"
>
> Arnie was being cruel, just cruel. She began, in spite of herself, to cry.
>
> "I don't want to go back home," Arnie went on. "I hate America."
>
> "But your father *died* for America," Grace Pemberton cried.
>
> "I guess he was a fool," said Arnie.

The protagonist's assertion that his father died pointlessly, in the name of a country where the full humanity of black people will never be recognized, is perhaps the bitterest moment in any African American short story about the Great War. And yet, this realization is also liberating. Hughes's devastating portrait of racist dogooders ends with Arnie making his escape into "the soft Paris air."

If World War I inspired what we might call a signature story, one that encapsulates the interpretive dilemmas that the conflict posed for Americans, then that story would have to be Ernest Hemingway's "Soldier's Home," the centerpiece of his audacious 1925 collection *In Our Time*. (Unfortunately, Hemingway's well-known tale of a soldier's troubled homecoming could not be included here.) Unlike the pieces in the latter two-thirds of *World War I in American Fiction,* "Soldier's Home" does not promote a particular construction of the Great War, either positive or negative. Instead, it highlights the absence of a master narrative through which Americans could come together and agree on the meaning of their recent past. If, as historian David Kennedy has argued, the Great War left a "hole in the fabric of American culture," then "Soldier's Home" stares squarely into that hole—a void that the other writers represented in this volume attempted to fill through their various and competing visions of the past.[10] Hemingway's protagonist, Harold Krebs, is an accomplished soldier with far more combat experience than the average doughboy, but thanks to occupation duty in Germany he returns to his hometown in Oklahoma long after the parades and fanfare associated with demobilization have ended. He drifts, unable to emulate other veterans who are becoming a "credit to the community," grows steadily more resentful of his patronizing parents (who allow him to use the family car for dating, provided he confine his romantic interests to "nice girls"), and at the story's climax tells his distraught mother he no longer loves her—or, for that matter, anyone.

With a nod to Cather, Hemingway might have called this bleak narrative "Krebs's Case" since the nature of the protagonist's psychological and/or spiritual malady is left open for the reader's diagnosis. Arguably, however, the true source of his maladjustment comes from without, not from within. Memory is the problem—not Krebs's personal recollections of the war, which are almost entirely positive, but the town's lack of coherent collective memory. While Krebs reads war histories, in an effort to situate his personal experience within a larger framework of meaning, his community acts as if the war had never happened at all. No one tries to understand the profound differences between the protagonist's experiences in a crack combat division and those of veterans who never saw action (the vast majority). No one makes an effort to vicariously *remember* what Krebs has gone through.

Forty-six years after the publication of "Soldier's Home," Harold Krebs reappears, in a sense, as the unnamed pilot in Richard Brautigan's story "The World War I Los Angeles Airplane" (1971), which serves as this anthology's epilogue. Like Hemingway's, Brautigan's narrative presents a chilling breakdown in collective memory. In the story's opening section, a first-person narrator describes the loss of his seventy-year-old father in law, once an aviator in World War I, and claims to have "done a lot of thinking about what his death means to all of us." But no sooner has the narrator made this statement then the story shifts into a series of numbered paragraphs that provide a terse chronology of the aviator's life.

Instead of infusing that life with meaning, these paragraphs flatten it into banality. All we get is the basic outline: the narrator's father-in-law grows up on a farm in South Dakota, becomes a teacher, marries and quickly divorces, serves as a pilot on the Western Front, marries again and has two children, starts up a chain of banks in Idaho, loses everything in the Great Depression, moves to Los Angeles, works as a clerk for a construction company, is laid off, becomes a school janitor and an alcoholic, and dies next to his television. The story's blasé and-so-on-and-so-on style of narration is redolent of cultural emptiness and implies that no one cares about the pilot's service in the Great War, a long-forgotten and irrelevant event, or the setbacks and tragedies that defined his life. History—memory—is dead. And yet, tucked within this apparently moribund past is a moment of remarkable beauty: once, when the pilot "was flying over France . . . a rainbow appeared behind the tail of his plane and every turn that the plane made, the rainbow also made the same turn and it followed after him through the skies of France for part of an afternoon in 1918." This brief intrusion of magical realism into an otherwise bland and colorless account perhaps suggests that the son-in-law, who seems oblivious to much, actually understands something profound—namely, that the pilot's time aloft, in his World War I airplane, represented the zenith of his life.

Ironically, the presence of the Great War in American culture seems in some ways greater today, now that its veterans are gone, than during the decade when Brautigan's story was published, a decade when American historians first began to refer to the conflict as "missing," "lost," or "forgotten." As evidenced by Steven Spielberg's *War Horse* (2011) and talk of a new remake of *All Quiet on the Western Front* (rumored to star Daniel Radcliffe), Hollywood has rediscovered World War I. Meanwhile, HBO has situated the conflict—or, rather, its ambiguous memory—at the center of the highly successful drama *Boardwalk Empire,* which follows former doughboys as they apply their violent skills in the service of a New Jersey crime syndicate. World War I commemoration has made a comeback as well. Designated the National World War I Museum in 2004, the Liberty Memorial in Kansas City, Missouri, an enormous facility created to honor the more than four hundred Kansas City citizens lost in the War to End All Wars, has become a lively focal point for remembrance, in which crowds of visitors from coast to coast congregate each weekend. This surging interest inspires ongoing discussion of a National World War I Memorial in Washington, D.C.

As Americans prepare for the centennial of the outbreak of the war and contemplate the various ways in which this conflict, now gone from living memory, has remained on so many levels unfinished business, it is hoped that this anthology will serve as a useful guide. The stories collected here offer insight into a war that changed America profoundly, but whose meaning remains elusive.

NOTES

1. See George L. Mosse, *Fallen Soldiers: Reshaping the Memory of the World Wars* (New York: Oxford University Press, 1990), 70–106.

2. For an excellent discussion of this book, *Ten Little Sausages* (1917) by British author Stanley L. Wood, see Celia Kingsbury, *For Home and Country: World War I Propaganda on the Home Front* (Lincoln: Univ. of Nebraska Press, 2010), 211–15.

3. See Robert K. Murry, *Red Scare: A Study in National Hysteria, 1919–1920* (Minneapolis: Univ. of Minnesota Press, 1955).

4. Willa Cather, *Not Under Forty* (New York: Knopf, 1936), 2.

5. Samuel Hynes, *A War Imagined: The First World War and English Culture* (London: Bodley Head, 1990), 439.

6. R. J. B. Bosworth, *Mussolini's Italy: Life under the Fascist Dictatorship, 1915–1945* (London: Penguin, 2006), 170.

7. For more on the American Legion's construction of collective memory, see Steven Trout, *On the Battlefield of Memory: The First World War and American Remembrance, 1919–1941* (Tuscaloosa: Univ. of Alabama Press, 2010), 63–89.

8. H. L. Mencken, "Portrait of an American Citizen," *Smart Set* 69 (Oct. 1922): 140–42.

9. For more on the Legion's right-wing political agenda and its relationship to the organization's remembrance activities, see Trout, *On the Battlefield of Memory*, 43–48.

10. David Kennedy, *Over Here: The First World War and American Society* (New York: Oxford Univ. Press, 1980), 230.

Willa Cather
(1873–1947)

Though Willa Cather is still best known for her novels set in late-nineteenth-century Nebraska, her literary imagination ranged far from the Midwest as well and included places and times as diverse as New Mexico in the 1850s and Quebec in the 1690s. She also wrote about the effects of the First World War, most famously in *One of Ours* (1922). This novel about a young man fleeing a staid midwestern life for the excitement of the American army and an opportunity to see Europe won the Pulitzer Prize and a wide audience. It was also criticized (privately) by Ernest Hemingway and (publicly) by H. L. Mencken for what they saw as its romantic treatment of war. Today critics are more attuned to the narrative's ironies and less disturbed by its protagonist's earnest longings. In Claude Wheeler, the protagonist of *One of Ours,* Cather dramatizes the romantic notions that impelled many young American men into war. "The Namesake" reveals the roots of that idealism in America's response to the Civil War. It was published in *McClure's Magazine* in March 1907.

The Namesake
Willa Sibert Cather

Seven of us, students, sat one evening in Hartwell's studio on the Boulevard St. Michel. We were all fellow-countrymen; one from New Hampshire, one from Colorado, another from Nevada, several from the farm lands of the Middle West, and I myself from California. Lyon Hartwell, though born abroad, was simply, as every one knew, "from America." He seemed, almost more than any other one living man, to mean all of it—from ocean to ocean. When he was in Paris, his studio was always open to the seven of us who were there that evening, and we intruded upon his leisure as often as we thought permissible.

Although we were within the terms of the easiest of all intimacies, and although the great sculptor, even when he was more than usually silent, was at all times the most gravely cordial of hosts, yet, on that long remembered evening, as the sunlight died on the burnished brown of the horse-chestnuts below the windows, a perceptible dullness yawned through our conversation.

We were, indeed, somewhat low in spirit, for one of our number, Charley Bentley, was leaving us indefinitely, in response to an imperative summons from home. To-morrow his studio, just across the hall from Hartwell's, was to pass into other hands, and Bentley's luggage was even now piled in discouraged resignation before his door. The various bales and boxes seemed literally to weigh upon us as we sat in his neighbor's hospitable rooms, drearily putting in the time until he should leave us to catch the ten o'clock express for Dieppe.

The day we had got through very comfortably, for Bentley made it the occasion of a somewhat pretentious luncheon at Maxim's. There had been twelve of us at table, and the two young Poles were so thirsty, the Gascon so fabulously entertaining, that it was near upon five o'clock when we put down our liqueur glasses for the last time, and the red, perspiring waiter, having pocketed the reward of his arduous and protracted services, bowed us affably to the door, flourishing his napkin and brushing back the streaks of wet, black hair from his rosy forehead. Our guests having betaken themselves belated to their respective engagements, the rest of us returned with Bentley—only to be confronted by the depressing array before his door. A glance about his denuded rooms had sufficed to chill the glow of the afternoon, and we fled across the hall in a body and begged Lyon Hartwell to take us in.

Bentley had said very little about it, but we all knew what it meant to him to be called home. Each of us knew what it would mean to himself, and each had felt something of that quickened sense of opportunity which comes at seeing another man in any way counted out of the race. Never had the game seemed so enchanting, the chance to play it such a piece of unmerited, unbelievable good fortune.

It must have been, I think, about the middle of October, for I remember that the sycamores were almost bare in the Luxembourg Gardens that morning, and the terraces about the queens of France were strewn with crackling brown leaves. The fat red roses, out the summer long on the stand of the old flower woman at the corner, had given place to dahlias and purple asters. First glimpses of autumn toilettes flashed from the carriages; wonderful little bonnets nodded at one along the Champs-Elysées; and in the Quarter an occasional feather boa, red or black or white, brushed one's coat sleeve in the gay twilight of the early evening. The crisp, sunny autumn air was all day full of the stir of people and carriages and of the cheer of salutations; greetings of the students, returned brown and bearded from their holiday, gossip of people come back from Trouville, from St. Valery, from Dieppe, from all over Brittany and the Norman coast. Everywhere was the joyousness of return, the taking up again of life and work and play.

I had felt ever since early morning that this was the saddest of all possible seasons for saying good-by to that old, old city of youth, and to that little corner of it on the south shore which since the Dark Ages themselves—yes, and before—has been so peculiarly the land of the young.

I can recall our very postures as we lounged about Hartwell's rooms that evening, with Bentley making occasional hurried trips to his desolated workrooms across the hall—as if haunted by a feeling of having forgotten something—or stopping to poke nervously at his *perroquets,* which he had bequeathed to Hartwell, gilt cage and all. Our host himself sat on the couch, his big, bronze-like shoulders backed up against the window, his shaggy head, beaked nose, and long chin cut clean against the gray light.

Our drowsing interest, in so far as it could be said to be fixed upon anything, was centered upon Hartwell's new figure, which stood on the block ready to be cast in bronze, intended as a monument for some American battlefield. He called it "The Color Sergeant." It was the figure of a young soldier running, clutching the folds of a flag, the staff of which had been shot away. We had known it in all the stages of its growth, and the splendid action and feeling of the thing had come to have a kind of special significance for the half dozen of us who often gathered at Hartwell's rooms—though, in truth, there was as much to dishearten one as to inflame, in the case of a man who had done so much in a field so amazingly difficult; who had thrown up in bronze all the restless, teeming force of that adventurous wave still climbing westward in our own land across the waters. We recalled his "Scout," his "Pioneer," his "Gold Seekers," and those monuments in which he had invested one and another of the heroes of the Civil War with such convincing dignity and power.

"Where in the world does he get the heat to make an idea like that carry?" Bentley remarked morosely, scowling at the clay figure. "Hang me, Hartwell, if I don't think it's just because you're not really an American at all, that you can look at it like that."

The big man shifted uneasily against the window. "Yes," he replied smiling, "perhaps there is something in that. My citizenship was somewhat belated and emotional in its flowering. I've half a mind to tell you about it, Bentley." He rose uncertainly, and, after hesitating a moment, went back into his workroom, where he began fumbling among the litter in the corners.

At the prospect of any sort of personal expression from Hartwell, we glanced questioningly at one another; for although he made us feel that he liked to have us about, we were always held at a distance by a certain diffidence of his. There were rare occasions—when he was in the heat of work or of ideas—when he forgot to be shy, but they were so exceptional that no flattery was quite so seductive as being taken for a moment into Hartwell's confidence. Even in the matter of opinions—the commonest of currency in our circle—he was niggardly and prone to qualify. No man ever guarded his mystery more effectually. There was a singular, intense spell, therefore, about those few evenings when he had broken through this excessive modesty, or shyness, or melancholy, and had, as it were, committed himself.

When Hartwell returned from the back room, he brought with him an unframed canvas which he put on an easel near his clay figure. We drew close about it, for the darkness was rapidly coming on. Despite the dullness of the light, we instantly recognized the boy of Hartwell's "Color Sergeant." It was the portrait of a very handsome lad in uniform, standing beside a charger impossibly rearing. Not only in his radiant countenance and flashing eyes, but in every line of his young body there was an energy, a gallantry, a joy of life, that arrested and challenged one.

"Yes, that's where I got the notion," Hartwell remarked, wandering back to his seat in the window. "I've wanted to do it for years, but I've never felt quite sure of myself. I was afraid of missing it. He was an uncle of mine, my father's half-brother, and I was named for him. He was killed in one of the big battles of Sixty-four, when I was a child. I never saw him—never knew him until he had been dead for twenty years. And then, one night, I came to know him as we sometimes do living persons—intimately, in a single moment."

He paused to knock the ashes out of his short pipe, refilled it, and puffed at it thoughtfully for a few moments with his hands on his knees. Then, settling back heavily among the cushions and looking absently out of the window, he began his story. As he proceeded further and further into the experience which he was trying to convey to us, his voice sank so low and was sometimes so charged with feeling, that I almost thought he had forgotten our presence and was remembering aloud. Even Bentley forgot his nervousness in astonishment and sat breathless under the spell of the man's thus breathing his memories out into the dusk.

"It was just fifteen years ago this last spring that I first went home, and Bentley's having to cut away like this brings it all back to me.

"I was born, you know, in Italy. My father was a sculptor, though I dare say you've not heard of him. He was one of those first fellows who went over after Story and Powers,—went to Italy for 'Art,' quite simply; to lift from its native bough the willing, iridescent bird. Their story is told, informingly enough, by some of those ingenuous marble things at the Metropolitan. My father came over some time before the outbreak of the Civil War, and was regarded as a renegade by his family because he did not go home to enter the army. His half-brother, the only child of my grandfather's second marriage, enlisted at fifteen and was killed the next year. I was ten years old when the news of his death reached us. My mother died the following winter, and I was sent away to a Jesuit school, while my father, already ill himself, stayed on at Rome, chipping away at his Indian maidens and marble goddesses, still gloomily seeking the thing for which he had made himself the most unhappy of exiles.

"He died when I was fourteen, but even before that I had been put to work under an Italian sculptor. He had an almost morbid desire that I should carry on his work, under, as he often pointed out to me, conditions so much more auspicious. He left me in the charge of his one intimate friend, an American gentleman in the consulate at Rome, and his instructions were that I was to be educated there and to live there until I was twenty-one. After I was of age, I came to Paris and studied under one master after another until I was nearly thirty. Then, almost for the first time, I was confronted by a duty which was not my pleasure.

"My grandfather's death, at an advanced age, left an invalid maiden sister of my father's quite alone in the world. She had suffered for years from a cerebral disease, a slow decay of the faculties which rendered her almost helpless. I decided to go to America and, if possible, bring her back to Paris, where I seemed on my way toward what my poor father had wished for me.

"On my arrival at my father's birthplace, however, I found that this was not to be thought of. To tear this timid, feeble, shrinking creature, doubly aged by years and illness, from the spot where she had been rooted for a lifetime, would have been little short of brutality. To leave her to the care of strangers seemed equally heartless. There was clearly nothing for me to do but to remain and wait for that slow and painless malady to run its course. I was there something over two years.

"My grandfather's home, his father's homestead before him, lay on the high banks of a river in Western Pennsylvania. The little town twelve miles down the stream, whither my great-grandfather used to drive his ox-wagon on market days, had become, in two generations, one of the largest manufacturing cities in the world. For hundreds of miles about us the gentle hill slopes were honeycombed with gas wells and coal shafts; oil derricks creaked in every valley and meadow; the brooks were sluggish and discolored with crude petroleum, and the air was impregnated by its searching odor. The great glass and iron manufactories had come up and up the river almost to our very door; their smoky exhalations brooded over us, and their crashing was always in our ears. I was plunged into the very incandescence of human energy. But, though my nerves tingled with the feverish, passionate endeavor which snapped in the very air about me, none of these great arteries seemed to feed me; this tumultuous life did not warm me. On every side were the great muddy rivers, the ragged mountains from which the timber was being ruthlessly torn away, the vast tracts of wild country, and the gulches that were like wounds in the earth; everywhere the glare of that relentless energy which followed me like a searchlight and seemed to scorch and consume me. I could only hide myself in the tangled garden, where the dropping of a leaf or the whistle of a bird was the only incident.

"The Hartwell homestead had been sold away little by little, until all that remained of it was garden and orchard. The house, a square brick structure, stood in the midst of a great garden which sloped toward the river, ending in a grassy bank which fell some forty feet to the water's edge. The garden was now little more than a tangle of neglected shrubbery; damp, rank, and of that intense blue-green peculiar to vegetation in smoky places where the sun shines but rarely, and the mists form early in the evening and hang late in the morning.

"I shall never forget it as I saw it first, when I arrived there in the chill of a backward June. The long, rank grass, thick and soft and falling in billows, was always wet until midday. The gravel walks were bordered with great lilac-bushes, mock-orange, and bridal-wreath. Back of the house was a neglected rose garden, surrounded by a low stone wall over which the long suckers trailed and matted. They had wound their pink, thorny tentacles, layer upon layer, about the lock and the hinges of the rusty iron gate. Even the porches of the house, and the very windows, were damp and heavy with growth: wistaria, clematis, honeysuckle, and trumpet vine. The garden was grown up with trees, especially that part of it which lay above the river. The bark of the old locusts was blackened by the smoke that crept continually up the valley, and their feathery foliage, so merry in its movement and so yellow and joyous in its color, seemed peculiarly precious under that somber sky. There were sycamores and copper beeches; gnarled apple-trees, too old to bear; and fall pear-trees, hung with a sharp, hard fruit in October; all with a leafage singularly rich and luxuriant, and peculiarly vivid in color. The oaks about the house had been old trees when my great-grandfather built his cabin there, more than a century before, and this garden was almost the only spot for miles along the river where any of the original forest growth still survived. The smoke from the mills was fatal to trees of the larger sort, and even these had the look of doomed things—bent a little toward the town and seemed to wait with head inclined before that on-coming, shrieking force.

"About the river, too, there was a strange hush, a tragic submission—it was so leaden and sullen in its color, and it flowed so soundlessly forever past our door.

"I sat there every evening, on the high veranda overlooking it, watching the dim outlines of the steep hills on the other shore, the flicker of the lights on the island, where there was a boat-house, and listening to the call of the boatmen through the mist. The mist came as certainly as night, whitened by moonshine or starshine. The tin water-pipes went splash, splash, with it all evening, and the wind, when it rose at all, was little more than a sighing of the old boughs and a troubled breath in the heavy grasses.

"At first it was to think of my distant friends and my old life that I used to sit there; but after awhile it was simply to watch the days and weeks go by, like the river which seemed to carry them away.

"Within the house I was never at home. Month followed month, and yet I could feel no sense of kinship with anything there. Under the roof where my father and grandfather were born, I remained utterly detached. The somber rooms never spoke to me, the old furniture never seemed tinctured with race. This portrait of my boy uncle was the only thing to which I could draw near, the only link with anything I had ever known before.

"There is a good deal of my father in the face, but it is my father transformed and glorified; his hesitating discontent drowned in a kind of triumph. From my first day in that house, I continually turned to this handsome kinsman of mine, wondering in what terms he had lived and had his hope; what he had found there to look like that, to bound at one, after all those years, so joyously out of the canvas.

"From the timid, clouded old woman over whose life I had come to watch, I learned that in the backyard, near the old rose garden, there was a locust-tree which my uncle had planted. After his death, while it was still a slender sapling, his mother had a seat built round it, and she used to sit there on summer evenings. His grave was under the apple-trees in the old orchard.

"My aunt could tell me little more than this. There were days when she seemed not to remember him at all.

"It was from an old soldier in the village that I learned the boy's story. Lyon was, the old man told me, but fourteen when the first enlistment occurred, but was even then eager to go. He was in the court-house square every evening to watch the recruits at their drill, and when the home company was ordered off he rode into the city on his pony to see the men board the train and to wave them good-by. The next year he spent at home with a tutor, but when he was fifteen he held his parents to their promise and went into the army. He was color sergeant of his regiment and fell in a charge upon the breastworks of a fort about a year after his enlistment.

"The veteran showed me an account of this charge which had been written for the village paper by one of my uncle's comrades who had seen his part in the engagement. It seems that as his company were running at full speed across the bottom lands toward the fortified hill, a shell burst over them. This comrade, running beside my uncle, saw the colors waver and sink as if falling, and looked to see that the boy's hand and forearm had been torn away by the exploding shrapnel. The boy, he thought, did not realize the extent of his injury, for he laughed, shouted something which his comrade did not catch, caught the flag in his left hand, and ran on up the hill. They went splendidly up over the breastworks, but just as my uncle, his colors flying, reached the top of the embankment, a second shell carried away his left arm at the arm-pit, and he fell over the wall with the flag settling about him.

"It was because this story was ever present with me, because I was unable to shake it off, that I began to read such books as my grandfather had collected upon the Civil War. I found that this war was fought largely by boys, that more men enlisted at eighteen than at any other age. When I thought of those battlefields—and I thought of them much in those days—there was always that glory of youth above them, that impetuous, generous passion stirring the long lines on the march, the blue battalions in the plain. The bugle, whenever I have heard it since, has always seemed to me the very golden throat of that boyhood which spent itself so gaily, so incredibly.

"I used often to wonder how it was that this uncle of mine, who seemed to have possessed all the charm and brilliancy allotted to his family and to have lived up its vitality in one splendid hour, had left so little trace in the house where he was born and where he had awaited his destiny. Look as I would, I could find no letters from him, no clothing or books that might have been his. He had been dead but twenty years, and yet nothing seemed to have survived except the tree he had planted. It seemed incredible and cruel that no physical memory of him should linger to be cherished among his kindred,—nothing but the dull image in the brain of that aged sister. I used to pace the garden walks in the evening, wondering that no breath of his, no echo of his laugh, of his call to his pony or his whistle to his dogs, should linger about those shaded paths where the pale roses exhaled their dewy, country smell. Sometimes, in the dim starlight, I have thought that I heard on the grasses beside me the stir of a footfall lighter than my own, and under the black arch of the lilacs I have fancied that he bore me company.

"There was, I found, one day in the year for which my old aunt waited, and which stood out from the months that were all of a sameness to her. On the thirtieth of May she insisted that I should bring down the big flag from the attic and run it up upon the tall flagstaff beside Lyon's tree in the garden. Later in the morning she went with me to carry some of the garden flowers to the grave in the orchard,—a grave scarcely larger than a child's.

"I had noticed, when I was hunting for the flag in the attic, a leather trunk with my own name stamped upon it, but was unable to find the key. My aunt was all day less apathetic than usual; she seemed to realize more clearly who I was, and to wish me to be with her. I did not have an opportunity to return to the attic until after dinner that evening, when I carried a lamp up-stairs and easily forced the lock of the trunk. I found all the things that I had looked for; put away, doubtless, by his mother, and still smelling faintly of lavender and rose leaves; his clothes, his exercise books, his letters from the army, his first boots, his riding-whip, some of his toys, even. I took them out and replaced them gently. As I was about to shut the lid, I picked up a copy of the Æneid, on the fly-leaf of which was written in a slanting, boyish hand, Lyon Hartwell, January, 1862. He had gone to the wars in Sixty-three, I remembered.

"My uncle, I gathered, was none too apt at his Latin, for the pages were dog-eared and rubbed and interlined, the margins mottled with pencil sketches—bugles, stacked bayonets, and artillery carriages. In the act of putting the book down, I happened to run over the pages to the end, and on the fly-leaf at the back I saw his name again, and a drawing—with his initials and a date—of the Federal flag; above it, written in a kind of arch and in the same unformed hand:

"Oh, say, can you see by the dawn's early light
What so proudly we hailed at the twilight's last gleaming?"

It was a stiff, wooden sketch, not unlike a detail from some Egyptian inscription, but, the moment I saw it, wind and color seemed to touch it. I caught up the book, blew out the lamp, and rushed down into the garden.

"I seemed, somehow, at last to have known him; to have been with him in that careless, unconscious moment and to have known him as he was then.

"As I sat there in the rush of this realization, the wind began to rise, stirring the light foliage of the locust over my head and bringing, fresher than before, the woody odor of the pale roses that overran the little neglected garden. Then, as it grew stronger, it brought the sound of something sighing and stirring over my head in the perfumed darkness.

"I thought of that sad one of the Destinies who, as the Greeks believed, watched from birth over those marked for a violent or untimely death. Oh, I could see him, there in the shine of the morning, his book idly on his knee, his flashing eyes looking straight before him, and at his side that grave figure, hidden in her draperies, her eyes following his, but seeing so much farther—seeing what he never saw, that great moment at the end, when he swayed above his comrades on the earthen wall.

"All the while, the bunting I had run up in the morning flapped fold against fold, heaving and tossing softly in the dark—against a sky so black with rain clouds that I could see above me only the blur of something in soft, troubled motion.

"The experience of that night, coming so overwhelmingly to a man so dead, almost rent me in pieces. It was the same feeling that artists know when we, rarely, achieve truth in our work; the feeling of union with some great force, of purpose and security, of being glad that we have lived. For the first time I felt the pull of race and blood and kindred, and felt beating within me things that had not begun with me. It was as if the earth under my feet had grasped and rooted me, and were pouring its essence into me. I sat there until the dawn of morning, and all night long my life seemed to be pouring out of me and running into the ground."

Hartwell drew a long breath that lifted his heavy shoulders, and then let them fall again. He shifted a little and faced more squarely the scattered, silent company before him. The darkness had made us almost invisible to each other, and, except for the occasional red circuit of a cigarette end traveling upward from the arm of a chair, he might have supposed us all asleep.

"And so," Hartwell added thoughtfully, "I naturally feel an interest in fellows who are going home. It's always an experience."

No one said anything, and in a moment there was a loud rap at the door,—the concierge, come to take down Bentley's luggage and to announce that the cab was below. Bentley got his hat and coat, enjoined Hartwell to take good care of his *per-roquets,* gave each of us a grip of the hand, and went briskly down the long flights of stairs. We followed him into the street, calling our good wishes, and saw him start on his drive across the lighted city to the Gare St. Lazare.

Richard Harding Davis

(1864–1916)

The son of Clarke Davis, a prominent Philadelphia journalist, and Rebecca Harding Davis, author of "Life in the Iron Mills" (1861) and numerous other works of fiction, Richard Harding Davis seems to have been born to his profession. As a journalist and fiction writer, Davis enjoyed tremendous commercial success. He popularized the romantic image of the warfront journalist, and though later writers ultimately rejected his optimistic view of America and his sentimental fictional aesthetic, his adventurous lifestyle prefigures that of other journalist-novelists such as Stephen Crane, Jack London, and Ernest Hemingway. His short fiction was first collected in *Gallegher and Other Stories* (1891), and his war correspondence appeared in several books. During the First World War, Davis reported vividly on the German army's occupation of Brussels in an account that has been frequently anthologized. Later, he covered the war from the Balkan front, and his story "The Man Who Had Everything" is based on an encounter with a young American in the British army. Biographer Arthur Lubow notes that this story is unlike most of Davis's other fiction in that it depicts "the sordid, unheroic reality of war.[1] The story originally appeared in *Metropolitan* in September 1916 and was collected in *Lost Road* (1916). It appeared in book form in 1917, with a new title as *The Deserter* and with an introduction by John T. McCutcheon.

---

1. Arthur Lubow, *The Reporter Who Would Be King: A Biography of Richard Harding Davis* (New York: Charles Scribner's Sons, 1992), 326.

The Man Who Had Everything

Richard Harding Davis

In Salonika, the American consul, the Standard Oil man, and the war correspondents formed the American colony. The correspondents were waiting to go to the front. Incidentally, as we waited, the front was coming rapidly toward us. There was "Uncle" Jim, the veteran of many wars, and of all the correspondents, in experience the oldest and in spirit the youngest, and there was the Kid, and the Artist. The Kid jeered at us, and proudly described himself as the only Boy Reporter who jumped from a City Hall assignment to cover a European War. "I don't know strategy," he would boast; "neither does the Man at Home. He wants 'human interest' stuff, and I give him what he wants. I write exclusively for the subway guard and the farmers in the wheat belt. When you fellows write about the 'Situation,' they don't understand it. Neither do you. Neither does Venizelos or the King. I don't understand it myself. So, I write my people heart-to-heart talks about refugees and wounded, and what kind of ploughs the Servian peasants use, and that St. Paul wrote his letters to the Thessalonians from the same hotel where I write mine; and I tell 'em to pronounce Salonika 'eeka,' and *not* put the accent on the 'on.' This morning at the refugee camp I found all the little Servians of the Frothingham unit in American Boy Scout uniforms. That's my meat. That's 'home week' stuff. You fellows write for the editorial page; and nobody reads it. I write for the man that turns first to Mutt and Jeff, and then looks to see where they are running the new Charlie Chaplin release. When that man has to choose between 'our military correspondent' and the City Hall Reporter, he chooses me!"

The third man was John, "Our Special Artist." John could write a news story, too, but it was the cartoons that had made him famous. They were not comic page, but front page cartoons, and before making up their minds what they thought, people waited to see what their Artist thought. So, it was fortunate his thoughts were as brave and clean as they were clever. He was the original Little Brother to the Poor. He was always giving away money. When we caught him, he would prevaricate. He would say the man was a college chum, that he had borrowed the money from him, and that this was the first chance he had had to pay it back. The Kid suggested it was strange that so many of his college chums should at the same moment turn up, dead broke, in Salonika, and that half of them should be women.

John smiled disarmingly. "It was a large college," he explained, "and coeducational." There were other Americans; Red Cross doctors and nurses just escaped through the snow from the Bulgars, and hyphenated Americans who said they had taken out their first papers. They thought hyphenated citizens were so popular with us, that we would pay their passage to New York. In Salonika they were transients. They had no local standing. They had no local lying-down place, either, or place to eat, or to wash, although they did not look as though that worried them, or place to change their clothes. Or clothes to change. It was because we had clothes to change, and a hotel bedroom, instead of a bench in a café, that we were ranked as residents and from the Greek police held a "permission to sojourn." Our American colony was a very close corporation. We were only six Americans against 300,000 British, French, Greek, and Servian soldiers, and 120,000 civilian Turks, Spanish Jews, Armenians, Persians, Egyptians, Albanians, and Arabs, and some twenty more other races that are not listed. We had arrived in Salonika before the rush, and at the Hotel Hermes on the water-front had secured a vast room. The edge of the stone quay was not forty feet from us, the only landing steps directly opposite our balcony. Everybody who arrived on the Greek passenger boats from Naples or the Piræus, or who had shore leave from a man-of-war, transport, or hospital ship, was raked by our cameras. There were four windows—one for each of us and his work table. It was not easy to work. What was the use? The pictures and stories outside the windows fascinated us, but when we sketched them or wrote about them, they only proved us inadequate. All day long the pinnaces, cutters, gigs, steam launches shoved and bumped against the stone steps, marines came ashore for the mail, stewards for fruit and fish, Red Cross nurses to shop, tiny midshipmen to visit the movies, and the sailors and officers of the Russian, French, British, Italian, and Greek war-ships to stretch their legs in the park of the Tour Blanche, or to cramp them under a café table. Sometimes the ambulances blocked the quay and the wounded and frost-bitten were lifted into the motor-boats, and sometimes a squad of marines lined the landing stage, and as a coffin under a French or English flag was borne up the stone steps stood at salute. So crowded was the harbor that the oars of the boatmen interlocked.

Close to the stone quay, stretched along the three-mile circle, were the fishing smacks, beyond them, so near that the anchor chains fouled, were the passenger ships with gigantic Greek flags painted on their sides, and beyond them transports from Marseilles, Malta, and Suvla Bay, black colliers, white hospital ships, burning green electric lights, red-bellied tramps and freighters, and, hemming them in, the grim, mouse-colored destroyers, submarines, cruisers, dreadnaughts. At times, like a wall, the cold fog rose between us and the harbor, and again the curtain would suddenly be ripped asunder, and the sun would flash on the brass work of the fleet, on the white wings of the aeroplanes, on the snow-draped shoulders of Mount Olympus. We often speculated as to how in the early days the gods and goddesses, dressed as they were, or as they were not, survived the snows of Mount Olympus. Or was it only their resort for the summer?

It got about that we had a vast room to ourselves, where one might obtain a drink, or a sofa for the night, or even money to cable for money. So, we had many strange visitors, some half starved, half frozen, with terrible tales of the Albanian trail, of the Austrian prisoners fallen by the wayside, of the mountain passes heaped with dead, of the doctors and nurses wading waist-high in snow-drifts and for food killing the ponies. Some of our visitors wanted to get their names in the American papers so that the folks at home would know they were still alive, others wanted us to keep their names out of the papers, hoping the police would think them dead; another, convinced it was of pressing news value, desired us to advertise the fact that he had invented a poisonous gas for use in the trenches. With difficulty we prevented him from casting it adrift in our room. Or, he had for sale a second-hand motorcycle, or he would accept a position as barkeeper, or for five francs would sell a state secret that, once made public, in a month would end the war. It seemed cheap at the price.

Each of us had his "scouts" to bring him the bazaar rumor, the Turkish bath rumor, the café rumor. Some of our scouts journeyed as far afield as Monastir and Doiran, returning to drip snow on the floor, and to tell us tales, one-half of which we refused to believe, and the other half the censor refused to pass. With each other's visitors it was etiquette not to interfere. It would have been like tapping a private wire. When we found John sketching a giant stranger in a cap and coat of wolf skin we did not seek to know if he were an Albanian brigand, or a Servian prince *incognito*, and when a dark Levantine sat close to the Kid, whispering, and the Kid banged on his typewriter, we did not listen.

So, when I came in one afternoon and found a strange American youth writing at John's table, and no one introduced us, I took it for granted he had sold the Artist an "exclusive" story, and asked no questions. But I could not help hearing what they said. Even though I tried to drown their voices by beating on the Kid's typewriter. I was taking my third lesson, and I had printed, "I Amm 5W writjng This, 5wjth my own lilly w?ite handS," when I heard the Kid saying:

"You can beat the game this way. Let John buy you a ticket to the Piræus. If you go from one Greek port to another you don't need a visé. But, if you book from here to Italy, you must get a permit from the Italian consul, and our consul, and the police. The plot is to get out of the war zone, isn't it? Well, then, my dope is to get out quick, and map the rest of your trip when you're safe in Athens."

It was no business of mine, but I had to look up. The stranger was now pacing the floor. I noticed that while his face was almost black with tan, his upper lip was quite white. I noticed also that he had his hands in the pockets of one of John's blue serge suits, and that the pink silk shirt he wore was one that once had belonged to the Kid. Except for the pink shirt, in the appearance of the young man there was nothing unusual. He was of a familiar type. He looked like a young business man from our Middle West, matter-of-fact and unimaginative, but capable and self-reliant. If had had a fountain pen in his upper waistcoat pocket, I would have guessed he was an insurance agent, or the publicity man for a new automobile. John picked up his hat, and said, "That's good advice. Give me your steamer ticket, Fred, and I'll have them change it." He went out; but he did not ask Fred to go with him.

Uncle Jim rose, and murmured something about the Café Roma, and tea. But neither did he invite Fred to go with him. Instead, he told him to make himself at home, and if he wanted anything the waiter would bring it from the cafe downstairs. Then the Kid, as though he also was uncomfortable at being left alone with us, hurried to the door. "Going to get you a suit-case," he explained. "Back in five minutes."

The stranger made no answer. Probably he did not hear him. Not a hundred feet from our windows three Greek steamers were huddled together, and the eyes of the American were fixed on them. The one for which John had gone to buy him a new ticket lay nearest. She was to sail in two hours. Impatiently, in short quick steps, the stranger paced the length of the room, but when he turned and so could see the harbor, he walked slowly, devouring it with his eyes. For some time, in silence, he repeated this manœuvre; and then the complaints of the typewriter disturbed him. He halted and observed my struggles. Under his scornful eye, in my embarrassment I frequently hit the right letter. "You a newspaper man, too?" he asked. I boasted I was, but begged not to be judged by my typewriting.

"I got some great stories to write when I get back to God's country," he announced. "I was a reporter for two years in Kansas City before the war, and now I'm going back to lecture and write. I got enough material to keep me at work for five years. All kinds of stuff—specials, fiction stories, personal experiences, maybe a novel."

I regarded him with envy. For the correspondents in the greatest of all wars the pickings had been meagre. "You are to be congratulated," I said. He brushed aside my congratulations. "For what?" he demanded. "I didn't go after the stories; they came to me. The things I saw I had to see. Couldn't get away from them. I've been with the British, serving in the R. A. M. C. Been hospital steward, stretcher bearer, ambulance driver. I've been sixteen months at the front, and all the time on the firing-line. I was in the retreat from Mons, with French on the Marne, at Ypres, all through the winter fighting along the Canal, on the Gallipoli Peninsula, and, just lately, in Servia. I've seen more of this war than any soldier. Because, sometimes, they give the soldier a rest; they never give the medical corps a rest. The only rest I got was when I was wounded."

He seemed no worse for his wounds, so again I tendered congratulations. This time he accepted them. The recollection of the things he had seen, things incredible, terrible, unique in human experience, had stirred him. He talked on, not boastfully, but in a tone, rather, of awe and disbelief, as though assuring himself that it was really he to whom such things had happened.

"I don't believe there's any kind of fighting I haven't seen," he declared; "hand-to-hand fighting with bayonets, grenades, gun butts. I've seen 'em on their knees in the mud choking each other, beating each other with their bare fists. I've seen every kind of airship, bomb, shell, poison gas, every kind of wound. Seen whole villages turned into a brickyard in twenty minutes; in Servia seen bodies of women frozen to death, bodies of babies starved to death, seen men in Belgium swinging from trees; along the Yzer for three months I saw the bodies of men I'd known sticking out of the mud, or hung up on the barb wire, with the crows picking them.

"I've seen some of the nerviest stunts that ever were pulled off in history. I've seen *real* heroes. Time and time again I've seen a man throw away his life for his officer, or for a chap he didn't know, just as though it was a cigarette butt. I've seen the women nurses of our corps steer a car into a village and yank out a wounded man while shells were breaking under the wheels and the houses were pitching into the streets." He stopped and laughed consciously.

"Understand," he warned me, "I'm not talking about myself, only of things I've seen. The things I'm going to put in my book. It ought to be a pretty good book—what?"

My envy had been washed clean in admiration.

"It will make a wonderful book," I agreed. "Are you going to syndicate it first?"

Young Mr. Hamlin frowned importantly.

"I was thinking," he said, "of asking John for letters to the magazine editors. So, they'll know I'm not faking, that I've really been through it all. Letters from John would help a lot." Then he asked anxiously: "They would, wouldn't they?"

I reassured him. Remembering the Kid's gibes at John and his numerous dependents, I said: "You another college chum of John's?" The young man answered my question quite seriously. "No," he said; "John graduated before I entered; but we belong to the same fraternity. It was the luckiest chance in the world my finding him here. There was a month-old copy of the *Balkan News* blowing around camp, and his name was in the list of arrivals. The moment I found he was in Salonika, I asked for twelve hours' leave, and came down in an ambulance. I made straight for John; gave him the grip, and put it up to him to help me."

"I don't understand," I said. "I thought you were sailing on the *Adriaticus?*"

The young man was again pacing the floor. He halted and faced the harbor.

"You bet I'm sailing on the *Adriaticus*," he said. He looked out at that vessel, at the Blue Peter flying from her foremast, and grinned. "In just two hours!"

It was stupid of me, but I still was unenlightened. "But your twelve hours' leave?" I asked.

The young man laughed. "They can take my twelve hours' leave," he said deliberately, "and feed it to the chickens. I'm beating it."

"What d'you mean, you're beating it?"

"What do you suppose I mean?" he demanded. "What do you suppose I'm doing out of uniform, what do you suppose I'm lying low in the room for? So's I won't catch cold?"

"If you're leaving the army without a discharge, and without permission," I said, "I suppose you know it's desertion."

Mr. Hamlin laughed easily. "It's not *my* army," he said. "I'm an American."

"It's your desertion," I suggested.

The door opened and closed noiselessly, and Billy, entering, placed a new travelling bag on the floor. He must have heard my last words, for he looked inquiringly at each of us. But he did not speak and, walking to the window, stood with his hands in his pockets, staring out at the harbor. His presence seemed to encourage the young man. "Who knows I'm deserting?" he demanded. "No one's ever seen me in Salonika before, and in these 'cits' I can get on board all right. And then they can't touch me. What do the folks at home care *how* I left the British army? They'll be so darned glad to get me back alive that they won't ask if I walked out or was kicked out. I should worry!"

"It's none of my business," I began, but I was interrupted. In his restless pacings the young man turned quickly.

"As you say," he remarked icily, "it *is* none of your business. It's none of your business whether I get shot as a deserter, or go home, or——"

"You can go to the devil for all I care," I assured him. "I wasn't considering you at all. I was only sorry that I'll never be able to read your book."

For a moment Mr. Hamlin remained silent, then he burst forth with a jeer.

"No British firing squad," he boasted, "will ever stand *me* up."

"Maybe not," I agreed, "but you will never write that book."

Again there was silence, and this time it was broken by the Kid. He turned from the window and looked toward Hamlin. "That's right!" he said.

He sat down on the edge of the table, and at the deserter pointed his forefinger.

"Son," he said, "this war is some war. It's the biggest war in history, and folks will be talking about nothing else for the next ninety years; folks that never were nearer it than Bay City, Mich. But you won't talk about it. And you've been all through it. You've been to hell and back again. Compared with what you know about hell, Dante is in the same class with Dr. Cook. But you won't be able to talk about this war, or lecture, or write a book about it."

"I won't?" demanded Hamlin. "And why won't I?"

"Because of what you're doing now," said Billy. "Because you're queering yourself.

Now, you've got everything." The Kid was very much in earnest. His tone was intimate, kind, and friendly. "You've seen everything, done everything. We'd give our eye-teeth to see what you've seen, and to write the things you can write. You've got a record now that'll last you until you're dead, and your grandchildren are dead—and then some. When you talk the table will have to sit up and listen. You can say 'I was there.' 'I was in it.' 'I saw.' 'I know.' When this war is over you'll have everything out of it that's worth getting—all the experiences, all the inside knowledge, all the 'nosebag' news; you'll have wounds, honors, medals, money, reputation. And you're throwing all that away!"

Mr. Hamlin interrupted savagely. "To hell with their medals," he said. "They can take their medals and hang 'em on Christmas trees. I don't owe the British army anything. It owes me. I've done *my* bit. I've earned what I've got, and there's no one can take it away from me."

"*You* can," said the Kid. Before Hamlin could reply the door opened and John came in, followed by Uncle Jim. The older man was looking very grave, and John very unhappy. Hamlin turned quickly to John.

"I thought these men were friends of yours," he began, "and Americans. They're fine Americans. They're as full of human kindness and red blood as a kippered herring!"

John looked inquiringly at the Kid.

"He wants to hang himself," explained Billy, "and because we tried to cut him down, he's sore."

"They talked to me," protested Hamlin, "as though I was a yellow dog. As though I was a quitter. I'm no quitter! But, if I'm ready to quit, who's got a better right? I'm not an Englishman, but there are several million Englishmen haven't done as much for England in this war as I have. What do you fellows know about it? You *write* about it, about the 'brave lads in the trenches'; but what do you know about the trenches? What you've seen from automobiles. That's all. That's where *you* get off! I've *lived* in the trenches for fifteen months, froze in 'em, starved in 'em, risked my life in 'em, and I've saved other lives, too, by hauling men out of the trenches. And that's no airy persiflage, either!"

He ran to the wardrobe where John's clothes hung, and from the bottom of it dragged a khaki uniform. It was still so caked with mud and snow that when he flung it on the floor it splashed like a wet bathing suit. "How would you like to wear one of those?" he demanded. "Stinking with lice and sweat and blood; the blood of other men, the men you've helped off the field, and your own blood."

As though committing hara-kiri, he slashed his hand across his stomach, and then drew it up from his waist to his chin. "I'm scraped with shrapnel from there to there," said Mr. Hamlin. "And another time got a ball in the shoulder. That would have been a 'blighty' for a fighting man—they're always giving *them* leave—but all I got was six weeks at Havre in hospital. Then it was the Dardanelles, and sunstroke and sand; sleeping in sand, eating sand, sand in your boots, sand in your teeth; hiding in holes in the sand like a dirty prairie dog. And then, 'Off to Servia!' And the next act opens in the snow and the mud! Cold? God, how cold it was! And most of us in sun helmets."

As though the cold still gnawed at his bones, he shivered.

"It isn't the danger," he protested. " It isn't *that* I'm getting away from. To hell with the danger! It's just the plain discomfort of it! It's the never being your own master, never being clean, never being warm." Again he shivered and rubbed one hand against the other. "There were no bridges over the streams," he went on, "and we had to break the ice and wade in, and then sleep in the open with the khaki frozen to us. There was no firewood; not enough to warm a pot of tea. There were no wounded; all our casualties were frost bite and pneumonia. When we take them out of the blankets their toes fall off. We've been in camp for a month now near Doiran, and it's worse there than on the march. It's a frozen swamp. You can't sleep for the cold; can't eat; the only ration we get is bully beef, and our insides are frozen so damn tight we can't digest it. The cold gets into your blood, gets into your brains. It won't let you think; or else, you think crazy things. It makes you afraid." He shook himself like a man coming out of a bad dream.

"So, I'm through," he said. In turn he scowled at each of us, as though defying us to contradict him. "That's why I'm quitting," he added. "Because I've done my bit. Because I'm damn well fed up on it." He kicked viciously at the water-logged uniform on the floor. "Any one who wants my job can have it!" He walked to the window, turned his back on us, and fixed his eyes hungrily on the *Adriaticus*. There was a long pause. For guidance we looked at John, but he was staring down at the desk blotter, scratching on it marks that he did not see.

Finally, where angels feared to tread, the Kid rushed in. "That's certainly a hard luck story," he said; "but," he added cheerfully, "it's nothing to the hard luck you'll strike when you can't tell why you left the army." Hamlin turned with an exclamation, but Billy held up his hand. "Now Wait," he begged, "we haven't time to get mussy. At six o'clock your leave is up, and the troop train starts back to camp, and——"

Mr. Hamlin interrupted sharply. "And the *Adriaticus* starts at five."

Billy did not heed him. "You've got two hours to change your mind," he said. "That's better than being sorry you didn't the rest of your life."

Mr. Hamlin threw back his head and laughed. It was a most unpleasant laugh. "You're a fine body of men," he jeered. "America must be proud of you!"

"If we *weren't* Americans," explained Billy patiently, "we wouldn't give a damn whether you deserted or not. You're drowning and you don't know it, and we're throwing you a rope. Try to see it that way. We'll cut out the fact that you took an oath, and that you're breaking it. That's up to you. We'll get down to results. When you reach home, if you can't tell why you left the army, the folks will darned soon guess. And that will queer everything you've done. When you come to sell your stuff, it will queer you with the editors, queer you with the publishers. If they know you broke your word to the British army, how can they know you're keeping faith with them? How can they believe anything you tell them? Every 'story' you write, every statement of yours will make a noise like a fake. You won't come into court with clean hands. You'll be licked before you start.

"Of course, you're for the Allies. Well, all the Germans at home will fear that; and when you want to lecture on your 'Fifteen Months at the British Front,' they'll look up your record; and what will they do to you? This is what they'll do to you. When you've shown 'em your moving pictures and say, 'Does any gentleman in the audience want to ask a question?' A German agent will get up and say, 'Yes, I want to ask a question. Is it true that you deserted from the British army, and that if you return to it, they will shoot you?'"

I was scared. I expected the lean and muscular Mr. Hamlin to fall on Billy, and fling him where he had flung the soggy uniform. But instead he remained motionless, his arms pressed across his chest. His eyes, filled with anger and distress, returned to the *Adriaticus*.

"I'm sorry," muttered the Kid.

John rose and motioned to the door, and guiltily and only too gladly we escaped. John followed us into the hall. "Let *me* talk to him," he whispered. "The boat sails in an hour. Please don't come back until she's gone."

We went to the moving picture place next door, but I doubt if the thoughts of any of us were on the pictures. For after an hour, when from across the quay there came the long-drawn warning of a steamer's whistle, we nudged each other and rose and went out.

Not a hundred yards from us the propeller blades of the *Adriaticus* were slowly churning, and the rowboats were falling away from her sides.

"Good-bye, Mr. Hamlin," called Billy. "You had everything and you chucked it away. I can spell your finish. It's 'check' for *yours*."

But when we entered our room, in the centre of it, under the bunch of electric lights, stood the deserter. He wore the water-logged uniform. The sun helmet was on his head.

"Good man!" shouted Billy.

He advanced, eagerly holding out his hand.

Mr. Hamlin brushed past him. At the door he turned and glared at us, even at John. He was not a good loser. "I hope you're satisfied," he snarled. He pointed at the four beds in a row. I felt guiltily conscious of them. At the moment they appeared so unnecessarily clean and warm and soft. The silk coverlets at the foot of each struck me as being disgracefully effeminate. They made me ashamed.

"I hope," said Mr. Hamlin, speaking slowly and picking his words, "when you turn into those beds to-night you'll think of me in the mud. I hope when you're having your five-course dinner and your champagne you'll remember my bully beef. I hope when a shell or Mr. Pneumonia gets me, you'll write a nice little sob story about the 'brave lads in the trenches.'"

He looked at us, standing like schoolboys, sheepish, embarrassed, and silent, and then threw open the door. "I hope," he added, "you all choke!"

With an unconvincing imitation of the college chum manner, John cleared his throat and said: "Don't forget, Fred, if there's anything I can do——"

Hamlin stood in the doorway smiling at us.

"There's something you can all do," he said

"Yes?" aside John heartily.

"You can all go to hell!" said Mr. Hamlin.

We heard the door slam, and his hobnailed boots pounding down the stairs. No one spoke. Instead, in unhappy silence, we stood staring at the floor. Where the uniform had lain was a pool of mud and melted snow and the darker stains of stale blood.

Fanny Kemble Johnson

(1868–1950)

A resident of West Virginia, Fanny Kemble Johnson was a poet and fiction writer. In addition to the novel *The Beloved Son* (1916), Johnson published a number of short stories in distinguished venues such as *Harper's Magazine* and the *Atlantic Monthly.* "The Strange-Looking Man" appeared in the *Pagan* in December 1917 and was later collected in *The Best Short Stories of 1917.*

The Strange-Looking Man

Fanny Kemble Johnson

A tiny village lay among the mountains of a country from which for four years the men had gone forth to fight. First the best men had gone, then the older men, then the youths, and lastly the school boys. It will be seen that no men could have been left in the village except the very aged, and the bodily incapacitated, who soon died, owing to the war policy of the Government which was to let the useless perish that there might be more food for the useful.

Now it chanced that while all the men went away, save those left to die of slow starvation, only a few returned, and these few were crippled and disfigured in various ways. One young man had only part of a face, and had to wear a painted tin mask, like a holiday-maker. Another had two legs but no arms, and another two arms but no legs. One man could scarcely be looked at by his own mother, having had his eyes burned out of his head until he stared like Death. One had neither arms nor legs, and was mad of his misery besides, and lay all day in a cradle like a baby. And there was a quite old man who strangled night and day from having sucked in poison-gas; and another, a mere boy, who shook, like a leaf in a high wind, from shell-shock, and screamed at a sound. And he too had lost a hand, and part of his face, though not enough to warrant the expense of a mask for him.

All these men, except he who had been crazed by horror of himself, had been furnished with ingenious appliances to enable them to be partly self-supporting, and to earn enough to pay their share of the taxes which burdened their defeated nation.

To go through that village after the war was something like going through a life-sized toy-village with all the mechanical figures wound up and clicking. Only instead of the figures being new, and gay, and pretty, they were battered and grotesque and inhuman.

There would be the windmill, and the smithy, and the public house. There would be the row of cottages, the village church, the sparkling waterfall, the parti-colored fields spread out like bright kerchiefs on the hillsides, the parading fowl, the goats and cows,—though not many of these last. There would be the women, and with them some children; very few, however, for the women had been getting reasonable, and were now refusing to have sons who might one day be sent back to them limbless and mad, to be rocked in cradles—for many years, perhaps.

Still the younger women, softer creatures of impulse, had borne a child or two. One of these, born the second year of the war, was a very blonde and bullet-headed rascal of three, with a bullying air, and of a roving disposition. But such traits appear engaging in children of sufficiently tender years, and he was a sort of village plaything, here, there, and everywhere, on the most familiar terms with the wrecks of the war which the Government of that country had made.

He tried on the tin mask and played with the baker's mechanical leg, so indulgent were they of his caprices; and it amused him excessively to rock the cradle of the man who had no limbs, and who was his father.

In and out he ran, and was humored to his bent. To one he seemed the son he had lost, to another the son he might have had, had the world gone differently. To others he served as a brief escape from the shadow of a future without hope; to others yet, the diversion of an hour. This last was especially true of the blind man who sat at the door of his old mother's cottage binding brooms. The presence of the child seemed to him like a warm ray of sunshine falling across his hand, and he would lure him to linger by letting him try on the great blue goggles which he found it best to wear in public. But no disfigurement or deformity appeared to frighten the little fellow. These had been his playthings from earliest infancy.

One morning, his mother, being busy washing clothes, had left him alone, confident that he would soon seek out some friendly fragment of soldier, and entertain himself till noon and hunger-time. But occasionally children have odd notions, and do the exact opposite of what one supposes.

On this brilliant summer morning the child fancied a solitary ramble along the bank of the mountain-stream. Vaguely he meant to seek a pool higher up, and to cast stones in it. He wandered slowly straying now and then into small valleys, or chasing wayside ducks. It was past ten before he gained the green-gleaming and foam-whitened pool, sunk in the shadow of a tall gray rock over whose flat top three pine-trees swayed in the fresh breeze. Under them, looking to the child like a white cloud in a green sky, stood a beautiful young man, poised on the sheer brink for a dive. A single instant he stood there, clad only in shadow and sunshine, the next he had dived so expertly that he scarcely splashed up the water around him. Then his dark, dripping head rose in sight, his glittering arm thrust up, and he swam vigorously to shore. He climbed the rock for another dive. These actions he repeated in pure sport and joy in life so often that his little spectator became dizzy with watching.

At length he had enough of it and stooped for his discarded garments. These he carried to a more sheltered spot and rapidly put on, the child still wide-eyed and wondering, for indeed he had much to occupy his attention.

He had two arms, two legs, a whole face with eyes, nose, mouth, chin, and ears, complete. He could see, for he had glanced about him as he dressed. He could speak, for he sang loudly. He could hear, for he had turned quickly at the whir of pigeon-wings behind him. His skin was smooth all over, and nowhere on it were the dark scarlet maps which the child found so interesting on the arms, face, and breast of the burned man. He did not strangle every little while, or shiver madly, and scream at a sound. It was truly inexplicable, and therefore terrifying.

The child was beginning to whimper, to tremble, to look wildly about for his mother, when the young man observed him.

"*Hullo!*" he cried eagerly, "if it isn't a child!"

He came forward across the foot-bridge with a most ingratiating smile, for this was the first time that day he had seen a child and he had been thinking it remarkable that there should be so few children in a valley, where, when he had travelled that way five years before, there had been so many he had scarcely been able to find pennies for them. So he cried "Hullo," quite joyously, and searched in his pockets.

But, to his amazement, the bullet-headed little blond boy screamed out in terror, and fled for protection into the arms of a hurriedly approaching young woman. She embraced him with evident relief, and was lavishing on him terms of scolding and endearment in the same breath, when the traveler came up, looking as if his feelings were hurt.

"I assure you, Madam," said he, "that I only meant to give your little boy these pennies." He examined himself with an air of wonder. "What on earth is there about me to frighten a child?" he queried plaintively.

The young peasant-woman smiled indulgently on them both, on the child now sobbing, his face buried in her skirt, and on the boyish, perplexed, and beautiful young man.

"It is because he finds the Herr Traveler so strange-looking," she said, curtsying. "He is quite small," she showed his smallness with a gesture, "and it is the first time he has even seen a whole man."

Edna Ferber
(1885–1968)

The author of a number of best-selling novels such as *So Big* (1924), *Show Boat* (1926), and *Giant* (1952), Edna Ferber began her career as a fiction writer with a series of stories featuring the character Emma McChesney, a traveling "salesman." Originally published in *American Magazine* and *Cosmopolitan* from 1911 to 1915, the McChesney stories were collected in three volumes: *Roast Beef, Medium* (1913), *Personality Plus* (1914), and *Emma McChesney & Co.* (1915). Ferber brings back Emma McChesney in "One Hundred Per Cent," which first appeared in *Metropolitan* in October 1918 and was collected in *Half Portions* (1920). In this last McChesney story, the popularity of Emma as a character allows Ferber to celebrate patriotic, home-front sacrifice.

One Hundred Per Cent
Edna Ferber

They had always had two morning papers—he his, she hers. The *Times*. Both. Nothing could illustrate more clearly the plan on which Mr. and Mrs. T. A. Buck conducted their married life. Theirs was the morning calm and harmony which comes to two people who are free to digest breakfast and the First Page simultaneously with no—"Just let me see the inside sheet, will you, dear?" to mar the day's beginning.

In the days when she had been Mrs. Emma McChesney, traveling saleswoman for the T. A. Buck Featherloom Petticoat Company, New York, her perusal of the morning's news had been, perforce, a hasty process, accomplished between trains, or in a small-town hotel 'bus, jolting its way to the depot for the 7:52; or over an

American-plan breakfast throughout which seven eighths of her mind was intent on the purchasing possibilities of a prospective nine o'clock skirt buyer. There was no need now of haste, but the habit of years still clung. From eight-thirty to eight thirty-five a.m. Emma McChesney Buck was always in partial eclipse behind the billowing pages of her newspaper. Only the tip of her topmost coil of bright hair was visible. She read swiftly, darting from war news to health hints, from stock market to sport page, and finding something of interest in each. For her there was nothing cryptic in a headline such as "Rudie Slams One Home"; and Do pfd followed by dotted lines and vulgar fractions were to her as easily translated as the Daily Hint From Paris. Hers was the photographic eye and the alert brain that can film a column or a page at a glance.

Across the table her husband sat turned slightly sidewise in his chair, his paper folded in a tidy oblong. He read down one column, top of the next and down that, seriously and methodically; giving to toast or coffee-cup the single-handed and groping attention of one whose interest is elsewhere. The light from the big bay window fell on the printed page and cameoed his profile. After three years of daily contact with it, Emma still caught herself occasionally gazing with appreciation at that clear-cut profile and the clean, shining line of his hair as it grew away from the temple.

"T. A.," she had announced one morning, to his mystification, "you're the Francis X. Bushman of the breakfast table. I believe you sit that way purposely."

"Francis X—?" He was not a follower of the films.

Emma elucidated. "Discoverer and world's champion exponent of the side face."

"I might punish you, Emma, by making a pun about its all being Greek to me, but I shan't." He returned to Page Two, Column Four.

Usually their conversation was comfortably monosyllabic and disjointed, as is the breakfast talk of two people who understand each other. Amicable silence was the rule, broken only by the rustle of paper, the clink of china, an occasional, "Toast, dear?" And when Buck, in a low, vibrating tone (slightly muffled by buttered corn muffin) said, "Dogs!" Emma knew he was perusing the daily *schrecklichkeit*.

Upon this cozy scene Conservation cast his gaunt shadow. It was in June, the year of America's Great Step, that Emma, examining her household, pronounced it fattily degenerate, with complications, and performed upon it a severe and skilful surgical operation. Among the rest:

"One morning paper ought to be enough for any husband and wife who aren't living on a Boffin basis. There'll be one copy of the *Times* delivered at this house in the future, Mr. Buck. We might match pennies for it, mornings."

It lay there on the hall table that first morning, an innocent oblong, its headlines staring up at them with inky eyes.

"Paper, T. A.," she said, and handed it to him.

"You take it, dear."

"Oh, no! No."

She poured the coffee, trying to keep her gaze away from the tantalizing tail-end of the headline at whose first half she could only guess.

"By Jove, Emma! Listen to this! Pershing says if we have one m——"

"Stop right there! We've become pretty well acquainted in the last three years, T. A. But if you haven't learned that if there's one thing I can't endure, it's being fed across the table with scraps of the day's news, I shall have to consider our marriage a failure."

"Oh, very well. I merely thought you'd be——"

"I am. But there's something about having it read to you——"

On the second morning Emma, hurriedly fastening the middle button of her blouse on her way downstairs, collided with her husband, who was shrugging himself into his coat. They continued their way downstairs with considerable dignity and pronounced leisure. The paper lay on the hall table. They reached for it. There was a moment—just the fraction of a minute—when each clutched a corner of it, eying the other grimly. Then both let go suddenly, as though the paper had burned their fingers. They stared at each other, surprise and horror in their gaze. The paper fell to the floor with a little slap. Both stooped for it, apologetically. Their heads bumped. They staggered back, semi-stunned.

Emma found herself laughing, rather wildly. Buck joined in after a moment—a rueful laugh. She was the first to recover.

"That settles it. I'm willing to eat trick bread and whale meat and drink sugarless coffee, but I draw the line at hating my husband for the price of a newspaper subscription. White paper may be scarce but so are husbands. It's cheaper to get two newspapers than to set up two establishments."

They were only two among many millions who, at that time, were playing an amusing and fashionable game called Win the War. They did not realize that the game was to develop into a grim and magnificently functioning business to whose demands they would cheerfully sacrifice all that they most treasured.

Of late, Emma had spent less and less time in the offices of the Featherloom Company. For over ten years that flourishing business, and the career of her son, Jock McChesney, had been the twin orbits about which her existence had revolved. But Jock McChesney was a man of family now, with a wife, two babies, and an uncanny advertising sense that threatened to put his name on the letterhead of the Raynor Advertising Company of Chicago. As for the Featherloom factory—it seemed to go of its own momentum. After her marriage to the firm's head, Emma's interest in the business was unflagging.

"Now look here, Emma," Buck would say. "You've given enough to this firm. Play a while. Cut up. Forget you're the 'And Company' in T. A. Buck & Co."

"But I'm so used to it. I'd miss it so. You know what happened that first year of our marriage when I tried to do the duchess. I don't know how to loll. If you take Featherlooms away from me I'll degenerate into a Madam Chairman. You'll see."

She might have, too, if the War had not come along and saved her. Still, she had consented not to go down to the office at 9:30 every morning with her husband. She spent only two or three hours daily in the offices and the big, bright showrooms and workrooms. And if you happened into the old brownstone house on East Sixty-third at five o'clock or thereabouts, you were very likely to hear the tinkle of teacups.

By mid-summer the workrooms were turning not only the accustomed grist of petticoats, but strange garments, such as gray and khaki flannel shirts, flannelette one-piece pajamas, and woolen bloomers, all intended for the needs of women war workers going abroad. Emma had been responsible for the success of two of these Featherloom products. The one-piece pajama was a Godsend to the women overseas working in the mist-haunted, damp-laden, heatless villages of France and Flanders. And a seemingly trivial item—the tailored, neck-fitting collar—made the Featherloom service shirt for women the standard for war workers.

Emma had dropped into the workroom one day and had picked up a half-finished gray flannel garment. She eyed it critically, her deft fingers manipulating the neckband. A little frown gathered between her eyes.

"Somehow a woman in a flannel shirt always looks as if she had quinsy. It's the collar. They cut them like a man's small-size. But a woman's neck is as different from a man's as her collarbone is."

She picked up a piece of flannel and smoothed it on the cutting-table. The head designer had looked on in disapproval while her employer's wife had experimented with scraps of cloth, and pins, and chalk, and scissors. She had her opinion of meddle-some matrons in Fifth Avenue hats and suits who upset the shop and tried to teach an experienced designer her business. But Emma had gone on serenely cutting and snipping and pinning. They made up samples of service shirts with the new neck-hugging collar and submitted them to Miss Nevins, the head of the woman's uniform department at Fyfe & Gordon's. That astute lady had been obliged to listen to scores of canteeners, nurses, secretaries, and motor leaguers who, standing before a long mirror in one of the many fitting-rooms, had gazed, frowned, fumbled at collar and topmost button, and said, "But it looks so—so lumpy around the neck."

Miss Kate Nevins, diplomat and department head (the terms are dependent one on the other), always came in for a final fitting. Her reply to this plaint was: "Oh, when you get your tie on——"

But the overseas worker, gloomily regarding the image in the mirror, felt her patriotism oozing. Then brightly: "Perhaps they'll let me wear a turn-down collar."

Miss Nevins would shake her head. "Absolutely against regulations. The rules strictly forbid anything but the high, close-fitting collar."

The fair war worker would sigh, mutter something about supposing they'd shoot you at sunrise for wearing a becoming shirt, and order six, grumbling. Fyfe & Gordon's had the official sanction of the government. They were the court of last resort. If you couldn't get it at the great outfitting establishment on Madison Avenue, New York could not produce it.

Kate Nevins had known Mrs. T. A. Buck in that lady's Emma McChesney days. At the end of the first day's trial of the new Featherloom shirt she had telephoned the Featherloom factory and had asked for Emma McChesney. People who had known her by that name never seemed able to get the trick of calling her by any other.

With every fitting-room in the Fyfe & Gordon establishment demanding her attention, Miss Nevins's conversation was necessarily brief.

"Emma McChesney? . . . Kate Nevins. . . . Who's responsible for the collar on those Featherloom shirts? . . . I was sure of it. . . . No regular designer could cut a collar like that. Takes a genius. . . . H'm? . . . Well, I mean it. I'm going to write to Washington and have 'em vote you a distinguished service medal. This is the first day since last I-don't-know-when that hasn't found me in the last stages of nervous exhaustion at six o'clock. . . . All these women warriors are willing to bleed and die for their country, but they want to do it in a collar that fits, and I don't blame 'em. After I saw the pictures of that Russian Battalion of Death, I understood why. . . . Yes, I know I oughtn't to say that, but . . ."

By autumn Emma was wearing one of those Featherloom service shirts herself. It was inevitable that a woman of her executive ability, initiative, and detail sense should be pressed into active service. November saw Fifth Avenue a-glitter with uniforms, and one third of them seemed to be petticoated. The Featherloom factory saw little of Emma now. She bore the title of Commandant with feminine captains, lieutenants, and girl workers under her; and her blue uniform, as she herself put it, was so a-jingle with straps, buckles, belts, bars, and bolts that when she first put it on she felt dressed up like a jail.

She left the house at eight in the morning now. Dinner time rarely found her back in Sixty-third Street. Buck was devoting four evenings a week to the draft board. At the time of the second Liberty Loan drive in the autumn he had deserted Featherlooms for bonds. His success was due to the commodity he had for sale, the type of person to whom he sold it, and his own selling methods and personality.

There was something about this slim, leisurely man, with the handsome eyes and the quiet voice, that convinced and impressed you.

"It's your complete lack of eagerness in the transaction, too," Emma remarked after watching him land a twenty-five-thousand-dollar bond pledge, the buyer a business rival of the Featherloom Petticoat Company. "You make it seem a privilege, not a favor. A man with your method could sell sandbags in the Sahara."

Sometimes the two dined downtown together. Sometimes they scarcely saw each other for days on end. One afternoon at 5:30, Emma, on duty bound, espied him walking home up Fifth Avenue, on the opposite side of the street. She felt a little pang as she watched the easy, graceful figure swinging its way up the brilliant, flag-decked street. She had given him so little time and thought; she had bestowed upon the house such scant attention in the last few weeks. She turned abruptly and crossed the street, dodging the late afternoon traffic with a sort of expert recklessness. She almost ran after the tall figure that was now a block ahead of her, and walking fast. She caught up with him, matched his stride, and touched his arm lightly.

"I beg your pardon, but aren't you Mr. T. A. Buck?"

His eyes danced, but he bowed gravely. "Yes."

She extended her hand. "How do you do! I'm Mrs. Buck."

Then they had giggled together deliciously, and he had put a firm hand on the smartly tailored blue serge sleeve.

"I thought so. That being the case, you're coming home along o' me, young 'ooman."

"Can't do it. I'm on my way to the Ritz to meet a dashing delegation from Serbia. You never saw such gorgeous creatures. All gold and green and red, with swords, and snake-work, and glittering boots. They'd make a musical-comedy soldier look like an undertaker."

There came a queer little look into his eyes. "But this isn't a musical comedy, dear. These men are——Look here, Emma. I want to talk to you. Let's walk home together and have dinner decently in our own dining room. There are things at the office——"

"S'impossible, Mr. Buck. I'm late now. And you know perfectly well there are two vice-commandants ready to snatch my shoulder-straps."

"Emma! Emma!"

At his tone the smiling animation of her face was dimmed. "What's gone wrong?"

"Nothing. Everything. At least, nothing that I can discuss with you at the corner of Fifth Avenue and Forty-fifth Street. When does this Serbian thing end? I'll call for you."

"There's no telling. Anyway, the Fannings will drive me home, thanks, dear."

He looked down at her. She was unbelievably girlish and distingué in the blue uniform; a straight, slim figure, topped by an impudent cocked hat. The flannel shirt of workaday service was replaced today by a severely smart affair of white silk, high-collared, stitched, expensively simple. And yet he frowned as he looked.

"Fisk got his exemption papers today." With apparent irrelevance.

"Yes?" She was glancing sharply up and down the thronged street. "Better call me a cab, dear. I'm awfully late. Oh, well, with his wife practically an invalid, and all the expense of the baby's illness, and the funeral—The Ritz, dear. And tell him to hurry." She stepped into the cab, a little nervous frown between her eyes.

But Buck, standing at the curb, seemed bent on delaying her. "Fisk told me the doctor said all she needs is a couple of months at a sanitarium, where she can be bathed and massaged and fed with milk. And if Fisk could go to a camp now he'd have a commission in no time. He's had training, you know. He spent his vacation last summer at Plattsburg."

"But he's due on his advance spring trip in two or three weeks, isn't he? . . . I really must hurry, T. A."

"Ritz," said Buck, shortly, to the chauffeur. "And hurry." He turned away abruptly, without a backward glance. Emma's head jerked over her shoulder in surprise. But he did not turn. The tall figure disappeared. Emma's taxi crept into the stream. But uppermost in her mind was not the thought of Serbians, uniforms, Fisk, or Ritz, but of her husband's right hand, which, as he turned away from the cab, had been folded tight into a fist.

She meant to ask an explanation of the clenched fingers; but the Serbians, despite their four tragic years, turned out to be as sprightly as their uniforms, and it was past midnight when the Fannings dropped her at her door. Her husband was rather ostentatiously asleep. As she doffed her warlike garments, her feminine canniness warned her that this was no time for explanations. Tomorrow morning would be better.

But next morning's breakfast turned out to be all Jock.

A letter from Grace, his wife. Grace McChesney had been Grace Galt, one of the youngest and cleverest women advertising writers in the profession. When Jock was a cub in the Raynor office she had been turning out compelling copy. They had been married four years. Now Jock ruled a mahogany domain of his own in the Raynor suite overlooking the lake in the great Michigan Avenue building. And Grace was saying, "Eat the crust, girlie. It's the crust that makes your hair grow curly."

Emma, uniformed for work, read hasty extracts from Grace's letter. Buck listened in silence.

"You wouldn't know Jock. He's restless, irritable, moody. And the queer part of it is he doesn't know it. He tries to be cheerful, and I could weep to see him. He has tried to cover it up with every kind of war work from Red Crossing to Liberty Loaning, and from writing free full-page national advertising copy to giving up his tobacco money to the smoke fund. And he's miserable. He wants to get into it. And he ought. But you know I haven't been really husky since Buddy came. Not ill, but the doctor says it will be another six months before I'm myself, really. If I had only myself to think of—how simple! But two kiddies need such a lot of things. I could get a job at Raynor's. They need writers. Jock says, bitterly, that all the worth-while men have left. Don't think I'm complaining. I'm just trying to see my way clear, and talking to someone who understands often clears the way."

"Well!" said Emma.

And, "Well?" said T. A.

She sat fingering the letter, her breakfast cooling before her. "Of course, Jock wants to get into it. I wish he could. I'd be so proud of him. He'd be beautiful in khaki. But there's work to do right here. And he ought to be willing to wait six months."

"They can't wait six months over there, Emma. They need him now."

"Oh, come, T. A.! One man——"

"Multiplied by a million. Look at Fisk. Just such another case. Look at——"

The shrill summons of the telephone cut him short. Emma's head came up alertly. She glanced at her wrist-watch and gave a little exclamation of horror.

"That's for me! I'm half an hour late! The first time, too." She was at the telephone a second later, explanatory, apologetic. Then back in the dining-room doorway, her cheeks flushed, tugging at her gloves, poised for flight. "Sorry, dear. But this morning was so important, and that letter about Jock upset me. I'm afraid I'm a rotten soldier."

"I'm afraid you are, Emma."

She stared at that. "Why——! Oh, you're still angry at something. Listen, dear—I'll call for you at the office tonight at five, and we'll walk home together. Wait for me. I may be a few minutes late——"

She was off. The front door slammed sharply. Buck sat very still for a long minute, staring down at the coffee cup whose contents he did not mean to drink. The light from the window cameoed his fine profile. And you saw that his jaw was set. His mind was a thousand miles away, in Chicago, Illinois, with the boy who wanted to fight and couldn't.

Emma, flashing down Fifth Avenue as fast as wheels and traffic rules would permit, saw nothing of the splendid street. Her mind was a thousand miles away, in Chicago, Illinois.

And a thousand miles away, in Chicago, Illinois, Jock McChesney, three hours later, was slamming down the two big windows of his office. From up the street came the sound of a bugle and of a band playing a brisk march. And his office windows looked out upon Michigan Avenue. If you know Chicago, you know the building that housed the Raynor offices—a great gray shaft, towering even above its giant neighbors, its head in the clouds, its face set toward the blue beauty of Lake Michigan. Until very recently those windows of his office had been a source of joy and inspiration to Jock McChesney. The green of Grant Park just below. The tangle of I. C. tracks beyond that, and the great, gracious lake beyond that, as far as the eye could see. He had seen the changes the year had brought. The lake dotted with sinister gray craft. Dog tents in Grant Park, sprung up overnight like brown mushrooms. Men—mere boys, most of them—awkward in their workaday clothes of office and shop, drilling, wheeling, marching at the noon hour. And parades, and parades, and parades. At first Jock, and, in fact, the entire office staff—heads of departments, writers, secretaries, stenographers, office boys—would suspend business and crowd to the windows to see the pageant pass in the street below. Stirring music, khaki columns, flags, pennants, horses, bugles. And always the Jackie band from the Great Lakes Station, its white leggings twinkling down the street in the lead of its six-foot-six contortionistic drum-major.

By October the window-gazers, watching the parades from the Raynor windows, were mostly petticoated and exclamatory. Jock stayed away from the window now. It seemed to his tortured mind that there was a fresh parade hourly, and that bugles and bands sounded a taunting note.

"Where are *you!* (sounded the bugle)?

Where are *you?*

Where are YOU?!!!

Where

  are

    you,

Where—are—you-u-u-u——"

He slammed down the windows, summoned a stenographer, and gave out dictation in a loud, rasping voice.

"Yours of the tenth at hand, and contents noted. In reply I wish to say——"

(Boom! Boom! And a boom-boom-boom!)

"—all copy for the Sans Scent Soap is now ready for your approval and will be mailed to you to-day under separate cover. We in the office think that this copy marks a new record in soap advertising——"

(Over there! Over there! Send the word, send the word over there!)

"Just read that last line will you, Miss Dugan?"

"Over th—I mean, 'We in the office think that this copy marks a new record in soap advertising——'"

"H'm. Yes." A moment's pause. A dreamy look on the face of the girl stenographer. Jock interpreted it. He knew that the stenographer was in the chair at the side of his desk, taking his dictation accurately and swiftly, while the spirit of the girl herself was far and away at Camp Grant at Rockford, Illinois, with an olive-drab unit in an olive-drab world.

"—and, in fact, in advertising copy of any description that has been sent out from the Raynor offices."

The girl's pencil flew over the pad. But when Jock paused for thought or breath she lifted her head and her eyes grew soft and bright, and her foot, in its absurd high-heeled gray boot, beat a smart left! Left! Left-right-left!

Something of this picture T. A. Buck saw in his untasted coffee cup. Much of it Emma visualized in her speeding motor car. All of it Grace knew by heart as she moved about the new, shining house in the Chicago suburb, thinking, planning; feeling his agony, and trying not to admit the transparency of the look about her hands and her temples. So much for Chicago.

At five o'clock Emma left the war to its own devices and dropped in at the loft building in which Featherlooms were born and grown up. Mike, the elevator man, twisted his gray head about at an unbelievable length to gaze appreciatively at the trim, uniformed figure.

"Haven't seen you around fur many the day, Mis' Buck."

"Been too busy, Mike."

Mike turned back to face the door. "Well, 'tis a great responsibility, runnin' this war, an' all." He stopped at the Featherloom floor and opened the door with his grandest flourish. Emma glanced at him quickly. His face was impassive. She passed into the reception room with a little jingling of buckles and strap hooks.

The work day was almost ended. The display room was empty of buyers. She could see the back of her husband's head in his office. He was busy at his desk. A stock girl was clearing away the piles of garments that littered tables and chairs. At the window near the door Fisk, the Western territory man, stood talking with O'Brien, city salesman. The two looked around at her approach. O'Brien's face lighted up with admiration. Into Fisk's face there flashed a look so nearly resembling resentment that Emma, curious to know its origin, stopped to chat a moment with the two.

Said O'Brien, the gallant Irishman, "I'm more resigned to war this minute, Mrs. Buck, than I've been since it began."

Emma dimpled, turned to Fisk, stood at attention. Fisk said nothing. His face was unsmiling. "Like my uniform?" Emma asked; and wished, somehow, that she hadn't.

Fisk stared. His eyes had none of the softness of admiration. They were hard, resentful. Suddenly, "Like it! God! I wish I could wear one!" He turned away abruptly. O'Brien threw him a sharp look. Then he cleared his throat, apologetically.

Emma glanced down at her own trim self—at her stitched seams, her tailored lengths, her shining belt and buckles, her gloved hands—and suddenly and unaccountably her pride in them vanished. Something—something——

She wheeled and made for Buck's office, her color high. He looked up, rose, offered her a chair. She felt strangely ill at ease there in the office to which she had given years of service. The bookkeeper in the glass-enclosed cubby-hole across the little hall smiled and nodded and called through the open door: "My, you're a stranger, Mrs. Buck."

"Be with you in a minute, Emma," said T. A. And turned to his desk again. She rose and strolled toward the door, restlessly. "Don't hurry." Out in the showroom again she saw Fisk standing before a long table. He was ticketing and folding samples of petticoats, pajamas, blouses, and night-gowns. His cigar was gripped savagely between his teeth and his eyes squinted half closed through the smoke.

She strolled over to him and fingered the cotton flannel of a garment that lay under her hand. "Spring samples?"

"Yes."

"It ought to be a good trip. They say the West is dripping money, war or no war."

"'S right."

"How's Gertie?"

"Don't get me started, Mrs. Buck. That girl!—say, I knew what she was when I married her, and so did you. She was head stenographer here long enough. But I never really knew that kid until now, and we've been married two years. You know what the last year has been for her; the baby and all. And then losing him. And do you know what she says! That if there was somebody who knew the Western territory and could cover it, she'd get a job and send me to war. Yessir! That's Gert. We've been married two years, and she says herself it's the first really happy time she's ever known. You know what she had at home. Why, even when I was away on my long spring trip she used to say it wasn't so bad being alone, because there was always my home-coming to count on. How's that for a wife!"

"Gertie's splendid," agreed Emma. And wondered why it sounded so lame.

"You don't know her. Why, when it comes to patriotism, she makes T. R. look like a pacifist. She says if she could sell my line on the road, she'd make you give her the job so she could send her man to war. Gert says a traveling man's wife ought to make an ideal soldier's wife, anyway; and that if I went it would only be like my long Western trip, multiplied by about ten, maybe. That's Gertie."

Emma was fingering the cotton-flannel garment on the table.

Buck crossed the room and stood beside her. "Sorry I kept you waiting. Three of the boys were called today. It crippled us pretty badly in the shipping room. Ready?"

"Yes. Good-night, Charley. Give my love to Gertie."

"Thanks, Mrs. Buck." He picked up his cigar, took an apprehensive puff, and went on ticketing and folding. There was a grin behind the cigar now.

Into the late afternoon glitter of Fifth Avenue. Five o'clock Fifth Avenue. Flags of every nation, save one. Uniforms of every blue from French to navy; of almost any shade save field green. Pongee-colored Englishmen, seeming seven feet high, to a man; aviators slim and elegant, with walking sticks made of the propeller of their shattered planes, with a notch for every Hun plane bagged. Slim girls, exotic as the orchids they wore, gazing limpid-eyed at these warrior *élégants*. Women uniformed to the last degree of tailored exquisiteness. Girls, war accoutered, who brought arms up in sharp salute as they passed Emma. Buck eyed them gravely, hat and arm describing parabolas with increasing frequency as they approached Fiftieth Street, slackening as the colorful pageant grew less brilliant, thinned, and faded into the park mists.

Emma's cheeks were a glorious rose-pink. Head high, shoulders back, she matched her husband's long stride every step of the way. Her eyes were bright and very blue.

"There's a beautiful one, T. A.! The Canadian officer with the limp. They've all been gassed, and shot five times in the thigh and seven in the shoulder, and yet look at 'em! What do you suppose they were when they were new if they can look like that, damaged!"

Buck cut a vicious little semi-circle in the air with his walking stick.

"I know now how the father of the Gracchi felt, and why you never hear him mentioned."

"Nonsense, T. A. You're doing a lot." She did not intend her tone to be smug; but if she had glanced sidewise at her husband, she might have seen the pained red mount from chin to brow. She did not seem to sense his hurt. They went on, past the plaza now. Only a few blocks lay between them and their home; the old brownstone house that had been New York's definition of architectural elegance in the time of T. A. Buck, Sr.

"Tell me, Emma. Does this satisfy you—the work you're doing, I mean? Do you think you're giving the best you've got?"

"Well, of course I'd like to go to France———"

"I didn't ask you what you'd like."

"Yes, sir. Very good, sir. I don't know what you call giving the best one has got. But you know I work from eight in the morning until midnight, often and often. Oh, I don't say that someone else couldn't do my work just as well. And I don't say, either, that it doesn't include a lot of dashing up and down Fifth Avenue, and teaing at the Ritz, and meeting magnificent Missions, and being cooed over by Lady Millionaires. But if you'd like a few statistics as to the number of hundreds of thousands of soldiers we've canteened since last June, I'd be pleased to oblige." She tugged at a capacious pocket and brought forth a smart leather-bound notebook.

"Spare me! I've had all the statistics I can stand for one day at the office. I know you're working hard. I just wondered if you didn't realize——"

They turned into their own street. "Realize what?"

"Nothing. Nothing."

Emma sighed a mock sigh and glanced up at the windows of her own house. "Oh, well, everybody's difficult these days, T. A., including husbands. That second window shade is crooked. Isn't it queer how maids never do. . . . I'll tell you what I can realize, though. I realize that we're going to have dinner at home, reg'lar old-fashioned befo'-de-war. And I can bathe before dinner. There's richness."

But when she appeared at dinner, glowing, radiant, her hair shiningly re-coifed, she again wore the blue uniform, with the service cap atop her head. Buck surveyed her, unsmiling. She seated herself at table with a little clinking of buckles and buttons. She flung her motor gloves on a nearby chair, ran an inquiring finger along belt and collar with a little gesture that was absurdly feminine in its imitation of masculinity.

Buck did not sit down. He stood at the opposite side of the table, one hand on his chair, the knuckles showing white where he gripped it.

"It seems to me, Emma, that you might manage to wear something a little less military when you're dining at home. War is war, but I don't see why you should make me feel like your orderly. It's like being married to a policewoman. Surely you can neglect your country for the length of time it takes to dine with your husband."

It was the bitterest speech he had made to her in the years of their married life. She flushed a little. "I thought you knew that I was going out again immediately after dinner. I left at five with the understanding that I'd be on duty again at 8:30."

He said nothing. He stood looking down at his own hand that gripped the chair back so tightly. Emma sat back and surveyed her trim and tailored self with a placidity that had in it, perhaps, a dash of malice. His last speech had cut. Then she reached forward, helped herself to an olive, and nibbled it, head on one side.

"D'you know, T. A., what I think? H'm? I think you're jealous of your wife's uniform."

She had touched the match to the dynamite.

He looked up. At the blaze in his eyes she shrank back a little. His face was white. He was breathing quickly.

"You're right! I am. I am jealous. I'm jealous of every buck private in the army! I'm jealous of the mule drivers! Of the veterinarians. Of the stokers in the transports. Men!" He doubled his hand into a fist. His fine eyes glowed. "Men!"

And suddenly he sat down, heavily, and covered his eyes with his hands.

Emma sat staring at him for a dull, sickening moment. Then she looked down at herself, horror in her eyes. Then up again at him. She got up and came over to him.

"Why, dear—dearest—I didn't know. I thought you were satisfied. I thought you were happy. You——"

"Honey, the only man who's happy is the man in khaki. The rest of us are gritting our teeth and pretending."

She put a hand on his shoulder. "But what do you want—what can you do that——"

He reached back over his shoulder and found her hand. He straightened. His head came up. "They've offered me a job in Bordeaux. It isn't a fancy job. It has to do with merchandising. But I think you know they're having a devil of a time with all the millions of bales of goods. They need men who know materials. I ought to. I've handled cloth and clothes enough. I know values. It would mean hard work—manual work lots of times. No pay. And happiness. For me." There was a silence. It seemed to fill the room, that silence. It filled the house. It roared and thundered about Emma's ears, that silence. When finally she broke it:

"Blind!" she said. "Blind! Deaf! Dumb! *And* crazy." She laughed, and two tears sped down her cheeks and dropped on the unblemished blue serge uniform. "Oh, T. A.! Where have I been? How you must have despised me. Me, in my uniform. In my uniform that was costing the government three strapping men. My uniform, that was keeping three man-size soldiers out of khaki. You, Jock, and Fisk. Why didn't you tell me, dear! Why didn't you tell me!"

"I've tried. I couldn't. You've always seen things first. I couldn't ask you to go back to the factory."

"Factory! Factory nothing! I'm going back on the road. I'm taking Fisk's Western territory. I know the Middle West better than Fisk himself. I ought to. I covered it for ten years. I'll pay Gertie Fisk's salary until she's able to come back to us as stenographer. We've never had one so good. Grace can give the office a few hours a week. And we can promote O'Brien to manager while I'm on the road."

Buck was staring at her, dully. "Grace? Now wait a minute. You're traveling too fast for a mere man." His hand was gripping hers, tight, tight.

Their dinner was cooling on the table. They ignored it. She pulled a chair around to his. They sat shoulder to shoulder, elbows on the cloth.

"It took me long enough to wake up, didn't it? I've got to make up for lost time. The whole thing's clear in my mind. Now get this: Jock gets a commission. Grace and the babies pack up and come to New York, and live right here, with me, in this house. Fisk goes to war. Gertie gets well and comes back to work for Featherlooms. Mr. T. A. Buck goes to Bordeaux. Old Emmer takes off her uniform and begins to serve her country—on the road."

At that he got up and began pacing the room. "I can't have you do that, dear. Why, you left all that behind when you married me."

"Yes, but our marriage certificate didn't carry a war guarantee."

"Gad, Emma, you're glorious!"

"Glorious nothing! I'm going to earn the living for three families for a few months, until things get going. And there's nothing glorious about that, old dear. I haven't any illusions about what taking a line on the road means these days. It isn't traveling. It's exploring. You never know where you're going to land, or when, unless you're traveling in a freight train. They're cock o' the walk now. I think I'll check myself through as first-class freight. Or send my pack ahead, with natives on foot, like an African explorer. But it'll be awfully good for me character. And when I'm eating that criminal corn bread they serve on dining cars on a train that's seven hours late into Duluth I'll remember when I had my picture, in uniform, in the Sunday supplements, with my hand on the steering wheel along o' the nobility and gentry."

"Listen, dear, I can't have you——"

"Too late. Got a pencil? Let's send fifty words to Jock and Grace. They'll wire back 'No!' but another fifty'll fetch 'em. After all, it takes more than one night letter to explain a move that is going to change eight lives. Now let's have dinner, dear. It'll be cold, but filling."

Perhaps in the whirlwind ten days that followed a woman of less energy, less determination, less courage and magnificent vitality might have faltered and failed in an undertaking of such magnitude. But Emma was alert and forceful enough to keep just one jump ahead of the swift-moving times. In a less cataclysmic age the changes she wrought within a period of two weeks would have seemed herculean. But in this time of stress and change, when every household in every street in every town in all the country was feeling the tremor of upheaval, the readjustment of this little family and business group was so unremarkable as to pass unnoticed. Even the members of the group itself, seeing themselves scattered to camp, to France, to New York, to the Middle West, shuffled like pawns that the Great Game might the better be won, felt strangely unconcerned and unruffled.

It was little more than two weeks after the night of Emma's awakening that she was talking fast to keep from crying hard, as she stuffed plain, practical blue serge garments (unmilitary) into a bellows suitcase ("Can't count on trunks these days," she had said. "I'm not taking any chances on a clean shirtwaist"). Buck, standing in the doorway, tried hard to keep his gaze from the contemplation of his khaki-clad self reflected in the long mirror. At intervals he said:

"Can't I help, dear?" Or, "Talk about the early Pilgrim mothers, and the Revolutionary mothers, and the Civil War mothers! I'd like to know what they had on you, Emma."

And from Emma: "Yeh, ain't I noble!" Then, after a little pause: "This house is going to be so full of wimmin folks it'll look like a Home for Decayed Gentlewomen. Buddy McChesney, aged six months, is going to be the only male protector around the place. We'll make him captain of the home guard."

"Gertie was in today. She says I'm a shrimp in my uniform compared to Charley. You know she always was the nerviest little stenographer we ever had about the place, but she knows more about Featherlooms than any woman in the shop, except you. She's down to ninety-eight pounds, poor little girl, but every ounce of it's pure pluck, and she says she'll be as good as new in a month or two, and I honestly believe she will."

Emma was counting a neat stack of folded handkerchiefs. "Seventeen—eighteen——When she comes back we'll have to pay her twice the salary she got when she left. But, then, you have to pay an errand boy what you used to pay a shipping clerk, and a stock girl demands money that an operator used to brag about."

Buck came over to her and put a hand on the bright hair that was rumpled, now, from much diving into bags and suitcases and clothes closets.

"All except you, Emma. You'll be working without a salary—working like a man—like three men——"

"Working for three men, T. A. Three fighting men. I've got two service buttons already," she glanced down at her blouse, "and Charley Fisk said I had the right to wear one for him. I'll look like a mosaic, but I'm going to put 'em all on."

The day before Emma's departure for the West Grace arrived, with bags, bundles, and babies. A wan and tired Grace, but proud, too, and with the spirit of the times in her eyes.

"Jock!" she repeated, in answer to their questions. "My dears, he doesn't know I'm alive. I visited him at camp the day before I left. He thinks he'll be transferred East, as we hoped. Wouldn't that be glorious! Well, I had all sorts of intimate and vital things to discuss with him, and he didn't hear what I was saying. He wasn't even listening. He couldn't wait until I had finished a sentence so that he could cut in with something about his work. I murmured to him in the moonlight that there was something I had long meant to tell him and he answered that dammit he forgot to report that rifle that exploded. And when I said, 'Dearest, isn't this hotel a *little* like the place we spent our honeymoon in—that porch, and all?' he said, 'See this feller coming, Gracie? The big guy with the mustache. Now mash him, Gracie. He's my Captain. I'm going to introduce you. He was a senior at college when I was a fresh.'"

But the peace and the pride in her eyes belied her words.

Emma's trip, already delayed, was begun ten days before her husband's date for sailing. She bore that, too, with smiling equanimity. "When I went to school," she said, "I thought I hated the Second Peloponnesian War worse than any war I'd ever heard of. But I hate this one so that I want everyone to get into it one hundred per cent, so that it'll be over sooner; and because we've won."

They said little on their way to the train. She stood on the rear platform just before the train pulled out. They had tried frantically to get a lower berth, but unsuccessfully. "Don't look so tragic about it," she laughed. "It's like old times. These last three years have been a dream—a delusion."

He looked up at her, as she stood there in her blue suit, and white blouse, and trim blue hat and crisp veil. "Gad, Emma, it's uncanny. I believe you're right. You look exactly as you did when I first saw you, when you came in off the road after father died and I had just taken hold of the business."

For answer she hummed a few plaintive bars. He grinned as he recognized "Silver Threads Among the Gold." The train moved away, gathered speed. He followed it. They were not smiling now. She was leaning over the railing, as though to be as near to him as the fast-moving train would allow. He was walking swiftly along with the train, as though hypnotized. Their eyes held. The brave figure in blue on the train platform. The brave figure in khaki outside. The blue suddenly swam in a haze before his eyes; the khaki a mist before hers. The crisp little veil was a limp little rag when finally she went in to search for Upper Eleven.

The white-coated figure that had passed up and down the aisle unnoticed and unnoticing as she sat hidden behind the kindly folds of her newspaper suddenly became a very human being as Emma regained self-control, decided on dinner as a panacea, and informed the white coat that she desired Upper Eleven made up early.

The White Coat had said, "Yas'm," and glanced up at her. Whereupon she had said:

"Why, William!"

And he, "Well, fo' de lan'! 'F 'tain't Mis' McChesney! Well, mah sakes alive, Mis' McChesney! Ah ain't seen yo' since yo' married. Ah done heah yo' married yo' boss an' got a swell brownstone house, an' ev'thing gran'——"

"I've got everything, William, but a lower berth to Chicago. They swore they couldn't give me anything but an upper."

A speculative look crept into William's rolling eye. Emma recognized it. Her hand reached toward her bag. Then it stopped. She smiled. "No. No, William. Time was. But not these days. Four years ago I'd have slipped you fifty cents right now, and you'd have produced a lower berth from somewhere. But I'm going to fool you. My boss has gone to war, William, and so has my son. And I'm going to take that fifty cents and buy thrift stamps for Miss Emma McChesney, aged three, and Mr. Buddy McChesney, aged six months. And I'll dispose my old bones in Upper Eleven."

She went in to dinner.

At eight-thirty a soft and deferential voice sounded in her ear.

"Ah got yo' made up, Mis' McChesney."

"But this is my——"

He beckoned. He padded down the aisle with that walk which is a peculiar result of flat feet and twenty years of swaying car. Emma followed. He stopped before Lower Six and drew aside the curtain. It was that lower which can always be produced, magically, though ticket sellers, Pullman agents, porters, and train conductors swear that it does not exist. The key to it is silver, but tonight Emma McChesney Buck had unlocked it with finer metal. Gold. Pure gold. For William drew aside the curtain with a gesture such as one of his slave ancestors might have used before a queen of Egypt. He carefully brushed a cinder from the sheet with one gray-black hand. Then he bowed like any courtier.

Emma sank down on the edge of the couch with a little sigh of weariness. Gratefulness was in it, too. She looked up at him—at the wrinkled, kindly, ape-like face, and he looked down at her.

"William," she said, "war is a filthy, evil, vile thing, but it bears wonderful white flowers."

"Yas'm!" agreed William, genially, and smiled all over his rubbery, gray-black countenance. "*Yas'm!*"

And who shall say he did not understand?

Dorothy Canfield

(1879–1958)

Born in Lawrence, Kansas, Dorothy Canfield (Fisher) completed undergraduate studies at Ohio State University and took classes at the Sorbonne and the École des Heutes Études in Paris before earning a PhD in Romance languages from Columbia University. Living most of her life in Vermont, she wrote several novels—including *The Squirrel-Cage* (1912), *The Brimming Cup* (1921), and *The Deepening Stream* (1930)—and a host of short stories. For more than two decades, she contributed to selecting the titles for the Book of the Month Club, thereby promoting a number of American writers. In France during World War I, she was active in war relief, and her story collections *Home Fires in France* (1918), in which "The Permissionaire" appeared, *The Day of Glory* (1919) were part of an effort by American authors to portray sympathetically the hardships of French citizens and to foster pro-intervention opinion in the United States.

The Permissionaire

Dorothy Canfield

"What was in the ground, alive, they could not kill."

Two weeks after the German retreat from the Aisne was rumored, five days after the newspapers were printing censored descriptions of the ravaged country they had left, and the very moment the official bulletin confirmed the news, Pierre Nidart presented himself to his lieutenant to ask for a furlough, the long-delayed furlough, due for more than two years now, which he had never been willing to take. His lieutenant frowned uneasily, and did not answer. After a moment's silence he said, gently, "You know, my old fellow, the Boches have left very little up there."

(Nidart was not an old fellow at all, being but thirty-four, and the father of two young children. His lieutenant used the phrase as a term of endearment, because he had a high opinion of his silent sergeant.) Nidart made no answer to his officer's remark. The lieutenant took it that he persisted in wanting his furlough. As he had at least three furloughs due him, it was hard to refuse. There was a long silence. Finally, fingering the papers on the dry-goods box which served him as desk, the lieutenant said: "Your wife is young. They say the Germans carried back to work in Germany all women under forty-five, or those who hadn't children under three."

Nidart swallowed hard, looked sick, and obstinately said nothing. His lieutenant turned with a sigh and motioned the *fourrier* to start the red tape for the authorization for the furlough. "All right, I think I can manage a three weeks' 'permission' for you. They're allowing that, I hear, to men from the invaded regions who haven't taken any furloughs since the beginning of the war."

"Yes, *mon Lieutenant*. Thank you, *mon Lieutenant*." Nidart saluted and went back to his squad.

His lieutenant shook his head, murmuring to the *fourrier*: "Those north-country men! There is no use saying a word to them. They won't believe that *their* homes and families aren't there, till they see with their own eyes . . . and when they do see. . . . I've heard that some of the men in these first regiments that followed up the Boche retreat across the devastated regions went crazy when they found their own villages. . . . Nidart has just one idea in his head, poor devil!—to go straight before him, like a homing pigeon, till . . ." He stopped, his face darkening.

"Oh, damn the Boches!" the *fourrier* finished the sentence fervently.

"You see, Nidart is a master-mason by trade, and he built their own little house. He carries around a snapshot of it, with his wife and a baby out in front."

"Oh, damn the Boches!" responded the *fourrier* on a deeper note.

"And like all those village workmen, they got half their living out of their garden and a field or two. And you've read what the Boches did to the gardens and fruit-trees."

"Isn't there anything else we can talk about?" said the *fourrier*.

Nidart passed through Paris on his way (those being before the days of strictly one-destination furloughs) and, extracting some very old bills from the lining of his shoe, he spent the five hours between his trains in hasty purchasing. At the hardware shop, where he bought an ax, a hammer, some nails, and a saw, the saleswoman's vivacious curiosity got the better of his taciturnity, and she screwed from him the information that he was going back to his home in the devastated regions.

At once the group of Parisian working-people and bourgeois who happened to be in the shop closed in on him sympathetically, commenting, advising, dissuading, offering their opinions with that city-bred, glib-tongued clatter which Nidart's country soul scorned and detested.

"No, no, my friend, it's useless to try to go back. The Germans have made a desert of it. My cousin's wife has a relative who was in the regiment that first followed the Germans after their retreat from Noyon, and he said . . ."

"The Government is going to issue a statement, saying that land will be given in other parts of France to people from those regions, because it's of no use to try to rebuild from under the ruins."

"No, not the Government, it's a society for the Protection of the People in the Invaded Regions; and they are Americans, millionaires, every one. And it's in America they are offering land, near New York."

"No, near Buenos Aires."

"The Americans want the regions left as a monument, as a place to see. You'll make much more money as a guide to tourists than trying to . . ."

"Your family won't be there, you know. The Boches took all the able-bodied women back with them; and the children were sent to . . ."

"*Give me my change, won't you!*" said Nidart with sudden fierceness, to the saleswoman. He turned his back roughly on the chattering group and went out. They shrugged their shoulders. "These country-people. Nothing on earth for them but their little hole of a village!"

Down the street, Nidart, quickening to an angry stride his soldierly gait, hurried along to a seed-store.

That evening when he got into the battered, dingy, third-class compartment of the train going north, he could hardly be seen for the innumerable packages slung about his person. He pulled out from one bulging pocket a square piece of bread, from another a piece of cheese, and proceeded to dine, bent forward with the weight of his burdens and his thoughts, gazing out through the dirty windows at the flat farming country jerking by him in the moonlight. It was so soon after the retreat that the train went no further north than Noyon, and Nidart had lived far beyond Noyon. About midnight, he rolled off the train, readjusted his packages and his knapsack, and, after showing his perfectly regular *sauf-conduit* to five or six sentries along the way, finally got out of town.

He found himself on the long, white road leading north. It was the road down which they had driven once a week, on market-days. Of all the double line of noble poplar-trees, not one was standing. The utterly changed aspect of the familiar road startled him. Ahead of him as he tramped rapidly forward, was what had been a cross-roads, now a gaping hole. Nidart, used to gaping holes in roads, walked down into this, and out on the other side. He was panting a little, but he walked forward steadily and strongly. . . .

The moon shone full on the place where the first village had stood, the one where his married sister had lived, where he and his wife and the children used to come for Sunday dinners once in a while. He stood suddenly before a low, confused huddle of broken bricks and splintered beams, and looked about him uncomprehending. The silence was intense. In the instant before he understood what he was seeing, he heard and felt a rapid vibration, his own heart knocking loudly. Then he understood.

A moment later, mechanically, he began to move about, clambering up and down, aimlessly, over the heaps of rubble. Although he did not know it, he was looking for the place where his sister's house had stood. Presently his knees gave way under him. He sat down suddenly on a tree-stump. The lopped-off trunk beside it showed it to have been an old cherry-tree. Yes, his sister's big cherry-tree, the pride of her garden. A long strip of paper, one end buried in a heap of bits of plaster, fluttered in the night-wind. It beat against his leg like some one calling feebly for help. The moon emerged from a cloud and showed it to be a strip of wall-paper; he recognized the pattern; he had helped his brother-in-law put it on the bedroom of the house. His sister's four children had been born within the walls of that bedroom. He tried to fix his mind on those children, not to think of any other children, not to remember his own, not to . . .

The paper beat insistently and rhythmically against his leg like a recurrent thought of madness—he sprang up with the gesture of a man terrified, and stumbling wildly among the formless ruins sought for the road again.

He walked heavily after this, lifting his feet with an effort. Several miles further, at the heap of débris which had been Falquières, where his wife's family had lived, he made a wide detour through the fields to avoid passing closer to the ruins. At the next, Bondry, where he had been born and brought up, he tried to turn aside, but against his will his feet carried him straight to the center of the chaos. When the first livid light of dawn showed him the two stumps of the big apple-trees before the door, which his grandfather had planted, he stopped short. Of the house, of the old walled garden, not a trace beyond the shapeless heap of stones and plaster. He stood there a long time, staring silently. The light gradually brightened, until across the level fields a ray of yellow sunshine struck ironically through the prone branches of the murdered trees upon the gray face of the man.

At this he turned and, walking slowly, dragging his feet, his head hanging, his shoulders bent, he followed the road which led like a white tape laid straight across the plain, towards—towards . . . The road had been mined at regular intervals, deep and broad craters stretching across it, enough to stop a convoy of camions, not enough to stop a single soldier, even though he stumbled along so wearily, his cumbersome packages beating against his legs and arms, even though he walked so slowly, more and more slowly as he came in sight of the next heaped and tumbled mound of débris. The sun rose higher. . . .

Presently it shone, with April clarity, on Nidart lying, face downwards, upon a heap of broken bricks.

For a long hour it showed nothing but that,—the ruins, the prostrate trees, the man, like them stricken and laid low.

Then it showed, poor and miserable under that pale-gold light, a wretched ant-like procession issuing from holes in the ground and defiling slowly along the scarred road towards the ruins; women, a few old men, a little band of pale and silent children. They approached the ruins and dispersed. One of the women, leading three children, picked her way wearily among the heaps of stone, the charred and twisted beams . . . stopped short, both hands at her heart.

And then the sun reeled in the sky to a sound which rang as strangely from that silent desolation as a burst of song out of hell, scream after scream of joy, ringing up to the very heavens, frantic, incredulous, magnificent joy.

There they stood, the man and wife, clasped in each other's arms in the ruins of their home, with red, swollen eyes, smiling with quivering lips, silent. Now that the first wild cries had gone rocket-like to the sky and fallen back in a torrent of tears, they had no words, no words at all. They clasped each other and the children, and wept, constantly wiping the tears from their white cheeks, to see each other. The two older children, a little shy of this father whom they had almost forgotten, drew away constrained, hanging their heads, looking up bashfully under their bent brows. Nidart sat down on a heap of stone and drew the little girl to him, stroking her hair. He tried to speak, but no voice issued from his lips. His wife sat down beside him, laying her head on his shoulder, spent with the excess of her relief. They were all silent a long time, their hearts beginning to beat in the old rhythm, a sweet, pale peace dropping down upon them.

After a time, the youngest child, cowering under the woman's skirts, surprised at the long silence, thrust out a little pale face from his shelter. The man looked down on him and smiled. "That's a Dupré," he said in his normal voice, with conviction, all his village lore coming back to him. "I know by the Dupré look of his nose. He looks the way my cousin Jacques Dupré used to, when he was little."

These were the first articulate words spoken. With them, he turned his back on the unfriendly, unknowable immensity of the world in which he had lived, exiled, for three years, and returned into the close familiar community of neighbors and kin where he had lived for thirty-four years,—where he had lived for hundreds of years. The pulverized wreck of this community lay all about him, but he opened its impalpable doors and stepped once more into its warm humanity. He looked at the little child whom he had never seen before and knew him for kin.

His wife nodded. "Yes, it's Louise and Jacques' baby. Louise was expecting him, you know, when the mobilization . . . he was born just after Jacques went away, in August. We heard Jacques was killed . . . we have heard everything . . . that Paris was taken, that London was burned. . . . I have heard twice that you were killed. Louise believed it, and never got out of bed at all after the baby came. She just turned over and let herself die. I took the baby. Somebody had to. That's the reason I'm here now. 'They' carried off all the women my age unless they had children under three. They thought the baby was mine."

"But Jacques isn't killed," said Nidart; "he's wounded, with one wooden leg, frantic to see Louise and the baby. . . ." He made a gesture of blame. "Louise always was a fool! Anybody's a fool to give up!" He looked down at the baby and held out his hand. "Come here, little Jeannot."

The child shrank away silently, burrowing deeper into his foster-mother's skirts.

"He's afraid," she explained. "We've had to make the children afraid so they would keep out of sight, and not break rules. There were so many rules, so many to salute and to bow to, the children couldn't remember; and when they forgot, they were so dreadfully cuffed, or their parents fined such big fines . . ."

"*I* never saluted!" said the boy of ten, wagging his head proudly. "You have to have something on your head to salute, they won't let you do it bareheaded. So I threw my cap in the fire."

"Yes, he's gone bareheaded since the first days, summer and winter, rain and shine," said his mother.

"Here, Jean-Pierre," said his father, wrestling with one of his packages, "I've got a hat for you. I've been saving it for you, lugged it all over because I wanted my boy to have it." He extracted from its brown canvas bag a German helmet with the spike, which he held out. "And I've got something for my little Berthe, too." He fumbled in an inner pocket. "I made it myself, near Verdun. The fellows all thought I was crazy to work over it so, when I didn't know if I'd ever see my little girl again; but I was pretty sure Maman would know how to take care of you, all right." He drew out from a nest of soft rags a roughly carved aluminum ring and slipped it on the child's forefinger.

As the children drew off a little, to compare and examine, their parents looked into each other's eyes, the deep, united, serious look of man and wife before a common problem.

"*Eh bien,* Paulette," said the man, "what shall we do? Give up? Move away?"

"Oh, Pierre!" cried his wife. "You *wouldn't?*"

For answer, he shook himself free of his packages and began to undo them, the ax, the hammer, the big package of nails, the saw, the trowel, the paper bags of seeds, the pickax. He spread them out on the clutter of broken bricks, plaster, splintered wood, and looked up at his wife. "That's what I bought on the way here."

His wife nodded. "But have you had your breakfast? You'd better eat something before you begin."

While he ate his bread and munched his cheese, she told him, speaking with a tired dullness, something of what had happened during the years of captivity. It came out just as she thought of it, without sequence, one detail obscuring another. "There wasn't much left inside the house when they finally blew it up. They'd been taking everything little by little. No, they weren't bad to women; they were horrid and rough and they stole everything they could, but they didn't mistreat us, only some of the foolish girls. You know that good-for-nothing family of Boirats, how they'd run after any man. Well, they took to going with the Boches; but any decent woman that kept out of sight as much as she could, no, I wasn't afraid of them much that way, unless they were drunk. Their officers were awfully hard on them about everything—*hard!* They treated them like dogs. *We were sorry for them sometimes.*"

Yes, this ignorant woman, white and thin and ragged, sitting on the wreck of her home, said this.

"Did you hear how they took every single thing in copper or brass—Grandfather's candlesticks, the andirons, the handles of the clothes-press, the door-knobs, and all, *every one* of my saucepans and kettles?" Her voice trembled at this item. "The summer after that, it was everything in linen. I had just the chemise I had on my back . . . even what was on the clothes-line, drying, they took. The American Committee distributed some cotton material and I made a couple for me and Berthe, and some drawers for Jean-Pierre and the baby. That was when we could still get thread. The winter after that, it was woolen they took, everything, especially mattresses. Their officers made them get every single mattress in town, except the straw ones. Alice Bernard's mother, they jerked her mattress right out from under her, and left her lying on the bed-ropes. And M. le Curé, he was sick with pneumonia and they took his, that way, and he died. But the Boches didn't dare not to. Their officers would have shot them if they hadn't."

"I can make beds for you," he said. "There must be trenches somewhere, near,"— she nodded,—"they'll have left some wire-netting in an *abri.* You make a square of wood, and put four legs to it, and stretch the wire-netting over it and put straw on that. But we had some wire-netting of our own that was around the chicken-yard."

"Oh, they took that," she explained,—"that, and the doors of the chicken-house, and they pried off our window-cases and door-jambs and carried those off the last days, too . . . but there was one thing they wouldn't do, no, not even the Boches, and that was *this* dirty work!" She waved her hand over the destruction about her, and pointed to the trees across the road in the field, all felled accurately at the same angle. "We couldn't understand much of what happened when they were getting ready to leave, but some of them had learned enough French to tell us they wouldn't 'do it'—we didn't know what. They told us they would go away and different troops would come. And Georges Duvalet's boy said they told *him* that the troops who were to come to 'do it' were criminals out of the prisons that the officers had let out if they would 'do it'—all this time we didn't know what, and somebody said it was to pour oil on us and burn us, the way they did the people in the barn at Vermad-derville. But there wasn't anything we could do to prevent it. We couldn't run away. So we stayed, and took care of the children. All the men who could work at all and all the women too, unless they had very little children, were marched away, off north, to Germany, with just what few extra things they could put in a big handkerchief. Annette Cagnon, she was eighteen, and had to go, but her mother stayed with the younger children—her mother has been sort of crazy ever since. She had such a long fainting turn when Annette went by, with a German soldier, we thought we never could bring her to life. . . ." The rough, tired voice shook a moment, the woman rested her head again on her husband's arm, holding to him tightly. "Pierre, oh Pierre, *if we had known what was to come,*—no, we couldn't have lived through it, not any of us!" He put his great, workingman's hand on her rough hair, gently.

She went on: "And then the troops who had been here did go away and the others came, and they made the few of us who were left go down into the cellars of those old houses down the road. They told us to stay there three days, and if we went out before we'd get shot. We waited for two whole days. The water they had given us was all gone, and then old Granny Arnoux said she was all alone in the world, so it wouldn't make any difference if she did get shot. She wanted to make sure that her house was all right. You know what she thought of her house! So she came up and we waited. And in half an hour we heard her crutches coming back on the road, and she was shrieking out. We ran up to see. She had fallen down in a heap. She hasn't known anything since; shakes all the time as if she were in a chill. She was the first one; she was all alone, when she saw what they had done . . . and *you* know . . ."

Nidart turned very white, and stood up. "God! yes, I know! *I* was alone!"

"Since then, ten days ago, the French soldiers came through. We didn't know them for sure, we were expecting to see the red trousers. I asked everybody about you, but nobody knew. There are so *many* soldiers in an army. Then Americans came in cars and brought us bread, and blankets and some shoes, but they have leather soles and I make the children keep them for best, they wear out so. And since then the Government has let the camions that go through to the front, leave bread and meat and once a bag of potatoes for us. The préfet came around and asked if we wanted to be sent to a refugee home in Paris or stay here, and of course I said stay here. The children and I have come every day to work. We've got the plaster and bricks cleared out from the corner of the fireplace, and I cook there, though there isn't any chimney of course, but I think the tiles of the kitchen floor are mostly all there still. And oh, Pierre, we have one corner of the garden almost cleared, *and the asparagus is coming up!* Come and see! They cut down everything they could see, even the lilac bushes, but what was in the ground, alive, they couldn't kill."

Nidart put the shovel in his wife's hand, and took up the pickax. "Time spent in traveling isn't counted on furloughs," he said, "so we have twenty-one days, counting to-day. The garden first, so's to get in the seeds."

They clambered over the infernal disorder of the ruins of the house, and picked their way down and back into what had been the garden. A few sections of the wall were still standing, its thick solidity resisting even dynamite petards.

"Oh, see, almost all of the pleached trees are saved!" cried Nidart, astonished, "that part of the wall didn't fall."

"I'm not sure I pruned those right," said his wife doubtfully, glancing at them. "I couldn't remember whether you left two or four buds on the peaches, and I just gave up on the big grapevine. It grew so, it got all ahead of me!"

"Did they bear well?" asked the man, looking across the trash heap at the well-remembered trees and vines. "We'd better leave those till some odd time, they won't need much care. I can do them between other things some time when I'm too tired to do anything else. Here is where the big job is." He looked the ground over with a calculating eye and announced his plan of campaign.

"We won't try to carry the rubbish out. It's too heavy for you, and my time has got to go as far as it can for the important things. We'll just pile it all up in a line along the line where the walls used to stand. All of us know that line! I'll use the pickax, and Maman the shovel. Jean-Pierre will throw the bigger pieces over on the line, and Berthe will go after and pick up the littler ones."

They set to work, silently, intensely. When they reached the currant-bushes, all laid low, Pierre gave a growl of wrath and scorn, but none of them slackened their efforts. About eleven the big convoy of camions on the way to the front came through, lurching along the improvised road laid out across the fields. The workers, lifting their eyes for the first time from their labors, saw at a distance on the main road the advance guard of the road-menders already there, elderly soldiers, gray-haired territorials, with rakes and shovels, and back of them, shuttle-like, the big trucks with road-metal coming and going.

Reluctantly leaving her work, Paulette went to get the supplies for dinner, and started an open-air fire in the cleared-out corner of the chimney. Over this she hung a big pot, and leaving it to boil she hurried back to her shovel. "The soup-kettle and the flat-irons," she told her husband, "they were too hard to break and too heavy to carry away, and they are about all that's left of what was in the house."

"No, I found an iron fork," said Berthe, "but it was all twisted. Jean-Pierre said he thought he could . . ."

"Don't talk," said their father firmly,—"you don't work so fast when you talk."

At noon they went back to the fire burning under the open sky, in the blackened corner of the fireplace where it had cooked the food during the years past. The man looked at it strangely, and turned his eyes away.

"Now where is your fork, little Berthe?" he said. "I'll straighten it for you. With that and my kit . . ."

"I have my jackknife too," said Jean-Pierre.

They ate thus, dipping up the stew in the soldier's *gamelle,* using his knife and fork and spoon and the straightened iron fork. The baby was fed on bread soaked in the gravy, and on bits of potato given him from the end of a whittled stick. In the twenty minutes' rest which their captain allowed the little force after the meal, he and Jean-Pierre whittled out two wooden forks, two-tined, from willow twigs. "That's one apiece now," said Nidart, "and the asparagus bed is all cleared off. We have made a beginning."

They went back to work, stooping, straining, heaving, blinded with the flying plaster, wounded with the sharp edges of the shattered stones. The sun shone down on them with heavenly friendliness, the light, sparkling air lifted the hair from their hot foreheads. After a time, Nidart, stopping for an instant to wipe away the sweat which ran down into his eyes, said: "The air has a different feel to it here. And the sun looks different. It *looks* like home."

At four they stopped to munch the piece of bread which is the supplementary meal of French working-people at that hour. Nidart embellished it with a slice of cheese for each, which made the meal a feast. They talked as they ate; they began to try to bridge over the gap between them. But they lacked words to tell what lay back of them; only the dry facts came out.

"Yes, I've been wounded, there's a place on my thigh, here, put your hand and feel, where there isn't any flesh over the bone, just skin. It doesn't bother me much, except when I try to climb a ladder. Something about that position I can't manage . . . and for a mason . . ."

"I'll climb the ladders," said Jean-Pierre.

"Yes, I was pretty sick. It got gangrene some. They thought I wouldn't live. I was first in a big hospital near the front, and then in a convalescent hospital in Paris.

It was awfully dull when I got better. They thought if I had made an application to be *réformé* and retired I could be like Jacques Dupré with his wooden leg. But with you and the children here . . . what could I have done with myself? So I didn't say anything, and when my time was up in the hospital I went back to the trenches. That was a year ago last winter."

"Berthe and Jean-Pierre had the mumps that winter," said their mother. "The baby didn't get it. I kept him away from them. The Boches shut us up as though we had the smallpox. They were terribly strict about any sickness. The Boche regimental doctor came every day. He took very good care of them."

"He wanted to give me a doll because I didn't cry when he looked in my throat," said Berthe.

"Of course she didn't take it," said Jean-Pierre. "I told her I'd break it all to pieces if she did."

"But she cried afterwards."

"Come," said the father, "we've finished our bread. Back to work."

That night, after the children were asleep on straw in the cellar down the road, their parents came back to wander about in the moonlight over their ravaged little kingdom. The wife said little, drawing her breath irregularly, keeping a strained grasp on her husband's arm. For the most part he succeeded in speaking in a steady voice of material plans for the future,—how he could get some galvanized roofing out of the nearest trench *abri;* how he could use the trunks of the felled trees to strengthen his hastily constructed brick walls, and for roof-beams; what they could plant in the garden and the field—things which she and the children could cultivate after he had gone back.

At this reminder of the inevitable farewell again before them, the wife broke out in loud wailings, shivering, clutching at him wildly. He drew her down on a pile of rubbish, put his arms around her, and said in a peremptory tone: "Paulette! Listen! *You are letting the Boches beat you!*" He used to her the tone he used for his squad, his new soldier's voice which the war had taught him, the tone which carried the laggards up over the top. At the steel-like ring of it his wife was silent.

He went on: "There's nothing any of us *can* do but to go on. The only thing to do is to go on without making a fuss. That's the motto in the army, you know. Don't make a fuss." He lifted his head and looked around at his home dismantled, annihilated. "*Not to give up,*—that and the flat-irons are about all the Boches have left us, don't you see?"

He was silent a moment and went on with his constructive planning. "Perhaps I can get enough lime sent on from Noyon to really rebuild the chimney. With that, and a roof, and the garden, and the allocation from the Government . . ."

"Yes, Pierre," said his wife in a trembling voice. She did not weep again.

He himself, however, was not always at this pitch of stoicism. There were times when he looked up suddenly and felt, as though for the first time, the downfall and destruction of all that had been his life. At such moments the wind of madness blew near him. The night after they had moved from the cellar into the half-roofed, half-walled hut, to sleep there on the makeshift beds, he lay all night awake, crushed with the immensity of the effort they would need to put forth and with the insignificance of any progress made. There came before him the long catalogue of what they had lost, the little decencies and comforts they had earned and paid for and owned. He sickened at the squalid expedients of their present life. They were living like savages; never again would they attain the self-respecting order which had been ravished from them, which the ravishers still enjoyed. With all his conscious self he longed to give up the struggle, but something more than his conscious self was at work. The tree had been cut down, but something was in the ground, alive.

At dawn he found himself getting out of bed, purposefully. To his wife's question he answered: "I'm going to Noyon to buy the seed for the field. We haven't half enough corn. And I can get young cabbage plants there, too, they say. I can make it in six hours if I hurry."

He was back by ten o'clock, exhausted, but aroused from his waking nightmare—for that time! But it came again and again.

On the day he began to spade up the field he noticed that two of his murdered fruit-trees, attached by a rag of bark to the stumps, were breaking out into leaf. The sight turned him sick with sorrow, as though one of his children had smiled at him from her deathbed. He bent over the tree, his eyes burning, and saw that all the buds were opening trustfully. His heart was suffocating. He said to himself: "They have been killed! They are dead! But they do not know they are dead, and they try to go on living. *Are we like that?*"

In an instant all his efforts to reanimate his assassinated life seemed pitiful, childish, doomed to failure. He looked across the field at the shapeless, roughly laid brick wall he had begun, and felt a shamed rage. He was half-minded to rush and kick it down.

"Papa, come! The peonies have begun to come up in the night. The whole row of them, where we were raking yesterday."

The man found his wife already there, bending over the sturdy, reddish, rounded sprouts pushing strongly through the loosened earth. She looked up at him with shining eyes. When they were betrothed lovers, they had together planted those peonies, pieces of old roots from her mother's garden. "You see," she said again; "I told you what was in the ground alive they couldn't kill!"

The man went back to his spading silently, and, as he labored there, a breath of sovereign healing came up to him from that soil which was his. The burning in his eyes, the taste of gall in his mouth, he had forgotten when, two hours later, he called across to his wife that the ground for the beans was all spaded and that she and Jean-Pierre could come now with their rakes, while he went back to building the house-wall.

But that quick scorching passage through fire was nothing compared with the hour which waited for him in his garden beside the wall on which the branches of his pleached trees and vines still spread out their carefully symmetrical patterns. He had put off caring for them till some odd moment. He and his wife, glancing at them from time to time, had made estimates of the amount of fruit they would yield, "and for *us* this time—we haven't had a single peach or apple from them. The Boche officers sent their soldiers to get them always."

"Queer they should have left those unharmed," said his wife once, and he had answered: "Perhaps the man they sent to kill them was a gardener like us. I know I couldn't cut down a fruit-tree in full bearing, not if it were in hell and belonged to the Kaiser. Anybody who's ever grown things knows what it is!"

One gray day of spring rains and pearly mists, the fire would not burn in the only half-constructed chimney. Paulette crouched beside it, blowing with all her might, and thinking of the big leathern bellows which had been carried away to Germany with all the rest. Jean-Pierre shaved off bits from a dry stick and Berthe fed them under the pot, but the flame would not brighten. Pierre, coming down, cold and hungry, from the top of the wall where he had been struggling with a section of roof, felt physically incapable of going on with that work until he had eaten, and decided to use the spare half-hour for pruning the pleached trees and vines. Almost at the end of his strength after the long-continued strained effort to accomplish the utmost in every moment and every hour, he shivered from the cold of his wet garments as he stood for a moment, fumbling to reach the pruning-shears. But he did not give himself the time to warm his hands at the fire, setting out directly again into the rain. He had been working at top speed ever since the breakfast, six hours before, of black coffee and dry bread.

Sodden with fatigue and a little light-headed from lack of food, he walked along the wall and picked out the grapevine as the least tiring to begin on. He knew it so well he could have pruned it in the dark. He had planted it the year before his marriage, when he had been building the house and beginning the garden. It had not been an especially fine specimen, but something about the situation and the soil had exactly suited it, and it had thriven miraculously. Every spring, with the first approach of warm weather, he had walked out, in the evening after his day's work, along the wall to catch the first red bud springing amazingly to life out of the brown, woody stems which looked so dead. During the summers as he had sprayed the leaves, and manured the soil and watered the roots and lifted with an appraising hand the great purple clusters, heavier day by day, he had come to know every turn of every branch. In the trenches, during the long periods of silent inaction, when the men stare before them at sights from their past lives, sometimes Nidart had looked back at his wife and children, sometimes at his garden on an early morning in June, sometimes at his family about the dinner-table in the evening, and sometimes at his great grapevine, breaking into bud in the spring, or, all luxuriant curving lines, rich with leafage, green and purple in the splendor of its September maturity.

It was another home-coming to approach it now, and his sunken, bloodshot eyes found rest and comfort in dwelling on its well-remembered articulations. He noticed that the days of sunshine, and now the soft spring rain, had started it into budding. He laid his hand on the tough, knotted, fibrous brown stem.

It stirred oddly, with a disquieting lightness in his hand. The sensation was almost as though one of his own bones turned gratingly on nothing. The sweat broke out on his forehead. He knelt down and took hold of the stem lower down. The weight of his hand displaced it. It swung free. It had been severed from the root by a fine saw. The sap was oozing from the stump.

The man knelt there in the rain, staring at this, as though he were paralyzed. He did not know what he was looking at, for a moment, conscious of nothing but a cold sickness. He got up heavily to his feet, then, and made his way to the next vine. Its stem gave way also, swinging loose with the horrible limpness of a broken limb.

He went to the next, a peach-tree, and to the next, a fine pleached pear. Everything, everything, peach-trees, apple-trees, grapevines, everything had been neatly and dextrously murdered, and their corpses left hanging on the wall as a practical joke.

The man who had been sent to do that had been a gardener indeed, and had known where to strike to reach the very heart of this other gardener who now, his hands over his face, staggered forward and leaned his body against the wall, against the dead vine which had been so harmless, so alive. He felt something like an inward bleeding, as though that neat, fine saw had severed an artery in his own body.

His wife stepped out in the rain and called him. He heard nothing but the fine, thin voice of a small saw, eating its way to the heart of living wood.

His wife seeing him stand so still, his face against the wall, came out towards him with an anxious face. "Pierre, Pierre!" she said. She looked down, saw the severed vine-stem and gave a cry of dismay. "Pierre, they haven't . . . they haven't . . . !"

She ran along the wall, touching them one by one, all the well-known, carefully tended stems. Her anger, her sorrow, her disgust burst from her in a flood of out-cries, of storming, furious words.

Her husband did not move. A deathlike cold crept over him. He heard nothing but the venomous, fine voice of the saw, cutting one by one the tissues which had taken so long to grow, which had needed so much sun and rain and heat and cold, and twelve years out of a man's life. He was sick, sick of it all, mourning not for the lost trees but for his lost idea of life. That was what people were like, could be like, what one man could do in cold blood to another—no heat of battle here, no delirium of excitement, cold, calculated intention! He would give up the effort to resist, to go on. The killing had been too thoroughly done.

His wife fell silent, frightened by his stillness. She forgot her own anger, her grief, she forgot the dead trees. They were as nothing. A strong, valiant tenderness came into her haggard face. She went up to him, close, stepping into his silent misery with the secure confidence only a wife can have in a husband. "Come, Pierre," she said gently, putting her red, work-scarred hand in his. She drew him away from the wall, his arms hanging listlessly. She drew him into the sheltered corner of the room he had half finished. She set hot food before him and made him eat and drink.

The rain poured down in a gray wall close before them. The heaped-up ruins were all around them. Inside the shelter the children ate greedily, heartily, talking, laughing, quarreling, playing. The fire, now thoroughly ablaze, flamed brightly beside them. The kettle steamed.

After a time Nidart's body began slowly to warm. He began to hear the children's voices, to see his wife dimly. The horror was an hour behind him. The blessed, blurring passage of the moments clouded thick between him and the sound of that neat small saw, the sight of that deft-handed man, coolly and smilingly murdering . . .

He looked at his wife attentively, as she tried to set in order their little corner saved from chaos. She was putting back on the two shelves he had made her the wooden forks and spoons which she had cleaned to a scrupulous whiteness; she was arranging neatly the wretched outfit of tin cans, receptacles, and formless paper packages which replaced the shining completeness of her lost kitchen; she was smoothing out the blankets on their rough camp-beds; she was washing the faces and hands of the children, of their own children and the little foster-son, the child of the woman who had given up, who had let herself be beaten, who had let herself be killed, who had abandoned her baby to be cared for by another, braver woman.

A shamed courage began slowly to filter back into his drained and emptied heart. With an immense effort he got up from the tree-stump which served for chair and went towards his wife, who was kneeling before the little child she had saved. He would begin again.

"Paulette," he said heavily, "I believe that if we could get some grafting wax at once, we might save those. Why couldn't we cover the stumps with wax to keep the roots from bleeding to death, till the tops make real buds, and then graft them on to the stumps? It's too late to do it properly with dormant scions, but perhaps we might succeed. It would be quicker than starting all over again. The roots are there, still."

He raged as he thought of this poor substitute for his splendid trees, but he set his teeth. "I could go to Noyon. They must have wax and resin there in the shops by this time, enough for those few stumps."

The little boy presented himself imploringly. "Oh, let me go! I could do it, all right. And you could get on faster with the roof. There aren't but ten days left, now."

He set off in the rain, a small brave spot of energy in the midst of death. His father went back to his house-building.

The roads were mended now, the convoys of camions rumbled along day after day, raising clouds of dust; staff-cars flashed by; once in a while a non-militarized automobile came through, sometimes with officials of the Government on inspection tours, who distributed miscellaneous lots of seeds, and once brought Paulette some lengths of cotton stuff for sheets; sometimes with reporters from the Paris newspapers; once with some American reporters who took photographs, and gave some bars of chocolate to the children. Several times people stopped, foreigners, Americans, English, sometimes women in uniforms, who asked a great many questions and noted down the answers. Pierre wondered why those able-bodied young men were not in some army. He had thought all the able-bodied men in the world were in some army.

For the most part he found all these people rather futile and uninteresting, as he had always found city people, and paid little attention to them, never interrupting his work to talk to them, his work, his sacred work, for which there remained, only too well known, a small and smaller number of hours. He took to laboring at night whenever possible.

The roof was all on the one tiny room before the date for his return. The chimney was rebuilt, the garden spaded, raked, and planted. But the field was not finished. It takes a long time to spade up a whole field. Pierre worked on it late at night, the moonlight permitting. When his wife came out to protest, he told her that it was no harder than to march all night, with knapsack and blanket-roll and gun. She took up the rake and began to work beside him. Under their tan they were both very white and drawn, during these last days.

The day before the last came, and they worked all day in the field, never lifting their eyes from the soil. But their task was not finished when night came. Pierre had never been so exacting about the condition of the ground. It must be fine, fine, without a single clod left to impede the growth of a single precious seed. This was not work which, like spading, could be done at night in an uncertain light. When their eyes, straining through the thickening twilight, could no longer distinguish the lumps of earth, he gave it up, with a long breath, and, his rake on his shoulder, little Berthe's hand in his, he crossed the mended road to the uncomely little shelter which was home.

Paulette was bending over the fire. She looked up, and he saw that she had been crying. But she said nothing. Nor did he, going to lean his rake against the reconstructed wall. He relinquished the implement reluctantly, and all through the meal kept the feel of it in his hand.

They were awake when the first glimmer of gray dawn shone through the empty square which was their window. Pierre dressed hurriedly and taking his rake went across the road to the field. Paulette blew alive the coals of last night's fire, and made coffee and carried it across to her husband with a lump of bread. He stopped work to drink and eat. It was in the hour before the sunrise. A gray, thin mist clung to the earth. Through it they looked at each other's pale faces, soberly.

"You must get the seed in as soon as you can, after I'm gone," said the husband.

"Yes," she promised, "we won't lose a minute."

"And I think you and Jean-Pierre can manage to nail in the window-frame when it comes. I thought I'd be able to do that myself."

"Yes, Jean-Pierre and I can do it."

"You'd better get my kit and everything ready for me to leave," he said, drinking the last of the coffee and setting his hand again to the rake.

They had reckoned that he would need to leave the house at ten o'clock if he were to make the long tramp to Noyon in time for the train. At a quarter of ten he stopped, and, the rake still tightly held in his hand, crossed the road. His knapsack, blanket-roll, all the various brown bags and *musettes* were waiting for him on the bench hewn from a tree-trunk before the door. He passed them, went around the little hut, and stepped into the garden.

Between the heaped-up lines of rubble, the big rectangle of well-tilled earth lay clean and brown and level. And on it, up and down, were four, long, straight lines of pale green. The peas were up. He was to see that before he went back.

He stooped over them. Some of them were still bowed double with the effort of thrusting themselves up against the encumbering earth. He felt their effort in the muscles of his own back. But others, only a few hours older, were already straightening themselves blithely to reach up to the sun and warmth. This also he felt—in his heart. Under the intent gaze of the gardener, the vigorous little plants seemed to be vibrating with life. His eyes were filled with it. He turned away and went back to the open door of the hut. His wife, very pale, stood there, silent. He heaved up his knapsack, adjusted his blanket-roll and *musettes,* and drew a long breath.

"Good-bye, Paulette," he said, kissing her on both cheeks, the dreadful long kiss which may be the last.

"I will—I will take care of things here," she said, her voice dying away in her throat.

He kissed his children, he stooped low to kiss the little foster-child. He looked once more across at the field, not yet seeded. Then he started back to the trenches.

He had gone but a few steps when he stopped short and came back hurriedly. The rake was still in his hand. He had forgotten his gun.

Carita Collins

(?)

Carita Owens Collins wrote the poem "This Must Not Be!" which was first published in the *Negro World* in 1919. Scholar Barbara Foley writes that the poem was controversial in its time, for it was mistakenly seen as inciting violence against whites.[1] Robert T. Kerlin, who reprinted it (under the title "Be a Man!") in *The Voice of the Negro 1919*, placed the poem within "the Negro's reaction . . . to the World War," as one voice expressing the "Negro . . . point of view, his way of thinking upon race relations, his grievances, his aspirations, his demands."[2] "This Must Not Be!" includes the lines: "And that same blood so freely spent on Flanders' field, / Shall yet redeem your race. / Be men, not cowards and demand your rights."[3] Collins's story "How Walter Regained His Manhood" exemplifies the theme of African American war service and racial pride. It was published in the May 1919 edition of the *Crusader*.

1. Barbara Foley, *Spectres of 1919: Class and Nation in the Making of the New Negro* (Urbana: Univ. of Illinois Press, 2003), 46.

2. Robert T. Kerlin, preface to *The Voice of the Negro 1919*, ed. Robert T. Kerlin (New York: Dutton, 1920), v.

3. Carita Owens Collins, "This Must Not Be!" *Negro World*, Sept. 13, 1919, 168, ll. 8–10.

How Walter Regained His Manhood

Carita Collins

Walter Cummings was "passing." If you don't know what "passing" means, an explanation is due.

In the United States of America there is a very common and prevalent ailment from which mainly white people suffer, known as color prejudice.

This disease so afflicts and distorts the victim's mind that he is unable to recognize any merit or capability in a person of African descent.

You will realize how dreadful and formidable this disease is when you learn that Walter Cummings was not as dark in color as many of the foreigners that flock to the shores of the U.S.A., and his blue eyes and brown, wavy hair in no way marked him as one whose foreparents had been enslaved.

When the door of opportunity was closed many, many times in Walter's face because he announced himself to be a Negro, the idea of "passing for white" presented itself to him. He had several friends who had in this way obtained lucrative positions. He thought of Margaret Evans, a stenographer, and Charles West, an engineer, and John Cummings, a cousin, who was serving the Emergency Fleet Corporation as auditor—all failing to claim kinship with the Negro race in order to earn their daily bread in the profession which they had chosen.

Hitherto Walter Cummings had nothing but scorn for these friends of his whom he termed "deserters," but when he found himself face to face with the same conditions that confronted them, he fought a desperate battle with his conscience—and lost.

Applying at the Pierce Arrow Company in Long Island City for a position as automobile salesman, in the space on the cards for applicants reserved for nationality, he placed the word "American," comforting his displeased Conscience with the fact that he was an American even if he did have Negro blood in his veins, and adding in an undertone as he noted many dark, swarthy countenances here and there in the great factory, "I am a darned sight better an American than many of these foreigners here."

Walter was a successful salesman, and soon his economic troubles vanished. Nevertheless his life was most miserable. His desk happened to be near a group of Negro-haters, and their frequent conversations on the subject tried Walter's soul. The following is a sample of one of the conversations:

"Say, William," said one of the salesmen, "come out and take a drink with me. My nerves are somewhat wobbly. I nearly ran down a damn nigger today, and——"

"Ha! Ha! Too bad you didn't succeed. Why in the hell didn't the black fool have sense enough to keep out of your way?" replied his friend.

"Oh I am not worrying about hurting a nigger. The trouble was that I had an old man and his daughter in the car demonstrating, as I thought to their perfect satisfaction, and when this accident happened, the girl insisted upon getting out of the car to see if the nigger was hurt. And that father of hers got out with her. When I made some remark about their showing so much concern over a nigger, they both glared at me and called the whole deal off. Damn it!"

Another day the men engaged in arguments concerning women suffrage, and several thought white women ought to vote, but most certainly not colored women. The thought of colored women voting was preposterous!

Many times, Walter had to leave the room in order to refrain from telling his fellow salesmen what unspeakable cowards they were and how ignorant they were of the culture and intelligence existing among Negroes.

While Walter was enduring these daily torments of the spirit, Fate prepared another for him.

As he slowly guided his car down a long road known as Jackson Avenue, suddenly around a corner darted a girl on a bicycle, and before Walter could swerve aside, there was a collision. The girl was thrown to one side of the roadway, and bringing his car to a sudden stop, Walter jumped out and hastened to aid her. As he knelt beside her, raising her in his arms, his alarmed gaze rested on what Walter believed to be the most beautiful girl he had ever seen.

She was unmistakably a Negro. She was as brown as the Indians who long ago followed this same road to Flushing Bay.

Her curly black hair lay in moist little ringlets about her face, and occasionally the soft June wind would secure a tendril and wave it aloft.

As Walter gazed into her face, her eyes opened, and she said feebly, "Where am I? What happened?", making an attempt to rise. Walter suddenly remembered that he was almost embracing a charming young lady whom he had never before seen, and gallantly assisted her to her feet.

When Iola Warfield attempted to stand up, she suddenly slipped forward, exclaiming, "Oh, my ankle!" And Walter, overjoyed that she was really alive, very willingly caught her in his arms. Then briefly explaining the accident and apologizing for his carelessness, stupidity and poor driving, he picked Iola up and deposited her in his car.

Iola was very much embarrassed. Her ankle was paining her and she couldn't walk, nevertheless she did not want this strange man, whom she found staring at her so intently whenever she glanced at him, to take her home in his car. Her embarrassment increased a hundred-fold when Walter handed her his card stating that he was a salesman for the Pierce Arrow Company. It suddenly dawned upon Iola that this man was white, and she cordially hated and distrusted all white people. She made another ineffectual attempt to leave the car, but by this time her ankle was swollen considerably and the pain was making her faint. Seeing her distress, but not realizing the entire cause, Walter secured Iola's home address at Corona, and in a few minutes, Mrs. Warfield, Iola's mother, started to the door in great agitation as she saw a man come up the walk, leading to the veranda with her daughter in his arms. Iola could not walk, and Walter was both sorry and glad of this opportunity.

He explained to Iola's mother, who hastily summoned a doctor, and took on himself the entire cause of the accident, although Iola occasionally from the divan in the sitting room interpolated, "It wasn't his fault at all mother, it was mine."

Finding that he had no excuse for lingering further, Walter left the house. The next day he telephoned an inquiry concerning Miss Warfield and was told that she had sprained her ankle, and was suffering somewhat from shock.

Immediately Walter inquired of the salesman nearest him, if people died from the shock of an accident when the physical injury amounted only to a sprained ankle.

"Sure," replied the salesman, as he winked to another, "a Pierce Arrow car gives a fellow that's hit a shock from which he sometimes never recovers."

"This car being the so-different-from-the-rest, best-on-earth, more-miles-for-your-money—"

The sight of Walter's grave face was too much for him, and he ended in a burst of laughter.

The next day Walter wondered if he could, with propriety, send Miss Warfield some flowers, and he crystallized this idea by going post-haste to the nearest florist and sending with his card one dozen American Beauties.

When the flowers came, Mrs. Warfield, with a smiling face and a troubled heart, took them up to Iola's room where Iola sat in a big chair alternately reading and looking out of the window.

"Oh, mother," exclaimed Iola, "who sent them?"

"Mr. Cummings, my dear," said the mother as she arranged them in a vase.

"Mr. Cummings," repeated Iola. "Why, why——I suppose it is very nice of him, but really, mother, I do not wish to accept flowers from a stranger—and a white man too. Please send them back."

"No, Iola," said the mother. "That would be most discourteous. I shall write him a note myself and thank him for them. You know, my dear, I have tried to teach you that there are kind hearts everywhere, even among white people.

"Believe good of all people, until you, yourself, find evil in them."

With these words, Mrs. Warfield descended the stairs, leaving Iola the prey to many conflicting emotions. No matter how often the thought of Walter's courtesy and gentleness presented itself to her mind, the thought that he was white and her aversion for his race persisted.

That night Mr. and Mrs. Warfield discussed the matter and Mr. Warfield wanted to go to see Cummings and tell him that he did not care to have him send flowers to his daughter, but his wife's counsel prevailed, and a calm and courteous note of thanks was dispatched by mail to Walter.

Walter wondered why Iola had not herself written the note, and then reflected that he supposed some mothers were like that, or maybe, it was some form of etiquette about which he did not know. And daily he telephoned inquiries about Iola's health and the latter part of the week, sent to the house a gorgeously decorated basket of fruit.

The daily telephone inquiries, and the flowers and the fruit, all served to anger Iola and to crystallize the fears that were slowly forming in the minds of Iola's parents. Years ago when Iola was but a little girl, a white man in their community had forced his attentions upon an attractive colored girl, only sixteen years of age, and helped to lynch her father who had sought redress. Shortly after this Mr. and Mrs. Warfield had migrated to the North, where they felt they could rear their daughter in safety and proper protection to human life could be secured. They did not feel that Walter's intentions could possibly be honorable, and even if they were, they felt that an intermarriage might be alright for some people, but they didn't want it in their family!

On Sunday afternoon the subject of their discussion blithely drove up to the gate, and found Mr. and Mrs. Warfield, and Iola, on the veranda.

He was duly presented to Mr. Warfield, who immediately invited him into the living room.

Mr. Warfield's stern countenance made Walter curious as to what he would say to him, and Mr. Warfield lost no time in beginning.

"Mr. Cummings, Mrs. Warfield and I are very grateful to you for your kind assistance to our daughter at the time when she carelessly ran into your machine. We realize that you are in no way to blame for the accident. We appreciate your inquiries and the other courtesies you have extended to us, but we do not wish you to continue them. You are a young white man, my daughter is a young colored girl. Between you two is the gulf of unreasoning race prejudice. We have no desire to span this gulf. I trust you understand me fully."

Walter listened with a sinking heart to Mr. Warfield. He had totally forgotten that they had no way of knowing that he too belonged to the Negro race, and he groaned inwardly as he thought, "I have indeed sold my birthright for a mess of pottage!"

"Mr. Warfield," he began. "I must tell you that I"—and here he paused. Suppose Mr. Warfield should inform his company that he was a Negro, he would lose his position. Then, too, Mr. Warfield might not believe him, and he knew of no mutual friend that would substantiate his statement.

"Mr. Warfield," he said. "I understand what you mean, and I assure you that you need have no fear of me. I do not know that I shall be in Long Island after this month. Permit me to shake your hand, sir."

Giving Mr. Warfield's hand a hearty grip, he passed out. Lifting his hat to the two ladies on the veranda, he went down the steps, entered his car and drove away, as they thought, out of their lives forever.

Mr. Warfield told his wife and daughter of his conversation and they expressed their approval of the course he had taken.

On the morning of October 15th, 1918, a group of colored soldiers from the 92nd Division occupied an advanced position in the northern part of France, just beyond the river Meuse. Pontoon bridges had to be built immediately in order to provide for an advance before nightfall. The stream, over which the bridge was to be constructed, was being swept by German shells, but the bridge was absolutely necessary. Not being willing to assign men to so dangerous a task, the Commanding Officer called for volunteers and Lieutenant Walter Cummings stepped forward and offered to direct the work. Other volunteers offered their services, and the men went to work. Under the most deadly fire they worked feverishly, dodging shells and laying the bridge, and in a few hours a triumphant company swept forward to victory over the bridge. But Lieutenant Cummings was being rushed to the nearest field hospital where he lay for weeks waging a now successful and now a losing battle with the grim monster Death. Often in his unconscious moments he would call pitifully for "Iola" and beg her to let him explain. The kind red cross nurse who attended him thought Iola was either his wife or his sweetheart, and in an effort to help straighten out matters looked in Lieutenant Cummings' address book, found Iola's address and wrote her a letter describing his brave deed and stating that his recovery was doubtful. She tactfully suggested that a letter from Iola might help a great deal. She told Iola that she was a southern white woman who had lost all her foolish prejudices. She had nothing but praise for the heroic deeds of the colored soldiers, and stated that Lieutenant Cummings was one of the bravest and most gallant colored gentlemen that she knew!

Iola read and re-read this letter. She knew there could be no mistake about the matter. She realized that Walter had not made known his identity because of his work; and she found herself hoping and praying for his recovery, and thinking how proud she would be to have his friendship if he ever returned. When she read the letter to her parents, asking their advice, both her mother and father urged her to write to him, and her father added, "Think I'll send him a little note in your letter myself."

While Walter was slowly convalescing, his nurse handed him a letter. Walter surveyed the girlish handwriting without much interest, and would have laid it aside, but his nurse insisted upon his reading it immediately.

He read a few lines, and then turning to the last page saw in letters of gold "Iola Warfield." When he had finished reading the letter for the fourth time, he remembered the nurse, and calling her, thanked her with tears in his eyes for the great happiness she had brought to him.

He told the nurse how he met Iola, how he loved her, how her father had disdained him. He said, "When I left Mr. Warfield, my heart was very heavy. I was denied the privilege of trying to win Iola's love because they thought me to be white."

"If I had told them that I was colored, Mr. Warfield might have doubted me, and I had no way of proving the fact. I had no friends who could substantiate my statements. I was alone and I had always hated the false position in which I had placed myself. The money I earned meant nothing to me. I did not care to associate with the men with whom I worked, and I could not make friends with my own people. It seemed to me that I was an outcast. I made up my mind that I would be a man and not a coward. I determined to throw in my lot with my people, and I thought if other Negroes can be successful, I can be so too. I resigned my position, telling them I was a Negro. I really did gain some satisfaction from the horror on the faces of my associates and their remarks, but it was grim amusement. Then the call came for colored officers and I went to Des Moines and became a Lieutenant. Then I came over here, and you know what happened here. I do not believe I can ever express my deep gratefulness to you. You have opened the door of hope for me."

"My experiences here in France have opened my eyes to the courageous manhood that exists among colored people, and I am truly glad that I have been of some little service to you," said the nurse.

Walter lost no time in writing to Iola. In the letters he wrote her during the months that followed, he told her all that he had told the nurse and more.

Early in February 1919, the great steamer Leviathan majestically swung anchor at New York. Among the convalescent troops which hung over the side of the steamer and enthusiastically cheered every building, large or small, every pier every body and everything that marked their return home, was a pale officer, with one arm in a sling and a painful limp that kept him from imitating the antics of his brother officers.

But his blue eyes were alight with hope and love as he crowded close to the railing of the ship in order to get a good view of the pier at which they were to dock.

Standing just behind the great ropes that keep anxious relatives and friends back, and that make a pathway for the heroes who come home, was Iola Warfield. Her father and mother were there too, but Walter saw no one in that throng but her. And so keen are the eyes of love that among 5,000 men, Iola saw Walter and waved a tremulous but joyful greeting.

Edith Wharton

(1862–1937)

In Paris during the war, Edith Wharton was active in relief charities and refugee resettlement. She made five tours of the front in 1915, firsthand experiences from which she wrote articles published in *Scribner's Magazine* and later collected in *Fighting France, from Dunkerque to Belfort* (1915). In recognition of her relief efforts, the French government named Wharton a chevalier of the Legion of Honor in 1916. She also wrote about the war in the novels *The Marne* (1918) and *A Son at the Front* (1923). "Writing a War Story" appeared in the September 1919 edition of *Woman's Home Companion,* and Wharton did not later collect it. Hermione Lee calls the story an "unkind satire" on the acceptance of war stories by female authors: "Women cannot write about the war and be taken seriously unless they turn themselves into men, Wharton suggests."[1]

Writing a War Story

Edith Wharton

Miss Ivy Spang of Cornwall-on-Hudson had published a little volume of verse before the war.

It was called "Vibrations," and was preceded by a "Foreword" in which the author stated that she had yielded to the urgent request of "friends" in exposing her first-born to the public gaze. The public had not gazed very hard or very long, but the Cornwall-on-Hudson "News-Dispatch" had a flattering notice by the wife of the rector of St. Dunstan's (signed "Asterisk"), in which, while the somewhat

---

1. Hermione Lee, *Edith Wharton* (New York: Knopf, 2007), 494.

unconventional sentiment of the poems was gently deprecated, a graceful and lady-like tribute was paid to the "brilliant daughter of one of our most prominent and influential citizens, who has voluntarily abandoned *the primrose way of pleasure* to scale *the rugged heights of Parnassus.*"

Also, after sitting one evening next to him at a bohemian dinner in New York, Miss Spang was honored by an article by the editor of "Zig-zag," the new "Weekly Journal of Defiance," in which that gentleman hinted that there was more than she knew in Ivy Spang's poems, and that their esoteric significance showed that she was a *vers-librist* in thought as well as in technique. He added that they would "gain incommensurably in meaning" when she abandoned the superannuated habit of beginning each line with a capital letter.

The editor sent a heavily-marked copy to Miss Spang, who was immensely flattered, and felt that at last she had been understood. But nobody she knew read "Zig-zag," and nobody who read "Zig-zag" seemed to care to know her. So nothing in particular resulted from this tribute to her genius.

Then the war came, and she forgot all about writing poetry.

The war was two years old, and she had been pouring tea once a week for a whole winter in a big Anglo-American hospital in Paris, when one day, as she was passing through the flower-edged court on her way to her ward, she heard one of the doctors say to a pale gentleman in civilian clothes and spectacles, "But I believe that pretty Miss Spang writes. If you want an American contributor, why not ask her?" And the next moment the pale gentleman had been introduced and, beaming anxiously at her through his spectacles, was urging her to contribute a rattling war story to "The Man-at-Arms," a monthly publication that was to bring joy to the wounded and disabled in British hospitals.

"A good rousing story, Miss Spang; a dash of sentiment of course, but nothing to depress or discourage. I'm sure you catch my meaning? A tragedy with a happy ending—that's about the idea. But I leave it to you; with your large experience of hospital work of course you know just what hits the poor fellows' taste. Do you think you could have it ready for our first number? And have you a portrait—if possible in nurse's dress—to publish with it? The Queen of Norromania has promised us a poem, with a picture of herself giving the baby Crown Prince his morning tub. We want the first number to be an 'actuality,' as the French say; all the articles written by people who've done the thing themselves, or seen it done. You've been at the front, I suppose? As far as Rheims, once? That's capital! Give us a good stirring trench story, with a Coming-Home scene to close with . . . a Christmas scene, if you can manage it, as we hope to be out in November. Yes—that's the very thing;

and I'll try to get Sargent to do us the wounded V. C. coming back to the old home on Christmas Eve—snow effect."

It was lucky that Ivy Spang's leave was due about that time, for, devoted though she was to her patients, the tea she poured for them might have suffered from her absorption in her new task.

Was it any wonder that she took it seriously?

She, Ivy Spang, of Cornwall-on-Hudson, had been asked to write a war story for the opening number of "The Man-at-Arms," to which Queens and Archbishops and Field Marshals were to contribute poetry and photographs and patriotic sentiment in autograph! And her full-length photograph in nurse's dress was to precede her prose; and in the table of contents she was to figure as "Ivy Spang, author of *Vibrations: A Book of Verse.*"

She was dizzy with triumph, and went off to hide her exultation in a quiet corner of Brittany, where she happened to have an old governess, who took her in and promised to defend at all costs the sacredness of her mornings—for Ivy knew that the morning hours of great authors were always "sacred."

She shut herself up in her room with a ream of mauve paper, and began to think.

At first the process was less exhilarating than she had expected. She knew so much about the war that she hardly knew where to begin; she found herself suffering from a plethora of impressions.

Moreover, the more she thought of the matter, the less she seemed to understand how a war story—or any story, for that matter—was written. Why did stories ever begin, and why did they ever leave off? Life didn't—it just went on and on.

This unforeseen problem troubled her exceedingly, and on the second morning she stealthily broke from her seclusion and slipped out for a walk on the beach. She had been ashamed to make known her projected escapade, and went alone, leaving her faithful governess to mount guard on her threshold while she sneaked out by a back way.

There were plenty of people on the beach, and among them some whom she knew; but she dared not join them lest they should frighten away her "Inspiration." She knew that "Inspirations" were fussy and contrarious, and she felt rather as if she were dragging along a reluctant dog on a string.

"If you wanted to stay indoors, why didn't you say so?" she grumbled to it. But the Inspiration continued to sulk.

She wandered about under the cliff till she came to an empty bench, where she sat down and gazed at the sea. After a while her eyes were dazzled by the light, and she turned them toward the bench and saw lying on it a battered magazine—the midsummer "All-Story" number of "Fact and Fiction." Ivy pounced upon it.

She had heard a good deal about not allowing one's self to be "influenced," about jealously guarding one's originality, and so forth; the editor of "Zig-zag" had been particularly strong on that theme. But her story had to be written, and she didn't know how to begin it; so she decided just to glance casually at a few beginnings.

The first tale in the magazine was signed by a name great in fiction, one of the most famous names of the past generation of novelists. The opening sentence ran: "In the month of October, 1914—" and Ivy turned the page impatiently. She may not have known much about story-writing, but she did know that *that* kind of a beginning was played out. She turned to the next.

"'My God!' roared the engineer, tightening his grasp on the lever, while the white, sneering face under the red lamp . . ."

No; that was beginning to be out of date, too.

"They sat there and stared at it in silence. Neither spoke; but the woman's heart ticked like a watch."

That was better; but best of all she liked: "Lee Lorimer leaned to him across the flowers. She had always known that this was coming . . ." Ivy could imagine tying a story on to *that*.

But she had promised to write a war story; and in a war story the flowers must be at the end and not at the beginning.

At any rate, there was one clear conclusion to be drawn from the successive study of all these opening paragraphs; and that was that you must begin in the middle, and take for granted that your reader knew what you were talking about.

Yes; but where was the middle, and how could your reader know what you were talking about when you didn't know yourself?

After some reflection, and more furtive scrutiny of "Fact and Fiction," the puzzled authoress decided that perhaps, if you pretended hard enough that you knew what your story was about, you might end by finding out toward the last page. "After all, if the reader can pretend, the author ought to be able to," she reflected. And she decided (after a cautious glance over her shoulder) to steal the magazine and take it home with her for private dissection.

On the threshold she met her governess, who beamed on her tenderly.

"Chérie, I saw you slip off, but I didn't follow. I knew you wanted to be alone with your Inspiration." Mademoiselle lowered her voice to add: "Have you found your plot?"

Ivy tapped her gently on the wrinkled cheek. "Dear old Madsy! People don't bother with plots nowadays."

"Oh, don't they, darling? Then it must be very much easier," said Mademoiselle. But Ivy was not so sure—

After a day's brooding over "Fact and Fiction," she decided to begin on the empiric system. ("It's sure to come to me as I go along," she thought.) So she sat down before the mauve paper and wrote "A shot rang out—"

But just as she was appealing to her Inspiration to suggest the next phrase a horrible doubt assailed her, and she got up and turned to "Fact and Fiction." Yes, it was just as she had feared, the last story in "Fact and Fiction" began: "A shot rang out—"

Its place on the list showed what the editor and his public thought of that kind of an opening, and her contempt for it was increased by reading the author's name. The story was signed "Edda Clubber Hump." Poor thing!

Ivy sat down and gazed at the page which she had polluted with that silly sentence.

And now (as they often said in "Fact and Fiction") a strange thing happened. The sentence was there—she had written it—it was the first sentence on the first page of her story, it *was* the first sentence of her story. It was there, it had gone out of her, got away from her, and she seemed to have no further control of it. She could imagine no other way of beginning, now that she had made the effort of beginning in that way.

She supposed that was what authors meant when they talked about being "mastered by their Inspiration." She began to hate her Inspiration.

On the fifth day an abased and dejected Ivy confided to her old governess that she didn't believe she knew how to write a short story.

"If they'd only asked me for poetry!" she wailed.

She wrote to the editor of "The Man-at-Arms," begging for permission to substitute a sonnet; but he replied firmly, if flatteringly, that they counted on a story, and had measured their space accordingly—adding that they already had rather more poetry than the first number could hold. He concluded by reminding her that he counted on receiving her contribution not later than September first; and it was now the tenth of August.

"It's all so sudden," she murmured to Mademoiselle, as if she were announcing her engagement.

"Of course, dearest—of course! I quite understand. How could the editor expect you to be tied to a date? But so few people know what the artistic temperament is; they seem to think one can dash off a story as easily as one makes an omelet."

Ivy smiled in spite of herself. "Dear Madsy, what an unlucky simile! So few people make good omelets."

"Not in France," said Mademoiselle firmly.

Her former pupil reflected. "In France a good many people have written good short stories, too—but I'm sure they were given more than three weeks to learn how. Oh, what shall I do?" she groaned.

The two pondered long and anxiously; and at last the governess modestly suggested: "Supposing you were to begin by thinking of a subject?"

"Oh, my dear, the subject's nothing!" exclaimed Ivy, remembering some contemptuous statement to that effect by the editor of "Zig-zag."

"Still—in writing a story, one has to have a subject. Of course I know it's only the treatment that really matters; but the treatment, naturally, would be yours, quite yours. . . ."

The authoress lifted a troubled gaze upon her Mentor. "What are you driving at, Madsy?"

"Only that during my year's work in the hospital here I picked up a good many stories—pathetic, thrilling, moving stories of our poor poilus; and in the evening, sometimes, I used to jot them down, just as the soldiers told them to me—oh, without any art at all . . . simply for myself, you understand. . . ."

Ivy was on her feet in an instant. Since even Mademoiselle admitted that "only the treatment really mattered," why should she not seize on one of these artless tales and transform it into Literature? The more she considered the idea, the more it appealed to her; she remembered Shakespeare and Molière, and said gayly to her governess: "You darling Madsy! Do lend me your book to look over—and we'll be collaborators!"

"Oh—collaborators!" blushed the governess, overcome. But she finally yielded to her charge's affectionate insistence, and brought out her shabby copybook, which began with lecture notes on Mr. Bergson's course at the Sorbonne in 1913, and suddenly switched off to "Military Hospital No. 13. November, 1914. Long talk with the Chasseur Alpin Emile Durand, wounded through the knee and the left lung at the Hautes Chaumes. I have decided to write down his story. . . ."

Ivy carried the little book off to bed with her, inwardly smiling at the fact that the narrative, written in a close, tremulous hand, covered each side of the page, and poured on and on without a paragraph—a good deal like life. Decidedly, poor Mademoiselle did not even know the rudiments of literature!

The story, not without effort, gradually built itself up about the adventures of Emile Durand. Notwithstanding her protests, Mademoiselle, after a day or two, found herself called upon in an advisory capacity, and finally as a collaborator. She gave the tale a certain consecutiveness, and kept Ivy to the main point when her pupil showed a tendency to wander; but she carefully revised and polished the rustic speech in which she had originally transcribed the tale, so that it finally issued forth in the language that a young lady writing a composition on the Battle of Hastings would have used in Mademoiselle's school days.

Ivy decided to add a touch of sentiment to the anecdote, which was purely military, both because she knew the reader was entitled to a certain proportion of "heart interest," and because she wished to make the subject her own by this original addition. The revisions and transpositions which these changes necessitated made the work one of uncommon difficulty; and one day, in a fit of discouragement, Ivy privately decided to notify the editor of "The Man-at-Arms" that she was ill and could not fulfill her engagement.

But that very afternoon the "artistic" photographer to whom she had posed for her portrait sent home the proofs; and she saw herself, exceedingly long, narrow and sinuous, robed in white and monastically veiled, holding out a refreshing beverage to an invisible sufferer with a gesture half way between Mélisande lowering her braid over the balcony and Florence Nightingale advancing with the lamp.

The photograph was really too charming to be wasted, and Ivy, feeling herself forced onward by an inexorable fate, sat down again to battle with the art of fiction. Her perseverance was rewarded, and after a while the fellow authors (though Mademoiselle disclaimed any right to the honors of literary partnership) arrived at what seemed to both a satisfactory result.

"You've written a very beautiful story, my dear," Mademoiselle sighed with moist eyes; and Ivy modestly agreed that she had.

The task was finished on the last day of her leave; and the next morning she traveled back to Paris, clutching the manuscript to her bosom, and forgetting to keep an eye on the bag that contained her passport and money, in her terror lest the precious pages should be stolen.

As soon as the tale was typed she did it up in a heavily-sealed envelope (she knew that only silly girls used blue ribbon for the purpose), and dispatched it to the pale gentleman in spectacles, accompanied by the Mélisande-Nightingale photograph. The receipt of both was acknowledged by a courteous note (she had secretly hoped for more enthusiasm), and thereafter life became a desert waste of suspense. The very globe seemed to cease to turn on its axis while she waited for "The Man-at-Arms" to appear.

Finally one day a thick packet bearing an English publisher's name was brought to her: she undid it with trembling fingers, and there, beautifully printed on the large rough pages, her story stood out before her.

At first, in that heavy text, on those heavy pages, it seemed to her a pitifully small thing, hopelessly insignificant and yet pitilessly conspicuous. It was as though words meant to be murmured to sympathetic friends were being megaphoned into the ear of a heedless universe.

Then she began to turn the pages of the review: she analyzed the poems, she read the Queen of Norromania's domestic confidences, and she looked at the portraits of the authors. The latter experience was peculiarly comforting. The Queen was rather good-looking—for a Queen—but her hair was drawn back from the temples as if it were wound round a windlass, and stuck out over her forehead in the good old-fashioned Royal Highness fuzz; and her prose was oddly built out of London drawing-room phrases grafted onto German genitives and datives. It was evident that neither Ivy's portrait nor her story would suffer by comparison with the royal contribution.

But most of all was she comforted by the poems. They were nearly all written on Kipling rhythms that broke down after two or three wheezy attempts to "carry on," and their knowing mixture of slang and pathos seemed oddly old-fashioned to the author of "Vibrations." Altogether, it struck her that "The Man-at-Arms" was made up in equal parts of tired compositions by people who knew how to write, and artless prattle by people who didn't. Against such a background "His Letter Home" began to loom up rather large.

At any rate, it took such a place in her consciousness for the next day or two that it was bewildering to find that no one about her seemed to have heard of it. "The Man-at-Arms" was conspicuously shown in the windows of the principal English and American book shops, but she failed to see it lying on her friends' tables, and finally, when her tea-pouring day came round, she bought a dozen copies and took them up to the English ward of her hospital, which happened to be full at the time.

It was not long before Christmas, and the men and officers were rather busy with home correspondence and the undoing and doing-up of seasonable parcels; but they all received "The Man-at-Arms" with an appreciative smile, and were most awfully pleased to know that Miss Spang had written something in it. After the distribution of her tale Miss Spang became suddenly hot and shy, and slipped away before they had begun to read her.

The intervening week seemed long; and it was marked only by the appearance of a review of "The Man-at-Arms" in the "Times"—a long and laudatory article—in which, by some odd accident, "His Letter Home" and its author were not so much as mentioned. Abridged versions of this notice appeared in the English and American newspapers published in Paris, and one anecdotic and intimate article in a French journal celebrated the maternal graces and literary art of the Queen of Norromania. It was signed "Fleur-de-Lys," and described a banquet at the Court of Norromania at which the writer hinted that she had assisted.

The following week, Ivy reentered her ward with a beating heart. On the threshold one of the nurses detained her with a smile.

"Do be a dear and make yourself specially nice to the new officer in Number 5; he's only been here two days, and he's rather down on his luck. Oh, by the way—he's the novelist, Harold Harbard; you know, the man who wrote the book they made such a fuss about."

Harold Harbard—the book they made such a fuss about! What a poor fool the woman was—not even to remember the title of "Broken Wings!" Ivy's heart stood still with the shock of the discovery; she remembered that she had left a copy of "The Man-at-Arms" in Number 5, and the blood coursed through her veins and flooded her to the forehead at the idea that Harold Harbard might at that very moment be reading "His Letter Home."

To collect herself, she decided to remain a while in the ward, serving tea to the soldiers and N. C. O.'s, before venturing into Number 5, which the previous week had been occupied only by a polo-player drowsy with chloroform and uninterested in anything but his specialty. Think of Harold Harbard lying in the bed next to that man!

Ivy passed into the ward, and as she glanced down the long line of beds she saw several copies of "The Man-at-Arms" lying on them, and one special favorite of hers, a young lance-corporal, deep in its pages.

She walked down the ward, distributing tea and greetings; and she saw that her patients were all very glad to see her. They always were; but this time there was a certain unmistakable emphasis in their gladness; and she fancied they wanted her to notice it.

"Why," she cried gayly, "how uncommonly cheerful you all look!"

She was handing his tea to the young lance-corporal, who was usually the spokesman of the ward on momentous occasions. He lifted his eyes from the absorbed perusal of "The Man-at-Arms," and as he did so she saw that it was open at the first page of her story.

"I say, you know," he said, "it's simply topping—and we're so awfully obliged to you for letting us see it."

She laughed, but would not affect incomprehension.

"That?" She laid a light finger on the review. "Oh, I'm glad—I'm awfully pleased, of course—you *do* really like it?" she stammered.

"Rather—all of us—most tremendously—!" came a chorus from the long line of beds.

Ivy tasted her highest moment of triumph. She drew a deep breath and shone on them with glowing cheeks.

"There couldn't be higher praise . . . there couldn't be better judges. . . . You think it's really like, do you?"

"Really like? Rather! It's just topping," rang out the unanimous response.

She choked with emotion. "Coming from you—from all of you—it makes me most awfully glad."

They all laughed together shyly, and then the lance-corporal spoke up.

"We admire it so much that we're going to ask you a most tremendous favor—"

"Oh, yes," came from the other beds.

"A favor—?"

"Yes; if it's not too much." The lance-corporal became eloquent. "To remember you by, and all your kindness; we want to know if you won't give one to each of us—"

("Why, of course, of course," Ivy glowed.)

"—to frame and take away with us," the lance-corporal continued sentimentally. "There's a chap here who makes rather jolly frames out of Vichy corks."

"Oh—" said Ivy, with a protracted gasp.

"You see, in your nurse's dress, it'll always be such a jolly reminder," said the lance-corporal, concluding his lesson.

"I never saw a jollier photo," spoke up a bold spirit.

"Oh, do say yes, nurse," the shyest of the patients softly whispered; and Ivy, bewildered between tears and laughter, said, "Yes."

It was evident that not one of them had read her story.

She stopped on the threshold of Number 5, her heart beating uncomfortably.

She had already recovered from her passing mortification: it was absurd to have imagined that the inmates of the ward, dear, gallant young fellows, would feel the subtle meaning of a story like "His Letter Home." But with Harold Harbard it was different. Now, indeed, she was to be face to face with a critic.

She stopped on the threshold, and as she did so she heard a burst of hearty, healthy laughter from within. It was not the voice of the polo-player; could it be that of the novelist?

She opened the door resolutely and walked in with her tray. The polo-player's bed was empty, and the face on the pillow of the adjoining cot was the brown, ugly, tumultuous-locked head of Harold Harbard, well-known to her from frequent photographs in the literary weeklies. He looked up as she came in, and said in a voice that seemed to continue his laugh: "Tea? Come, that's something like!" And he began to laugh again.

It was evident that he was still carrying on the thread of his joke, and as she approached with the tea she saw that a copy of "The Man-at-Arms" lay on the bed at his side, and that he had his hand between the open pages.

Her heart gave an apprehensive twitch, but she determined to carry off the situation with a high hand.

"How do you do, Captain Harbard? I suppose you're laughing at the way the Queen of Norromania's hair is done."

He met her glance with a humorous look, and shook his head, while the laughter still rippled the muscles of his throat.

"No—no; I've finished laughing at that. It was the next thing; what's it called? 'His Letter Home,' by—" The review dropped abruptly from his hands, his brown cheek paled, and he fixed her with a stricken stare.

"Good lord," he stammered out, "but it's *you!*"

She blushed all colors, and dropped into a seat at his side. "After all," she faltered, half-laughing too, "at least you read the story instead of looking at my photograph."

He continued to scrutinize her with a reviving eye. "Why—do you mean that everybody else—"

"All the ward over there," she assented, nodding in the direction of the door.

"They all forgot to read the story for gazing at its author?"

"Apparently." There was a painful pause. The review dropped from his lax hand.

"Your tea—?" she suggested, stiffly.

"Oh, yes; to be sure. . . . Thanks."

There was another silence, during which the act of pouring out the milk, and the dropping of the sugar into the cup, seemed to assume enormous magnitude, and make an echoing noise. At length Ivy said, with an effort at lightness, "Since I know who you are, Mr. Harbard,—would you mind telling me what you were laughing at in my story?"

He leaned back against the pillows and wrinkled his forehead anxiously.

"My dear Miss Spang, not in the least—if I *could.*"

"If you could?"

"Yes; I mean in any understandable way."

"In other words, you think it so silly that you don't dare to tell me anything more?"

He shook his head. "No; but it's queer—it's puzzling. You've got hold of a wonderfully good subject; and that's the main thing, of course—"

Ivy interrupted him eagerly. "The subject is the main thing?"

"Why, naturally; it's only the people without invention who tell you it isn't."

"Oh," she gasped, trying to readjust her carefully acquired theory of esthetics.

"You've got hold of an awfully good subject," Harbard continued; "but you've rather mauled it, haven't you?"

She sat before him with her head drooping, and the blood running back from her pale cheeks. Two tears had gathered on her lashes.

"There!" the novelist cried out irritably. "I knew that as soon as I was frank you'd resent it! What was the earthly use of asking me?"

She made no answer, and he added, lowering his voice a little, "Are you very angry with me, really?"

"No, of course not," she declared with a stony gayety.

"I'm so glad you're not; because I do want most awfully to ask you for one of these photographs," he concluded.

She rose abruptly from her seat. To save her life she could not conceal her disappointment. But she picked up the tray with feverish animation.

"A photograph? Of course—with pleasure. And now, if you've quite finished, I'm afraid I must run back to my teapot."

Harold Harbard lay on the bed and looked at her. As she reached the door he said, "Miss Spang!"

"Yes?" she rejoined, pausing reluctantly.

"You were angry just now because I didn't admire your story; and now you're angrier still because I do admire your photograph. Do you wonder that we novelists find such an inexhaustible field in Woman?"

Hugh Wiley

(1884–1968)

Published in the March 8, 1919, *Saturday Evening Post*, "The Four-Leaved Wild-cat" is the first in Hugh Wiley's popular series of stories featuring "Wildcat" Vitus Marsden, a member of the First Service Battalion. Originally presented in *The Saturday Evening Post* and later in *The American Legion Monthly*, these stories were also collected in *The Wildcat* (1920) and *The Prowler* (1924). The Wildcat stories did much to create white America's image of black doughboys. Wiley was born in Zanesville, Ohio, and served in France during World War I as a member of the 18th Engineer Regiment. In the 1930s, he created the Chinese detective James Lee Wong for a number of stories published in *Colliers*. The Wong character was later played by Boris Karloff in a string of low-budget films.

The Four-Leaved Wildcat

Hugh Wiley

"I don't bother work, work don't bother me, Ise fo' times as happy as a buh-humble-bee."

Vitus Marsden proclaimed to the world the content that filled his heart. Work was good enough for field hands and river niggers. Cutting the lawns that fronted white folks' residences on Legal Hill or taking an occasional r'ar at the gallopin' dominoes when the sevens and 'levens were feeling anxious to oblige a boy were the sources of an income sufficient for the day. And no man has seen to-morrow.

Vitus walked along a shaded back street. The sidewalk was made of soft red brick, which wore down unevenly so that young grass cutters would flap along and flap along until an old brick would try to bump hisself in an' live with a boy's toes.

In the left pocket of his adhesive shirt three silver dollars lay heavy as a croco-
dile's conscience. "Black shoes is three dollars, yaller shoes is three-fifty," thought
Vitus. "Ketch me one mo' law—then watch out, yaller shoes! Ise a wil'cat f'r yaller,
an' Ise on my prowl!"

The Wildcat was captured at the corner of Fourth and Elm by Mis' Minnie Morrison. "Name's Mis' Minny but folks minds like she was a ol' whale an' them Jonah."

"Vitus, come here!"

The Wildcat responded with the muscular activity of his namesake. "Mis' Minny,
here I is."

"This lawn needs trimming. It must be trimmed evenly and with precision—
eliminating, as far as your inferior technic will permit, the incongruous undulations
consequent to a preponderance of clover."

"Yas'm! Is you got a whetstone?" The Wildcat's intellect sagged for an instant
with the effort of remembering some of the heavy-set words for future use at the
Argumentative Pleasure Club.

Ordinarily the business of trimming a lawn meant no more to the Wildcat than
shuffling half a mile through a grass-strewn bit of life, but Mis' Minnie's specifications had made this a different proposition. Her vocabulary had made work out
of a little old job of cutting grass.

"I don't bother work, work don't conflooperate no bumblebee-ee, I'll lend me
a lawn-mowin' machine f'r this here ol' elephant of a lawn."

For half an hour after the lawn mower had been borrowed—on the strength of a
promise to sharpen it up free "to show how good kin I make ol' grass eater cut"—the
Wildcat marched with his feet flopping into a cascade of blue grass and clover which
gushed from the whirling knives. He roughed down the incongruous undulations
and trimmed the edges as best he could with the lawn mower, and was so relieved at
the improvement he had wrought that he resolved to sacrifice the edge of his shavin'
razor in an attack on the floppity bunches of grass along the margin of the lawn.
He produced the razor with a movement similar to that which a fat man employs
in scratching his back, and in a few minutes the margin of the lawn was enjoying
the bristly status of its interior. The Wildcat raked up the results of the grass eater's
activity, returned the machine to its owner with a request that he try it and see how
good kin she cut now, and sat down to rest himself until Mis' Minnie might bestow
the fifty cents.

"Black shoes, three dollars. Yaller shoes, three-fifty. Fifty cents, where at is you?"

He regarded the flappy sole of his left shoe and discovered that the contents of
the shoe consisted of about equal parts of foot and clover. He removed the shoe
and shook the grass out of it.

Mis' Minnie appeared with the fifty cents. "From a casual inspection it would appear that your reputation has been substantiated in this instance by equivalent performance."

The Wildcat batted his eyes. "Yas'm, Mis' Minnie. Thank you!"

The fifty-cent piece clinked to its place in the pocket of the adhesive shirt beside the three silver dollars. Mis' Minnie walked into the house and Vitus sat down to put on his left shoe, from which the clover had been emptied. "Yaller shoes, three-fifty." The three-fifty clinked nobly as the Wildcat bent over to put on his shoe.

Pressed against the sole inside of the Wildcat's left shoe, outlining in placid green the perfection of its promise, lay a four-leaved clover.

"Cloveh! Li'l cloveh, us needs action!"

The three-fifty clinked in cadence with the Wildcat's gallop toward a place where sevens and 'levens were feeling anxious to oblige.

In the back room of Willie Webster's barber shop the Wildcat knelt in a circle of his kind, getting action on the three-fifty. A pair of mercury dice introduced by a lodge brother failed to respond. The Wildcat shot a dollar and let it lay for three passes. He picked up the accumulated wealth and warmed the dice with the breath of victory.

"Ise a fo'-leaf wil'cat, an' Ise on my prowl! Shoots five dollars!"

The lodge brother recalled the words of the guaranty that accompanied the mercury dice. "Boy," he said, "roll 'em!"

The Wildcat rolled 'em, and his proprietary interest in the five dollars died a natural death. The lodge brother galloped the dominoes for two passes and whittled the Wildcat down to the measly fifty-cent piece that Mis' Minnie had given him for manicuring the ol' elephant.

The Wildcat massaged the dice between his magenta palms. "Little gallopers, speak to me! Shoots fifty cents!"

The little gallopers spoke to him. Their speech was not that which charms the ears of fortune's paramour. It sounded like the language of a steamboat man or deppity sheriff. The lodge brother grunted: "Wildcat, you is had your prowl."

The Wildcat retreated from the circle and made his way to the front room of the barber shop.

"Willie, how's chances for gettin' me a haircut on credit till I cuts me another lawn?"

The proprietor, wise to the financial condition of the victim who emerged from the back room of the shop, lost no time in stating his terms.

"We sells haircuts f'r cash; wartimes an' folks movin' away has me about bust now. They ain't no more credit 'til after the war is over."

The Wildcat shuffled out of the shop and prowled homeward. He paused in front of a grocery store long enough to figger he might eat a can of sardine fishes. He read the sign above the door—"Cash Grocery"—and resumed his course.

At the boarding house a white man waited for the Wildcat. The man carried a sheaf of folded-up papers in his left hand. The Wildcat recalled the fact that white men with folded-up papers never meant any luck for a boy.

"Ain't no 'stallment man—I finished up that 'stallment banjo an' that ol' 'stallment gold watch—how come this white man here?"

The white man challenged: "Boy, your name Vitus Marsden?"

The Wildcat saw no avenue of escape.

The white man pointed the folded-up papers at him. "You are drafted for the First Service Battalion. Report to the provost marshal in Memphis by to-morrow noon. You're 953,497."

"I sure is considerable. What is this here Fust Service Battalion?" Vitas Marsden, the Wildcat, mentally recorded his number.

"Service Battalions are front-line construction troops. Your uniform and equipment will be issued as soon as you pass the medical examination."

"Front line—'quipment—'zamination!" The Wildcat took hold of his Adam's apple, figgerin' it might keep jumpin' round until it got lost. "You mean Ise a wah soldier f'r workin' in dis yere wah?"

"Wouldn't say you'll be in the war, boy,"—the white man had his joy in his work—"you'll be sort of on the edge of it—the front edge, buildin' railroads f'r haulin' dead Germans away from in front of our cannons."

The Wildcat lost his health during the next three seconds. "Mister, my misery has got me bad ag'in——"

"Before noon to-morrow at Memphis; the provost marshal's office. And if you ain't there you get a military burial to-morrow at sundown."

The white man offered this casual interruption to the Wildcat's complaint and departed in search of the next winner in the lottery.

The military Wildcat curled up on his bed and removed his shoes so as to be footloose in his misery. Inside the left shoe, distinct against the dark leather background of the sole, lay the four-leaved clover.

"Cloveh, you fo'-leaf liar, wuz you a hawg I'd barbecue you with a rock."

The Wildcat scraped the four-leaved clover from the inside of his shoe. He clenched the talisman in a savage fist and heaved it from him. It fell on the foot of the bed and attached itself to the surface of a blanket. The Wildcat flopped himself down and tried to groan himself to death. He felt sleepy. He was pretty handy when there was any jobs of eating or sleeping to be done. Presently he dreamed of yaller shoes and cascades of four-leaved clover.

"Ise a mil'tary Wildcat, an' Ise on my prowl! Wah Germans is like gallopin' dominoes—only us boys hauls dead ones on railroads! Shoots five dollars—I needs action!"

The Wildcat's lower jaw sagged down something less than a foot. Without half trying he slept until an hour past noon of the next day.

The Wildcat awakened to face a threatening past and a tolerably measly future. The window of the room was clouded with a drizzle of rain. The smell of something frying in hot grease suggested that a little grub might come in handy for a hungry prowler. "Ain't et me nothing a-tall since Mis' Minnie consecrated me to cuttin' that ol' elephant of a lawn."

Dressing consisted of the simple business of putting on his shoes and hat. The floppity front of the left shoe was lashed to contact with the sole of the Wildcat's foot by means of a piece of string. "Yaller shoes, three-fifty; I don't need you nohow in the summertime."

Downstairs the empress of the boarding house was rendering grease from some bacon rinds that a white lady had bestowed upon her. The Wildcat looked things over and suggested that a little breakfast might build up his run-down constitution.

The Amazon eyed him with the caressing look of an active rattlesnake. "Brekfus'—you beggin' brekfus,' an' dinner cleared up an hour ago! Youse rollin' heavy if you gits any supper, you triflin' fiddle-footed mushrat! Clear outen here!"

The Wildcat lost interest in breakfast. The white man had said something about a military burial in case the rendezvous at the provost marshal's office in Memphis was delayed beyond noon.

"Miss Lou, what time does the clock say now?"

"Inch past two o'clock."

Number 953,497 selected from the several evils which confronted him that one which led away from the military burial. Eliminating the Memphis quadrant from the circle of fate, there remained the railroad track which led south; the impossible Mississip', on the west; and the Swamp Road leading east. The Swamp Road was pretty fair except that a boy traveling that way had to pass the hangin' tree, where a piece of rope still dangled from a lower limb.

The Wildcat rolled up a blanket from the bed where he had slept and tossed it gently out of the window. In making his exit he was careful to avoid Mis' Lou. He sneaked down the back street with his blanket and headed for the railroad track which led south.

Farewell, muddy horseshoe bend in the rollin' Mississip'; farewell, hangin' tree on the Swamp Road; farewell, military burial.

Number 953,497 reached the railroad yards and headed down the track. The Wildcat was on his prowlin' way.

"*I don't bother work, work don't bother me——*"

At the lower end of the yard a soldier stepped from between a pair of box cars and pointed a shiny new bayonet at the Wildcat's digestive system. Behind the bayonet was the biggest rifle the Wildcat had ever seen.

The soldier strayed a little from the words of the manual. "Nigger," he demanded, "where in hell is you headed for?"

After a while the Wildcat regained partial control of his lower jaw. "Provo' man's place in Memphis f'r 'quipmant," he stated.

"Corp'l the guard—Post Number Six!" the sentry bawled. The Wildcat rolled his eyes. The corporal appeared, convoying an automatic pistol whose sagging volume was eloquent of military burials.

"White man with a paper tol' me my number an' could I git to Memphis. I got headed round somehow——"

"Boy, head round again, an' head quick!" The Wildcat executed an efficient but technically imperfect About Face.

Ten minutes later, in a box car filled with twenty more high numbers, he was en route for Memphis. In an hour the car was disgorging its accumulation under the smoky train shed in the Memphis station. A group of officers confronted the Wildcat and his associates. One of these gentlemen with a long paper in his hand was reading numbers.

"Number 953,497."

"Gin'ral, here I is." The Wildcat stepped forward to whatever kind of military funeral might await him.

The officer consulted his list. "Son, is your name Vitus Marsden?"

"Gin'ral, yassir."

"Line up over there with those other boys—and don't call me 'gin'ral.'"

"Gin'ral, yassir!"

Anything to oblige was the present policy. The "gin'ral" had a low voice, like a good poker player. The Wildcat decided that the "gin'ral" was white folks.

That night the Wildcat slept in a long cotton shed. At quarter to ten a lusty bugler blew the call to quarters.

"Whut dat horn mean?" the Wildcat suddenly demanded of an experienced soldier in soldier clothes.

"Sign they's buryin' some noisy nigger," the experienced soldier informed him.

Taps blared with a suddenness to be expected of Gabriel only. "Buryin' us boys as fast as they ketch us," the Wildcat decided. He rolled his blanket around his head and resigned himself to whatever hand the fates might deal from their stacked deck.

Something tickled his ear. "Cotton creeper, mos' likely." He reached for the offending insect and inspected it. It was the four-leaved clover, considerably the worse for wear, which he had cast from him the night before in the boarding house. "Cloveh, you hell-raisin' houn'—Ise gonna eat you!" He ground the four-leaved nemesis to a pulp.

The sergeant in charge of quarters turned out the lights. The Wildcat kept thinkin' and ponderin' about military burials and hauling dead Germans in front of cannons. In his misery he decided to let the gin'ral help him worry. There was one man what acted like white folks. He fell asleep with the gin'ral between him and the military funeral and the dead Germans and the hangin' tree and the rest of the pesterin' things that wildcats hate.

So far the Wildcat had missed four meals.

Reveille sounded. The Wildcat blinked himself into the cold realities of life and sat up.

"Boy," he said to the ginger-faced youth next to him, "boy, what us needs is some side meat an' gravy an' biscuits an'——When does us eat?"

He put on his shoes and sought out a soldier with three chevrons on his sleeve. "Podneh, where at is us boys' brekfus' 'quipment?"

The sergeant, old in the service, gave the Wildcat his second lesson in military etiquette. The Wildcat figgered that if there was any card lower than a deuce in the military deck he was it. For the balance of the day he waited for some other boy to start something. In the afternoon he passed the medical examination and stood in line for an hour until his uniform and equipment were issued to him. He was assigned to Company C of the battalion. At four o'clock the company formed for the first time. The Wildcat sized down to Squad Seven and took his place in the front rank.

"Company—'en-shun!" The sergeant observed a sudden epidemic of protruding stomachs.

"Co'pals will be selected at retreat for their mil'tary bearin.' When I tells you 'At ease,' you eases; when I tells you 'At rest,' you talks. At Rest!"

The boy behind the Wildcat talked. He talked at the Wildcat.

"Cap'n find that meat plow you's totin' you'll be at res'—after the funeral."

The weight of the Wildcat's shaving razor suddenly rested heavy between the shoulder blades of his conscience. "How come?"

"You know how come; an' it stickin' out agin' yo' coat like ol' hawg's backbone."

The Wildcat straightened up. At retreat he had shifted his razor, but was still acutely straight. The captain's "Tenshun!" nearly threw him over backward.

Because of his military bearing the Wildcat became corporal of his squad.

One minute after taps the Wildcat gave his first command. "Lootenant says, 'Shut up when taps horn blows.' She done blow. Shut up!"

Out of the darkness came an impudent inquiry: "Who is you?"

"Ise yo' co'pal."

From another corner of the tent there came a whisper of derision: "Huh—when de lootenant's gone day ain't no co'pals!"

The Wildcat fumbled around for an instant and then walked softly toward the source of the whisper. He lighted a match with his left hand. In his right there waved a razor with the meanest blade Squad Seven had ever seen. The match burned out. Until reveille Squad Seven snored heavily.

As near as the Wildcat could see, the war consisted of free rations, free clothes, a little prancin' round and considerable work with picks and shovels. Trench practice was the order of the day, and for three weeks the company dug trenches. A jack-rabbit, springing from section F-63 of an advance sector, running through the Skagg's pasture, led two members of the Wildcat's family a chase that terminated in the guardhouse. With this exception the squad had an excellent record. The colonel was pleased to remark the fact within hearing of the Wildcat; with cyclones selling at two cents a ton the Wildcat figured Squad Seven was about twelve dollars' worth.

Then, following rumor, care orders.

Box cars to an Atlantic port, a few hours on the long pier against which the transport lay, and then four decks below the surface of the harbor the Wildcat realized that as a boiled egg he was something under ninety seconds. All the steamboats he was ever on were made of wood and a nigger could look over the side and see land once in a while, but this old elephant of an iron boat was a jail with four or five cellars.

"What grieves my gizzard mos' is why is ol' boat so res'less an' uncertain where is she goin'," the Wildcat objected. "Rockin' round all the time like a bog-down mule."

The third day out a strange bugle call floated down from the deck above.

"Co'pal, what dat horn sayin'?" a startled member of Squad Seven demanded.

The Wildcat was pretty well scared himself but he managed to pick his cue from a yell in the far corner of the compartment, where the sergeants bunked.

"Pay day, boy. Ain't you been a soldier long enough to rekonize money when she sings at you?"

An hour later pay day had gravitated to a group of hardboiled professionals whose skill as crap shooters was advertised by their several accumulations of paper money. The Wildcat, still in the game and going stronger every second, was rolling some eloquent ivory. Restricted in the calisthenics of chance by the fact that his guardian knees covered two bales of greenbacks, about all he could do was to sweat and win money. Coming out, his opening palm spelled seven or eleven with monotonous regularity.

"Shoots fifty dollars; shower down, brothers, shower down! . . . Five spot an' a li'l deuce. . . . I lets her lay. . . . Shower down, brothers, shower down! . . . An' I six-aces fo' my home on high! Fade me, niggers, fade me! Ise a mil'tary wil'cat, an' I shoots it all. . . . Five an' six is 'leven! Li'l green leaves come back where at you growed. I rolls a hund'ed an' de boat rolls me. Shower down yo' money, brothers———"

"Ten-shun!"

At the foot of the companionway stood the lieutenant. Presently he began to read out loud from a paper:

"Special Orders Number Seven—Headquarters First Service Battalion: Gambling on board this ship by members of this battalion is forbidden. Offenders will be placed in arrest, in confinement and tried by special court. Signed: Colonel Commanding."

The lieutenant added an emphatic verbal indorsement: "If I find any of you niggers shootin' craps I'll skin the livin' hell out of you."

The Wildcat sat on the edge of his bunk and counted up as high as he could. "I figgers I wins sumpin' like a thousan' dollars; an' here is me an' the money, safe an' sound."

From a sack of mail delivered on board at the hour of the ship's departure a letter addressed to the Wildcat reached him as he finished counting his money. He laid the money beside him and summoned a school nigger.

"Boy, read me this here letter what she say."

The school nigger opened the pages of the letter and read it.

"Letter come from Mis' Lou at de boa'din' house sayin' 'Where at that blanket you took an' three dollars boa'd an' here is a fo'-leaf cloveh fo' good luck, an' how is you all? Good-by, an' Lawd bless yo,' savin' you a jar of pussonal preserves what you likes.'"

"Where at de cloveh?"

The school nigger shook a flattened green talisman from the envelope. The Wildcat picked it up.

"Cloveh! Li'l cloveh, here is you an' here's mo' money what I ever see. . . . Money, where is you at!"

The bale of greenbacks had disappeared.

Mess call blew a minute later but the Wildcat wasn't hungry.

· · ·

Ten days later at a base port in France the ship discharged her brunet cargo.

"Feet, lemme see kin you trod de ground!" The Wildcat felt middlin' good in spite of the incidental discomforts of the voyage. Explosive eggs, stewed liver, and

the restless rockin' round of the uncertain boat were forgotten, and in their place
a hundred happier impressions formed:

I eats when I kin git it,
I sleeps mos' all de time,
I don't give a dog-gone if de sun don't neveh shine,
Dat's why I'm as happy as a buh-humblebee-ee—
I don't bother work, an' work don't bother me!

"Fall in!"

"Company C formed and counted off as far down the line as the tenth squad
without getting balled up, and executed a Squads Right that found only about half
its members running wild, and finally hit up a route step for the long hill that led
to camp.

"Where at is we headed fo', co'pal?"

"Res' camp; us needs rest."

At nine o'clock that night the company reached camp and dined on bully beef
and coffee. For the next three hours they erected tents and dug ditches around them,
True to tradition the evening clouds of the Gironde condensed to a cold rain which
endured throughout the night. At midnight Squad Seven, drenched and middlin'
miserable, lay down on some wet straw and pulled some wet blankets over its wet
anatomy.

"Whut did de lootenant call dis camp, co'pal?"

"Res' camp."

"Anyhow, alongside that ol' boat dis yere dry lan' feels steady like an'nacheral."
The Wildcat diverted a rivulet of rainwater that suddenly flowed under his neck.

"Whut you mean—'dry' lan'? Git to sleep!"

At midnight three hundred miles farther along the road to Berlin a general commanding brigade headquarters lay down on a potato sack in the corner of a roofless
stone barn and smoked the front ends of three cigarettes. Then in a sulphuric bass
rich with the tremolo of passion he cursed the qualified rain and the Service of
Supply and called for an orderly.

"Ask one of the artillery officers to come in here a moment, and then get G. H.
Q. on the wire." The orderly saluted and faded into the adjoining room, where, in a
stall once tenanted by a large red cow, a signal-corps man sat in front of a twenty-
pair board.

"Git G. H. Q. an' ring the Ol' Man when you git 'em," he ordered. He sought
another section of the barn and addressed an officer who was stuttering some

orders on a rusty typewriter: "Sir, the general presents his compliments and wishes to see you in his quarters."

The general was sitting up on his potato sack when the artillery colonel reported. "Jim, what's the maximum barrage range for to-morrow's advance?" he asked.

"Eight miles, general; not over eight."

"Our Front is four miles ahead of your guns—leaving four to go. I've ordered two miles kicked out of the line. Two miles is two miles on paper, but when the babies start it's hard to hold 'em—and if they make it five or six where in hell are they at?"

"Beyond the barrage—where you said; the ones who get through."

The telephone beside the potato sack rang. The general spoke slowly: "General commanding censored Brigade speaking. Let me have Artillery Staff. . . . This is General commanding censored Brigade. How in hell do you expect me to move my guns with these deleted, gas-damned Skiddite tractors in mud ten feet deep!"

Artillery Staff at G. H. Q. yawned and asked the general what he could suggest.

The general spoke a little faster: "I suggest that you fill my requisition for mules—that's what I suggest! Fill it quick and don't send any two-legged ones just because you're overstocked. I want some mules!"

He hung up the receiver and spoke to the artillery officer standing beside him: "I'll try to get you some mules, Jim, but until they get here do your best to keep the guns moved up. That's all. Good-night."

The General lay down on his potato sack and pulled his trench coat over his head.

A hundred miles away Artillery Staff smiled. "The old squirrel is lonesome; but I'll get him some mules."

At reveille the Wildcat moved himself round slowly and warped himself into shape and figgered could he sleep till 'zactly one minute before the breakfast bugle should start a stampede. The company circled round the cook tent absorbing "seconds" until even the grease was gone from the bacon pans and the coffee a matter of dehydrated grounds. The Wildcat returned to his tent after breakfast and squirmed himself into his nest of saturated blankets.

"Res' camp, here is where at I takes all the rest you got."

A moment after he had settled himself for a good sleep the captain's striker summoned him to company headquarters. "Cap'n said come a-runnin', boy."

"What for all dis runnin' business?" the Wildcat protested. "I never seed such a pesterin' wah. Where at is all dat res' camp business the lootenant was speakin' about?"

Five minutes after the Wildcat had reported to his captain he left camp in the wake of a French officer and interpreter and headed for a remount station. In the Wildcat's charge were seven other members of C Company. At the remount station the Wildcat and each of his companions were presented with eight mules, which they conducted to a train of dinky little freight cars. Presently the squad had witnessed the flop-eared charges safely loaded on board the train. An hour later after splitting the air with whistles the engineer succumbed to the plaintive charms of the conductor's tin-horn solo and the braying of sixty-four mules. The train departed through a maze of tracks that complicated its escape from the terminal.

The Wildcat sat in the open side door of his box car. Behind him at right and left were grouped the restless hind legs of eight mules. This sinister formation endured throughout the first day with but one interruption, during which the train stopped in the freight yards of a little town that the mules might be watered and fed.

On the evening of the third day the French officer, who had traveled with his interpreter in the passenger car at the head of the train, addressed the Wildcat and his two-legged associates.

"You will detrain at once. The night will be spent here!" said the interpreter. "At dawn the convoy will form and depart for headquarters, deleted Artillery Brigade, thirty kilometers to the east."

The interpreter and the French officer sought quarters for the night in the central part of the town.

The Wildcat fed his eight mules on some hay which he borrowed from a stack in an adjoining field. At nine o'clock it began to rain. The inviting shelter of a deserted stone barn half a mile away had painted itself into the Wildcat's mental picture of his surroundings, and at ten o'clock the eight mules and the Wildcat were comfortably billeted.

"At ease, mules! At ease! Don't you know a res'-camp barn when you sees it? At res'!"

The Wildcat wrapped his overcoat round him and crawled into a pile of straw. "Artillery parade thirty calamities east of here; mules, you makes it easy by to-morrow. At res'!"

The Wildcat busted his previous records for long-time sleep. Thirty hours later he woke up and felt some rested. The mules were evidently all right and it was still dark, so he went back to sleep.

"Us needs rest."

About this time the Wildcat's captain read a telegram which stated that the corporal of the convoy furnished by Company C together with eight mules had become lost.

"If I ketch that nigger, I'll hit him with a court-martial sentence that'll age him gray in hell. I'll lose him so he'll stay lost!"

I kin ride a freight train,
I don't pay no fare,
I kin ride a freight train mos' anywhere,

Dat's why Ise as happy as a buh-humble-bee-ee—
I don't bother work, an' work don't bother me.

"Mules, squad yo'self east an' west an' see kin you eat dis heah cloveh field in fifteen minnits. Us leaves fo' ol' artillery parade soon as I 'sorb my travel rations. You-all's got thirty calamities between you an' supper; us has to travel."

The Wildcat devoted the next hour to his rations. Then he strolled leisurely down to the railroad tracks to see if the convoy was ready to leave. The shock of surprise which he experienced at discovering that his companions had departed was absorbed by the knowledge that he could sleep mos' anywhere and that Uncle Sam had provided him with travel rations.

He returned to the stone barn and rounded up his eight mules. He headed for the main street of the village. In the middle of the street in front of a café stood a negro soldier in a blue overcoat. The soldier carried a French rifle to which was attached a long curved bayonet.

The Wildcat leading a string of seven mules rode the eighth mount to where the soldier stood.

"Podneh, where at is the artillery parade from here?"

The soldier with the rifle glanced at the soldier on the mule, but did not reply.

"Uppity, I ax you where at is de artillery parade where Ise consecrated to carry dese mules?"

The Senegalese soldier with the rifle grunted and shook his head. The disgusted Wildcat yanked at his string of mules.

"Ise seed niggers what couldn't read and niggers what couldn't write, but I never seed one befoh what couldn't talk! Come 'long here, mules! Us heads east like de lootenant said, where de sun shines early in de mawnin.'"

The Wildcat traveled down an excellent road lined on both sides with trees. He rode for three hours, encountering the motor traffic common to the roads of France in the zone of advance. Presently he came to a stretch of road where the smooth surface gave way to a rougher construction. The trees were no longer leafy coverings above the road. Some of them were shattered stumps.

At evening, seeing nothing that remotely resembled the headquarters of an artillery brigade, the Wildcat addressed the driver of a motor truck that had halted beside the road.

"Where at is dis yere artillery parade what needs mules?"

The driver answered without turning his head. "Up the road about ten miles." He knew nothing of artillery location, but his reply was enough to discourage further travel. The Wildcat hazed his charges along the road until he discovered a ditch in which there was a few inches of water.

"Mules, us camps here."

Night had fallen. The mules were picketed after the Wildcat had eaten a gratifying segment of his own rations. The chill of the hour before dawn awakened him. He collected some splinters of wood from beneath a shattered tree that stood beside the road and lighted a fire. For perhaps five minutes he lay beside the fire, absorbing its grateful heat.

Then from the sky above his head there came the moan of a motor—a rising note that whined for an instant before the world blew up about him.

The next thing he remembered was the docile manner in which his mules submitted to his will as they galloped in the dark along the broken road.

The mules were thinking over their several sinful lives, and the Wildcat was thinking could a mule outrun an earthquake. The procession endured for nearly an hour. Never for a moment was the steady gallop interrupted until the light of dawn dispelled the terror of the night.

The Wildcat looked round with an apprehensive eye. He did not like the look of the country. The terrain was marked with craters that fringed the road and expanded into the hills on either side. Strands of broken barbed wire hung from succeeding lines of posts and on either hand irregular trenches narrowed to the horizon.

"Sho' is poor farmin' lan'—wonder to me how folks makes any crop a-tall on lan' like dis yere. Sho' wastin' lots of good fencin' wire."

Against a strand of wire from which hung shreds of stained gray cloth the Wildcat found a saber, red with rust. The owner was nowhere to be seen and the Wildcat appropriated the weapon.

"Good soa'd; come in mighty handy f'r leadin' parades with when us gits home. Git up, mule!"

The Wildcat waved his saber. His mules accelerated their pace with a lunge, and then, urged to extreme endeavor—not by the Wildcat's yells or by his waving blade, but by the barrage of the zero hour which rocked the earth round them—the eight mules charged across a field that suddenly began to bloom with shrapnel.

"Mules, de Lawd is our shepherd; us needs some gin!"

The Wildcat saw some gray-clad figures running toward him out of the smoke. They were without weapons and their arms were upraised.

"White folks, come heah!" With his saber the Wildcat waved at the men in gray. They came running toward him. "How does us git out of dis heah wah?"

"Kamerad! Kamerad!"

"'Gimme ride! Gimme ride!' Git on dese heah mules an' ride. Us gwine fr'm dis wah sudden. Git on. Us leaves now!"

The Wildcat and seven mules loaded with boche started away from the war. Each mule except that one which the Wildcat rode carried two or three riders, and alongside the group, seeking the false security of companionship, twenty additional prisoners had coagulated from the mob of their fellows.

Thus escorted the Wildcat rode through the wave of the first advance and their supports. He arrived finally at a zone of comparative quiet within the French lines, where he was confronted by a group of French officers standing beside a mud-splashed racing car. One of them, a tired looking gentleman whose stars of rank were as bright as the keen gray eyes with which he surveyed the Wildcat, spoke to an officer beside him. The officer approached the Wildcat.

"It is that you alone, monsieur, armed only with a saber, retrieve these prisoners?"

The Wildcat did not understand many of these high sounding words. "Yassir, gin'ral—me an' dese yere artillery-parade mules was alone an' runnin', an' up come some white folks: 'Gimme ride! Gimme ride!' An' I lets 'em ride; an' here us is."

The French officer patted the Wildcat on the shoulder: "My brave! Of such is your glorious Army! The general shall be informed. Your name, and of what regiment?"

The Wildcat fished for his identity tag. "Cop'al Vitus Marsden, 953,497, Company C, Fust Service Battalion, fr'm Memphis, Ten-o-see."

The officer recorded the data in his notebook. He held his hand out to the Wildcat in parting. "And now, brave corporal, adieu!"

"Yassir, gin'ral; an' kin you-all tell me where at is headquarters artillery parade?"

"Headquarters? . . . Ah, yes, it is of the adjoining artillery headquarters that you speak. A courier shall accompany you as guide."

The Wildcat accumulated his mules. The "gimme-ride" white folks had disappeared. A French soldier mounted one of the mules.

"Come wiz me," he said.

As the Wildcat rode past the French officers they saluted him. "Adieu, soldier of what bravery!"

At Brigade Headquarters the adjutant accomplished a memorandum receipt for the eight mules and signed a travel order for the Wildcat. An orderly delivered the documents.

"What does I do now?" asked the Wildcat when the orders were handed him.

"Read your orders."

"Cain't read dis yere writin'. What does she say?"

The orderly glanced at the pages. "She says git t'hell back where you come from."

"Where at does I go?"

"Ketch a truck to Chemin Blanc and hit the rattler fr'm there south."

"Where at does I git me a ticket an' rations?"

"You don't need no ticket except them orders, and you draws rations wherever you're at from the A. E. F. troops. On your way! On your way!"

The arrangement was perfect except that the Wildcat's orders were not transportation on French passenger trains and that A. E. F. troops were not serving meals at all points along the lines of the S. O. S. south of Chemin Blanc.

The Wildcat completed the two-day journey in eight days and landed A. W. O. L. in the guardhouse at the base port from which his company had marched to their rest camp.

The provost marshal telephoned the commanding officer of the Wildcat's company.

"Nigger with some stale orders by the name of Vitus Marsden just picked up, captain. Will you come down to-morrow and get him?"

The captain cooled down enough to explain that the blankety-blank Wildcat wasn't due for anything less than a lynching, and that the provost marshal might as well keep him penned up until sentence had been imposed.

The sergeant of the guard locked the Wildcat in a special apartment reserved for bad military eggs.

"Sergeant, I'se hongry; when does I draw my rations?"

"You won't need no rations after the firin' squad gits through with you."

The Wildcat tried to figure out the nature of his offenses.

"Guess mebbe us oughta lef' ol' soa'd layin' 'gin' de wire. Nobody 'ceptin' gin'rals carrys soa'ds as fine as dat. . . . Wondeh when does the firin' squad shoot me? . . . Wisht I could see de lootenant. . . ."

That night, alone save for the cooties abandoned by a former occupant of the solitary, the Wildcat slept middlin' miserable.

The Captain made quick work of the Wildcat's case. The Manual of Courts-martial yielded several gratifying charges, amplified by a series of specifications which bade fair to imprison the Wildcat for a hundred years.

Except for a ride both ways in a truck and a chance to plead guilty to every-thing, the Wildcat gained nothing from the trial of his case. The Special Court dished out a copious measure of punishment in a brief sentence, and the documents went forward to the general commanding the base section.

There came a morning later in the week when upon the general's wide desk the charge sheets in the Wildcat's case awaited the signature of the base commander. Attached to the charge sheets were three letters. Beside these documents lay two small packages.

The General glanced through the charges and specifications. He read the sentence of the court and reached for his pen. The attached letters fixed his attention. He read the first letter and sat forward in his chair. He threw away his cigarette and jabbed at a push button.

"Take my car down to the provost marshal's place at once and return with a negro prisoner who is in confinement—Vitus Marsden, First Service Battalion."

The colonel saluted and departed on his mission.

The general opened one of the small packages that lay on his desk. He read the third letter attached to the charge sheets of the Special Court. "Well, I'm damned!" He opened the other package and removed its contents. "Doubly damned!" He again read each of the three letters, after which he jabbed at the push button. Another colonel entered the room.

"I want all of my staff officers in here at once; the officers attached, the French liaison officers, and any members of Headquarters Staff who may be in the building."

He reached for his telephone and talked for a few seconds to the French general commanding the district.

Presently the great room was filled with half a hundred colonels, lieutenant-colonels and majors. The French general and his staff entered the room, and for a moment the assemblage stood at rigid attention.

And then, itching promiscuously and looking pretty measly alongside of so much congested military rank, the Wildcat shuffled into the room.

The general raised his hand. The officers in the room snapped to attention.

"Sergeant Vitus Marsden," the general began, "in effecting the capture of thirty-seven of the enemy you have won the Distinguished Service Cross."

The General pinned the decoration on the Wildcat's blouse above the place where the Wildcat's heart was missing every fourth flop. The French general and his adjutant stepped forward.

"Sergeant Vitus Marsden, brave soldier of the American forces, in the name of the French Republic, by orders of the commanders of the Armies, for extraordinary heroism, receive the Croix de Guerre!"

The general took the decoration from its case and pinned it fast beside the Distinguished Service Cross.

The Wildcat sensed the reversal of his fate.

"Gin'ral, I is sho' glad to meet you." He glanced downward at the green cross upon his breast. "Looks a lot like a fo'-leafed cloveh."

That night in Company C the Wildcat was a nach'ral seven.

Scratching himself industriously he looked long at the sergeant's chevrons on his sleeve and at the colored ribbons with their pendant crosses.

"Dat's why I'm as happy as a bumble-bee-ee."

F. Scott Fitzgerald

(1896–1940)

Born in St. Paul, Minnesota, F. Scott Fitzgerald early formed an ambition to become a writer. He attended Princeton University before being commissioned in the army in which he rose to the rank of first lieutenant. In army camps he wrote drafts of the novel that was eventually published as *This Side of Paradise* (1920) and which made him almost instantly famous. The war ended before Fitzgerald could ship for France, and all of his life he regretted that he did not face combat. The Great War became a theme in much of his fiction, including in chapter 13 of *Tender Is the Night* (1934), in which protagonist Dick Diver tours a trench and longs for the war as a great but tragic event that he missed. "May Day" originally appeared in *The Smart Set* in July 1920 and was collected in *Tales of the Jazz Age* (1922).

May Day

F. Scott Fitzgerald

There had been a war fought and won and the great city of the conquering people was crossed with triumphal arches and vivid with thrown flowers of white, red, and rose. All through the long spring days the returning soldiers marched up the chief highway behind the strump of drums and the joyous, resonant wind of the brasses, while merchants and clerks left their bickerings and figurings and, crowding to the windows, turned their white-bunched faces gravely upon the passing battalions.

Never had there been such splendor in the great city, for the victorious war had brought plenty in its train, and the merchants had flocked thither from the South and West with their households to taste of all the luscious feasts and witness the lavish entertainments prepared—and to buy for their women furs against the next winter and bags of golden mesh and varicolored slippers of silk and silver and rose satin and cloth of gold.

So gaily and noisily were the peace and prosperity impending hymned by the scribes and poets of the conquering people that more and more spenders had gathered from the provinces to drink the wine of excitement, and faster and faster did the merchants dispose of their trinkets and slippers until they sent up a mighty cry for more trinkets and more slippers in order that they might give in barter what was demanded of them. Some even of them flung up their hands helplessly, shouting:

"Alas! I have no more slippers! and alas! I have no more trinkets! May heaven help me, for I know not what I shall do!"

But no one listened to their great outcry, for the throngs were far too busy—day by day, the foot-soldiers trod jauntily the highway and all exulted because the young men returning were pure and brave, sound of tooth and pink of cheek, and the young women of the land were virgins and comely both of face and of figure.

So during all this time there were many adventures that happened in the great city, and, of these, several—or perhaps one—are here set down.

I

At nine o'clock on the morning of the first of May, 1919, a young man spoke to the room clerk at the Biltmore Hotel, asking if Mr. Philip Dean were registered there, and if so, could he be connected with Mr. Dean's rooms. The inquirer was dressed in a well-cut, shabby suit. He was small, slender, and darkly handsome; his eyes were framed above with unusually long eyelashes and below with the blue semicircle of ill health, this latter effect heightened by an unnatural glow which colored his face like a low, incessant fever.

Mr. Dean was staying there. The young man was directed to a telephone at the side.

After a second his connection was made; a sleepy voice hello'd from somewhere above.

"Mr. Dean?"—this very eagerly—"it's Gordon, Phil. It's Gordon Sterrett. I'm down-stairs. I heard you were in New York and I had a hunch you'd be here."

The sleepy voice became gradually enthusiastic. Well, how was Gordy, old boy! Well, he certainly was surprised and tickled! Would Gordy come right up, for Pete's sake!

A few minutes later Philip Dean, dressed in blue silk pajamas, opened his door and the two young men greeted each other with a half-embarrassed exuberance. They were both about twenty-four, Yale graduates of the year before the war; but there the resemblance stopped abruptly. Dean was blond, ruddy, and rugged under his thin pajamas. Everything about him radiated fitness and bodily comfort. He smiled frequently, showing large and prominent teeth.

"I was going to look you up," he cried enthusiastically. "I'm taking a couple of weeks off. If you'll sit down a sec I'll be right with you. Going to take a shower."

As he vanished into the bathroom his visitor's dark eyes roved nervously around the room, resting for a moment on a great English travelling bag in the corner and on a family of thick silk shirts littered on the chairs amid impressive neckties and soft woolen socks.

Gordon rose and, picking up one of the shirts, gave it a minute examination. It was of very heavy silk, yellow, with a pale blue stripe—and there were nearly a dozen of them. He stared involuntarily at his own shirt-cuffs—they were ragged and linty at the edges and soiled to a faint gray. Dropping the silk shirt, he held his coat-sleeves down and worked the frayed shirt-cuffs up till they were out of sight. Then he went to the mirror and looked at himself with listless, unhappy interest. His tie, of former glory, was faded and thumb-creased—it served no longer to hide the jagged buttonholes of his collar. He thought, quite without amusement, that only three years before he had received a scattering vote in the senior elections at college for being the best-dressed man in his class.

Dean emerged from the bathroom polishing his body.

"Saw an old friend of yours last night," he remarked. "Passed her in the lobby and couldn't think of her name to save my neck. That girl you brought up to New Haven senior year."

Gordon started.

"Edith Bradin? That whom you mean?"

"'At's the one. Damn good looking. She's still sort of a pretty doll—you know what I mean: as if you touched her she'd smear."

He surveyed his shining self complacently in the mirror, smiled faintly, exposing a section of teeth.

"She must be twenty-three anyway," he continued.

"Twenty-two last month," said Gordon absently.

"What? Oh, last month. Well, I imagine she's down for the Gamma Psi dance. Did you know we're having a Yale Gamma Psi dance to-night at Delmonico's? You better come up, Gordy. Half of New Haven'll probably be there. I can get you an invitation."

Draping himself reluctantly in fresh underwear, Dean lit a cigarette and sat down by the open window, inspecting his calves and knees under the morning sunshine which poured into the room.

"Sit down, Gordy," he suggested, "and tell me all about what you've been doing and what you're doing now and everything."

Gordon collapsed unexpectedly upon the bed; lay there inert and spiritless. His mouth, which habitually dropped a little open when his face was in repose, became suddenly helpless and pathetic.

"What's the matter?" asked Dean quickly.

"Oh, God!"

"What's the matter?"

"Every God damn thing in the world," he said miserably. "I've absolutely gone to pieces, Phil. I'm all in."

"Huh?"

"I'm all in." His voice was shaking.

Dean scrutinized him more closely with appraising blue eyes.

"You certainly look all shot."

"I am. I've made a hell of a mess of everything." He paused. "I'd better start at the beginning—or will it bore you?"

"Not at all; go on." There was, however, a hesitant note in Dean's voice. This trip East had been planned for a holiday—to find Gordon Sterrett in trouble exasperated him a little.

"Go on," he repeated, and then added half under his breath, "Get it over with."

"Well," began Gordon unsteadily, "I got back from France in February, went home to Harrisburg for a month, and then came down to New York to get a job. I got one—with an export company. They fired me yesterday."

"Fired you?"

"I'm coming to that, Phil. I want to tell you frankly. You're about the only man I can turn to in a matter like this. You won't mind if I just tell you frankly, will you, Phil?"

Dean stiffened a bit more. The pats he was bestowing on his knees grew perfunctory. He felt vaguely that he was being unfairly saddled with responsibility; he was not even sure he wanted to be told. Though never surprised at finding Gordon Sterrett in mild difficulty, there was something in this present misery that repelled him and hardened him, even though it excited his curiosity.

"Go on."

"It's a girl."

"Hm." Dean resolved that nothing was going to spoil his trip. If Gordon was going to be depressing, then he'd have to see less of Gordon.

"Her name is Jewel Hudson," went on the distressed voice from the bed. "She used to be 'pure,' I guess, up to about a year ago. Lived here in New York—poor family. Her people are dead now and she lives with an old aunt. You see it was just about the time I met her that everybody began to come back from France in droves—and all I did was to welcome the newly arrived and go on parties with 'em.

That's the way it started, Phil, just from being glad to see everybody and having them glad to see me."

"You ought to've had more sense."

"I know," Gordon paused, and then continued listlessly. "I'm on my own now, you know, and Phil, I can't stand being poor. Then came this darn girl. She sort of fell in love with me for a while and, though I never intended to get so involved, I'd always seem to run into her somewhere. You can imagine the sort of work I was doing for those exporting people—of course, I always intended to draw; do illustrating for magazines; there's a pile of money in it."

"Why didn't you? You've got to buckle down if you want to make good," suggested Dean with cold formalism.

"I tried, a little, but my stuff's crude. I've got talent, Phil; I can draw—but I just don't know how. I ought to go to art school and I can't afford it. Well, things came to a crisis about a week ago. Just as I was down to about my last dollar this girl began bothering me. She wants some money; claims she can make trouble for me if she doesn't get it."

"Can she?"

"I'm afraid she can. That's one reason I lost my job—she kept calling up the office all the time, and that was sort of the last straw down there. She's got a letter all written to send to my family. Oh, she's got me, all right. I've got to have some money for her."

There was an awkward pause. Gordon lay very still, his hands clenched by his side.

"I'm all in," he continued, his voice trembling. "I'm half crazy, Phil. If I hadn't known you were coming East, I think I'd have killed myself. I want you to lend me three hundred dollars."

Dean's hands, which had been patting his bare ankles, were suddenly quiet—and the curious uncertainty playing between the two became taut and strained.

After a second Gordon continued:

"I've bled the family until I'm ashamed to ask for another nickel."

Still Dean made no answer.

"Jewel says she's got to have two hundred dollars."

"Tell her where she can go."

"Yes, that sounds easy, but she's got a couple of drunken letters I wrote her. Unfortunately she's not at all the flabby sort of person you'd expect."

Dean made an expression of distaste.

"I can't stand that sort of woman. You ought to have kept away."

"I know," admitted Gordon wearily.

"You've got to look at things as they are. If you haven't got money you've got to work and stay away from women."

"That's easy for you to say," began Gordon, his eyes narrowing. "You've got all the money in the world."

"I most certainly have not. My family keep darn close tab on what I spend. Just because I have a little leeway I have to be extra careful not to abuse it."

He raised the blind and let in a further flood of sunshine.

"I'm no prig, Lord knows," he went on deliberately. "I like pleasure—and I like a lot of it on a vacation like this, but you're—you're in awful shape. I never heard you talk just this way before. You seem to be sort of bankrupt—morally as well as financially."

"Don't they usually go together?"

Dean shook his head impatiently.

"There's a regular aura about you that I don't understand. It's a sort of evil."

"It's an air of worry and poverty and sleepless nights," said Gordon, rather defiantly. "I don't know."

"Oh, I admit I'm depressing. I depress myself. But, my God, Phil, a week's rest and a new suit and some ready money and I'd be like—like I was. Phil, I can draw like a streak, and you know it. But half the time I haven't had the money to buy decent drawing materials—and I can't draw when I'm tired and discouraged and all in. With a little ready money I can take a few weeks off and get started."

"How do I know you wouldn't use it on some other woman?"

"Why rub it in?" said Gordon, quietly.

"I'm not rubbing it in. I hate to see you this way."

"Will you lend me the money, Phil?"

"I can't decide right off. That's a lot of money and it'll be darn inconvenient for me."

"It'll be hell for me if you can't—I know I'm whining, and it's all my own fault but—that doesn't change it."

"When could you pay it back?"

This was encouraging. Gordon considered. It was probably wisest to be frank.

"Of course, I could promise to send it back next month, but—I'd better say three months. Just as soon as I start to sell drawings."

"How do I know you'll sell any drawings?"

A new hardness in Dean's voice sent a faint chill of doubt over Gordon. Was it possible that he wouldn't get the money?

"I supposed you had a little confidence in me."

"I did have—but when I see you like this I begin to wonder."

"Do you suppose if I wasn't at the end of my rope I'd come to you like this? Do you think I'm enjoying it?" He broke off and bit his lip, feeling that he had better subdue the rising anger in his voice. After all, he was the suppliant.

"You seem to manage it pretty easily," said Dean angrily. "You put me in the position where, if I don't lend it to you, I'm a sucker—oh, yes, you do. And let me tell you it's no easy thing for me to get hold of three hundred dollars. My income isn't so big but that a slice like that won't play the deuce with it."

He left his chair and began to dress, choosing his clothes carefully. Gordon stretched out his arms and clenched the edges of the bed, fighting back a desire to cry out. His head was splitting and whirring, his mouth was dry and bitter and he could feel the fever in his blood resolving itself into innumerable regular counts like a slow dripping from a roof.

Dean tied his tie precisely, brushed his eyebrows, and removed a piece of tobacco from his teeth with solemnity. Next he filled his cigarette case, tossed the empty box thoughtfully into the waste basket, and settled the case in his vest pocket.

"Had breakfast?" he demanded.

"No; I don't eat it any more."

"Well, we'll go out and have some. We'll decide about that money later. I'm sick of the subject. I came East to have a good time.

"Let's go over to the Yale Club," he continued moodily, and then added with an implied reproof: "You've given up your job. You've got nothing else to do."

"I'd have a lot to do if I had a little money," said Gordon pointedly.

"Oh, for Heaven's sake drop the subject for a while! No point in glooming on my whole trip. Here, here's some money."

He took a five-dollar bill from his wallet and tossed it over to Gordon, who folded it carefully and put it in his pocket. There was an added spot of color in his cheeks, an added glow that was not fever. For an instant before they turned to go out their eyes met and in that instant each found something that made him lower his own glance quickly. For in that instant they quite suddenly and definitely hated each other.

II

Fifth Avenue and Forty-fourth Street swarmed with the noon crowd. The wealthy, happy sun glittered in transient gold through the thick windows of the smart shops, lighting upon mesh bags and purses and strings of pearls in gray velvet cases; upon gaudy feather fans of many colors; upon the laces and silks of expensive dresses; upon the bad paintings and the fine period furniture in the elaborate show rooms of interior decorators.

Working-girls, in pairs and groups and swarms, loitered by these windows, choosing their future boudoirs from some resplendent display which included even a man's silk pajamas laid domestically across the bed. They stood in front of the jewelry stores and picked out their engagement rings, and their wedding rings and their platinum wrist watches, and then drifted on to inspect the feather fans and opera cloaks; meanwhile digesting the sandwiches and sundaes they had eaten for lunch.

All through the crowd were men in uniform, sailors from the great fleet anchored in the Hudson, soldiers with divisional insignia from Massachusetts to California, wanting fearfully to be noticed, and finding the great city thoroughly fed up with soldiers unless they were nicely massed into pretty formations and uncomfortable under the weight of a pack and rifle. Through this medley Dean and Gordon wandered; the former interested, made alert by the display of humanity at its frothiest and gaudiest; the latter reminded of how often he had been one of the crowd, tired, casually fed, overworked, and dissipated. To Dean the struggle was significant, young, cheerful; to Gordon it was dismal, meaningless, endless.

In the Yale Club they met a group of their former classmates who greeted the visiting Dean vociferously. Sitting in a semicircle of lounges and great chairs, they had a highball all around.

Gordon found the conversation tiresome and interminable. They lunched together en masse, warmed with liquor as the afternoon began. They were all going to the Gamma Psi dance that night—it promised to be the best party since the war.

"Edith Bradin's coming," said some one to Gordon. "Didn't she used to be an old flame of yours? Aren't you both from Harrisburg?"

"Yes." He tried to change the subject. "I see her brother occasionally. He's sort of a socialistic nut. Runs a paper or something here in New York."

"Not like his gay sister, eh?" continued his eager informant. "Well, she's coming to-night—with a junior named Peter Himmel."

Gordon was to meet Jewel Hudson at eight o'clock—he had promised to have some money for her. Several times he glanced nervously at his wrist watch. At four, to his relief, Dean rose and announced that he was going over to Rivers Brothers to buy some collars and ties. But as they left the Club another of the party joined them, to Gordon's great dismay. Dean was in a jovial mood now, happy, expectant of the evening's party, faintly hilarious. Over in Rivers' he chose a dozen neckties, selecting each one after long consultations with the other man. Did he think narrow ties were coming back? And wasn't it a shame that Rivers couldn't get any more Welsh Margotson collars? There never was a collar like the "Covington."

Gordon was in something of a panic. He wanted the money immediately. And he was now inspired also with a vague idea of attending the Gamma Psi dance. He wanted to see Edith—Edith whom he hadn't met since one romantic night at the Harrisburg Country Club just before he went to France. The affair had died, drowned in the turmoil of the war and quite forgotten in the arabesque of these three months, but a picture of her, poignant, debonnaire, immersed in her own inconsequential chatter, recurred to him unexpectedly and brought a hundred memories with it. It was Edith's face that he had cherished through college with a sort of detached yet affectionate admiration. He had loved to draw her—around his room had been a dozen sketches of her—playing golf, swimming—he could draw her pert, arresting profile with his eyes shut.

They left Rivers' at five-thirty and paused for a moment on the sidewalk.

"Well," said Dean genially, "I'm all set now. Think I'll go back to the hotel and get a shave, haircut, and massage."

"Good enough," said the other man, "I think I'll join you."

Gordon wondered if he was to be beaten after all. With difficulty he restrained himself from turning to the man and snarling out, "Go on away, damn you!" In despair he suspected that perhaps Dean had spoken to him, was keeping him along in order to avoid a dispute about the money.

They went into the Biltmore—a Biltmore alive with girls—mostly from the West and South, the stellar débutantes of many cities gathered for the dance of a famous fraternity of a famous university. But to Gordon they were faces in a dream. He gathered together his forces for a last appeal, was about to come out with he knew not what, when Dean suddenly excused himself to the other man and taking Gordon's arm led him aside.

"Gordy," he said quickly, "I've thought the whole thing over carefully and I've decided that I can't lend you that money. I'd like to oblige you, but I don't feel I ought to—it'd put a crimp in me for a month."

Gordon, watching him dully, wondered why he had never before noticed how much those upper teeth projected.

"—I'm mighty sorry, Gordon," continued Dean, "but that's the way it is."

He took out his wallet and deliberately counted out seventy-five dollars in bills.

"Here," he said, holding them out, "here's seventy-five; that makes eighty all together. That's all the actual cash I have with me, besides what I'll actually spend on the trip."

Gordon raised his clenched hand automatically, opened it as though it were a tongs he was holding, and clenched it again on the money.

"I'll see you at the dance," continued Dean. "I've got to get along to the barber shop."

"So-long," said Gordon in a strained and husky voice.

"So-long."

Dean began to smile, but seemed to change his mind. He nodded briskly and disappeared.

But Gordon stood there, his handsome face awry with distress, the roll of bills clenched tightly in his hand. Then, blinded by sudden tears, he stumbled clumsily down the Biltmore steps.

III

About nine o'clock of the same night two human beings came out of a cheap restaurant in Sixth Avenue. They were ugly, ill-nourished, devoid of all except the very
lowest form of intelligence, and without even that animal exuberance that in itself
brings color into life; they were lately vermin-ridden, cold, and hungry in a dirty
town of a strange land; they were poor, friendless; tossed as driftwood from their
births, they would be tossed as driftwood to their deaths. They were dressed in the
uniform of the United States Army, and on the shoulder of each was the insignia
of a drafted division from New Jersey, landed three days before.

The taller of the two was named Carrol Key, a name hinting that in his veins,
however thinly diluted by generations of degeneration, ran blood of some potenti-
ality. But one could stare endlessly at the long, chinless face, the dull, watery eyes,
and high cheek-bones, without finding a suggestion of either ancestral worth or
native resourcefulness.

His companion was swart and bandy-legged, with rat-eyes and a much-broken
hooked nose. His defiant air was obviously a pretense, a weapon of protection borrowed from that world of snarl and snap, of physical bluff and physical menace,
in which he had always lived. His name was Gus Rose.

Leaving the café they sauntered down Sixth Avenue, wielding toothpicks with
great gusto and complete detachment.

"Where to?" asked Rose, in a tone which implied that he would not be surprised
if Key suggested the South Sea Islands.

"What you say we see if we can getta holda some liquor?" Prohibition was not
yet. The ginger in the suggestion was caused by the law forbidding the selling of
liquor to soldiers.

Rose agreed enthusiastically.

"I got an idea," continued Key, after a moment's thought, "I got a brother somewhere."

"In New York?"

"Yeah. He's an old fella." He meant that he was an elder brother. "He's a waiter
in a hash joint."

"Maybe he can get us some."

"I'll say he can!"

"B'lieve me, I'm goin' to get this darn uniform off me to-morra. Never get me in
it again, neither. I'm goin' to get me some regular clothes."

"Say, maybe I'm not."

As their combined finances were something less than five dollars, this intention can be taken largely as a pleasant game of words, harmless and consoling.

It seemed to please both of them, however, for they reinforced it with chuckling and mention of personages high in biblical circles, adding such further emphasis as "Oh, boy!" "You know!" and "I'll say so!" repeated many times over.

The entire mental pabulum of these two men consisted of an offended nasal comment extended through the years upon the institution—army, business, or poorhouse—which kept them alive, and toward their immediate superior in that institution. Until that very morning the institution had been the "government" and the immediate superior had been the "Cap'n"—from these two they had glided out and were now in the vaguely uncomfortable state before they should adopt their next bondage. They were uncertain, resentful, and somewhat ill at ease. This they hid by pretending an elaborate relief at being out of the army, and by assuring each other that military discipline should never again rule their stubborn, liberty-loving wills. Yet, as a matter of fact, they would have felt more at home in a prison than in this new-found and unquestionable freedom.

Suddenly Key increased his gait. Rose, looking up and following his glance, discovered a crowd that was collecting fifty yards down the street. Key chuckled and began to run in the direction of the crowd; Rose thereupon also chuckled and his short bandy legs twinkled beside the long, awkward strides of his companion.

Reaching the outskirts of the crowd they immediately became an indistinguishable part of it. It was composed of ragged civilians somewhat the worse for liquor, and of soldiers representing many divisions and many stages of sobriety, all clustered around a gesticulating little Jew with long black whiskers, who was waving his arms and delivering an excited but succinct harangue. Key and Rose, having wedged themselves into the approximate parquet, scrutinized him with acute suspicion, as his words penetrated their common consciousness.

"—What have you got outa the war?" he was crying fiercely. "Look arounja, look arounja! Are you rich? Have you got a lot of money offered you?—no; you're lucky if you're alive and got both your legs; you're lucky if you came back an' find your wife ain't gone off with some other fella that had the money to buy himself out of the war! That's when you're lucky! Who got anything out of it except J. P. Morgan an' John D. Rockerfeller?"

At this point the little Jew's oration was interrupted by the hostile impact of a fist upon the point of his bearded chin and he toppled backward to a sprawl on the pavement.

"God damn Bolsheviki!" cried the big soldier-blacksmith who had delivered the blow. There was a rumble of approval, the crowd closed in nearer.

The Jew staggered to his feet, and immediately went down again before a half-dozen reaching-in fists. This time he stayed down, breathing heavily, blood oozing from his lip where it was cut within and without.

There was a riot of voices, and in a minute Rose and Key found themselves flowing with the jumbled crowd down Sixth Avenue under the leadership of a thin civilian in a slouch hat and the brawny soldier who had summarily ended the oration. The crowd had marvelously swollen to formidable proportions and a stream of more non-committal citizens followed it along the sidewalks lending their moral support by intermittent huzzas.

"Where we goin'?" yelled Key to the man nearest him.

His neighbor pointed up to the leader in the slouch hat.

"That guy knows where there's a lot of 'em! We're goin' to show 'em!"

"We're goin' to show 'em!" whispered Key delightedly to Rose, who repeated the phrase rapturously to a man on the other side.

Down Sixth Avenue swept the procession, joined here and there by soldiers and marines, and now and then by civilians, who came up with the inevitable cry that they were just out of the army themselves, as if presenting it as a card of admission to a newly formed Sporting and Amusement Club.

Then the procession swerved down a cross street and headed for Fifth Avenue and the word filtered here and there that they were bound for a Red meeting at Tolliver Hall.

"Where is it?"

The question went up the line and a moment later the answer floated back. Tolliver Hall was down on Tenth Street. There was a bunch of other sojers who was goin' to break it up and was down there now!

But Tenth Street had a faraway sound and at the word a general groan went up and a score of the procession dropped out. Among these were Rose and Key, who slowed down to a saunter and let the more enthusiastic sweep on by.

"I'd rather get some liquor," said Key as they halted and made their way to the sidewalk amid cries of "Shell hole!" and "Quitters!"

"Does your brother work around here?" asked Rose, assuming the air of one passing from the superficial to the eternal.

"He oughta," replied Key. "I ain't seen him for a coupla years. I been out to Pennsylvania since. Maybe he don't work at night anyhow. It's right along here. He can get us some o'right if he ain't gone."

They found the place after a few minutes' patrol of the street—a shoddy tablecloth restaurant between Fifth Avenue and Broadway. Here Key went inside to inquire for his brother George, while Rose waited on the sidewalk.

"He ain't here no more," said Key emerging. "He's a waiter up to Delmonico's."

Rose nodded wisely, as if he'd expected as much. One should not be surprised at a capable man changing jobs occasionally. He knew a waiter once—there ensued a long conversation as they walked as to whether waiters made more in actual wages than in tips—it was decided that it depended on the social tone of the joint wherein the waiter labored. After having given each other vivid pictures of millionaires dining at Delmonico's and throwing away fifty-dollar bills after their first quart of champagne, both men thought privately of becoming waiters. In fact, Key's narrow brow was secreting a resolution to ask his brother to get him a job.

"A waiter can drink up all the champagne those fellas leave in bottles," suggested Rose with some relish, and then added as an afterthought, "Oh, boy!"

By the time they reached Delmonico's it was half past ten, and they were surprised to see a stream of taxis driving up to the door one after the other and emitting marvelous, hatless young ladies, each one attended by a stiff young gentleman in evening clothes.

"It's a party," said Rose with some awe. "Maybe we better not go in. He'll be busy."

"No, he won't. He'll be o'right."

After some hesitation they entered what appeared to them to be the least elaborate door and, indecision falling upon them immediately, stationed themselves nervously in an inconspicuous corner of the small dining-room in which they found themselves. They took off their caps and held them in their hands. A cloud of gloom fell upon them and both started when a door at one end of the room crashed open, emitting a comet-like waiter who streaked across the floor and vanished through another door on the other side.

There had been three of these lightning passages before the seekers mustered the acumen to hail a waiter. He turned, looked at them suspiciously, and then approached with soft, catlike steps, as if prepared at any moment to turn and flee.

"Say," began Key, "say, do you know my brother? He's a waiter here."

"His name is Key," annotated Rose.

Yes, the waiter knew Key. He was up-stairs, he thought. There was a big dance going on in the main ballroom. He'd tell him.

Ten minutes later George Key appeared and greeted his brother with the utmost suspicion; his first and most natural thought being that he was going to be asked for money.

George was tall and weak chinned, but there his resemblance to his brother ceased. The waiter's eyes were not dull, they were alert and twinkling, and his manner was suave, indoor, and faintly superior. They exchanged formalities. George was married and had three children. He seemed fairly interested, but not impressed by the news that Carrol had been abroad in the army. This disappointed Carrol.

"George," said the younger brother, these amenities having been disposed of, "we want to get some booze, and they won't sell us none. Can you get us some?"

George considered.

"Sure. Maybe I can. It may be half an hour, though."

"All right," agreed Carrol, "we'll wait."

At this Rose started to sit down in a convenient chair, but was hailed to his feet by the indignant George.

"Hey! Watch out, you! Can't sit down here! This room's all set for a twelve o'clock banquet."

"I ain't goin' to hurt it," said Rose resentfully. "I been through the delouser."

"Never mind," said George sternly, "if the head waiter seen me here talkin' he'd romp all over me."

"Oh."

The mention of the head waiter was full explanation to the other two; they fingered their overseas caps nervously and waited for a suggestion.

"I tell you," said George, after a pause, "I got a place you can wait; you just come here with me."

They followed him out the far door, through a deserted pantry and up a pair of dark winding stairs, emerging finally into a small room chiefly furnished by piles of pails and stacks of scrubbing brushes, and illuminated by a single dim electric light. There he left them, after soliciting two dollars and agreeing to return in half an hour with a quart of whiskey.

"George is makin' money, I bet," said Key gloomily as he seated himself on an inverted pail. "I bet he's making fifty dollars a week."

Rose nodded his head and spat.

"I bet he is, too."

"What'd he say the dance was of?"

"A lot of college fellas. Yale College."

They both nodded solemnly at each other.

"Wonder where that crowda sojers is now?"

"I don't know. I know that's too damn long to walk for me."

"Me too. You don't catch me walkin' that far."

Ten minutes later restlessness seized them.

"I'm goin' to see what's out here," said Rose, stepping cautiously toward the other door.

It was a swinging door of green baize and he pushed it open a cautious inch.

"See anything?"

For answer Rose drew in his breath sharply.

"Doggone! Here's some liquor I'll say!"

"Liquor?"

Key joined Rose at the door, and looked eagerly.

"I'll tell the world that's liquor," he said, after a moment of concentrated gazing.

It was a room about twice as large as the one they were in—and in it was prepared a radiant feast of spirits. There were long walls of alternating bottles set along two white covered tables; whiskey, gin, brandy, French and Italian vermouths, and orange juice, not to mention an array of syphons and two great empty punch bowls. The room was as yet uninhabited.

"It's for this dance they're just starting," whispered Key; "hear the violins playin'? Say, boy, I wouldn't mind havin' a dance."

They closed the door softly and exchanged a glance of mutual comprehension. There was no need of feeling each other out.

"I'd like to get my hands on a coupla those bottles," said Rose emphatically.

"Me too."

"Do you suppose we'd get seen?"

Key considered.

"Maybe we better wait till they start drinkin' 'em. They got 'em all laid out now, and they know how many of them there are."

They debated this point for several minutes. Rose was all for getting his hands on a bottle now and tucking it under his coat before any one came into the room. Key, however, advocated caution. He was afraid he might get his brother in trouble. If they waited till some of the bottles were opened it'd be all right to take one, and everybody'd think it was one of the college fellas.

While they were still engaged in argument George Key hurried through the room and, barely grunting at them, disappeared by way of the green baize door. A minute later they heard several corks pop, and then the sound of cracking ice and splashing liquid. George was mixing the punch.

The soldiers exchanged delighted grins.

"Oh, boy!" whispered Rose.

George reappeared.

"Just keep low, boys," he said quickly. "I'll have your stuff for you in five minutes."

He disappeared through the door by which he had come.

As soon as his footsteps receded down the stairs, Rose, after a cautious look, darted into the room of delights and reappeared with a bottle in his hand.

"Here's what I say," he said, as they sat radiantly digesting their first drink. "We'll wait till he comes up, and we'll ask him if we can't just stay here and drink what he brings us—see. We'll tell him we haven't got any place to drink it—see. Then we can sneak in there whenever there ain't nobody in that there room and tuck a bottle under our coats. We'll have enough to last us a coupla days—see?"

"Sure," agreed Key enthusiastically. "Oh, boy! And if we want to we can sell it to sojers any time we want to."

They were silent for a moment thinking rosily of this idea. Then Key reached up and unhooked the collar of his O. D. coat.

"It's hot in here, ain't it?"

Rose agreed earnestly.

"Hot as hell."

IV

She was still quite angry when she came out of the dressing-room and crossed the intervening parlor of politeness that opened onto the hall—angry not so much at the actual happening which was, after all, the merest commonplace of her social existence, but because it had occurred on this particular night. She had no quarrel with herself. She had acted with the correct mixture of dignity and reticent pity which she always employed. She had succinctly and deftly snubbed him.

It had happened when their taxi was leaving the Biltmore—hadn't gone half a block. He had lifted his right arm awkwardly—she was on his right side—and attempted to settle it snugly around the crimson fur-trimmed opera cloak she wore. This in itself had been a mistake. It was inevitably more graceful for a young man attempting to embrace a young lady of whose acquiescence he was not certain, to first put his far arm around her. It avoided that awkward movement of raising the near arm.

His second *faux pas* was unconscious. She had spent the afternoon at the hairdresser's; the idea of any calamity overtaking her hair was extremely repugnant—yet as Peter made his unfortunate attempt the point of his elbow had just faintly brushed it. That was his second *faux pas*. Two were quite enough.

He had begun to murmur. At the first murmur she had decided that he was nothing but a college boy—Edith was twenty-two, and anyhow, this dance, first of its kind since the war, was reminding her, with the accelerating rhythm of its associations, of something else—of another dance and another man, a man for whom her feelings had been little more than a sad-eyed, adolescent mooniness. Edith Bradin was falling in love with her recollection of Gordon Sterrett.

So she came out of the dressing-room at Delmonico's and stood for a second in the doorway looking over the shoulders of a black dress in front of her at the groups of Yale men who flitted like dignified black moths around the head of the stairs. From the room she had left drifted out the heavy fragrance left by the passage to and fro of many scented young beauties—rich perfumes and the fragile memory-laden dust of fragrant powders. This odor drifting out acquired the tang of cigarette smoke in the hall, and then settled sensuously down the stairs and permeated the ballroom where the Gamma Psi dance was to be held. It was an odor she knew well, exciting, stimulating, restlessly sweet—the odor of a fashionable dance.

She thought of her own appearance. Her bare arms and shoulders were powdered to a creamy white. She knew they looked very soft and would gleam like milk against the black backs that were to silhouette them to-night. The hairdressing had been a success; her reddish mass of hair was piled and crushed and creased to an arrogant marvel of mobile curves. Her lips were finely made of deep carmine; the irises of her eyes were delicate, breakable blue, like china eyes. She was a complete, infinitely delicate, quite perfect thing of beauty, flowing in an even line from a complex coiffure to two small slim feet.

She thought of what she would say to-night at this revel, faintly prestiged already by the sounds of high and low laughter and slippered footsteps, and movements of couples up and down the stairs. She would talk the language she had talked for many years—her line—made up of the current expressions, bits of journalese and college slang strung together into an intrinsic whole, careless, faintly provocative, delicately sentimental. She smiled faintly as she heard a girl sitting on the stairs near her say: "You don't know the half of it, dearie!"

And as she smiled her anger melted for a moment, and closing her eyes she drew in a deep breath of pleasure. She dropped her arms to her side until they were faintly touching the sleek sheath that covered and suggested her figure. She had never felt her own softness so much nor so enjoyed the whiteness of her own arms.

"I smell sweet," she said to herself simply, and then came another thought—"I'm made for love."

She liked the sound of this and thought it again; then in inevitable succession came her new-born riot of dreams about Gordon. The twist of her imagination which, two months before, had disclosed to her her unguessed desire to see him again, seemed now to have been leading up to this dance, this hour.

For all her sleek beauty, Edith was a grave, slow-thinking girl. There was a streak in her of that same desire to ponder, of that adolescent idealism that had turned her brother socialist and pacifist. Henry Bradin had left Cornell, where he had been an instructor in economics, and had come to New York to pour the latest cures for incurable evils into the columns of a radical weekly newspaper.

Edith, less fatuously, would have been content to cure Gordon Sterrett. There was a quality of weakness in Gordon that she wanted to take care of; there was a helplessness in him that she wanted to protect. And she wanted someone she had known a long while, someone who had loved her a long while. She was a little tired; she wanted to get married. Out of a pile of letters, half a dozen pictures and as many memories, and this weariness, she had decided that next time she saw Gordon their relations were going to be changed. She would say something that would change them. There was this evening. This was her evening. All evenings were her evenings.

Then her thoughts were interrupted by a solemn undergraduate with a hurt look and an air of strained formality who presented himself before her and bowed unusually low. It was the man she had come with, Peter Himmel. He was tall and humorous, with horned-rimmed glasses and an air of attractive whimsicality. She suddenly rather disliked him—probably because he had not succeeded in kissing her.

"Well," she began, "are you still furious at me?"

"Not at all."

She stepped forward and took his arm.

"I'm sorry," she said softly. "I don't know why I snapped out that way. I'm in a bum humor to-night for some strange reason. I'm sorry."

"S'all right," he mumbled, "don't mention it."

He felt disagreeably embarrassed. Was she rubbing in the fact of his late failure?

"It was a mistake," she continued, on the same consciously gentle key. "We'll both forget it." For this he hated her.

A few minutes later they drifted out on the floor while the dozen swaying, sighing members of the specially hired jazz orchestra informed the crowded ballroom that "if a saxophone and me are left alone why then two is com-pan-ee!"

A man with a mustache cut in.

"Hello," he began reprovingly. "You don't remember me."

"I can't just think of your name," she said lightly—"and I know you so well."

"I met you up at—" His voice trailed disconsolately off as a man with very fair hair cut in. Edith murmured a conventional "Thanks, loads—cut in later," to the *inconnu*.

The very fair man insisted on shaking hands enthusiastically. She placed him as one of the numerous Jims of her acquaintance—last name a mystery. She remembered even that he had a peculiar rhythm in dancing and found as they started that she was right.

"Going to be here long?" he breathed confidentially.

She leaned back and looked up at him.

"Couple of weeks."

"Where are you?"

"Biltmore. Call me up some day."

"I mean it," he assured her. "I will. We'll go to tea."

"So do I—Do."

A dark man cut in with intense formality.

"You don't remember me, do you?" he said gravely.

"I should say I do. Your name's Harlan."

"No-ope. Barlow."

"Well, I knew there were two syllables anyway. You're the boy that played the ukulele so well up at Howard Marshall's house party."

"I played—but not—"

A man with prominent teeth cut in. Edith inhaled a slight cloud of whiskey. She liked men to have had something to drink; they were so much more cheerful, and appreciative and complimentary—much easier to talk to.

"My name's Dean, Philip Dean," he said cheerfully. "You don't remember me, I know, but you used to come up to New Haven with a fellow I roomed with senior year, Gordon Sterrett."

Edith looked up quickly.

"Yes, I went up with him twice—to the Pump and Slipper and the Junior prom."

"You've seen him, of course," said Dean carelessly. "He's here to-night. I saw him just a minute ago."

Edith started. Yet she had felt quite sure he would be here.

"Why, no, I haven't——"

A fat man with red hair cut in.

"Hello, Edith," he began.

"Why—hello there——"

She slipped, stumbled lightly.

"I'm sorry, dear," she murmured mechanically.

She had seen Gordon—Gordon very white and listless, leaning against the side of a doorway, smoking and looking into the ballroom. Edith could see that his face was thin and wan—that the hand he raised to his lips with a cigarette was trembling. They were dancing quite close to him now.

"—They invite so darn many extra fellas that you—" the short man was saying.

"Hello, Gordon," called Edith over her partner's shoulder. Her heart was pounding wildly.

His large dark eyes were fixed on her. He took a step in her direction. Her partner turned her away—she heard his voice bleating——

"—but half the stags get lit and leave before long, so——"

Then a low tone at her side.

"May I, please?"

She was dancing suddenly with Gordon; one of his arms was around her; she felt it tighten spasmodically; felt his hand on her back with the fingers spread. Her hand holding the little lace handkerchief was crushed in his.

"Why Gordon," she began breathlessly.

"Hello, Edith."

She slipped again—was tossed forward by her recovery until her face touched the black cloth of his dinner coat. She loved him—she knew she loved him—then for a minute there was silence while a strange feeling of uneasiness crept over her. Something was wrong.

Of a sudden her heart wrenched, and turned over as she realized what it was. He was pitiful and wretched, a little drunk, and miserably tired.

"Oh——" she cried involuntarily.

His eyes looked down at her. She saw suddenly that they were blood-streaked and rolling uncontrollably.

"Gordon," she murmured, "we'll sit down; I want to sit down."

They were nearly in mid-floor, but she had seen two men start toward her from opposite sides of the room, so she halted, seized Gordon's limp hand and led him bumping through the crowd, her mouth tight shut, her face a little pale under her rouge, her eyes trembling with tears.

She found a place high up on the soft-carpeted stairs, and he sat down heavily beside her.

"Well," he began, staring at her unsteadily, "I certainly am glad to see you, Edith."

She looked at him without answering. The effect of this on her was immeasurable. For years she had seen men in various stages of intoxication, from uncles all the way down to chauffeurs, and her feelings had varied from amusement to disgust, but here for the first time she was seized with a new feeling—an unutterable horror.

"Gordon," she said accusingly and almost crying, "you look like the devil."

He nodded, "I've had trouble, Edith."

"Trouble?"

"All sorts of trouble. Don't you say anything to the family, but I'm all gone to pieces. I'm a mess, Edith."

His lower lip was sagging. He seemed scarcely to see her.

"Can't you—can't you," she hesitated, "can't you tell me about it, Gordon? You know I'm always interested in you."

She bit her lip—she had intended to say something stronger, but found at the end that she couldn't bring it out.

Gordon shook his head dully. "I can't tell you. You're a good woman. I can't tell a good woman the story."

"Rot," she said, defiantly. "I think it's a perfect insult to call any one a good woman in that way. It's a slam. You've been drinking, Gordon."

"Thanks." He inclined his head gravely. "Thanks for the information."

"Why do you drink?"

"Because I'm so damn miserable."

"Do you think drinking's going to make it any better?"

"What you doing—trying to reform me?"

"No; I'm trying to help you, Gordon. Can't you tell me about it?"

"I'm in an awful mess. Best thing you can do is to pretend not to know me."

"Why, Gordon?"

"I'm sorry I cut in on you—it's unfair to you. You're pure woman—and all that sort of thing. Here, I'll get some one else to dance with you."

He rose clumsily to his feet, but she reached up and pulled him down beside her on the stairs.

"Here, Gordon. You're ridiculous. You're hurting me. You're acting like a— like a crazy man——"

"I admit it. I'm a little crazy. Something's wrong with me, Edith. There's something left me. It doesn't matter."

"It does, tell me."

"Just that. I was always queer—little bit different from other boys. All right in college, but now it's all wrong. Things have been snapping inside me for four months like little hooks on a dress, and it's about to come off when a few more hooks go. I'm very gradually going loony."

He turned his eyes full on her and began to laugh, and she shrank away from him.

"What *is* the matter?"

"Just me," he repeated. "I'm going loony. This whole place is like a dream to me—this Delmonico's——"

As he talked she saw he had changed utterly. He wasn't at all light and gay and careless—a great lethargy and discouragement had come over him. Revulsion seized her, followed by a faint, surprising boredom. His voice seemed to come out of a great void.

"Edith," he said, "I used to think I was clever, talented, an artist. Now I know I'm nothing. Can't draw, Edith. Don't know why I'm telling you this."

She nodded absently.

"I can't draw, I can't do anything. I'm poor as a church mouse." He laughed, bitterly and rather too loud. "I've become a damn beggar, a leech on my friends. I'm a failure. I'm poor as hell."

Her distaste was growing. She barely nodded this time, waiting for her first possible cue to rise.

Suddenly Gordon's eyes filled with tears.

"Edith," he said, turning to her with what was evidently a strong effort at self-control, "I can't tell you what it means to me to know there's one person left who's interested in me."

He reached out and patted her hand, and involuntarily she drew it away.

"It's mighty fine of you," he repeated.

"Well," she said slowly, looking him in the eye, "any one's always glad to see an old friend—but I'm sorry to see you like this, Gordon."

There was a pause while they looked at each other, and the momentary eagerness in his eyes wavered. She rose and stood looking at him, her face quite expressionless.

"Shall we dance?" she suggested, coolly.

—Love is fragile—she was thinking—but perhaps the pieces are saved, the things that hovered on lips, that might have been said. The new love words, the tendernesses learned, are treasured up for the next lover.

V

Peter Himmel, escort to the lovely Edith, was unaccustomed to being snubbed; having been snubbed, he was hurt and embarrassed, and ashamed of himself. For a matter of two months he had been on special delivery terms with Edith Bradin, and knowing that the one excuse and explanation of the special delivery letter is its value in sentimental correspondence, he had believed himself quite sure of his ground. He searched in vain for any reason why she should have taken this attitude in the matter of a simple kiss.

Therefore when he was cut in on by the man with the mustache he went out into the hall and, making up a sentence, said it over to himself several times. Considerably deleted, this was it:

"Well, if any girl ever led a man on and then jolted him, she did—and she has no kick coming if I go out and get beautifully boiled."

So he walked through the supper room into a small room adjoining it, which he had located earlier in the evening. It was a room in which there were several large bowls of punch flanked by many bottles. He took a seat beside the table which held the bottles.

At the second highball, boredom, disgust, the monotony of time, the turbidity of events, sank into a vague background before which glittering cobwebs formed. Things became reconciled to themselves, things lay quietly on their shelves; the troubles of the day arranged themselves in trim formation and at his curt wish of dismissal, marched off and disappeared. And with the departure of worry came brilliant, permeating symbolism. Edith became a flighty, negligible girl, not to be worried over; rather to be laughed at. She fitted like a figure of his own dream into the surface world forming about him. He himself became in a measure symbolic, a type of the continent bacchanal, the brilliant dreamer at play.

Then the symbolic mood faded and as he sipped his third highball his imagination yielded to the warm glow and he lapsed into a state similar to floating on his back in pleasant water. It was at this point that he noticed that a green baize door near him was open about two inches, and that through the aperture a pair of eyes were watching him intently.

"Hm," murmured Peter calmly.

The green door closed—and then opened again—a bare half inch this time.

"Peek-a-boo," murmured Peter.

The door remained stationary and then he became aware of a series of tense intermittent whispers.

"One guy."

"What's he doin'?"

"He's sittin' lookin'."

"He better beat it off. We gotta get another li'l' bottle."

Peter listened while the words filtered into his consciousness.

"Now this," he thought, "is most remarkable."

He was excited. He was jubilant. He felt that he had stumbled upon a mystery. Affecting an elaborate carelessness he arose and waited around the table—then, turning quickly, pulled open the green door, precipitating Private Rose into the room.

Peter bowed.

"How do you do?" he said.

Private Rose set one foot slightly in front of the other, poised for fight, flight, or compromise.

"How do you do?" repeated Peter politely.

"I'm o'right."

"Can I offer you a drink?"

Private Rose looked at him searchingly, suspecting possible sarcasm.

"O'right," he said finally.

Peter indicated a chair.

"Sit down."

"I got a friend," said Rose, "I got a friend in there." He pointed to the green door.

"By all means let's have him in."

Peter crossed over, opened the door and welcomed in Private Key, very suspicious and uncertain and guilty. Chairs were found and the three took their seats around the punch bowl. Peter gave them each a highball and offered them a cigarette from his case. They accepted both with some diffidence.

"Now," continued Peter easily, "may I ask why you gentlemen prefer to lounge away your leisure hours in a room which is chiefly furnished, as far as I can see, with scrubbing brushes. And when the human race has progressed to the stage where seventeen thousand chairs are manufactured on every day except Sunday—"

he paused. Rose and Key regarded him vacantly. "Will you tell me," went on Peter, "why you choose to rest yourselves on articles intended for the transportation of water from one place to another?"

At this point Rose contributed a grunt to the conversation.

"And lastly," finished Peter, "will you tell me why, when you are in a building beautifully hung with enormous candelabra, you prefer to spend these evening hours under one anemic electric light?"

Rose looked at Key; Key looked at Rose. They laughed; they laughed uproariously; they found it was impossible to look at each other without laughing. But they were not laughing with this man—they were laughing at him. To them a man who talked after this fashion was either raving drunk or raving crazy.

"You are Yale men, I presume," said Peter, finishing his highball and preparing another.

They laughed again.

"Na-ah."

"So? I thought perhaps you might be members of that lowly section of the university known as the Sheffield Scientific School."

"Na-ah."

"Hm. Well, that's too bad. No doubt you are Harvard men, anxious to preserve your incognito in this—this paradise of violet blue, as the newspapers say."

"Na-ah," said Key scornfully, "we was just waitin' for somebody."

"Ah," exclaimed Peter, rising and filling their glasses, "very interestin'. Had a date with a scrublady, eh?"

They both denied this indignantly.

"It's all right," Peter reassured them, "don't apologize. A scrublady's as good as any lady in the world. Kipling says 'Any lady and Judy O'Grady under the skin.'"

"Sure," said Key, winking broadly at Rose.

"My case, for instance," continued Peter, finishing his glass. "I got a girl up here that's spoiled. Spoildest darn girl I ever saw. Refused to kiss me; no reason whatsoever. Led me on deliberately to think sure I want to kiss you and then plunk! Threw me over! What's the younger generation comin' to?"

"Say tha's hard luck," said Key—"that's awful hard luck."

"Oh, boy!" said Rose.

"Have another?" said Peter.

"We got in a sort of fight for a while," said Key after a pause, "but it was too far away."

"A fight?—tha's stuff!" said Peter, seating himself unsteadily. "Fight 'em all! I was in the army."

"This was with a Bolshevik fella."

"Tha's stuff!" exclaimed Peter, enthusiastic. "That's what I say! Kill the Bolshevik! Exterminate 'em!"

"We're Americuns," said Rose, implying a sturdy, defiant patriotism.

"Sure," said Peter. "Greatest race in the world! We're all Americans! Have another."

They had another.

VI

At one o'clock a special orchestra, special even in a day of special orchestras, arrived at Delmonico's, and its members, seating themselves arrogantly around the piano, took up the burden of providing music for the Gamma Psi Fraternity. They were headed by a famous flute-player, distinguished throughout New York for his feat of standing on his head and shimmying with his shoulders while he played the latest jazz on his flute. During his performance the lights were extinguished except for the spotlight on the flute-player and another roving beam that threw flickering shadows and changing kaleidoscopic colors over the massed dancers.

Edith had danced herself into that tired, dreamy state habitual only with débutantes, a state equivalent to the glow of a noble soul after several long highballs. Her mind floated vaguely on the bosom of her music; her partners changed with the unreality of phantoms under the colorful shifting dusk, and to her present coma it seemed as if days had passed since the dance began. She had talked on many fragmentary subjects with many men. She had been kissed once and made love to six times. Earlier in the evening different undergraduates had danced with her, but now, like all the more popular girls there, she had her own entourage—that is, half a dozen gallants had singled her out or were alternating her charms with those of some other chosen beauty; they cut in on her in regular, inevitable succession.

Several times she had seen Gordon—he had been sitting a long time on the stairway with his palm to his head, his dull eyes fixed at an infinite speck on the floor before him, very depressed, he looked, and quite drunk—but Edith each time had averted her glance hurriedly. All that seemed long ago; her mind was passive now, her senses were lulled to trance-like sleep; only her feet danced and her voice talked on in hazy sentimental banter.

But Edith was not nearly so tired as to be incapable of moral indignation when Peter Himmel cut in on her, sublimely and happily drunk. She gasped and looked up at him.

"Why, *Peter!*"

"I'm a li'l' stewed, Edith."

"Why, Peter, you're a *peach*, you are! Don't you think it's a bum way of doing—when you're with me?"

Then she smiled unwillingly, for he was looking at her with owlish sentimentality varied with a silly spasmodic smile.

"Darlin' Edith," he began earnestly, "you know I love you, don't you?"

"You tell it well."

"I love you—and I merely wanted you to kiss me," he added sadly.

His embarrassment, his shame, were both gone. She was a mos' beautiful girl in whole worl'. Mos' beautiful eyes, like stars above. He wanted to 'pologize—firs', for presuming try to kiss her; second, for drinking—but he'd been so discouraged 'cause he had thought she was mad at him——

The red-fat man cut in, and looking up at Edith smiled radiantly.

"Did you bring any one?" she asked.

No. The red-fat man was a stag.

"Well, would you mind—would it be an awful bother for you to—to take me home to-night?" (This extreme diffidence was a charming affectation on Edith's part—she knew that the red-fat man would immediately dissolve into a paroxysm of delight.)

"Bother? Why, good Lord, I'd be darn glad to! You know I'd be darn glad to."

"Thanks *loads!* You're awfully sweet."

She glanced at her wrist-watch. It was half-past one. And, as she said "half-past one" to herself, it floated vaguely into her mind that her brother had told her at luncheon that he worked in the office of his newspaper until after one-thirty every evening.

Edith turned suddenly to her current partner.

"What street is Delmonico's on, anyway?"

"Street? Oh, why Fifth Avenue, of course."

"I mean, what cross street?"

"Why—let's see—it's on Forty-fourth Street."

This verified what she had thought. Henry's office must be across the street and just around the corner, and it occurred to her immediately that she might slip over for a moment and surprise him, float in on him, a shimmering marvel in her new crimson opera cloak and "cheer him up." It was exactly the sort of thing Edith reveled in doing—an unconventional, jaunty thing. The idea reached out and gripped at her imagination—after an instant's hesitation she had decided.

"My hair is just about to tumble entirely down," she said pleasantly to her partner; "would you mind if I go and fix it?"

"Not at all."

"You're a peach."

A few minutes later, wrapped in her crimson opera cloak, she flitted down a side-stairs, her cheeks glowing with excitement at her little adventure. She ran by a couple who stood at the door—a weak-chinned waiter and an over-rouged young lady, in hot dispute—and opening the outer door stepped into the warm May night.

VII

The over-rouged young lady followed her with a brief, bitter glance—then turned again to the weak-chinned waiter and took up her argument.

"You better go up and tell him I'm here," she said defiantly, "or I'll go up myself."

"No, you don't!" said George sternly.

The girl smiled sardonically.

"Oh, I don't, don't I? Well, let me tell you I know more college fellas and more of 'em know me, and are glad to take me out on a party, than you ever saw in your whole life."

"Maybe so——"

"Maybe so," she interrupted. "Oh, it's all right for any of 'em like that one that just ran out—God knows where *she* went—it's all right for them that are asked here to come or go as they like—but when I want to see a friend they have some cheap, ham-slinging, bring-me-a-doughnut waiter to stand here and keep me out."

"See here," said the elder Key indignantly, "I can't lose my job. Maybe this fella you're talkin' about doesn't want to see you."

"Oh, he wants to see me all right."

"Anyways, how could I find him in all that crowd?"

"Oh, he'll be there," she asserted confidently. "You just ask anybody for Gordon Sterrett and they'll point him out to you. They all know each other, those fellas."

She produced a mesh bag, and taking out a dollar bill handed it to George.

"Here," she said, "here's a bribe. You find him and give him my message. You tell him if he isn't here in five minutes I'm coming up."

George shook his head pessimistically, considered the question for a moment, wavered violently, and then withdrew.

In less than the allotted time Gordon came down-stairs. He was drunker than he had been earlier in the evening and in a different way. The liquor seemed to have hardened on him like a crust. He was heavy and lurching—almost incoherent when he talked.

"'Lo, Jewel," he said thickly. "Came right away. Jewel, I couldn't get that money. Tried my best."

"Money nothing!" she snapped. "You haven't been near me for ten days. What's the matter?"

He shook his head slowly.

"Been very low, Jewel. Been sick."

"Why didn't you tell me if you were sick. I don't care about the money that bad. I didn't start bothering you about it at all until you began neglecting me."

Again he shook his head.

"Haven't been neglecting you. Not at all."

"Haven't! You haven't been near me for three weeks, unless you been so drunk you didn't know what you were doing."

"Been sick. Jewel," he repeated, turning his eyes upon her wearily.

"You're well enough to come and play with your society friends here all right. You told me you'd meet me for dinner, and you said you'd have some money for me. You didn't even bother to ring me up."

"I couldn't get any money."

"Haven't I just been saying that doesn't matter? I wanted to see *you*, Gordon, but you seem to prefer your somebody else."

He denied this bitterly.

"Then get your hat and come along," she suggested.

Gordon hesitated—and she came suddenly close to him and slipped her arms around his neck.

"Come on with me, Gordon," she said in a half whisper. "We'll go over to Devineries' and have a drink, and then we can go up to my apartment."

"I can't, Jewel,——"

"You can," she said intensely.

"I'm sick as a dog!"

"Well, then, you oughtn't to stay here and dance."

With a glance around him in which relief and despair were mingled, Gordon hesitated; then she suddenly pulled him to her and kissed him with soft, pulpy lips.

"All right," he said heavily. "I'll get my hat."

VIII

When Edith came out into the clear blue of the May night she found the Avenue deserted. The windows of the big shops were dark; over their doors were drawn great iron masks until they were only shadowy tombs of the late day's splendor. Glancing down toward Forty-second Street she saw a commingled blur of lights from the all-night restaurants. Over on Sixth Avenue the elevated, a flare of fire, roared across the street between the glimmering parallels of light at the station and streaked along into the crisp dark. But at Forty-fourth Street it was very quiet.

Pulling her cloak close about her Edith darted across the Avenue. She started nervously as a solitary man passed her and said in a hoarse whisper—"Where bound, kiddo?" She was reminded of a night in her childhood when she had walked around the block in her pajamas and a dog had howled at her from a mystery-big back yard.

In a minute she had reached her destination, a two-story, comparatively old building on Forty-fourth, in the upper window of which she thankfully detected a wisp of light. It was bright enough outside for her to make out the sign beside the window—the *New York Trumpet.* She stepped inside a dark hall and after a second saw the stairs in the corner.

Then she was in a long, low room furnished with many desks and hung on all sides with file copies of newspapers. There were only two occupants. They were sitting at different ends of the room, each wearing a green eye-shade and writing by a solitary desk light.

For a moment she stood uncertainly in the doorway, and then both men turned around simultaneously and she recognized her brother.

"Why, Edith!" He rose quickly and approached her in surprise, removing his eye-shade. He was tall, lean, and dark, with black, piercing eyes under very thick glasses. They were far-away eyes that seemed always fixed just over the head of the person to whom he was talking.

He put his hands on her arms and kissed her cheek.

"What is it?" he repeated in some alarm.

"I was at a dance across at Delmonico's, Henry," she said excitedly, "and I couldn't resist tearing over to see you."

"I'm glad you did." His alertness gave way quickly to a habitual vagueness. "You oughtn't to be out alone at night though, ought you?"

The man at the other end of the room had been looking at them curiously, but at Henry's beckoning gesture he approached. He was loosely fat with little twinkling eyes, and, having removed his collar and tie, he gave the impression of a Middle-Western farmer on a Sunday afternoon.

"This is my sister," said Henry. "She dropped in to see me."

"How do you do?" said the fat man, smiling. "My name's Bartholomew, Miss Bradin. I know your brother has forgotten it long ago."

Edith laughed politely.

"Well," he continued, "not exactly gorgeous quarters we have here, are they?"

Edith looked around the room.

"They seem very nice," she replied. "Where do you keep the bombs?"

"The bombs?" repeated Bartholomew, laughing. "That's pretty good—the bombs.

Did you hear her, Henry? She wants to know where we keep the bombs. Say, that's pretty good."

Edith swung herself onto a vacant desk and sat dangling her feet over the edge. Her brother took a seat beside her.

"Well," he asked, absent-mindedly, "how do you like New York this trip?"

"Not bad. I'll be over at the Biltmore with the Hoyts until Sunday. Can't you come to luncheon to-morrow?"

He thought a moment.

"I'm especially busy," he objected, "and I hate women in groups."

"All right," she agreed, unruffled. "Let's you and me have luncheon together."

"Very well."

"I'll call for you at twelve."

Bartholomew was obviously anxious to return to his desk, but apparently considered that it would be rude to leave without some parting pleasantry.

"Well"—he began awkwardly.

They both turned to him.

"Well, we—we had an exciting time earlier in the evening."

The two men exchanged glances.

"You should have come earlier," continued Bartholomew, somewhat encouraged. "We had a regular vaudeville."

"Did you really?"

"A serenade," said Henry. "A lot of soldiers gathered down there in the street and began to yell at the sign."

"Why?" she demanded.

"Just a crowd," said Henry, abstractedly. "All crowds have to howl. They didn't have anybody with much initiative in the lead, or they'd probably have forced their way in here and smashed things up."

"Yes," said Bartholomew, turning again to Edith, "you should have been here."

He seemed to consider this a sufficient cue for withdrawal, for he turned abruptly and went back to his desk.

"Are the soldiers all set against the Socialists?" demanded Edith of her brother. "I mean do they attack you violently and all that?"

Henry replaced his eye-shade and yawned.

"The human race has come a long way," he said casually, "but most of us are throw-backs; the soldiers don't know what they want, or what they hate, or what they like. They're used to acting in large bodies, and they seem to have to make demonstrations. So it happens to be against us. There've been riots all over the city to-night. It's May Day, you see."

"Was the disturbance here pretty serious?"

"Not a bit," he said scornfully. "About twenty-five of them stopped in the street about nine o'clock, and began to bellow at the moon."

"Oh"—She changed the subject. "You're glad to see me, Henry?"

"Why, sure."

"You don't seem to be."

"I am."

"I suppose you think I'm a—a waster. Sort of the World's Worst Butterfly." Henry laughed.

"Not at all. Have a good time while you're young. Why? Do I seem like the priggish and earnest youth?"

"No—" she paused, "—but somehow I began thinking how absolutely different the party I'm on is from—from all your purposes. It seems sort of—of incongruous, doesn't it?—me being at a party like that, and you over here working for a thing that'll make that sort of party impossible ever any more, if your ideas work."

"I don't think of it that way. You're young, and you're acting just as you were brought up to act. Go ahead—have a good time!"

Her feet, which had been idly swinging, stopped and her voice dropped a note.

"I wish you'd—you'd come back to Harrisburg and have a good time. Do you feel sure that you're on the right track——"

"You're wearing beautiful stockings," he interrupted. "What on earth are they?"

"They're embroidered," she replied, glancing down. "Aren't they cunning?" She raised her skirts and uncovered slim, silk-sheathed calves. "Or do you disapprove of silk stockings?"

He seemed slightly exasperated, bent his dark eyes on her piercingly.

"Are you trying to make me out as criticizing you in any way, Edith?"

"Not at all——"

She paused. Bartholomew had uttered a grunt. She turned and saw that he had left his desk and was standing at the window.

"What is it?" demanded Henry.

"People," said Bartholomew, and then after an instant: "Whole jam of them. They're coming from Sixth Avenue."

"People?"

The fat man pressed his nose to the pane.

"Soldiers, by God!" he said emphatically. "I had an idea they'd come back."

Edith jumped to her feet, and running over joined Bartholomew at the window.

"There's a lot of them!" she cried excitedly. "Come here, Henry!"

Henry readjusted his shade, but kept his seat.

"Hadn't we better turn out the lights?" suggested Bartholomew.

"No. They'll go away in a minute."

"They're not," said Edith, peering from the window. "They're not even thinking of going away. There's more of them coming. Look—there's a whole crowd turning the corner of Sixth Avenue."

By the yellow glow and blue shadows of the street lamp she could see that the sidewalk was crowded with men. They were mostly in uniform, some sober, some enthusiastically drunk, and over the whole swept an incoherent clamor and shouting.

Henry rose, and going to the window exposed himself as a long silhouette against the office lights. Immediately the shouting became a steady yell, and a rattling fusillade of small missiles, corners of tobacco plugs, cigarette-boxes, and even pennies beat against the window. The sounds of the racket now began floating up the stairs as the folding doors revolved.

"They're coming up!" cried Bartholomew.

Edith turned anxiously to Henry.

"They're coming up, Henry."

From down-stairs in the lower hall their cries were now quite audible.

"—God damn Socialists!"

"Pro-Germans! Boche-lovers!"

"Second floor, front! Come on!"

"We'll get the sons——"

The next five minutes passed in a dream. Edith was conscious that the clamor burst suddenly upon the three of them like a cloud of rain, that there was a thunder of many feet on the stairs, that Henry had seized her arm and drawn her back toward the rear of the office. Then the door opened and an overflow of men were forced into the room—not the leaders, but simply those who happened to be in front.

"Hello, Bo!"

"Up late, ain't you?"

"You an' your girl. Damn *you!*"

She noticed that two very drunken soldiers had been forced to the front, where they wobbled fatuously—one of them was short and dark, the other was tall and weak of chin.

Henry stepped forward and raised his hand.

"Friends!" he said.

The clamor faded into a momentary stillness, punctuated with mutterings.

"Friends!" he repeated, his far-away eyes fixed over the heads of the crowd, "you're injuring no one but yourselves by breaking in here to-night. Do we look like rich men? Do we look like Germans? I ask you in all fairness——"

"Pipe down!"

"I'll say you do!"

"Say, who's your lady friend, buddy?"

A man in civilian clothes, who had been pawing over a table, suddenly held up a newspaper.

"Here it is!" he shouted, "They wanted the Germans to win the war!"

A new overflow from the stairs was shouldered in and of a sudden the room was full of men all closing around the pale little group at the back. Edith saw that the tall soldier with the weak chin was still in front. The short dark one had disappeared.

She edged slightly backward, stood close to the open window, through which came a clear breath of cool night air.

Then the room was a riot. She realized that the soldiers were surging forward, glimpsed the fat man swinging a chair over his head—instantly the lights went out, and she felt the push of warm bodies under rough cloth, and her ears were full of shouting and trampling and hard breathing.

A figure flashed by her out of nowhere, tottered, was edged sideways, and of a sudden disappeared helplessly out through the open window with a frightened, fragmentary cry that died staccato on the bosom of the clamor. By the faint light streaming from the building backing on the area Edith had a quick impression that it had been the tall soldier with the weak chin.

Anger rose astonishingly in her. She swung her arms wildly, edged blindly toward the thickest of the scuffling. She heard grunts, curses, the muffled impact of fists.

"Henry!" she called frantically, "Henry!"

Then, it was minutes later, she felt suddenly that there were other figures in the room. She heard a voice, deep, bullying, authoritative; she saw yellow rays of light sweeping here and there in the fracas. The cries became more scattered. The scuffling increased and then stopped.

Suddenly the lights were on and the room was full of policemen, clubbing left and right. The deep voice boomed out:

"Here now! Here now! Here now!"

And then:

"Quiet down and get out! Here now!"

The room seemed to empty like a wash-bowl. A policeman fast-grappled in the corner released his hold on his soldier antagonist and started him with a shove toward the door. The deep voice continued. Edith perceived now that it came from a bull-necked police captain standing near the door.

"Here now! This is no way! One of your own sojers got shoved out of the back window an' killed hisself!"

"Henry!" called Edith, "Henry!"

She beat wildly with her fists on the back of the man in front of her; she brushed between two others; fought, shrieked, and beat her way to a very pale figure sitting on the floor close to a desk.

"Henry," she cried passionately, "what's the matter? What's the matter? Did they hurt you?"

His eyes were shut. He groaned and then looking up said disgustedly——

"They broke my leg. My God, the fools!"

"Here now!" called the police captain. "Here now! Here now!"

IX

"Childs', Fifty-ninth Street," at eight o'clock of any morning differs from its sisters by less than the width of their marble tables or the degree of polish on the frying-pans. You will see there a crowd of poor people with sleep in the corners of their eyes, trying to look straight before them at their food so as not to see the other poor people. But Childs', Fifty-ninth, four hours earlier is quite unlike any Childs' restaurant from Portland, Oregon, to Portland, Maine. Within its pale but sanitary walls one finds a noisy medley of chorus girls, college boys, débutantes, rakes, *filles de joie*—a not unrepresentative mixture of the gayest of Broadway, and even of Fifth Avenue.

In the early morning of May the second it was unusually full. Over the marble-topped tables were bent the excited faces of flappers whose fathers owned individual villages. They were eating buckwheat cakes and scrambled eggs with relish and gusto, an accomplishment that it would have been utterly impossible for them to repeat in the same place four hours later.

Almost the entire crowd were from the Gamma Psi dance at Delmonico's except for several chorus girls from a midnight revue who sat at a side table and wished they'd taken off a little more make-up after the show. Here and there a drab, mouse-like figure, desperately out of place, watched the butterflies with a weary, puzzled curiosity. But the drab figure was the exception. This was the morning after May Day, and celebration was still in the air.

Gus Rose, sober but a little dazed, must be classed as one of the drab figures. How he had got himself from Forty-fourth Street to Fifty-ninth Street after the riot was only a hazy half-memory. He had seen the body of Carrol Key put in an ambulance and driven off, and then he had started up town with two or three soldiers. Somewhere between Forty-fourth Street and Fifty-ninth Street the other soldiers had met some women and disappeared. Rose had wandered to Columbus Circle and chosen the gleaming lights of Childs' to minister to his craving for coffee and doughnuts. He walked in and sat down.

All around him floated airy, inconsequential chatter and high-pitched laughter. At first he failed to understand, but after a puzzled five minutes he realized that this was the aftermath of some gay party. Here and there a restless, hilarious young man wandered fraternally and familiarly between the tables, shaking hands indiscriminately and pausing occasionally for a facetious chat, while excited waiters, bearing cakes and eggs aloft, swore at him silently, and bumped him out of the way. To Rose, seated at the most inconspicuous and least crowded table, the whole scene was a colorful circus of beauty and riotous pleasure.

He became gradually aware, after a few moments, that the couple seated diagonally across from him, with their backs to the crowd, were not the least interesting pair in the room. The man was drunk. He wore a dinner coat with a disheveled tie and shirt swollen by spillings of water and wine. His eyes, dim and blood-shot, roved unnaturally from side to side. His breath came short between his lips.

"He's been on a spree!" thought Rose.

The woman was almost if not quite sober. She was pretty, with dark eyes and feverish high color, and she kept her active eyes fixed on her companion with the alertness of a hawk. From time to time she would lean and whisper intently to him, and he would answer by inclining his head heavily or by a particularly ghoulish and repellent wink.

Rose scrutinized them dumbly for some minutes, until the woman gave him a quick, resentful look; then he shifted his gaze to two of the most conspicuously hilarious of the promenaders who were on a protracted circuit of the tables. To his surprise he recognized in one of them the young man by whom he had been so ludicrously entertained at Delmonico's. This started him thinking of Key with a vague sentimentality, not unmixed with awe. Key was dead. He had fallen thirty-five feet and split his skull like a cracked cocoanut.

"He was a darn good guy," thought Rose mournfully. "He was a darn good guy, o'right. That was awful hard luck about him."

The two promenaders approached and started down between Rose's table and the next, addressing friends and strangers alike with jovial familiarity. Suddenly Rose saw the fair-haired one with the prominent teeth stop, look unsteadily at the man and girl opposite, and then begin to move his head disapprovingly from side to side.

The man with the blood-shot eyes looked up.

"Gordy," said the promenader with the prominent teeth, "Gordy."

"Hello," said the man with the stained shirt thickly.

Prominent Teeth shook his finger pessimistically at the pair, giving the woman a glance of aloof condemnation.

"What'd I tell you Gordy?"

Gordon stirred in his seat.

"Go to hell!" he said.

Dean continued to stand there shaking his finger. The woman began to get angry.

"You go 'way!" she cried fiercely. "You're drunk, that's what you are!"

"So's he," suggested Dean, staying the motion of his finger and pointing it at Gordon.

Peter Himmel ambled up, owlish now and oratorically inclined.

"Here now," he began as if called upon to deal with some petty dispute between children. "Wha's all trouble?"

"You take your friend away," said Jewel tartly. "He's bothering us."

"What's 'at?"

"You heard me!" she said shrilly. "I said to take your drunken friend away."

Her rising voice rang out above the clatter of the restaurant and a waiter came hurrying up.

"You gotta be more quiet!"

"That fella's drunk," she cried. "He's insulting us."

"Ah-ha, Gordy," persisted the accused. "What'd I tell you." He turned to the waiter. "Gordy an' friends. Been tryin' help him, haven't I, Gordy?"

Gordy looked up.

"Help me? Hell, no!"

Jewel rose suddenly, and seizing Gordon's arm assisted him to his feet.

"Come on, Gordy!" she said, leaning toward him and speaking in a half whisper. "Let's us get out of here. This fella's got a mean drunk on."

Gordon allowed himself to be urged to his feet and started toward the door. Jewel turned for a second and addressed the provoker of their flight.

"I know all about *you!*" she said fiercely. "Nice friend, you are, I'll say. He told me about you."

Then she seized Gordon's arm, and together they made their way through the curious crowd, paid their check, and went out.

"You'll have to sit down," said the waiter to Peter after they had gone.

"What's 'at? Sit down?"

"Yes—or get out."

Peter turned to Dean.

"Come on," he suggested. "Let's beat up this waiter."

"All right."

They advanced toward him, their faces grown stern. The waiter retreated.

Peter suddenly reached over to a plate on the table beside him and picking up a handful of hash tossed it into the air. It descended as a languid parabola in snowflake effect on the heads of those near by.

"Hey! Ease up!"

"Put him out!"

"Sit down, Peter!"

"Cut out that stuff!"

Peter laughed and bowed.

"Thank you for your kind applause, ladies and gents. If some one will lend me some more hash and a tall hat we will go on with the act."

The bouncer bustled up.

"You've gotta get out!" he said to Peter.

"Hell, no!"

"He's my friend!" put in Dean indignantly.

A crowd of waiters were gathering. "Put him out!"

"Better go, Peter."

There was a short struggle and the two were edged and pushed toward the door.

"I got a hat and a coat here!" cried Peter.

"Well, go get 'em and be spry about it!"

The bouncer released his hold on Peter, who, adopting a ludicrous air of extreme cunning, rushed immediately around to the other table, where he burst into derisive laughter and thumbed his nose at the exasperated waiters.

"Think I just better wait a l'il' longer," he announced.

The chase began. Four waiters were sent around one way and four another. Dean caught hold of two of them by the coat, and another struggle took place before the pursuit of Peter could be resumed; he was finally pinioned after overturning a sugar-bowl and several cups of coffee. A fresh argument ensued at the cashier's desk, where Peter attempted to buy another dish of hash to take with him and throw at policemen.

But the commotion upon his exit proper was dwarfed by another phenomenon which drew admiring glances and a prolonged involuntary "Oh-h-h!" from every person in the restaurant.

The great plate-glass front had turned to a deep creamy blue, the color of a Maxfield Parrish moonlight—a blue that seemed to press close upon the pane as if to crowd its way into the restaurant. Dawn had come up in Columbus Circle, magical, breathless dawn, silhouetting the great statue of the immortal Christopher, and mingling in a curious and uncanny manner with the fading yellow electric light inside.

                                    x

Mr. In and Mr. Out are not listed by the census-taker. You will search for them in vain through the social register or the births, marriages, and deaths, or the grocer's credit list. Oblivion has swallowed them and the testimony that they ever existed at all is vague and shadowy, and inadmissible in a court of law. Yet I have it upon the best authority that for a brief space Mr. In and Mr. Out lived, breathed, answered to their names and radiated vivid personalities of their own.

During the brief span of their lives they walked in their native garments down the great highway of a great nation; were laughed at, sworn at, chased, and fled from. Then they passed and were heard of no more.

They were already taking form dimly, when a taxicab with the top open breezed down Broadway in the faintest glimmer of May dawn. In this car sat the souls of Mr. In and Mr. Out discussing with amazement the blue light that had so precipitately colored the sky behind the statue of Christopher Columbus, discussing with bewilderment the old, gray faces of the early risers which skimmed palely along the street like blown bits of paper on a gray lake. They were agreed on all things, from the absurdity of the bouncer in Childs' to the absurdity of the business of life. They were dizzy with the extreme maudlin happiness that the morning had awakened in their glowing souls. Indeed, so fresh and vigorous was their pleasure in living that they felt it should be expressed by loud cries.

"Ye-ow-ow!" hooted Peter, making a megaphone with his hands—and Dean joined in with a call that, though equally significant and symbolic, derived its resonance from its very inarticulateness.

"Yo-ho! Yea! Yoho! Yo-buba!"

Fifty-third Street was a bus with a dark, bobbed-hair beauty atop; Fifty-second was a street cleaner who dodged, escaped, and sent up a yell of, "Look where you're aimin'!" in a pained and grieved voice. At Fiftieth Street a group of men on a very white sidewalk in front of a very white building turned to stare after them, and shouted:

"Some party, boys!"

At Forty-ninth Street Peter turned to Dean. "Beautiful morning," he said gravely, squinting up his owlish eyes.

"Probably is."

"Go get some breakfast, hey?"

Dean agreed—with additions.

"Breakfast and liquor."

"Breakfast and liquor," repeated Peter, and they looked at each other, nodding. "That's logical."

Then they both burst into loud laughter.

"Breakfast and liquor! Oh, gosh!"

"No such thing," announced Peter.

"Don't serve it? Ne'mind. We force 'em serve it. Bring pressure bear."

"Bring logic bear."

The taxi cut suddenly off Broadway, sailed along a cross street, and stopped in front of a heavy tomb-like building in Fifth Avenue.

"What's idea?"

The taxi-driver informed them that this was Delmonico's.

This was somewhat puzzling. They were forced to devote several minutes to intense concentration, for if such an order had been given there must have been a reason for it.

"Somep'm 'bouta coat," suggested the taxi-man.

That was it. Peter's overcoat and hat. He had left them at Delmonico's. Having decided this, they disembarked from the taxi and strolled toward the entrance arm in arm.

"Hey!" said the taxi-driver.

"Huh?"

"You better pay me."

They shook their heads in shocked negation.

"Later, not now—we give orders, you wait."

The taxi-driver objected; he wanted his money now. With the scornful condescension of men exercising tremendous self-control they paid him.

Inside Peter groped in vain through a dim, deserted check-room in search of his coat and derby.

"Gone, I guess. Somebody stole it."

"Some Sheff student."

"All probability."

"Never mind," said Dean, nobly. "I'll leave mine here too—then we'll both be dressed the same."

He removed his overcoat and hat and was hanging them up when his roving glance was caught and held magnetically by two large squares of cardboard tacked to the two coat-room doors. The one on the left-hand door bore the word "In" in big black letters, and the one on the right-hand door flaunted the equally emphatic word "Out."

"Look!" he exclaimed happily——

Peter's eyes followed his pointing finger.

"What?"

"Look at the signs. Let's take 'em."

"Good idea."

"Probably pair very rare an' valuable signs. Probably come in handy."

Peter removed the left-hand sign from the door and endeavored to conceal it about his person. The sign being of considerable proportions, this was a matter of some difficulty. An idea flung itself at him, and with an air of dignified mystery he turned his back. After an instant he wheeled dramatically around, and stretching out his arms displayed himself to the admiring Dean. He had inserted the sign in his vest, completely covering his shirt front. In effect, the word "In" had been painted upon his shirt in large black letters.

"Yoho!" cheered Dean. "Mister In."

He inserted his own sign in like manner.

"Mister Out!" he announced triumphantly. "Mr. In meet Mr. Out."

They advanced and shook hands. Again laughter overcame them and they rocked in a shaken spasm of mirth.

"Yoho!"

"We probably get a flock of breakfast."

"We'll go—go to the Commodore."

Arm in arm they sallied out the door, and turning east in Forty-fourth Street set out for the Commodore.

As they came out a short dark soldier, very pale and tired, who had been wandering listlessly along the sidewalk, turned to look at them.

He started over as though to address them, but as they immediately bent on him glances of withering unrecognition, he waited until they had started unsteadily down the street, and then followed at about forty paces, chuckling to himself and saying "Oh, boy!" over and over under his breath, in delighted, anticipatory tones.

Mr. In and Mr. Out were meanwhile exchanging pleasantries concerning their future plans.

"We want liquor; we want breakfast. Neither without the other. One and indivisible."

"We want both 'em!"

"Both 'em!"

It was quite light now, and passers-by began to bend curious eyes on the pair. Obviously they were engaged in a discussion, which afforded each of them intense amusement, for occasionally a fit of laughter would seize upon them so violently that, still with their arms interlocked, they would bend nearly double.

Reaching the Commodore, they exchanged a few spicy epigrams with the sleepy-eyed doorman, navigated the revolving door with some difficulty, and then made their way through a thinly populated but startled lobby to the dining-room, where a puzzled waiter showed them an obscure table in a corner. They studied the bill of fare helplessly, telling over the items to each other in puzzled mumbles.

"Don't see any liquor here," said Peter reproachfully.

The waiter became audible but unintelligible.

"Repeat," continued Peter, with patient tolerance, "that there seems to be unexplained and quite distasteful lack of liquor upon bill of fare."

"Here!" said Dean confidently, "let me handle him." He turned to the waiter—"Bring us—bring us—" he scanned the bill of fare anxiously. "Bring us a quart of champagne and a—a—probably ham sandwich."

The waiter looked doubtful.

"Bring it!" roared Mr. In and Mr. Out in chorus.

The waiter coughed and disappeared. There was a short wait during which they were subjected without their knowledge to a careful scrutiny by the head-waiter. Then the champagne arrived, and at the sight of it Mr. In and Mr. Out became jubilant.

"Imagine their objecting to us having champagne for breakfast—jus' imagine."

They both concentrated upon the vision of such an awesome possibility, but the feat was too much for them. It was impossible for their joint imaginations to conjure up a world where any one might object to any one else having champagne for breakfast. The waiter drew the cork with an enormous *pop*—and their glasses immediately foamed with pale yellow froth.

"Here's health, Mr. In."

"Here's same to you, Mr. Out."

The waiter withdrew; the minutes passed; the champagne became low in the bottle.

"It's—it's mortifying," said Dean suddenly.

"Wha's mortifying?"

"The idea their objecting us having champagne breakfast."

"Mortifying?" Peter considered. "Yes, tha's word—mortifying."

Again they collapsed into laughter, howled, swayed, rocked back and forth in their chairs, repeating the word "mortifying" over and over to each other—each repetition seeming to make it only more brilliantly absurd.

After a few more gorgeous minutes they decided on another quart. Their anxious waiter consulted his immediate superior, and this discreet person gave implicit instructions that no more champagne should be served. Their check was brought.

Five minutes later, arm in arm, they left the Commodore and made their way through a curious, staring crowd along Forty-second Street, and up Vanderbilt Avenue to the Biltmore. There, with sudden cunning, they rose to the occasion and traversed the lobby, walking fast and standing unnaturally erect.

Once in the dining-room they repeated their performance. They were torn between intermittent convulsive laughter and sudden spasmodic discussions of politics, college, and the sunny state of their dispositions. Their watches told them that it was now nine o'clock, and a dim idea was born in them that they were on a memorable party, something that they would remember always. They lingered over the second bottle. Either of them had only to mention the word "mortifying" to send them both into riotous gasps. The dining-room was whirring and shifting now; a curious lightness permeated and rarefied the heavy air.

They paid their check and walked out into the lobby.

It was at this moment that the exterior doors revolved for the thousandth time that morning, and admitted into the lobby a very pale young beauty with dark circles under her eyes, attired in a much-rumpled evening dress. She was accompanied by a plain stout man, obviously not an appropriate escort.

At the top of the stairs this couple encountered Mr. In and Mr. Out.

"Edith," began Mr. In, stepping toward her hilariously and making a sweeping bow, "darling, good morning."

The stout man glanced questioningly at Edith, as if merely asking her permission to throw this man summarily out of the way.

"'Scuse familiarity," added Peter, as an afterthought. "Edith, good-morning." He seized Dean's elbow and impelled him into the foreground.

"Meet Mr. In, Edith, my bes' frien'. Inseparable. Mr. In and Mr. Out."

Mr. Out advanced and bowed; in fact, he advanced so far and bowed so low that he tipped slightly forward and only kept his balance by placing a hand lightly on Edith's shoulder.

"I'm Mr. Out, Edith," he mumbled pleasantly. "S'misterin Misterout."

"'Smisterinanout," said Peter proudly.

But Edith stared straight by them, her eyes fixed on some infinite speck in the gallery above her. She nodded slightly to the stout man, who advanced bull-like and with a sturdy brisk gesture pushed Mr. In and Mr. Out to either side. Through this alley he and Edith walked.

But ten paces farther on Edith stopped again—stopped and pointed to a short, dark soldier who was eying the crowd in general, and the tableau of Mr. In and Mr. Out in particular, with a sort of puzzled, spell-bound awe.

"There," cried Edith. "See there!"

Her voice rose, became somewhat shrill. Her pointing finger shook slightly.

"There's the soldier who broke my brother's leg."

There were a dozen exclamations; a man in a cutaway coat left his place near the desk and advanced alertly; the stout person made a sort of lightning-like spring toward the short, dark soldier, and then the lobby closed around the little group and blotted them from the sight of Mr. In and Mr. Out.

But to Mr. In and Mr. Out this event was merely a particolored iridescent segment of a whirring, spinning world.

They heard loud voices; they saw the stout man spring; the picture suddenly blurred.

Then they were in an elevator bound skyward.

"What floor, please?" said the elevator man.

"Any floor," said Mr. In.

"Top floor," said Mr. Out.

"This is the top floor," said the elevator man.

"Have another floor put on," said Mr. Out.
"Higher," said Mr. In.
"Heaven," said Mr. Out.

XI

In a bedroom of a small hotel just off Sixth Avenue Gordon Sterrett awoke with a pain in the back of his head and a sick throbbing in all his veins. He looked at the dusky gray shadows in the corners of the room and at a raw place on a large leather chair in the corner where it had long been in use. He saw clothes, disheveled, rumpled clothes on the floor and he smelt stale cigarette smoke and stale liquor. The windows were tight shut. Outside the bright sunlight had thrown a dust-filled beam across the sill—a beam broken by the head of the wide wooden bed in which he had slept. He lay very quiet—comatose, drugged, his eyes wide, his mind clicking wildly like an unoiled machine.

It must have been thirty seconds after he perceived the sunbeam with the dust on it and the rip on the large leather chair that he had the sense of life close beside him, and it was another thirty seconds after that before that he realized that he was irrevocably married to Jewel Hudson.

He went out half an hour later and bought a revolver at a sporting goods store. Then he took a took a taxi to the room where he had been living on East Twenty-seventh Street, and, leaning across the table that held his drawing materials, fired a cartridge into his head just behind the temple.

Ema S. Hunting

(1885–1923)

The daughter of a Congregational minister and the older sister of writer Ruth Suckow (1892–1960), Emma Suckow Hunting was born in Iowa and graduated from Grinnell College. In addition to publishing three short stories in the *Midland: A Magazine of the Middle West* ("Dissipation," May 1920, and "True Love," June 1922), she was the author of the plays *A Dickens Revival* (1914), *Her Superior Intelligence: A Comedy* (1914) and *Double Dummy: A Comedietta in One Act* (1917). "The Soul That Sinneth" was published in the *Midland* in August 1920. In her memoir, Ruth Suckow discusses her pacifism during the Great War, which estranged her for a time from her father, who preached in favor of the war. Ema's views on the war may be discerned from "The Soul That Sinneth" and its depiction of the consequences of a son's death.

The Soul That Sinneth

Ema S. Hunting

The soul that sinneth, it shall die.
—Ezekiel 18:4.

Henry Schultz drove into the yard and unhitched the team from the plough. It was coming sunset already—the dusty, cool October sunset that so early sent him in from the fields. In the meadow back of the barn, which they had never been able to drain because there was no place lower to drain into, innumerable frogs croaked and chorused. Visitors from towns had sometimes found the sound dreary coming through the hush and low wind of twilight: and indeed Henry thought it unpleasant since it reminded him of the half acre of waste land his ditches and tiles could not make profitable. But in the main, he paid no more attention to the frogs than he paid to the colors in the level, deep prairie sunsets, or to the scent of rank vegetation, past its prime, from the roadsides. He smelled the sweat on his team, and the odor from the open barn, partly of animals and partly from the hay and grains stored there, and he caught from the house a whiff of potatoes frying in fat.

He drove the liberated team over to the trough to drink. After that they must be fed and bedded, this team and two other teams and Johnny's driving horse besides. Then there was the milking and the separating and the pigs. It was dark, with a cold whisper of wind in the trees, when he turned towards the house.

He was a humane man, Henry Schultz, and fed his animals before he fed himself, or before his wife could eat or get her work put aside. A silent man, partly deaf, who drove regularly to church on Sundays, seldom spoke, and for recreation improvised chords and modulations on the reed organ in the parlor, evenings and Sunday afternoons. He owned three farms: but the last one, the one in Minnesota where land was still cheaper than in Iowa, that would be a long while getting paid for now that he had everything to do alone and might even have to hire a man.

He stood at the bench outside the kitchen door where there was a pail of water, a tin dipper and basin, and took a long drink of the cool, deep well water tasting of iron. Everything to do—yes, just when Johnny was getting over his nonsense and settling down into some help to a man. The girls, of course, that was natural—girls get married and go and what can you say? Besides, Carrie managed the work by herself: but how could he manage one hundred and sixty acres, and the cattle and the pigs, and the cream to haul, and the repairing, and all? How could any man? He had never thought so much of Johnny's help, always talking about school and machinery, and driving that Klinefelter girl to church—a little fellow, anyhow, short in the legs: it was a wonder they took him. But of course they would take him, take *his* boy, the only one he had to do anything. He stood by the bench with the water running out of the dipper beside him and stared at the grey sky where the sun had long disappeared. In Texas, they said he was, a big camp, thousands of young chaps he had written his mother. Well, let them go, the thousands, if they wanted to be fools: but let them let *him* alone, him and his, his acres and his barns and his boy.

The frogs were quiet, but the cottonwoods in the grove bent and thrashed and shed their dry leaves on the wind.

He poured water into the basin and splashed face and hands, and groped his way into the kitchen to dry on the towel behind the door.

There was no light in the kitchen except the glow in the cook stove and a bar of yellow in the slit of the dining room door. Supper was waiting, pushed back to keep hot, but Carrie might have been there watching for him. He took up the comb hanging on a chain beside the towel and combed his wet hair. He could hear the rockers of a chair in the next room, rocking, rocking on the bare floor. That was the grandmother, too old to do anything, sitting as she always sat, waiting to be fed. He dropped the comb and pushed open the room door.

A lamp with a white china shade stood on the supper table throwing yellow light in a circle across the dishes and the red and white table cloth and leaving the room dim. The grandmother sat in her corner, not rocking now, sitting still like a cat. He could see her face peering at him. Even then he did not speak, did not say, "Where's Carrie?" nor shout for her as another man might have done. It was true he was ready for his supper after a hard day's work—

He saw the door of the parlor open and his wife look at him. She too said nothing. But he saw that she was white with swollen patches of red about her eyes. She had something—a bit of paper—in her hand.

Then he spoke. He said, "What's the matter?" She made a little sound in her throat, but it was not a word, and gave him the yellow paper: and even then, instead of going into the kitchen, she went back into the parlor and pulled the door shut.

He carried the paper to the table and sat down and began reading it, held close to the light.

Private John Schultz—of pneumonia—October 6—

There was not a sound from the grandmother, not a sound from the parlor, not a sound from the man at the table reading—

And then there came a cry, and an awful curse, and a blow that set the lampshade rattling and the light flickering in the room.

"You!" he screamed at the grandmother. "Here eleven years and worth nothing. You there in your corner, hanging on, and Johnny dead. Dead." He ran out of the room and through the kitchen, and in the yard they could hear him, screaming.

Carrie crept in from the parlor and touched her mother.

"Kommen Sie mit, ma. Go to bett."

"Ja. Ja. I go. I go." She scrambled up and clung to her daughter and they went through the dark, shut parlor to the bedroom. The pipes of the reed organ gleamed with gilt in the corner. Their feet were noiseless on the ingrain carpet padded underneath with straw.

"At Carl's," whispered the Grandmother, "there are the children, so many. Und seine Frau—but I go, I go there. Ich denke—"

"Ja. But never mind tonight, ma" Go to bett."

"Ja, zum bett. I go."

All night, at times Carrie heard him: but in the morning he came in to his breakfast, fed in silence, and went out to the chores and the ploughing. She carried him his lunch and put it down in the corner of the field, and she swept and burnished the house, and called up her two daughters on their farms to tell them.

"Johnny?" they said. "But, ma—he just went! *Johnny?* Oh, ma!"

"Yes. But don't come over tonight. Wait a day or two." She knew the neighbors would be listening in—"rubbering." "There's to be a big funeral. The telegram said so. An escort of honor. They are coming with him all the way from Texas."

"Oh, ma! With Johnny!"

"He was a soldier already. I swept today and tomorrow I'll bake up some biscuit."

"We'll come to help you."

"Yes. But not tomorrow. Wait a day or two."

In spite of Carrie, whispers ran about the neighborhood. Henry Schultz was crazed. All day he ploughed in his fields while Johnny lay dead. Old Grandma Haar was to be sent to her son's, nine miles away, where there were seven children and the farm was poor. She would die there, they said. Henry had pulled down the flag from the window and burned it.

"No one but May Klinefelter has dared go near the place," they whispered. "It looks funny, her not married to Johnny. But she went over to help Carrie while Henry ploughed in the south eighty."

Then a rumour from the village. Henry Schultz had telegraphed to the camp in Texas that he would have no soldiers with the body. They would have come—an escort of honor for Johnny Schultz, two weeks a soldier. Now there would be no one.

Few dared, when the coffin arrived draped in the flag, one young officer its sole escort, few dared go to the Schultz place for the funeral. The two girls, Annie and Linda, were there as in duty bound, with their husbands, and James McGovern, the only Scotchman in the county, came stumping fiercely on his lame leg. Carrie had fitted herself out in black, and the grandmother was still there, mumbling and shrinking into her bonnet. The house was shining and ready, with a row of chairs set 'round the parlor. But the wagon with the coffin had driven down the long lane between the cottonwoods and the young officer had stepped out on the porch, and the men from town who had volunteered as pall bearers were just ready to lift the body, before Henry Schultz appeared. He came around the corner of the porch in his overalls and boots. He said terrible things to the young officer. He tore the great flag from the coffin and trampled it and threw it away. And then he went back again to his field and ploughed all day until dark.

The young officer was very kind. He put his arm around Carrie and took her into the house, and when they brought in the coffin, he held her while she looked at Johnny. And Johnny lay white and smiling in his uniform, not at all thin for he had been sick only four days, with his big blue eyes just closed and his brown hair brushed back from his forehead.

It was three days later when the insurance man from town, Art Fedderman, drove out to settle about Johnny's insurance. There was a thousand dollars coming for Johnny. Art brought the new lawyer, young Harvey, with him. Art was getting pretty fat and puffy what with big land deals and maybe a bottle under the seat, and perhaps he didn't care about coming alone.

Carrie told him Henry was in the barn mending harness—it was rainy that day—and sure enough, there they found him with the golden dust from the mows sifting around him.

"Well, Mr. Schultz, this is too bad." said Art. It's too bad."

"What do you want?"

"Why—the insurance, you know, Mr. Schultz. Johnny's insurance."

"Then say the insurance, the thousand dollars. Three days in his grave and you just getting here."

"My God, three days, Mr. Schultz! Is there another company, only but just the Mutual, that comes around with a check in three days!"

"Then let's see the check."

They settled somehow about the insurance—young Harvey took himself off to the car—and Art came out of the barn looking mottled and shaky and was for driving straight off. But Carrie called to them to come in to dinner—it was past noon and raining—and young Harvey said, "Better take a bite. You look done."

They ate alone at the table in the dining room with the grandmother shriveled in her corner and Carrie waiting on them, back and forth, between the table and the stove in the kitchen. Art kept a lookout through the window toward the barn: and even when they were through and going out to the car, he said in a whisper, "Start her up, Harve. I want to get out of here."

"What's the matter?" young Harvey asked as they turned out of the lane of cotton-woods on the public road. "Out of his head?"

"Is he? Say, he darned near put me out of mine. What d'you think he thinks this check is I brought him from the Mutual—twenty payment life he carried for the kid? Thinks it's Gov'ment money. Got it all mixed up with War Risk Insurance and that stuff. Laughed his head off—d'you hear him? My land, the barn shook. 'Two weeks they had him,' he says, 'and it cost 'em a thousand dollars! And it's not for his mother,' he says. 'Don't you believe that.' Raved around about Johnny's being murdered. 'Stole him, stole him!' he yelled. Turned a man's blood cold. And then, by George, if he wasn't going to strangle me getting me to promise I wouldn't tell he had the money. Said the Red Cross and that gang would be right on him, and he had to pay for Johnny's farm—some deal he had on up in Minnesota. Kept on telling how poor he is, how he has to work now Johnny's gone. Oh, he's a bug all right! And yet, you know—poor old nut—a man feels sorry for him." The car slid around another turn in the road, and Art, recovering, became reflective. "Yes, sir, he must have thought a lot more of that kid than anybody knew about. Kept talking about his legs. Says his mother says he worked too hard when he was a kid and it made him short. And if he hasn't got it half in his head the kid ain't dead! Yes—told me a dozen times. 'They're hiding him,' he says, 'his mother and that Klinefelter girl. They've sneaked him off to school. Always at me about school—school.' Smart boy, Johnny Schultz was. Well—" Art sighed and reached a fat hand under the seat. "Poor devil, it's his own loss. But I'd hate to live with him."

"Yes."

And the two fell silent: not thinking perhaps of the lost crazed man in the barn, sitting in his rain of golden dust: but of Carrie going back and forth, back and forth, between the table and the kitchen stove: and of the grandmother mumbling in her corner. And of the silence in the house, and the long cold winds in the cottonwoods.

Laurence Stallings
(1894–1968)

Laurence Stallings joined the U.S. Marine Corps after graduating from Wake Forest University. At the Battle of Belleau Wood, he was struck by machine gun fire, and the resulting wounds led to the eventual amputation of his right leg. His only novel, *Plumes* (1924), focuses on the treatment received by a wounded soldier. With Maxwell Anderson he cowrote the popular play *What Price Glory* (1924), which was made into a film in 1926. His screenplay for the war film *The Big Parade* (1925) was inspired by his short story of that title published in the *New Republic* on September 17, 1924. In addition to his work as a playwright and screenwriter, he wrote two notable histories of the war: *The First World War: A Photographic History* (1933) and *The Doughboys: The Story of the AEF, 1917–1918* (1963).

The Big Parade
Laurence Stallings

There were nine of them left after twenty days, and the lieutenant made them ten. They were not isolated, for there were soldiers all about them. The lieutenant must have held ninety in his platoon, in addition to the nine. He could not tell the number to a man, because replacements were being rushed into the line and wounded hushed out of the line at all night hours in the twenty-four. In stages of ten and twenty each night, and conscript nondescripts they were, too. Casuals, the army called them; as if they had some faltering genius for mortality.

The lieutenant could not count them in the night time, for the blanket darkness was pinioned down about them by masses of shell smoke, thunderous vapors turgid with phosgene. Under the pall of this blanket, where the lieutenant alternately ral-

lied and gagged upon the fruity mellowness of gas, the ninety lay so quietly in the
coverts that counting them was impossible. Scuttling sparrows, along the sunken
road bisecting the arc of the lieutenant's position which fringed the cringing limes
and poplars of a broken wood.

The nine had first ventured into the broken wood when its trees were fluted
evenly against the ruddy seas of a startled dawn, trees now gat-toothed under the
bludgeonings of man. There had been fifty-seven men with the lieutenant. Forty-
eight of those were gone. Gone, oh, anywhere: to hell if you like, and ninety had
filled their places. The nine were the lieutenant's own, for he had brought them
from overseas as his own. When they sailed, his father had turned up by some
acute discovery, had seen them pass along the brutally cobbled, wintry streets of
Hoboken. Had said: "A fine body of men you have there, my son." The lieutenant
knew that never, even though by a miracle he continued to live, could men be so
close again. He understood the nine's divination of his helplessness, of the odd
points of his strength. When he was minted and stamped, as expendable as a bright
new penny, as cheaply held, these nine had been among those first given him. As
the Spartan boy had been given away; the boy who was later to feel the teeth of
a small red fox lacerating the belly of his ethical pride. Where there was utterly
no safety, he liked having them with him for the sense of security they lent him
amidst these ninety casuals of the night.

Most of all, the lieutenant liked having Gianonni. The boy was eager; a dark,
unleashed undertaker's assistant from Brooklyn. Gianonni was wonderful about
the dead; put them out of sight before morning, threw light mantles of earth over
their drained faces, replenished mantles of other nights where desecrating shells
had churned the light, odorous loam of spring. Gianonni could also carry messages. He could carry messages anywhere. He was the best runner in the world,
the lieutenant boasted to each of his three captains. In turn, Gianonni had thrown
the last mantles over two of these captains in the darkness of the night, heavier in
accordance with their rank. The lieutenant felt lonely with the third captain, unless
Gianonni was near. For the captain was himself a casual acquisition of the darkness.

Night after night Gianonni strayed anywhere, everywhere, having pleasantly
appointed his horrid chores. A mile up to the left of the line to examine curiously
the Moroccans who sometimes wore enemy eyes as bangles of prowess. Or three
miles to the rear of the lines, to slake his gullet with limpid water from chalky
wells, to purchase chocolate with money given him by surgeons in return for
souvenirs of the chase. The lieutenant knew the source of the souvenirs. Gianonni
chattered. Gianonni, he knew, was a ghoul. The undertaker's apprentice picked
enemy dead clean, thrust his nimble hands into the pockets of swollen Germans
who had grown beards while lying with faces turned to drink the warm spring

rains. The lieutenant knew that Gianonni was not a killer, had never fired his runner's automatic, had never been seized with the hysteria of hatred. Others killed. Gianonni robbed. The lieutenant felt Gianonni closer to him than any other of the nine. The lieutenant was not a killer.

The lieutenant considered taking all nine with him when the message came. Certainly all nine were deserving of going, as deserving as the lieutenant himself. The message specified that the lieutenant and eight other ranks were to present themselves at battalion headquarters at midnight to entrain for Paris. They were to form a squad in a composite company representing the regiment in a Fourth of July parade. The lieutenant was aware of the sinister moral of such an expedition. Dirtied Americans, smelling of blood, were to be exhibited along the Champs Elysées fresh from the lines. The French, become connoisseurs in enervated faces, could find proof of active American participation in the seven kinds of hell prepared for a sister republic. The lieutenant read, understood. He whipped out a steel mirror he wore next his heart. He studied puttied cheeks, eyes yellowed by a thousand end-to-end cigarettes, nose swollen from picric fumes, lips seared from thirst, hair brittle with sweat. The French could label him exhibit A.

The message was inconsiderate. Eight were not enough. The lieutenant considered taking eight and hinting to Gianonni that he might make his own dispositions for following close on. He was confident of Gianonni's ability to desert. But there were complications, other considerations. Gianonni once removed from immediate responsibility, once remote from intimate control, might never in the course of his peregrinations become tangent to the line again. Trust the amiable embalmer's novice. Gianonni was too intelligent, too calloused, to fling free on his own once. The best runner, the lieutenant reflected in the late afternoon as he fingered the message, the best runner in France would spend the remainder of his life of service swinging his quick short legs along the boulevards.

The lieutenant decided to make the nine draw straws for it. He sat back in his fox-hole and carefully partitioned a wheat straw into nine pieces. Eight parts were graduated from one inch to three. The butt of the ninth straw was frayed into a five inch length. This longest, it pleased him to decide, would give its holder instant joy. The shortest straw would obligate its owner to remain behind with the ninety casuals.

The lieutenant carefully placed the nine pieces of straw in his notebook, and tucked it under some miscellany of gear at the bottom of his fox-hole. He crawled across an open space and sought out the nine among the listless coveys of men. He located eight, one after another. "When it's pitch black tonight," he whispered to each in turn, "come to my P. C."

Gianonni had strayed again. Would some one pass the word to Gianonni? The lieutenant wormed his long dirty body back to the fox-hole and sat stonily for three hours, aching for sleep. At dusk a formation of silvered albatross droned in the high violet of evening; birds winging to lay steel eggs into the nests of Paris. The lieutenant from his boredom envied the enemy airmen their light blue war of the skies. A bomber did his dirty work upon a full night's sleep, a full evening's belly. The albatross were pillowed in feathery clouds. Machine gunners were tuning in for the night, lining up targets for the fear watches. The lieutenant noted with precision the beaten zones of the night's play. Darkness came on slowly, random star shells mimicked the bloodstone of the evening star. Anxious machine gunners began their intermittent alarm. The blanket of night was pinioned down again. The lieutenant blew the sand from the magazine of his automatic, and snapped the trigger twice for inspection, sighting on the evening star. On the last Sunday night at home he had played from the score of Tannhäuser for the offertory.

Presently the eight appeared, one by one enriching the fox-hole's smell of roots and blood, of canned salmon and phosgene as each lurched down the crater. They were stoics, apathetic. Then they were sceptics, wary. It was clear to them that the meeting of the nine was signal, portentous. A job, some sort of a sweet job, was awaiting men who knew the ground of contention. The senior corporal spoke first: "Dirty work, Mister?"

The lieutenant was important. "Trip to Paris," he said laconically.

None said a word. In the darkness all breathed fiercely at the jest. There was a detonation fifteen yards away which broke the senior corporal's inhibitions into bits. "In a pig's" . . . he began. He stopped short. All breathed more easily. There might be something in the lieutenant's remark after all.

The lieutenant explained. The eight were eager to live. They believed. They crouched, rifles grounded, and a current of credulity ran through the circle, bridging gap after gap until the smell of the fox-hole became acrid in the darkness with burning insulation.

"Who'll draw for Gianonni?" the lieutenant asked. "He rates this trip. He's one of you."

The eight heated the darkness like so many radiators. "It's the kinda lay-out," said the youngest of the two corporals after two detonations and a machine gunner's ecstacy had warmed him, "that could mean Hoboken or hell, getting away like this. Three of mine today . . . that God-damned one pounder again. I wouldn't like to pluck a raspberry for little Caruso."

A shower of earth tinkled upon the lieutenant's tin hat. A voice whispered cheerily into the fox-hole. "Theesa you, Meester," came down the layers of darkness. "I no get da message soon." Gianonni's small feet struggled down through the gloom, wriggled for a purchase in the centre of the ring. He rose to the drama of his entrance into the ring. Merrily, lightly, his spirits responded.

"A gooda job, eh?"

Pleasantly, his breath smelled of milk chocolate and jam. As he settled into the ring the masses of French currency on him clinked affluently. He began feeling arm chevrons, shoulder straps; identifying the arrangement of his companions. The lieutenant opened his note book craftily, gathering the straws into his left hand, fringing them evenly in the channel of thumb and forefinger. He bent his long dirty body over as a shade, and drew from his tunic a small electric torch. He splayed the tiny beam, millions of candles in the darkness, for an instant full upon his left hand extending forward into the circle. He cried, jauntily:

"A straw for each of you old timers. The shortest one marks the man who stays behind."

Gianonni, with the gambler's instinct for chance, seized a straw's tip with a whizz-bang's quickness. A shell exploded forward. The lieutenant snubbed the torch, feeling the longest straw whip through his hand. Its frayed end telegraphed that Gianonni was safe. The eight drew methodically. Straws were compared. The lieutenant was struck with anger. Gianonni was extending a straw a half inch shorter than any broken by the lieutenant. Triumphantly Gianonni thrust his small brown hand forward. Fatuous in his deception—a double deception—Gianonni cried:

"I stay behind with lieutenant's bag. Youse guys weel be bump off on damned gooda job!"

Gianonni had said nothing to the lieutenant. He accepted the condolences of the eight, who were cut that he had felt for an instant the false joy of safety. Until he had broken the straw, war had been happy turns, pleasures, excitements for Gianonni. He wandered out of the lines ten minutes after the eight had disappeared into the darkness filing behind the lieutenant on their way to the railhead. He loped parallel to them, twice picking them out as stalking shadows, when they stood still under the baleful glow of vagrant star shells. He tired of running parallel with them in the darkness, as a dog tires when quartering a stubble for his horsemen. He drew across odorous fields in the darkness, stumbling over furrows, turning aside for shell holes, throwing himself expertly flat when some shell left the droves above him to rush screaming down upon his solitary figure. He grew thirsty from dust and fumes, from the dry fields quilted in lazy patterns of smoke. He gained the dismantled village of the fields, and wriggled his small body through the water details clustered about the town fountain. The details were cursing, fretting under the warming they had sustained while cantering with their long poles, strung with clanking canteens and chains. He wriggled through them and thrice drank his canteen cup dry, apathetic to the thirst of the ninety left behind. Three quarts of water logged his small belly until it was distended puppy fashion within the girdle of his runner's belt. He was enervated, sleepy, sorrowful. He walked through the wrecked wall of a farm-house, stumbled into the best room, and stretched his body along an overturned grandfather's clock. He slept. Presently he awoke, as the hunted will awake, instantly. They were sending over heavy metal. He could hear its screaming overhead, bursting along the roads where water details, ammunition wagons, ration parties would not be scouring for friendly cover. A pang seized him when he understood that he had not awakened cheerily.

He counted his money as it grew light. There were nearly two thousand francs. He could never spend them all upon chocolate at the Y. M. C. A. wagons. Across the room a ladder ran to a loft. He mounted it curiously, and in the faint streamers of dawn filtering through displaced slates he saw two officers sleeping gently, maps and artillery glasses unslung beside them, telephone headpieces clapped upon one's dulled ears. He descended, moved about the house and found the room they occupied. There was a blanket roll in one corner. He unrolled it deftly, pleased when it discharged the uniform of a major of United States Field Artillery. The boots, their gloss slightly mildewed, were only a size too large for his small feet. But they were beautiful boots. He tiptoed in them; whispered martial commands at his image in a greenish pane of the casement. . . .

The long parade briskly climbed the hill of the Arc de Triomphe, the lieutenant haggard as was intended, stiff shoes galling his neglected toes, forehead sweating against his stinking tin hat. Somewhere in back of him were eight of his men, eight he had brought from overseas. The rest were gone, oh, anywhere, to hell if you like.

It was a dashing fine parade with heads up and tails over the dashboard. He could not look back pridefully, paternally. It was too fine a parade for an officer to relax his head for an instant, to turn a single degree out of the perfect alignment of heads identical with his own. Nor did he care to look back. For there should have been nine of his men. At the halt in the Place de la Concorde he had found himself checking up the eight as they leaned disconsolately, faces dulled, upon their rifles. Nine should have been there, with ninety back in the seven kinds of hell prepared for a Fourth of July moral. Nine here in the fragrance of scented women, where soft breasts brushed the lieutenant's elbow as he walked handsomely beside his right guide between shoals of women banking the channel of fresh blood . . . Scent of gloves, ribbons, silks, of violets, muguet, roses, and not a trace of salmon and phosgene and dank red earth.

The long parade was tortured past the Arc de Triomphe, moving outward towards the Bois. The lieutenant pranced to the strains of Stars and Stripes Forever, to the stains of the Marseillaise, Madelon, Over There, and Hot Time in the Old

Town Tonight. Gianonni seemed prancing at his heels. No need for the lieutenant to turn his head. Gianonni was there. He felt Gianonni's nearness, saw Gianonni with eyes in the back of his head.

The twisting mass of weary men streamed through avenues of green, canyons of white stucco, hordes of clacking tongues. The lieutenant grew weary, faint, bored again. He would have continued walking through eternity had he been offered the alternative to the lines. The parade halted near the Gare du Nord, a long earthworm disintegrating. Lists were checked. Officers barked. Sergeants swore. Men lifted aching feet from underneath other aching feet and cursed solid sheets of profanity. Sweat enriched the smells of them again, and the lieutenant cursed too. They were restoring his eight to him, and Gianonni was not among them.

The men limped into the station, to be parceled back to the ninety. The lieutenant was seized with anguish. Gianonni was dead. It was certain, for he looked at the clock over the train compound and saw that its hands were at five o'clock sharp, just when Gianonni would have begun straying about the lines having awakened from a day's sleep. The lieutenant fancied that he had returned, that a sergeant had given him Gianonni's watch. The sergeant would be saying that it was stopped at five o'clock sharp by the shell which had destroyed him. The lieutenant would find Gianonni's body before it was hastily covered with a light mantle of earth. . . .

The eight and their officer crowded into a third class compartment. They unslung equipment and relaxed upon the hard boards, grotesquely woven into a mass of tired beasts. The eight were instantly, triumphantly asleep. The lieutenant looked out upon the station crowds. He envied the small, sprightly artillery major who, back turned to him, was conversing animatedly with a piquante blonde. The pair stood beside a carriage marked Deauville. It was evident that the officer would presently mount the carriage and be whirled with her to cool sands, blissful hours.

Suddenly the eight awoke to the sound of the lieutenant's bellow of rage. The major was leaning half out of the window of the departing Deauville train, gesticulating to the lieutenant, saluting, grimacing. The lieutenant shook his fist savagely, frantically. But he knew, no matter what the alertness of the military police of Deauville, that the services of the best runner in France were lost to him forever. Presently the nine slept, returning to the ninety, in a lurching train.

George L. Stout
(1897–1978)

George Leslie Stout is best known as a pioneering art conservationist and museum director. He was born in Winterset, Iowa, and served in an army hospital unit during the First World War. After the war, he studied art at the University of Iowa and at Harvard University. He later joined the staff of the Fogg Art Museum, where he helped to develop art conservation as a scientific field of study. While at the University of Iowa, he met John T. Frederick, editor of the highly regarded literary journal *Midland: A Magazine of the Middle West,* and he provided the illustrations for Frederick's novel *Green Bush* (1925). He published two World War I stories in the *Midland* in May 1924. "Dust" and "Plumes" are companion pieces in that the former is set in an Iowa army camp and the latter in a field hospital at the front, representing a soldier's beginning and ending. Once again on active duty during World War II, Stout was an instrumental member of a group of Allied officers who saved masterpieces of European art from the destruction of war and the theft of the Nazis, a heroic effort detailed by Robert M. Edsel in *The Monuments Men.*

Dust
George L. Stout

Anyone familiar with Camp Dodge of the summer of 1918 knew a place of abounding dust. It lay on barren drill areas and beat into barracks leaving a pale crust on men and things. This had been flat prairie beneath a long low hill. Now its grass was trampled and sand clouds swept the open spaces.

Through this dust on an August day Mr. David Calvers trudged up an incline of a cantonment street. The sun was hot. Turfless soil and raw board buildings reflected it with bluish glow. There was no place of relief. The uniformity of heat and light, dust and bare boards, seemed endless, omnipotent. One of Mr. Calvers's pudgy hands brushed at his white moustache. His other hand held a parcel. He walked jerkily with a positive settling of his bulk on one side then the other. A captain passed and Mr. Calvers saluted with awkward cordiality; civilian workers were not bound to that observance. Some distance away a line of troops with full equipment passed into an obscurity of buildings and sand.

Over a small knoll where the street seemed to reach into the sky, a man came toward him. He was old yet there was something spirited about his gait, and about his thin aged figure. He wore dark civilian clothing. Dust enveloped him but he came on.

When the two were abreast Mr. Calvers spoke. He received no audible reply but something in the other's manner seemed to halt him, some unspoken command. They stopped. He looked at the eyes of the older man. Mr. Calvers always looked at eyes expectantly. They were likely to be gay or brooding, to say something. These, however, were silent: small, thick-lidded, inscrutable. The man sought there had apparently withdrawn behind the film of age, secure from an observing world. Yet they were kindly. At the band of the man's black hat was a line of sweat where dust had gathered. Mr. Calvers said nothing. There seemed to be nothing to say. The other raised one hand. A heavy thumb and forefinger pressed the edge of his blue coat. He spoke.

"Do you know a boy named Howard Lucas? . . ." The voice was low. "He's my boy. I've come over from Nebraska to see him."

"You have his regiment and company?"

"No." A weary suggestion of a smile met this query. "Howard never wrote but once." The man fumbled in his pocket. It was a movement of expectancy. The other waited. But after a pause the old man seemed to withdraw himself again. He only said, "Then he didn't tell me."

Mr. Calvers was not amazed at this. A camp full of young men sees little that is unusual. It was strange indeed that so many of them did scrawl out letters home. They were young, forgetful, caught in the romance of war, the fatigue of training. The old was not forgotten but it might well be thought to continue unchanged, not to be touched by this strange progression of sleep, trumpets, duty, men in uniform, men and barracks, everywhere.

Mr. Calvers looked into the faded eyes. One had to decide against impulse at times. Moreover the boys came first. It was for them that he had wheedled boards into acceptance of himself, schoolmaster of sixty, as a civilian employe. Shifting the weight of his package he began to speak, giving instructions about procedure at a personnel office. The smaller man nodded, dully. David Calvers turned away towards the rise of ground. Wind had slightly abated leaving the air more clear, and a bare slope at the knoll's top caught a pattern of shadow that made it look like a withered face. Mr. Calvers glanced back. The old man was questioning an officer in boots. Hardly with volition Mr. Calvers turned and pursued him.

"Excuse me." The larger man breathed heavily. "Your name?"

"It's Lucas. I'm Howard's father."

"Yes, of course. You must be tired."

"I might be." The old man laughed, a dry chuckle that came from deep in the throat. "I been tramping around for two days now."

"Then I make a suggestion. My place is at the Y. M. C. A. station a little way beyond. It's cool and quiet there. Come up with me. Tonight I've other matters but in the morning we'll take this to headquarters." Mr. Calvers looked for some light of hope or relief in the eyes. None was apparent. He shifted the packet again. "Will you go?"

"Yes, I'm much obliged to you."

They climbed the knoll together. Beyond it their progress was blocked by a company of riflemen returning from the range. The men moved at route step. They were sweaty. The backs of their flannel shirts were dark with sweat, and dust had settled on them. Under campaign hats were sunburned faces, dirty, damp with effort, strained or tired or careless. It was the end of a day. They were typical of the soldiery of those camps: seasoned sergeants, border service men, recruits from drafts, here and there a volunteer.

The last were different. Others might be in that column for many reasons; they were in it because they wanted to be. They wanted to be among men, doing what seemed to be a man's turn. In their faces, in their profane jibes, in the swing of their walk, was this fusing of youth and romance.

Wearily Mr. Lucas scanned each face. He apparently forgot his companion and the rows of barracks in the sun. The column passed. "There's a powerful lot of them." Mr. Calvers made no answer. They proceeded, quaint figures on the cantonment street, one in drab uniform ill-fitted to his stooping, heavy frame, the other walking with aged erectness behind an unreadable face. Then Mr. Lucas spoke again. "They drill different than we did. I was with Sherman." There was something positive, unquestionable, about that low, monotonous voice.

"Ah, indeed." Mr. Calvers puffed. "I was crawling then."

"We fought in daytime." He of the quiet eyes seemed not to have heard. ". . . . on horseback or in ranks, and when one went down we closed in. Now, some of the boys was telling me yesterday, they dig in trenches. And the gas—it must be bad." The two had been approaching an angular frame building which was painted dark green.

"We go in here." Jerkily, Mr. Calvers led the way up wooden steps. Inside were rows of plank writing benches. It was almost deserted. The heavy man took his visitor to a shaded corner where a breeze came in and eastern windows looked upon field and timber. "I have routine work to do. You'll find newspapers."

"This is a good place. You are coming back?"

"Yes, in about an hour. Have you gripsacks?"

"No. I get a clean collar at the store in the city, and go to a barber shop. I didn't figure to be away so long." He adjusted a pair of silver-bowed spectacles and reached for a newspaper. Mr. Calvers looked back. Sitting stiffly on a bench the old man was reading. His chin was raised. A lock of thin, grey hair fell forward almost touching his mild eyes.

Two enlisted men, the only other occupants of the room, were playing checkers. Passing, Mr. Calvers heard one say:

"Our last's tomorrow; major from Washington. . . . what I heard. He inspected the signal battalion Saturday, and they left Monday. Believe me, it can't be too damn' soon."

"Sure about goin'?"

"Surer 'n hell. Brother's with 'em. Camp Mills, then over." It was common talk at the time. The ——th division, made of drafts, regulars, and volunteers, was, outfit at a time, clambering on long shrieking troop trains and travelling to the East.

Mr. Calvers followed the cantonment street. He came to a hill at the north which overlooked the plain. Away from him stretched lines of barracks, irregular, serpentine. The lowering sun caught the barracks themselves in its red rays, throwing purple shadows on their eastern sides. They appeared trifling as they lay—thousands of them—playthings on the soil. Figures walked about them. Mr. Calvers heard footfalls behind him. An enlisted man passed. With his boy's face he was hardly an item in the playground below, yet linked with him were others, some dead, some living, family, future, a station in life. The youth went down the hill to the barracks in sunlight.

"Didn't mean to rouse you."

"You haven't, Mr. Lucas. We want to be down for breakfast at 5:30. The company with which I'm eating goes to the range today." Mr. Calvers smoothed the blankets on his cot. He sat down brushing at the white moustache with drowsy movements. A leather legging wrinkled into place under his thumbs. "You're dressed early."

"I'm used to it."

Mr. Calvers looked at his guest. The grey locks of hair were damp and combed; there was no other change. Calm of daybreak lay on the place like a translucent tone, touching faces, things, spirits. Beyond a gable window the eastern sky bloomed with its first crimson. Mr. Calvers began to move a razor along a strop. He could see the other man's head and shoulders at a window, silhouetted against the silver of morning, which held a distance of low gables over men asleep.

Mr. Calvers felt a wonder at the tenacity of life in this man. Something about him seemed eternal. Now near death he still went on, securely believing that the events of his days would come and go with fairness. Yet all of it lay masked. Any sleep that came in the night had not broken the barrier of his eyes. It was a kindly barrier, but it stood. Something beyond it was kept hidden from men, to go out of knowledge at his death. Mr. Calvers thought of the razor. He had been stropping it regularly for ten minutes and neither of them had noticed.

"I get up with the birds." Mr. Lucas turned from the window. "Howard was no hand to wake of a morning. Didn't know but he'd get into trouble down here with his sleepy-headedness. Reckon if he had, though, the boy'd 'a' let me know."

"Yes." Taking a scrap of paper from a neatly ordered pile, Mr. Calvers slid lather from the blade. "You don't know even his branch of service?"

"Couldn't make out. . . . Here's what he states in the letter." For the second time his hand fumbled in a side pocket of the blue coat. It drew forth an envelope which was dirty and worn. Big fingers removed the paper and set the silver bowed spectacles. He read.

"'I'm in the army at Camp Dodge. I couldn't stay away any more. I guess George can come over and help on the place though he like enough won't want to. They say here we're going over to France before long. I haven't anything against you.'" The old man folded the single sheet along edges perforated by wear. He looked up, his chin high, eyes discernible under the lenses. "That was all. He run off to go. . . . told his brothers first and they made a fuss; allowed I'd be mad about him leavin'. They're older and live on other places, sons of my first wife. I didn't know how it was till lately. They're older of course but it seems Howard and I was better acquainted. If it hadn't been for them I presume he'd have told me. There's many years between us but I understand the boy." He removed the spectacles and straightened a little. Dawn grey at the windows was warmed by approaching sunlight. "Me mad? Don't I know how it was? . . . Time I went to join Sherman." They descended into the street and strode away in gathering light.

At the notes of a bugle, barracks woke around them. Men in uniform came out. They formed lines, grinding cigarettes under boot heels, elbowing, cursing, laughing, bantering. Officers, puff-eyed from sleep, stood before commands. The two figures on the street paused at the flank of a company. In an open parade ground musicians gathered. The flag staff looked black against long-fingered purple clouds. A guard passed; disappeared behind a row of barracks. These angular buildings seemed at the moment to be the only homes of men like these, to encompass all youth in big board forms whose ruddy windows held the glow of its animation. A throb of drums and trumpets began in the open space. It continued a moment, then the full band broke into a reveille march. A flag rippled against purple and gold and grey. The companies stayed in line—there were formalities—but the two old men went down the street.

Taking it up with headquarters proved slower than Mr. Calvers had expected. It was a busy place. Men were leaving in thousands, and records were to be sent to Washington or to regimental officers or to fumbling company clerks. And men were arriving in tens of thousands: Scandinavians with names made of consonants, Greeks with names full of diphthongs, and negroes with no names at all and small hopes of finding any.

The orderly was curt. "Lucas? Howard? Try his regiment. Don't? Private; corporal? Don't know? Oh, my Gawd. Well, do the best we can. No, not today. Maybe tomorrow. Best we can. Hell's bells. Say, might try the base hospital. We don't keep records of patients—changes too fast."

A long corridor smelling of drugs lay sickly in the warmth of afternoon. Occasional doors were hung with forbidding white sheets. A cart passed bearing a prone man senseless from ether. Mr. Calvers looked at his companion. The tired eyes were unchanged.

"Seems Howard won't be in a place like this." Mr. Lucas was speaking. "He never could stand to be around sickness. Time his mother died, my second wife, he was all done up. She went quick: like a mornin' glory, I said. Howard and me and the doctor was with her through the night. Then a little after she was taken I found Howard lying across the sitting room doorway, clear unconscious. Things took him strong. I suppose that's why he listened to the older boys' talk."

A fingering of records at the office and receiving station showed that Howard Lucas was not in the place. Mr. Calvers caught himself saying, "So Howard isn't here." He had never seen the boy, yet he spoke of him like that.

"Still I guess he'll make a good fighter." The older man picked up his thread of retrospection. They were again in the street with its pouring sunlight and its sandy dust. "We used to sit by the well of warm evenings after the work was done, me telling him about the days with Sherman. I was his orderly, one of them. At Chattanooga I was hit early and finished out the day carryin' messages on horseback, with a broken leg."

Here Mr. Lucas gave that chuckling laugh from the throat. "And seemed like whatever else we'd be talkin' about, most always when it got dusk and the stars begin to come out, Howard'd say, 'Tell me again about Chattanooga, Pa.'"

Vague promises of personnel officials brought no result the third day. Men drilled on barren fields; sunlight glared through the hours, died; dusk dropped its veil on spaces and buildings; then the uniforms of men and the dresses of visitors moved through a clear darkness of starry night.

David Calvers was alone. He stood before a barrack, darker than the rest, where a single lamp threw its pale yellow on corner windows. The light attracted him. He went in.

Desks in the large office appeared huge and animate in the dark. Mr. Calvers knocked at a rickety door bordered by lines of silver. A voice said "Come," and he entered. At the desk of the small corner office sat a young man behind a litter of papers. The man was a captain. His shirt was open at the neck. The lamp above cast blocks of shadow in the sockets of his large eyes, under his full lips, and a strand of black hair on his brow glistened in the mellow rays.

"Well?"

"Captain, I have come here often, and with not much success. There is an old man looking for his boy whom we can't find anywhere. The man is from Nebraska."

"Hm—, too bad; but we can't get sentimental. Our job's to put men in the field." He ran his fingers through his hair. Mr. Calvers waited. "First night this week that our full force didn't work till taps. They need rest. But, damn it, we've got to get men in the field."

"I know, captain, what you say is true." Mr. Calvers looked wearily towards the door. "Yet I wish you could see this man. He's at my quarters now. All day, for many days, he has walked over this place. He's tired. But he'll do it again tomorrow. . . . He'll do the same thing tomorrow."

"Yes?" The captain's words were slow, and distant. "Well, war going on, you know." His lips were very red.

"I know there is a war." Mr. Calvers felt himself speaking emphatically. "I know what you've got to do. And I know about me also." The young man leaned forward; began to write. "I must do something. He's old. Why, he's at the end of a life. He came here to see this boy who is left to him in age. That is something, Captain." Mr. Calvers hesitated. The electric lamp seemed to flare with a white light. Of course it only seemed to. The man at the desk went on writing. "You see . . . some action. He can't go on so. And, in truth, that old man is unshaken. Nothing appears to halt him. Yet he must have something to take back to his farm . . . some assurance. Indeed, sir, it seems to me that all of fatherhood is looking at his chance, and waiting, too. I hope you'll pardon me." He turned to the door.

"Queer case." The officer spoke. He leaned back and his face went into shadow. He sat there for some time fingering a full under lip. "The man's old, is he?"

"He was in the war of the Rebellion. His age must be near eighty." Mr. Calvers had turned the knob. He waited then. Something in the other man's attitude was auspicious.

". . . . Well. I don't know. Come over in the morning. Bring him too. I'll see." Mr. Calvers made a movement towards the speaker. This small consideration seemed assurance. He felt tearful. He wanted to clasp the young officer's hand, to say some words of friendliness, but that man was very reserved. Mr. Calvers held back.

He said, "In the morning?"

"Yes." The officer made a notation of name, and possible dates. "At about ten."

"Good night, captain, and thank you."

A night breeze cooled Mr. Calvers's face. He looked up at the sky which seemed blue-purple and far away. Then his thoughts returned to the man he had left in quarters. At the moment Mr. Calvers pictured him asleep and felt somehow sure of the picture. He would sleep. That was the strength of him. The board walk, empty at that hour, appeared to welcome an impact of boot heels and resounded to them loudly. Another picture came: Mr. Lucas on his farm, a slight figure, moving among buildings, speaking to animals, looking at clouds, facing solitude with his boundless capacity to live, to accept life. The starry sky glowed venerably as if it alone in all that night could fathom the spirit of man.

In the hot morning a battalion stood at "rest" under full equipment. One man chanted "Over There" in a mocking voice. Another yelled: "Good Gawd, ain't we never goin' to move?" It was near ten o'clock. Sounds of their voices carried through the windows of headquarters barrack, where, by the shafts of yellow light, sat two old men on a raw board bench.

Mr. Lucas's hands were resting on his knees. They made Mr. Calvers think of wind-blown branches. He wanted to say something, for they had been silent, but he could think of nothing to say.

Mr. Lucas regarded his dust-covered shoes. "I'll have to get back before long. A man was going to say on the place for a week. But it won't take Howard and me much time. We can say what we've got to say." A fly settled on one of the large fingers, staying there unheeded while a square spot of sunlight shifted over floor cracks. The door opened and an orderly came out. The captain would see them.

That officer sat in a starched uniform as inviolate as the printed orders strewn before him. He nodded to the old men. They stood and waited. Sounds from the nearby formation had stopped. There was a quiet broken only by the rustle of papers in the building; the click of typewriters. Then sharp orders echoed between barracks and the street took up the shuffling thud of men on the march. Through the window was visible a line of trees far away and wavering in heat that beat upon intervening plain. The captain rose facing the two men, one of whom fixed him with quiet eyes.

Nervously the young officer moved some papers before him; glanced at a wrist watch; cleared his throat. "I found a record of Howard Lucas," he said. Mr. Calvers wished somehow that the man would stop speaking; he felt as if he dared not move. The officer continued. "It's unfortunate, but you can't see him. His regiment left five days ago."

Mr. Calvers turned to the father. He saw that straight figure unmoved. The deep-lined face seemed to be working on an uncertain problem. A momentary pallor had covered it, like a blue light on granite, something like that. He asked, "Does this mean that Howard will go to France?"

"Yes."

The old man's head sank, then lifted, showing eyes which held an unremitting calm. To David Calvers the trim captain appeared very familiar and impotent and far away, and his own shoes with wrinkled tips seemed utterly futile things. Dully through the room sounded the tread of troops outside.

Then Mr. Lucas said: "Now I'd better go back to the place. Howard will know where to come."

The two men parted outside of the building as the last of the battalion crossed the street. Barracks glared pale blue under the mid-day sun. Reaching an eminence Mr. Calvers turned and looked behind him. A swirl of dust blew about the straight old figure now moving at some distance, but the man walked surely on.

Claude McKay

(1890–1948)

Best known as a leading poet in the Harlem Renaissance, Claude McKay was born in Jamaica, where he published his first two books of poetry in 1912. In 1914 he moved to the United States, living most often in New York City. While working on Max Eastman's magazine the *Liberator* he published the poem that made him famous, "If We Must Die," in 1919. After some time in England and then in Harlem, McKay traveled throughout the Soviet Union on a lecture tour. His first novel, *Home to Harlem* (1928), a best-seller about a black soldier who deserts from the army, daringly portrayed African Americans in negative as well as positive terms. McKay's harsh realism and his outrage at white racism are clearly shown in "The Soldier's Return," which was translated into Russian and published in Moscow in a volume titled *Sudom Lincha* (1925). The extant English version is a retranslation into English that appeared in *Trial by Lynching: Stories about Negro Life in North America* (1977).

The Soldier's Return

Claude McKay

The soldiers returned from the war. In the small, rural town of Great Neck in Georgia, great excitement reigned. All that three thousand people could talk about was the return of the soldiers.

Everyone knew that our American boys had travelled across the ocean in order to sweep the Kaiser off the face of the earth, for on the trains and steamships in which the troops travelled, placards could be seen everywhere: We're off to Berlin. We'll break through the Hindenburg Line. Democracy Against the Huns. And so on.

The boys kept their word. They smashed the Kaiser and now were returning home in triumph. Like a hundred other American cities, Great Neck prepared itself for a triumphant "Welcome Home." The white population had sent 75 men to the front, the blacks 100; but 1,300 whites came to the station to welcome the white soldiers, and 700 blacks prepared to welcome the black soldiers. The authorities undertook everything that was necessary for the reception of 60 whites and 75 negroes, for of the total number of men mobilized, 40 fewer men were returning to their native town of Great Neck.

On the white blocks, special committees for welcoming white soldiers were created, and the various women's groups made common cause in order to plan a worthy welcome.

At four o'clock, with banners and flags waving, the train rolled into the station. The orchestra of freemasons started to play a national march with bravura. The mayor, the district attorney, the judge, the sheriff, the clergy of various denominations, all were on hand in order to give a triumphant welcome to the proud, victorious warriors of Great Neck. Automobiles carried the soldiers, together with the representatives of authority and "high society," to City Hall while enthusiastic, ordinary citizens ran behind, shouting and singing themselves hoarse.

The mayor gave a cordial welcome speech. His face was unnaturally red, as if it had been stimulated by alcohol. But it wasn't alcohol, since Georgia was a "dry" state. A law had been passed in the state forbidding the sale of alcoholic beverages, and the mayor, the chief pillar of the local Methodist Church, couldn't allow the law to be broken by anyone.

Mrs. Patricia Riglesby, in the name of a group of local ladies, presented to the young people a splendidly embroidered silk flag. When everyone had sat down to eat, the pastor of the Methodist Church tried the grape juice first, in order to reassure himself that there was no alcohol in it. Among the rows of tables, black waiters—male and female—slid silently and quickly. White aprons shone beautifully on the black suits of the men and black dresses of the women.

Towards eight o'clock in the evening the banquet was finished. The more important people began to disperse to their homes, while the soldiers and a crowd of their friends set out for one of the streets set aside as a place for carousing. The houses were decorated with American flags. Multicolored flags and lanterns swung on ropes extended over the street. Refreshments were served: ice cream, pies, and grape juice. Here and there girls, red from excitement, surrounded the soldiers, chattered gaily with them, and flirted.

Ah, how those young men who weren't wearing khaki that night envied them! Some of the young men had very old parents; others worked for defense, and

those who had "friends" in high places had doctors' certificates which testified
to their supposed lack of fitness for military service on account of varicose veins
or lung ailments. Now they burned with shame and indignation and swore at the
circumstances thanks to which they had not fallen at the front, since all the young
girls turned away from them and were interested only in the "heroes."

The orchestra began to play a one-step, and then a fox trot, and all the young
people began to turn in the whirlwind of the dance.

II

Two weeks later, on the four o'clock train, fifteen more black soldiers arrived in Great
Neck. The Black Belt at once started bustling, in order to give a proper welcome
to its worthy sons. Fraternal orders took upon themselves the duty of making the
necessary preparations. Among the general masses which met the black soldiers as
they arrived, five negro pastors stood out as representatives of the various denominations. Joyful black faces warmly greeted the soldiers when they got off the train.

A black mother in tears rushed to embrace her splendid, swarthy son. "The
Heavenly Father, Jesus has protected you my dear little son!" she exclaimed joyfully.

Among the black faces here and there stood out swarthy, half-white faces, and
there were also several octoroon girls whom it was difficult to distinguish from
whites. Four soldiers were mulattoes, and one was an octoroon whose commanding
officer had twice recommended for transfer to white regiments. But both times he
refused such an "honour," pleading that African blood flowed in his veins. Among
the white population of Great Neck the refusal of Frederick, the octoroon soldier,
produced lively rumours.

The procession set out for the African Methodist Church, and in front went
the orchestra, playing the march "Onward, Christian Soldiers!"

The black procession had been given permission to walk along the main street
of the white section, and the whites watched from behind closed shutters and
quietly snickered. Then the marchers stopped in front of the mayor's house, and
the mayor came out on the veranda and made a speech in which he welcomed
the black "boys" who had returned from the front. He declared that the war was
over, and so now they must take off their uniforms and return to the work which
they had done before the war. The negro pastor with black, shining features and
grey sideburns, replied briefly to the mayor, and then the procession again turned
towards the Black Belt and set out for the grey church on the hill. After the service
a banquet was given in the hall of the Daughters of Bathsheeba, and then the guests
broke up into small groups and conversed amiably.

III

Frederick Taylor, the octoroon solider, drove in a small cart along the road which led through a beautiful area of Georgia about half a mile from Great Neck. It was a splendid summer day; the air was saturated with the wonderful smell of southern roses and grasses. Frederick passed by an abandoned, semi-ruined, slave-owning manor. He had not succeeded in getting more than a few feet further when suddenly he heard an awful, heart-rending scream in back of him. He turned around in surprise and saw that, on the side opposite him, a white girl was running, screaming. He recognized her as the half-witted daughter of the postmaster. Frederick couldn't understand why the girl was screaming, but he didn't think about it much, and continued on his way to Richard Palmer's house. Palmer was a well-off negro farmer whose swarthy daughter Frederick was courting.

It was already evening when Frederick returned to Great Neck. The stars shone brightly in the sky. The evening chill on his face felt refreshingly pleasant. When he entered the main street which led to the white section and started to turn into a side street in the direction of the Black Belt, he was suddenly stopped by Sheriff Walker.

"Just tell me, Frederick, what did you want to do to Joe Campbell's daughter?" He turned towards the young man: "You'll have to come with me."

Frederick said that he had seen a girl running, but couldn't understand why she was running and screaming. The sheriff wasn't satisfied with his reply, ordered Frederick to follow him, and placed him in prison. He claimed that the girl had said that Frederick had stopped her on the lonely road and wanted to kiss her and take her with him in his cart. Every one knew that girl, Pauline, was half-witted and madly in love, but it was strange that she insisted so strongly on what she had said to the sheriff. Notwithstanding, Frederick was put in jail.

That same night the prison was surrounded by armed townsmen who appeared with torches, lanterns, a rope, and a can of kerosene. They demanded that the warden of the prison surrender Frederick to them, but he hurried off to inform the sheriff.

The sheriff tried in vain to quiet the crowd down; he pleaded in vain with those who had come that they should return to their homes. At the head of the armed band was the postmaster, Campbell, who had come, he said, to avenge the attempt to sully the virtue of his daughter. With terrible whooping and howling the crowd burst into the jail, got into Frederick's cell, and dragged him outside. While receiving blows on the head and kicks from all sides, Frederick pleaded for mercy, declaring his innocence.

Cries of "Lynch him. Lynch him!" came from everywhere, and soon the crowd began to grow with new men, women, and children. At the very peak of passions the mayor appeared, and succeeded in quieting the crowd in a minute. Climbing up on the stoop of the jail, he turned to the crowd and said that he himself had passed by the abandoned manor yesterday and seen how Pauline had run off screaming, but that there was no apparent cause for it.

This quieted the crowd, and it quickly dispersed; Frederick, Postmaster Campbell, the mayor, the prison head, the sheriff, and several idle spectators were left.

"Well, Frederick," the sheriff said as he turned towards him. "If they had lynched you, you would have had only yourself to blame. Pauline was frightened by seeing you wearing soldier's uniform. You know that in our town we don't like it when niggers wear soldier's uniforms. Indeed, you were told that you should quickly change your outfit, but for some reason what your elders said went in one ear and came out the other."

"Yes, Frederick," the mayor interrupted, "in our town there's plenty of work, thank God, and work clothes don't cost much. My brother has splendid work clothes in his store. But for some reason, you don't like to do anything and, moreover, you drive about in a buggy. One would think you were really some white gentleman. It seems to me, Frederick, that it's still necessary to place you under arrest and try you for vagrancy. We will take the uniform of a solider of the U.S. off you and give you an outfit which is more appropriate for you. In any case, we have to set an example. Niggers never learn prudence by themselves until we show them, good and proper, their place. There is still plenty of work for niggers in Great Neck. We won't put up with even one of them loafing without work and putting on airs, even if he was in France, and they treated him there just like a white man. You'll have to work in a chain gang for a few months, Frederick. Tomorrow we will give you that pleasure. It will be for your own good."

"Lock him up," he added, turning to the prison head.

Thomas Boyd

(1898–1935)

Born in Defiance, Ohio, Thomas Boyd enlisted in the Marine Corps in 1917. He fought in a number of major engagements, and in October 1918 was gassed during the battle at Blanc Mount. Through the intercession of his friend F. Scott Fitzgerald, Scribner's published Boyd's anti-war novel *Through the Wheat* (1923), which reviewers favorably compared to Stephen Crane's *The Red Badge of Courage*. Boyd also wrote biographies, short stories, and historical novels, including *Samuel Drummond* (1925). After his sudden death in 1935, *In Time of Peace* was published as a sequel to *Through the Wheat*. "The Kentucky Boy" first appeared in *Scribner's Magazine* in January 1925 and was collected in *Points of Honor* (1925).

The Kentucky Boy

Thomas Boyd

The letters S O S, so grouped, have a multitude of meanings. Coming from a ship at sea they are a signal of distress and a plea for help; used in common speech they apply to subjects which have become distasteful through repetition. But to John Goodwin those letters described the hellish invention of some especially adept fiend.

Draw a wavering line from Verdun through Château-Thierry, and in the area south of that line, from Toul to Marseilles, you will have Goodwin's S O S. It was a maze of training camps where men were taught to load a rifle; warehouses of food, clothing, and ammunition, general and sectional headquarters, military police, and hospitals—the service of supplies. And all of it filled Goodwin with a sharp disgust.

He would have said, as he lay in one of a row of white iron beds and glared at the swarthy hospital apprentice who was trying to bluster a wounded man into taking hold of a broom, that he had always hated the S O S, hated it instinctively from the moment he had heard of it. But this would not have been true. There had been a time, from March to June, when the service of supplies seemed a desirable place to be. Unexplored, it was greatly preferable to standing in a muddy trench four hours out of every eight, sleeping in a watery dugout, and eating corned beef and canned tomatoes. It had made Goodwin anxious for a minor wound which would take him to a bed with sheets and dry blankets, where his food would be cooked and served on a plate, and toward the middle of June, as he crouched in a shell hole, to the left of Vaux, his desire was fulfilled by the German artillery. One moment he heard a softly whirring noise, an explosion, and then through a cloud of thick, pungent gas he had rolled from his shelter, choking and gasping.

There was this to be admitted in favor of the S O S: at the evacuation hospital Goodwin had been given a bath and a clean suit of pajamas. And on the hospital train the Red Cross had given him a bar of chocolate. Other than that, nothing was to its credit. He had been made to stand in line for his food, his unlaced shoes sinking in the mud, a blanket thrown over his shoulders. He was told to make his own bed. The hospital attendants were bullies and thieves, the nurses were inattentive to the privates, and the doctors could have been less slip-shod in their treatment of the patients.

"All right, soldier. Snap out of it. Almost time for inspection."

Goodwin looked up, prepared to scowl, to curse, if necessary. But it was Hawthorne, so he asked with interest: "Got a cigarette?"

"Sure, I got a carton, but what good does that do? Yuh can't smoke in here." Hawthorne thrust his big brown hand in his jacket pocket and exhibited a package of cigarettes.

"Lord," Goodwin sighed. "But I wish I had my clothes."

"Git 'em," said Hawthorne with succinctness. "Git 'em."

Goodwin sat up, interested. " 'y gosh, I believe I will."

"Go ahead," encouraged Hawthorne. "An' we'll beat it outa here."

"Gosh——"

"Attention!" The hospital apprentice in charge of the ward shouted warning of the inspector's approach. A row of heads on either side of the room looked sharply toward the door; the patients in uniform stood stiffly by the foot of their beds, nervously smoothing out the wrinkles in the counterpane, and the medical officer, with a nurse and a sergeant following his bulbous hips, marched sternly into the room.

Goodwin, lying with his feet together and his hands flat at his sides, wondered whether Hawthorne would go, or whether he had only spoken lightly. A trip alone through the network of the S O S, with its military police and its railroad-transportation officers, would be disagreeable, but with Hawthorne to accompany him he could have "a hell of a lot of fun." And Hawthorne, even from the little he knew of him, was not the sort of person to say what he didn't mean. The inspecting doctor was approaching and he had to decide quickly.

"Sir, can I get my clothes?" He tried to work his features into an expression of health, eagerness, of a burning desire to fight in a holy cause.

The hips wedged in between the two beds, wedged out again, and from the wide aisle the sergeant wrote out a requisition and handed it to Goodwin, leaving him to wait, restlessly, until the undignified formality was finished for the day.

"Carry on," called the hospital apprentice as the inspecting officer left the ward. The bodies relaxed, turning to one another to rid themselves of pent-up speech. Hawthorne approached, pushing his unloved overseas cap to one side of his head.

"D'ja git it?"

Goodwin showed him the slip of paper.

"Come on, then. We'll see what we kin talk outa the quartermaster. You wanta take everything you can lay your hands on."

"Do you mean it, sure enough to go back to the outfit?"

"Mean it? Hell, yes, soldier. Jist watch me."

And with this assurance they walked out of the ward to the commissary, indistinguishable from the other buildings in its sallow complexion, its tarred roof, its eight little windows cut in the side, and the setting of drab mud where neither trees nor grass could be seen. Only officers, nurses, and important-looking non-coms of the medical corps strolled in twos and threes, planning dances at the hideous Y. M. C. A. or reminiscing over reckless supper-parties in the near-by town.

Inside the quartermaster building a bespectacled youth and a red-faced corporal stood behind a rough plank counter on which were articles of clothing. Goodwin handed the paper to the corporal, who passed it to the youth with spectacles.

"Size blouse ya wear?" asked the corporal.

Goodwin knew; he wasn't to be tricked into accepting ill-fitting garments. "Blouse, thirty-eight; underclothes, thirty-six; hat, seven and a quarter——"

"Matter a damn about that, buddy. I asked ya what size blouse you wore."

"I wouldn't let him call me buddy," Hawthorne seriously advised Goodwin. "I'd tell 'im the story of the apple and the——"

"Hey, let them pants alone," admonished the youth to Hawthorne, who was examining the stack of breeches on the counter. But Hawthorne imperturbably continued: "Git a good pair while you're at it, soldier. Here—" He drew a pair of whip-cord breeches from the pile and handed them to Goodwin. "Regular officer's britches, and they're jist your size. Now we'll pick out a blouse."

Half an hour later the pair walked out of the building, enjoying the luxury of cigarettes. "How do I look?" asked Goodwin.

"Well, the hat's ridin' a little high an' the britches look like they was full of bricks, but the coat an' leggin's fit you fine." Hawthorne regarded him closely. "Pull up the britches and tear the band outa your hat an' you'll look like a Jigadier Brindle."

Goodwin unbuttoned his new blouse and pulled at his breeches until there was an unbroken line between the end of his spiral puttees and his hips. "Guess I'll throw away that rain-coat," he said, tearing out his hatband.

Hawthorne took the rain-coat from him, drawing off in an attitude of surprise. "Soldier, you hurt me when you talk thataway. Why, that there rain-coat's good for forty francs any place in this country."

"You mean sell it?" asked Goodwin.

"Sell it? Not if we seen some pore ol' woman with ten orphans standin' out in the rain without anything to eat an' no place to go. No, we'd give it away then. But if we don't see this ol' woman, the forty francs is ourn."

Goodwin chuckled. "An' this extra pair of shoes ought to bring fifty."

Before the thought of their departure, its risks, the danger of arrest, the high-keying sensation of travelling alone through foreign countries, outwitting M. P.'s and officers, and the prospect of arriving again among their own, everything else dissolved in a mist. On other days the meals were grumbled over, but to-day the dinner's bad qualities, the lumps of tomato, the uncooked pieces of beef, were unnoticed. And in high excitement, they dipped their mess-kits in the lukewarm water, dried them on a borrowed towel, and marched busily to the extreme end of the camp, vaulted a wall, and were on the highroad, bursting with deviltry and joy.

This highroad would have conquered less robust spirits. For miles ahead of them and behind it ran a straight course. The mud was an inch thick, and very slushy; under their feet and out on the brown stubble of grass, large chunks of it had been thrown by the wheels of passing cars. In rear of them, Goodwin heard the chug of a heavy motor, and he looked in vain for a spot on which he might stand and be safe from the mud. The truck came on.

"Wait," said Hawthorne. "Let's ask 'em for a ride. Look and see if there's an officer in the front seat." There was none, nothing but red cords; and both men signaled wildly. The truck slowed down, and they climbed over the end gate and were hauled aboard.

"Hello, Artillery." Hawthorne's voice was neither high nor deep. It was rather a voice, medium to begin with, which had acquired terrible clarity through sounding over long fields and wide valleys. "How far ye goin'?"

"Le Mans," said the sergeant in charge.

"Where's that at, Artillery? On the way to Paris?"

"It's on the way, as you might say," answered Artillery. "You can take a train from there."

"That's the place we'll go; huh, Goodwin?"

They settled down in the end of the bumping, careening truck, smoking cigarettes until they could hold the shortened stubs no longer, and staring restively at the flat, damp ground on either side of the road. A few miles ahead, Le Mans was already to be seen, the buildings gray in the afternoon light. It had the appearance of great size, and Goodwin wondered if the entrances were patrolled by military police, who, no doubt, would arrest them when they were discovered to be without travelling orders. But they could do nothing but chance it now.

The truck rolled over the pavement of the city, past the steep-roofed houses, and stopped at the beginning of a row of small shops. "Far as we go," said Artillery.

"Much obliged," said Hawthorne. They climbed down from the truck and walked along the street. To the right and left and on the main thoroughfare Le Mans was filled with American soldiers who lounged in doorways, swaggered along the sidewalk, explored narrow streets, overflowed the bakeries and cafés, until it seemed unlikely that room could be found for two more.

"This is no place for us," said Goodwin. "Let's find the railroad-station."

"Let's have a drink first."

"There'll be a café near the station," said Goodwin nervously. "I don't like this town myself."

They walked on, unnoticed in the throng, until they saw the railroad tracks, two pairs of them on a black, cindery bed which rose above the street.

A picket fence secured the station from trespassers, but it was low and easily surmounted, Goodwin noticed with gratification. Nevertheless, it would be better to wait for evening to get a train. There were bound to be officers about the station. And the inevitable M. P.!

"There's the café," announced Hawthorne. "Now where's the drink?"

"Let's guess," said Goodwin, striding after Hawthorne's long legs, which were rapidly shortening the distance to a dilapidated brick building with musty windows.

The front room of the café was deserted, but in the rear a group of soldiers sat about a rectangular table, their blouses unfastened, their hats pushed high on their foreheads, with small glasses before them. One man, whom baldness had visited early and whose remaining hair grew about the scalp like a horseshoe, was talking with a great deal of smugness:

"Yes, and why shouldn't we be the best division in France? In the first place, we're selected men, and, in the second place, we're from New York. There's no bums among us. We didn't have to come into the army to make a livin'; we made ours in business."

Hawthorne sat listening, his drink untouched before him. He seemed very grave, as if he were intent on understanding all that was being spoken. Finally he asked, curious: "How long you been over here?"

The bald man stopped talking, smiled knowingly about the table, and answered: "Oh, about as long as you have, I guess."

"Have you ever been up to the front?" asked Hawthorne calmly.

"If we had you'd a seen our names in the paper, brother," said the bald man.

"What outfit did you say you was from?"

"New York's Own—selected division," said the man proudly. "What division are you from?"

"The First Division of Regulars," said Hawthorne.

"Oh," said the bald man superiorly. "You with them yellowbellies?"

Hawthorne got slowly to his feet, reached for the iron coffee-stand, and threw it deliberately at the bald spot. The iron weapon struck the wall, jangling harshly to the floor a moment after the bald head disappeared under the table.

"Why, damn you," said Hawthorne. He started to climb over the table, but Goodwin encircled his waist and coaxed: "Come on, Hawthorne. Let the poor fool alone. Can't you see he don't know any better? He don't mean anything; he jist ain't got any sense." Goodwin breathed hard through his exertion, but his arms remained straining about Hawthorne's narrow waist.

The bald head appeared at the corner of the table nearest the door, then ran. Hawthorne lunged to free himself, to reach the door, but Goodwin held on fast as the bald head bobbed out of sight.

"Gosh," said Goodwin, "I never seen anybody git under cover as fast as that in all my life."

"Damn lucky he did or I'd a brained him."

"Damned lucky he did or you'd be in jail long after the war is over." The consequences of such an act struck a cold chill down Goodwin's spine. "Gosh!" he shivered. "That iron thing would a killed him sure." In that event he too would have had to go to jail!

Madame came in to light the lamps, frowning over her task, every one of her movements showing disapproval of what had happened. She, too, would have been affected if the coffee-stand had struck the bald man. She would have been arrested by the American officers for selling cognac and her café would have been closed.

Goodwin pushed his glass away. "Let's git outa here."

In the street the evening made outlines of houses and shadows of doorways. A bell from the railway-station, somewhere over the raised ground and beyond the picket fence, struck up a warning of an approaching train. "Let's hop it," said Goodwin. He led the way up the grassy embankment, and grasping hold of the top bar climbed over the fence. There were red and green signal-lights, and men with lanterns moving about on the platform of the dimly lighted station. Then the train rushed in, throwing up a maze of ruddy sparks out of the mouth of the squat chimney. Goodwin, between the two tracks, followed the waiting line of coaches to the first-class compartments. "Hurry up," he called, unfastening the door, "We'll ride in style." It swung open and they hurried inside as the shrill little whistle made infuriated noises. The wheels turned and the train rolled out of the station.

Through a thick, concave glass inset in the roof of the compartment, the electric lights gleamed coolly on the gray covering of the seats, each with its triangular bit of lace for a headrest and separated from its neighbor by a padded arm. There were six seats in the compartment, three on each side, but Hawthorne and Goodwin were the only passengers. They sat facing each other by the window. Goodwin smoked, but Hawthorne gazed out at the hurtling scene like a shy but eager child. Colored lights on the railroad track, pin-points of gold through the darkness, clusters, fields of blinking lights in the distance, pale faces of girls outside the compartment as the train stopped for a moment, then went on. It was all very fascinating and mysterious. He grinned.

"Gosh!" Goodwin unexpectedly remarked. "Gosh, but I got a good outfit. A fine bunch. Wy, we wouldn't have a guy like that skunk in the café around us for more'n two minutes."

"So've I," said Hawthorne. "There's only one fellah in the whole lot that I can't git along with."

"Who's that?" asked Goodwin.

"Our damn mess sergeant."

"Oh," said Goodwin. "That's the way with all mess sergeants."

"No." Hawthorne slowly shook his head, as if he had fully considered Goodwin's explanation and found it lacking in truth. "No, soldier, I don't think so. Now you take our mess sergeant when we was up in the trenches last Febuary. We had it pearty tough up there, standin' watch four on and eight off, sleepin' in the mud and bein' et up by cooties, but do you think that damn mess sergeant'd ever send us down warm chow? No, sir. It wasn't that he couldn't a. The kitchen was in a forty-foot dugout where they had plenty of wood and plenty of grease-balls to keep things hot. But whenever I sent up a coupla men from my relief to git the chow, they'd always bring it back cold. No damn sense in it at all. So one day I goes up there with the chow detail. He was settin' down eatin' a big pie. 'Lenz,' I says to him, 'Lenz, how come we never get any hot chow?' He looked at me and mumbled: 'I guess your chow's hot enough.' 'Lenz,' I says, 'you're a damn liar and you know it. An' I'll tell you somepm else; if our chow's not hot to-day I'm gonna raise hell.' Well, he stands up at that and begins to git excited. 'Don't you call me a liar or I'll put ya out of here.' That made me peeved. I never liked 'im anyways. 'Lenz, you come here,' I said; and when he didn't come I went after 'im an' we tangled. I pounded that guy until my knuckles looked like raw meat, an' then I set out to kick hell out of 'im. I'd a done it too if they hadn't a ganged up on me, but what kin ya do aginst four grease-balls and a damn lieutenant?" Hawthorne made a deprecatory gesture with his big, brown hands, his first movement since he had begun his story. In fact, he made no expression of any sort, his voice remaining at the same droning pitch.

"Je's," said Goodwin. "Too bad you didn't wait till some dark night. I suppose they socked you in the hoosegow?"

"Sure they did. 'You'll fight the war from the bull-pen, Hawthorne,' says the lieutenant. 'Yes, sir,' I said, 'and it's a damn good thing for that Lenz too, because if I ever git at 'im agin you won't have no evidence left to try me with.'"

"Gosh," said Goodwin, "you oughtn't to have said that. I'll bet that one crack put three more months on your sentence. No, sir, I wouldn't a said that, Hawthorne."

Hawthorne grinned. "So they put me in the bull-pen, an' it was a hell of a sight better'n doin' four on an' eight off. It was at first, anyways, 'cause I didn't have any work to do. Then we moved back to a rest camp where the rest of the gang drilled an' dug trenches all day long. I was jist gittin' used to settin' around again when they sticks me in front of a guy with a bayonet, give me an axe an' puts me on the wood-pile, splittin' rails for the kitchen stove. An' there wasn't nothin' else to do but swing that axe all day. Then on the second day I was out there at work with that sentry behind me an' I saw Lenz comin' along. He didn't see me at first, an' I went right on choppin' until he got within about ten feet of me. He was walkin' along, lookin' at the ground, and all at once he looks up an' sees me. He laughed, so I jist let loose of that axe an' shied it at 'im."

"Je's," said Goodwin, horror-struck. "Did it hit 'im?"

"No, damn it. Only the handle. An' off he limped to report me to the O. D."

Goodwin shook his head. "That'd mean a general court in my outfit. We've had guys sent to Leavensworth for less than that."

"It's a general in ours, too," said Hawthorne coolly. "An' I'd a got it except that we got shoved up to the front again. The day before we left, the captain comes in the bull-pen an' says: 'Hawthorne, we're goin' up to the front to do a job that'll make that other time we was in the trenches look like a sewin'-bee. Now you can take your choice: you can stay back here in the guard-house or you can go up in the front line an' let me see what you're made of.' 'All right, sir,' I says, 'I'm rarin' to go, but you better keep me away from that damn Lenz or I'll take him for a Squarehead.' 'Lenz won't be up there, you needn't worry about that,' says the captain, an' the next day we broke camp." Hawthorne paused.

"I guess your outfit wasn't up with us at Cantigny, was it?"

"No," said Goodwin. "We was up around Château-Thierry."

"Well, anyway, we went into the trenches at Cantigny the next day, an' them Squareheads seemed to know the minute we got there. They throwed everything they had at us: sea-bags, Jack Johnsons, whizz-bangs, Lord only knows what. An' there we was, in that old muddy trench, listenin' to them shells bustin' all around. Pow! pow! powie! they went, an' when they stopped an' we stuck our heads up over the firin' bay there was a nice thick line a Dutchmen pokin' along up to our trench. Y'ever seen 'em come over? They don't look human, do they? Maybe it's them long gray coats or maybe it's them funny-lookin' helmets that come down over their heads like flower-pots, but they sure don't look human. Then it might be the long bayonets—" Hawthorne speculated carefully: "Well, I don't know, only I say they don't look human. 'N'en I got a crazy feeling that they was goin' to come right over an' step right down in our trench an' chase us out. 'Cause you couldn't kill nowheres near all of 'em even if we did smoke up the old barrels of our rifles till they was too hot to hold.

"But as I was gonna say, on they come, an' it looked like good night for us, when our own artillery opens up and lays down a barrage so thick it looked like rain. You could see the Squareheads sort of stop an' break up a little an' then come on agin, but our machine-guns caught 'em in an enfilade fire, an' the first thing we knowed somebody blowed a whistle in our trench an' everybody started yellin' 'Forward.'

"'So it's up an' at 'em!' I says to Crawford in a kind of a joke, but he hadn't anything to say. Something had walloped him in the head. Well, it was tough work gittin' outa that trench. The mud was so soft an' the trench so deep an' the barb wire so tough I thought I never would git out. An' then we starts over that yellow ground, dodgin' into shell holes and gittin' up and runnin' like rabbits toward the Squareheads' trench. I got about half-way there an' that was all. They got me jist below the knee with a machine-gun bullet." Hawthorne stopped talking, bent over, and carefully unwrapped his cloth puttee. Between the calf and the knee was a bandage, already soiled around the edges, in the centre of which a crimson bit of rust was showing.

"Gosh," said Goodwin, "you better be takin' care of that dressing or you won't have any leg left." He paused, staring down at his hobnailed boots in a bewildered manner. "You sure was lucky, Hawthorne. You got away with murder," he said slowly. Of course it was Hawthorne's own business if he wanted to carry on in that way, but Goodwin could not approve of it. There was something about Hawthorne's experience that flouted natural laws. It was almost an insult to the whole body of soldiery that he could pummel a non-com, be arrested, and, while under guard, deliberately throw an axe at the same non-com, and then not be punished for anything. But Hawthorne had learned his lesson; no doubt about that.... Poor old Hawthorne. He sure would be in bad if he and Goodwin were taken up by one of the military police. Why, with his record, he would get life imprisonment. He never should have gone with him on this escapade. He wouldn't if he had known the trouble Hawthorne had been in. But now that he had gone, had abetted him, almost, it devolved upon him to keep Hawthorne from the clutches of the M. P.'s.

"Hawthorne," he said earnestly, "I don't think we oughta go to Paris. It's too damned dangerous. I guess it's a great city, all right, but we ought to see it from the picture-cards this time."

"Soldier, you don't wanna miss Gay Paree. It's a bon *sector*. That's where everybody goes."

"I know it is. The M. P.'s is there, too."

"How will we git back to our outfits if we don't go to Paris?"

"Well, I didn't mean not to go there, exactly, Hawthorne. Course we got to go there to change trains. But there'll be a lot of M.P.'s at the station we come in at, an' I thought we could jump off at a suburb an' take a street-car through town to the other station."

"I s'pose it's all right," said Hawthorne, "but I'd like to see some of the town."

"Well, we can see it from the street-car."

"Lord, soldier, I don't mean thataway," said Hawthorne gloomily. "Besides, they'll see us at the station we go out at, anyways."

"Yeh," considered Goodwin. "But they don't bother yuh if you're goin'; it's only when you're comin' in that they pick yuh up."

"I thought you wanted to see Paris, soldier?"

"I did." How strongly he wanted to see Paris, how long he had been fascinated by tales of the Café de la Paix and the Folies Bergère, the Apache district! For a moment he weakened, but a moment only, for at the end of this merriment he saw Hawthorne in Saint Anne's Prison, with a service record that was black as ink, and charged with being absent without leave. "I don't want to now, though."

"Cold feet?" asked Hawthorne.

Goodwin gulped: Cold feet! But the train was speeding to Paris, Saint Denis was the next stop, and the matter must be decided at once. "Yeh," admitted Goodwin.

"All right," grinned Hawthorne, "I won't ditch ya, soldier. When do we git off?"

The train was slowing down, and before it had fully stopped they had jumped from the compartment to the cinder walk where an Ancient in a horizon-blue cape patrolled the premises with a swinging lantern.

Before them was a five-foot fence which terminated in a gate beside the brick wall of the station. The sign, Sortie, was above the gate, and before it stood the ticket-collector taking slips of pasteboard from the passengers.

"Don't let 'im stop us," cautioned Goodwin.

Stepping quickly, with a sense of onslaught, they approached the gate, smiled at the collector, and—were halted. A ticket was demanded.

"Americain soldat," answered Hawthorne.

The explanation did not serve. Barring the exit, the collector repeated his demand.

"What?" asked Hawthorne, leaning over the Frenchman, as if he thought distance to be all that prevented him from understanding.

"Ticket, comme ça, comme ça!" The Frenchman, growing irritated, held out a ticket which he had taken from another passenger, to show what he wanted.

"No savvy. I don't git ya, mister." Hawthorne slowly shook his head.

The collector danced in his exasperation over these Americans. "Ticket, ticket," he shouted.

"I don't know what you mean!" Hawthorne's voice was yet louder. "Here, how's this?" He reached in his pocket, withdrew his hospital order for a wound chevron, and held it forth.

The Frenchman violently shook his head.

"Tell 'im we're goin' back to our outfit, Hawthorne. Mussear, Bosche! Bing, bing! Toot sweet! Allemande. Knock hell out of the whole bunch!" Goodwin gritted his teeth at imaginary Germans, lunged with an imaginary bayonet, pressed an imaginary trigger, and smiled ingratiatingly.

The Frenchman cursed, waved his hands, and despaired. They passed out into the street, gay in their achievement.

No street-cars were to be seen, but an English soldier whom Goodwin hailed piloted them to the Metro and gave them directions to the Gare de L'Est. And so, while the stage of the Folies Bergère was a tantalizing mist of gauze and flesh, while a field clerk paid for the dinner of a cocotte at the Moulin Rouge, while a respectable line-officer lay prone on a bench by the Sacre Cour, and while the military police sleuthed the streets, Goodwin and Hawthorne rumbled through the bowels of Paris—the city of their latter dreams—to take the train for Toul.

Goodwin saw the dawn from a third-class coach in which he sat half-smothered by a detachment of French soldiers. He wondered how it was possible for Hawthorne to sleep. His charge was sprawled on the floor of the coach, his head resting on the feet of a snoring poilu and his legs serving as a pillow for another.

Not that Hawthorne's position was too uncomfortable for rest. Goodwin himself had lain that way innumerable times. His wonder was that Hawthorne could forget about his peril. He was, as Goodwin saw it, in a dangerous position. If the least thing happened to him to cause his arrest, his past record would certainly be the cause of his going to jail. At this instant, if they were seen by a military police, a railroad-transportation officer, in fact, any commissioned man, Hawthorne would be arrested, and when the court-martial board saw his record he might be tried for desertion. How could he explain that he was going back to the front? Goodwin worried, looking out the window at the green and brown rectangular fields, the gray farmhouses, the villages clustered on the quiet hilltops.

Soon they would arrive in Toul, and if they got off the train and through the city without being challenged, Hawthorne would be comparatively safe. But Toul was a divisional headquarters. Officers and soldiers would be at the station. It would be useless to attempt to pass the ticket-collector. But they could, by leaving the train by the left side instead of the right and walking across the tracks, avoid the collector completely. So Goodwin schemed for the welfare of his friend while the friend slept on, in a mass between the seats, ignorant of Goodwin's scheming.

Toul tells its mediæval story by the thick walls, the moat which surrounds it, the turrets, with long slits for the archers, rising above the walls and looking out over the calm, fertile country of wood and farm. Goodwin saw it from the window; shook Hawthorne by the shoulder. "Get up, Hawthorne, here we are," he called.

"Huh! Where?" Hawthorne disentangled himself and sat up, staring at Goodwin.

"We'll be at Toul in a minute an' we'll have to git off the minute the train stops."

Hawthorne grinned. "All right, soldier, I guess I kin say 'No savvy' to the Frogs."

"I gotta stunt, Hawthorne. When the train stops we'll get off on the wrong side an' beat it while the coaches are still standin' between us an' the station."

The train slackened, jerked, the bumpers of the coaches struck and recoiled. Goodwin raised the latch and opened the door.

With Goodwin leading, they trotted across the tracks, cleared the fence, and followed the street which led through the outer gate at the north. Suddenly Hawthorne halted.

"I don't know about you, soldier, but my laig hurts and I want some chow."

"Come on, Hawthorne," Goodwin coaxed. "We're nearly there now. We'll be at our outfits by noon. Maybe we can find a farmhouse along the way."

"Hell," said Hawthorne sceptically, "we won't see our outfits afore night, an' you know it. Besides, it's nearly all evacuated district between here an' the front."

"Come on, Hawthorne. The streets'll be full of soldiers in a minute an' we'll git run in," Goodwin pleaded.

Hawthorne resigned himself. "An' me with a gimpy laig," he said.

They walked under the heavy gateway to the road, a white ridge bending along green slopes past the walled town and through a wood where the ground levelled. There, the road was straight, with an appearance of coolness beneath the overhanging boughs. They walked without speaking. Hawthorne, because of the not-quite-healed wound in his leg, employed a kind of ploughing gait, and from time to time Goodwin would regard him stealthily, jealously, then look straight ahead again to the point where the road narrowed into nothingness. He was satisfied with himself, pleased with his success in bringing Hawthorne back to his outfit safely. If it hadn't been for him, Hawthorne would certainly have been arrested. And with his record! He would have been thrown in jail for the rest of his life. But now Hawthorne could go back to his outfit and live down his attack on the mess sergeant. At any rate, Hawthorne had learned his lesson.

In rear of them the revolutions of a motor sounded, and as they looked back they saw an ambulance speeding toward them. The brakes tightened, the rubber seared, skidding on the gravel, and an obliging driver stopped.

At the back of the car they sat facing each other on the long, leather-covered seats. Signs of the front grew more numerous each moment. The evacuation hospital, the camouflaged supply dump, the long-range guns hidden in a cellar and covered with leaves, the mended road, the concrete machine-gun emplacement—they passed all of them.

At a crossroad the ambulance stopped. To the left was a shell-raked farmhouse, headquarters of the brigade to which Hawthorne belonged. To the right, far beyond the blue-black woods, lay Goodwin's troops. Goodwin held out his hand.

"Well, Hawthorne, what'll you do when you git back to your outfit?"

"Hell," said Hawthorne, tightening his webbed belt and grinning, "I'll report for duty an' then carve my name all over the face of that Lenz."

"Who?" asked Goodwin.

"Lenz, the mess sergeant."

"Oh," said Goodwin dully, far down in his throat. . . . "Well, so long, Hawthorne."

As he turned to the right he was sickeningly aware of the distance he had yet to go and the fact that he was very hungry.

Elliot White Springs
(1896–1959)

Elliot White Springs was born into a wealthy family in South Carolina. While a student at Princeton, he joined what would become the U.S. Army Air Service. He saw combat as a pilot and was credited with eleven enemy kills. His first book, *War Birds: Diary of an Unknown Aviator* (1926), was largely autobiographical, though purported to be about and by another pilot. His numerous short stories about World War I pilots were collected in *Nocturne Militaire* (1927) and *Above the Bright Blue Sky: More about the War Birds* (1928). His novel *Leave Me with a Smile* (1928) describes the homecoming of a veteran combat pilot. "Big Eyes and Little Mouth" appeared in *Nocturne Militaire*.

Big Eyes and Little Mouth
Elliot White Springs

At odd times during my trip abroad with the A.E.F. and B.E.F. I made some notes. And at odd times since I have taken up these notes and tried to piece together a connected narrative dealing with some of the events and persons that appeared on my horizon. But I was never able to finish one story until recently, when Chance, or perhaps Fate, made a tale of what was but a few scattered names and dates, and furnished a climax to some drab events.

But this is not strictly a war story. It is a story which may bring back to you the distant rumble of the guns or stir the memory of some long-forgotten music; but it is not martial. My friends do no great deeds of valor. They are not called out before the regiment and kissed on both cheeks by General Foch. They are not invited to lunch with the Prince of Wales. With this assurance you may proceed.

There are several sheets of notes made in Scotland. Back in January of 1918 there were twelve American Flyers stationed at Ayr, at the Royal Flying Corps School of Aerial Fighting and Pilots' Pool. My notes mention names, approximate flying time and the number of statues of Robert Burns in Ayr. Then there is a long list of funerals and a part of this strange tale.

Ayr was the last step in the training of the British pilots before they were sent to the front. After an officer had taken his ground school course at Oxford or Reading for eight weeks, had learned to fly at the training squadrons, and had passed his aerial gunnery tests at Turnberry, he was sent to Ayr to be taught the delicate art of aerial maneuver and stunting *de luxe*. There he was kept until needed at the front.

The twelve of us were the first contingent of a hundred and fifty Americans who had been sent to England from the American flying fields in midsummer to take the complete training course with the R.F.C. This we had done. We had taken the ground course at Oxford, the machine-gun course at Grantham, and learned to fly at Hounslow, Croydon, and London Colney. Now we were getting the final polish and waiting for orders to the front.

Tap Johnson, Jim Watson, and I were rooming together. We had done so off and on for nearly a year. We had met at the Curtiss school at Newport News where we began our careers as pilots under Vic Carstrom, whose tragic death was one of our first shocks of the war. We were sent to different Ground Schools and met again at Mineola to be mobilized for the trip to England. We were together at Oxford and had spent our holidays together in London when the weather was too bad for flying at the squadrons in the suburbs. Now we were trying to arrange to go out to the front together.

We had finished the necessary stunt flying and were awaiting orders from the American Headquarters in Paris. But Paris would have none of us. We hoped to go out with the R.F.C. We did not share General Pershing's ambition for an Army all our own. We considered ourselves a part of the R.F.C. and we liked the British. And to us it seemed that the British had a real grievance against the Huns. We saw the wounded and gassed, and witnessed a few bomb raids. Our own reasons for entering the war were rather obscure to us.

The British Officers—Canadian, Australian, New Zealand, and South African, as well as English and Scot, passed through in several days. On a good day at the front, when the skies were clear, rival patrols would meet high above the clouds, and several dozen of the youngsters would be sent out to take the places of those who did not return. A week of bad weather at the front when no flying was possible, and several hundred would be waiting. It was a perpetual wake, as every night there must be a farewell party to those who left on the midnight express.

While we waited we kept in practice by fighting sham battles over the harbor. We flew the little Camels, so called because they had a hump on the body where the two machine guns were mounted. They were very small and very fast. One man could just squeeze in behind these guns which fired straight ahead through the propeller. They were so small that the torque of the big hundred and forty horsepower rotary motor would turn them over if the pilot took his hands or mind off the controls. And for that reason they could not turn to the right, which was against the torque.

We had a week of good weather and bad flying. The little Camels killed six good pilots who, like Lot's wife, turned—not back but to the right. The younger pilots were nervous and avoided the airdrome. Those who did venture aloft were unduly careful. And this is the face of the impending trip to the front where undue care was not welcome! Careful pilots were good only as instructors, and we were not to be instructors until we had lost our nerve or a limb. The colonel diagnosed this condition as a common complaint—the "wind-up." It must be cured, so he ordered all pilots on the airdrome.

Now this particular colonel had lost a leg and an eye. He wore the V.C. and the D.S.O. There was a rumor that he came by all these things when he was doing something that the others were afraid to do. And it had required the unerring aim of the great Richthofen himself to stop him.

The colonel herded us together and made a little speech. He told us that there was no need to be nervous over a Camel. They were very gentle little machines, a mere toy in the hands of a good pilot. And they would turn beautifully if we would only do it properly. All we had to do was to hold the nose up and skid—very simple—watch, he would show us!

He limped out to a machine and, without donning either helmet or coat, took off. As he cleared the trees he pulled up in a steep climb, called a zoom, and gently pulled his nose over to the right with the rudder. It was a skid, not a turn, and nothing but the powerful motor pulled the little Camel around to the right and straightened out its course just as the nose began to drop. Then he went wild. He looped and rolled so low that he would appear to be diving into the ground just as he would pull up with a roar. Then he would climb and spin, first to the right and then to the left, coming out into a quick dive and a roaring right skid only when it looked too late. We were all dizzy when he landed and advised us to practice these simple tricks which would help us in a tight corner at the front.

He told Jim to go up and show us what he could do. Jim was pretty good. He could fly upside down longer than any one else at Ayr. So he got in the same machine and took off. He skimmed over the surface of the field until he had his full speed and then pulled up in the same zoom and skid. His zoom was steep and his skid sharp. As his nose wavered he pulled it sharply to the right. He was nearly straight again when his motor choked and cut off. Then we saw him push the nose of the machine down to try to regain his speed. The motor was spluttering as his right wing dropped and it came on again with a great burst of smoke. But it was too late. There was a terrific crash as he hit the ground, and a pillar of flames shot into the air a hundred feet. We could see it from where we stood.

With leaden feet Tap and I walked over to the line of machines and inspected them in a perfunctory way. Then we, too, went up. We stunted madly, following each other wildly from loop to dive in an effort to avoid the horrible nightmares that otherwise would have followed us. For to see a crash is often to lose your nerve. The sooner you fly again and dispel the phantom of fear, the sooner you will get over it. Some men have put off this test flight for a day—and have never flown again.

Then came the funeral and the official inquiry. We were ordered to pack Jim's effects, pay his debts, examine his mail, and write to his family. It was a gruesome task and reduced us to a shameful state of drunkenness before we finished it. We opened his mail and extracted all valuable enclosures and bills. The letters were burned unread. They were mostly from his wife, who had married him in New York four days before he sailed. We contemplated this fresh victim of war and became maudlin.

There was a package from London. It contained a handsome wrist-watch, with a card inscribed: "Love from Sheila."

I knew all about Sheila. Jim had met her at a dance at the Grafton Galleries and was much excited about her. She had proceeded to fall madly in love with him, and he had spent most of his time in London with her after that. He said something about having her come up to Ayr and take a house. This brought on a long argument. I told Jim that I thought it was pretty rotten sportsmanship.

"But," said Jim, "haven't you heard the news? There's a war on! All is fair in love and war. And here we have a surprising amount of both of these commodities. I didn't start this war and I won't finish it. I am the proverbial bystander that always gets crowned by the flying fragments. Shall I bury my talent? My allotted span of fourscore years and ten is about to be all shot to hell to make Democracy safe for the Belgians. What do I get out of it? Requiescat in pace! All right, but I am not dead yet. Haven't you seen the pictures of the boys picking flowers on their way up to the front? Well, that's me. And, oh, boy, what an armful of tiger lilies and snapdragons I have picked! Sometimes I think that war is not as bad as it has been painted. If it just wasn't so dangerous!"

"Yes," I said, "that's all right for you. Some like 'em hot and some like 'em cold. But you forget that your wife is entitled to something more than a ring. You might at least have a little dignity."

"It's a shame you haven't a wife. You and Tap could uphold all the traditions that you so painfully view me upsetting."

"Then why did you get married?"

"Oh, there are lots of things that will ever be obscure. Why did you enlist? Now don't tell me, I'll guess. By the way, she has a friend, a nice well-behaved little friend who just loves aviators. I am going to give you the privilege of making it a foursome."

"No, thanks," I told him; "I am virile enough to pick my own. I pity your wife."

"No need to," he replied. "Can't you see that as far as she is concerned I am dead already? She's in America. You know what chance any of us have of getting back. We're half ghosts already."

And so the argument had ended. But he and Tap got quite heated on the subject and after that it was avoided.

"I guess," said Tap glumly, as we discussed the wrist-watch and went over his personal property, "there may have been something in what Jim said, after all. If there is anything to make this damn war worth while, I'm for it from now on. The more the powder, the brighter the fireworks. I vote we save her a pair of his wings to go back with the watch. And we ought to write her, too."

"All right," I said, "but just how will you address her? I haven't the faintest idea what her name is or where she lives. Have you?"

"No," he admitted, "I haven't. I've never met the lady. But we'll keep them and find her when we get to London."

But this didn't solve the problem. Several letters came from Sheila and then a telegram: "Where are you?" But we couldn't answer, so there was nothing to do but wait.

The weather was rotten during January and but little flying was done. We sat around the Dalblair Bar for a few days and mourned for those who followed Jim on the back of the Camel. Then Carol Banks came over from Turnberry and moved into Jim's room. We were glad to see him, and he set out at once to inject the necessary cheer into our dismal mess by making gallons of eggnog.

Our orders came through the last of February, and we went down to London to get our back pay and new assignments. We were not to go out to the front yet; Paris had not decided what they would do with us; but the British were short of pilots and were to use us to ferry planes to the front.

We inquired for Sheila without success and in three days I got the first assignment. I was to go to Norwich and get a Camel from the factory and fly it over to the front via Folkestone and Boulogne. Then I would get an old one and fly it back. It would be used for a school bus. This was the job of the ferry pilot and, outside of the thirty miles over the Channel, was pretty easy.

I ran into some bad weather, and it was five days before I was back in London. Tap was still at the Savoy and was well wrecked. His eyes were bleary and his hand shook as if he had crashed. He said he had. I got the story out of him with some difficulty and it required much unraveling. It was hard to tell which was Tap and which was the liquor speaking.

It seemed that the day I left he had gone into the Savoy lobby looking for some one to eat lunch with him. There was always a crowd there—pilots on leave, pilots out of hospitals for the afternoon, headquarters officers and various girls—always some one we knew. But Tap didn't see any one that he knew, and pilots are always lonely. He was sitting over by the window trying to make up his mind whether to go on into the bar and light up or use the telephone, when a very pretty girl sat down beside him. Here the story would halt indefinitely. Tap wanted to convince me that she was beautiful. I would admit it but he would refuse to leave the subject. She has big blue eyes and a little rosebud mouth. That was all he seemed to have noticed. And lots of blonde hair of a rather uncertain shade. She certainly wasn't a lunch-eater, Tap decided, but he couldn't take his eyes off her. He was fascinated. Finally she spoke to him:

"I can see that you are an aviator," she began. "Would you mind talking to me a little?"

Tap assured her that nothing else in the world would give him as much pleasure at that moment. Then she asked him where Jim Watson was. Tap told her rather carelessly. She blew up and got hysterical. Tap got her out of the Savoy and into a taxi and rode her around for a while. He tried to soothe her, but you couldn't imagine Tap soothing any one.

"There, there," said Tap, making a few passes at her shoulder, "don't cry. We've been looking for you everywhere. You've heard of us from Jim, haven't you? Well, we've been trying to find you but we didn't know your name and we didn't know your address and we couldn't find any one that knew you, so we couldn't very well tell you about it, could we? But we knew how cut up you would be over it and we brought you his wings and the wrist-watch you sent him. They are at the hotel, and I'll get them for you later."

Tap said she didn't seem to like this a bit. She wanted to know how he got the wrist-watch and why. She wanted to know just how he happened to hear of her and exactly how much he knew about the whole matter. She made him go over it several times and still she wasn't satisfied. She began to cry again, and Tap tried another tack.

"I suppose you know he was married," Tap said, but she only cried the more. "Yes, married just before he sailed. We never saw her as it was sort of sudden." This seemed to really upset her, so Tap tried to soothe her by going on:

"You mustn't let that worry you. Everybody at home got so excited about the war and tried to get married. All the girls wanted to marry a soldier—any soldier would do. It was supposed to be patriotic. Meant little or nothing. Just a game of catch-as-catch-can. Not as much as you and Jim. I dare say Jim was lots fonder of you. Oh, yes, he was. Must have been. Talked about you a lot. He was a prince,

Jim was. Everybody liked him. But I thought I had better tell you about his wife and tell you not to write home to his people. A girl did that when Kester was killed and it caused no end of trouble. So don't write his family. That's a good girl. I knew you wouldn't. Be a good girl and stop crying, too. You give me the willies. I'll be wishing I was Jim in a few minutes. It's after hours and we can't get any lunch, but we can get some tea in the Court, and you ought to have something to eat. It will make you feel better, and I have some real sugar in my suite."

She did quiet down and he took her up to his suite in the Savoy Court. Nothing could be served in the dining-room after hours, as the new Food Control Regulations had gone into effect. The Savoy Court was an annex of the Savoy Hotel and contained only suites. We all used to stay there when in London and usually turned the Court into a large house-party.

Tap ordered some tea, and the girl began to pull herself together. A little brandy seemed to help her and suddenly she started out in a new direction.

"It's rotten of me," she said, "to take on like this. I won't do it any more, for I am a big girl now. Please excuse me. I act as if I were the only woman who has lost her—er—lover. And it is not very kind to you. You are still here and I mustn't make you sad—give you the willies, I believe you said. I ought to be cheering you up, for you must carry on until it is your turn. Your last days in London should be gay. They must be gay! Tell me about yourself. Is there some one to look after you and weep when you crash? Is there some one at home to wait for you in vain? Some one who is dreadfully patriotic? Maybe you won't be killed and then you'll be in a worse fix! You aviators seem to have a bad time in between funerals. Is she blonde or brunette?" She was biting her lips to keep back the tears but conquered them at last and tossed her head derisively in victory.

"No," said Tap, "I'm a free-lance. I don't want anything to interfere with the business at hand. Women always seem to ruin a good pilot—take his mind off his work. And besides that, I've never noticed that traffic was jammed by any rush in my direction. The only person who worries over me is an aunt in Georgia and even she is unable to give the job her undivided attention. Let's have a little more of this brandy. I'm a bit shaky, if you don't mind my saying so. I saw the crash and it has stuck with me longer than I expected."

"None for me," she told him, "but help yourself if that will do you any good. And you are shaky. I don't blame you. I must have given you a bad time. But I'll make up for it now."

The tea was brought in, and they talked on for some time. Tap told her all about himself. She was a good listener, and he poured out all his joys and fears under the stimulation of her gentle smile. For she did seem interested and would prod him gently with some question whenever he would stop.

For the first time in months Tap realized that he really was lonely. The excitement had kept away the pangs, but now he knew there was something missing. And the girl before him made the pangs acute. He was fascinated by her presence, and just a little embarrassed by it as well.

"But surely you get homesick sometimes," she told him, "even though you don't have much time for it."

"Yes," he admitted, "sometimes when the other fellows get their mail from home I feel right blue. It must be sort of nice to have some one to really care what you are doing."

"All right," she told him and joined him on the sofa, "from now on I am going to worry over you. That is, if you'll let me. And I'll do my best. You can't go on alone. It isn't right. I won't let you. I am going to make up to you what you'll miss, while there is still time. And you will help me over the bumps. We'll help each other along the way. And I need you more than you need me."

She was crying again, and Tap thought she was going to get hysterical. But she didn't. Something seemed to have hit her. He tried the "there, there, little girl," but it was out of place. Before he knew it, his arms were around her and his lips sought hers.

Then his head cooled off and he pushed her away. He apologized.

"Please forget it," he told her, "I am very sorry. But you looked so lovable that I forgot myself."

But Tap assured me several times that she didn't seem to be the least bit in need of his apology. In fact, she rather liked the treatment. Tap told her she was out of her head and insisted on taking her home. She refused to go. He told her she was not behaving properly, that as far as he was concerned she might as well be Jim's widow. She asked him what difference that would make, and he couldn't think of an answer. Finally, she left him open-mouthed, after declining his offer of escort with the information that she would meet him for lunch the next day.

Of course, Tap got drunk. What else could he do? And he got mad. How dared she flirt with him? He had a vague idea that she should be mounting the funeral pyre or something of a like nature. Instead of that, as soon as she got her tears dried she had started to flirt with him. And he had fallen for it! Well, there were plenty of men in London, and she could have her pick of them! But not him!

He was fighting a fearful hangover when he met her for lunch. She was bright and gay and almost charmed him out of his determination. He was afraid he was in love with her and it made him mad. He had never loved any woman and he was determined that the woman he would some day come to love must be a little better and a little finer than those he had known. She must be worthy of the great love he would give her. And yet here he was in the throes of a peculiar power which was drawing him towards a woman he could never love—and a light-hearted flirt at that!

He drank too much, and when she tried to display some little affection he quite lost his temper. So she had left.

Then he knew he loved her. But he also hated her for cheating him of his dream of love.

So he got drunk again, this time very drunk.

The next day she came around to the Savoy again for lunch. She was very jauntily dressed and seemed very gay.

"Please go away and leave me," he begged her, after lunch, "I'm not myself. You made me get drunk. Can't you see I love you? Well, go on away. You can't be mine. You'll never love me. This is cheap. I won't have it. I can't treat you like Jim did! And you shan't treat me as you did him!"

Tap would break down at this point of the story and become entirely incoherent. So I never found out exactly what happened next. She put her hand over his mouth to stop him and then gently quieted him down.

"Don't you dare think my love is cheap," she told him, "but you are too much of a fool to think otherwise. You don't know love when you see it. I see my mistake. You are right—I can never be your little Elsie. So I'll leave. But I'll get news of you and I'll worry over you. And I'll love you—for a long time." And she had kissed him and left.

So my last few days with him were not very pleasant. He insisted that I might help him find her. But it was a hopeless task, and we wandered about in vain.

"She's crazy," he kept telling me, "just plain knocked cuckoo. His death just unbalanced her mind. My God, how she must have loved him to have felt it like that! You'd have to look at her to realize how far she is knocked. Why, man, she practically offered herself to me. I suppose she just wanted some one to take his place. Well, why not? But there's no reason why she should love me. But she said she did! And I let her go! I'm cuckoo myself. Women and war! They get you sooner or later. Well, bring on your war, the Hun has lost his sting!"

By the third day he had made up his mind to sit in the Savoy lobby and wait until she should come in again. He said he would wait forever, or longer if necessary.

Paris finally decided we were to go out to the front with the R.F.C. as regular British pilots, which news brought great joy and the excuse for a series of farewell parties. Ten of us were ordered to France at once. Tap was sent to Birmingham to ferry Bristol Fighters. He was disgusted with this luck and cursed the big two-seaters and the Paris office and himself and everything.

"But I'll have more time to find her," he consoled himself, "and I'll find her, too. She's got big blue eyes and a little mouth. I'll find her."

I was delayed a while in London and then went out from Hounslow with an S.E. squadron when the Huns broke through and started for Amiens and the call came for all available pilots. Sixty-two machines were lost the first day of the fighting.

2

The flying corps at the front was one big family. A pair of wings made us all brothers. And we all spoke the same language and had been along the same road. We had the same joys and fears, as well as the same friends and memories. So it was not surprising that news traveled fast up and down the front. For on every dud day when no flying was possible, everybody went calling. Transportation was plentiful and rapid. We dined out at other squadrons about half of the time. We moved frequently and always lived with another squadron for a few days while we were getting settled. There was usually another squadron living with us. And every one gathered at Charlie's Bar or at the Folkestone in Boulogne.

Henri, who presided over the bar at the Folkestone, was the newspaper of the flying corps. He knew everything. If some one shot down a Hun in flames, Henri would announce it to the gathered pilots within the hour. He could tell you the details of a wedding in your home town and when the Huns would attack again, meanwhile shaking your cocktail. He would tell you anything except how he concocted his drinks and where he got his rye. If, by chance, there was some obscure bit of information you wanted that Henri could not give, there were any number of pilots present that could supply the deficiency. For every rainy afternoon they all came in for a coffee cocktail and news of the war. There were pilots just over from England going to the pool, pilots on leave and from the hospital at Wimmeroux; and later on Americans from everywhere—usually lost.

And so it was at the Folkestone that I got news of Tap. His letters were brief and simply stated that he was still ferrying. But from Henri and others I heard a different story.

Wherever he went there was a beautiful lady with him. They had been seen together in far places. They were seen at the few fashionable places that were open in London, at Brighton and Eastbourne, on the terrace at Skindles, and in electric punts on the river at Maidenhead. One pilot had seen them at Liverpool. Another saw them at Oxford. All claimed that she was very beautiful and had tried to meet her, but none had succeeded. Tap was very wary and guarded his lady carefully. They were always alone.

They drank champagne in large quantities. Several times they had been seen leaving a dance just between a waver and a stagger. There was even a rumor that she flew with him on his ferry trips, disguised as a mechanic. But no one really believed this as it was too hard to do. I know of one pilot who did it, but he had a crash the second trip and was caught. The British fined him ten shillings, or some such terrible punishment, and issued orders that all passengers in ferry planes be registered. They became quite a famous pair, did Tap and his beautiful lady, and I heard much of them for the next two months.

In May Tap came out to a Bristol squadron located near us. I had been transferred to a Camel squadron. Every one was afraid of Camels at that time. We were losing men faster than any of the other squadrons, and the Camel was avoided as a war chariot. This machine was much slower than the Hun Fokkers and was often forced to fight against odds. And when the Camels joined a fight they couldn't leave, whereas the faster S.E. scouts and the Bristols could run home at will. Every one liked to pick his fight and leave when he had enough. But, on the other hand, the little Camels could put up a stiff fight against odds when cornered, and the Hun pilots liked them no better than we did.

We were having a big binge in honor of our new colonel, and Tap came over for it. A binge consisted of a formal dinner in the squadron mess. Special invitations were issued, and the guest of honor was usually a colonel or a general. There was not much food available, but there was plenty of "likker" to make up for it. Every one present was supposed to make a speech, particularly our guests. The game was to ply the guest of honor with potent beverages until he was sufficiently enthusiastic to abandon his dignity and lead the frolic. Sometimes we would call in a body on another squadron. We would usually be resisted by force, and a battle with signal pistols would follow. Sometimes the opposing major would discover to his horror that he was rubbing sand into the face of his commanding general. This would give us a technical victory, and we would proceed to raid their bar. Or perhaps we would stage a miniature battle in the old trenches back of the hangars where the infantry, in their haste, had left a plentiful supply of hand grenades, Mills bombs, and aminol. And sometimes another squadron, thirsting for revenge, would raid our mess and break up our party. Later on in the summer, the guest of honor at one of these binges was killed by a Very pistol, and we were ordered to disarm.

Tap refused to tell me very much of what had happened. "Oh, yes," he admitted, "she came back to see me again. I asked her to marry me. She said she would never marry any one that had anything to do with a plane. But I couldn't give her up. And I didn't. That's all, except that she has taken a house on the River down at Maidenhead and is going to wait there for me. I'll get leave in three months. I'll marry her then."

I was a flight commander now and had six machines and six pilots in my flight. I had just lot two men, so I suggested to Tap that he join my flight. I knew I could get him transferred, as American Camel pilots were scarce. But he didn't seem to care for the idea.

"You Camel merchants can go on with your suicide clubs," he told me; "you all seem to be having a private war of your very own. Don't let me cheat the Fokkers out of their daily cold meat, but I have business to attend to after the war is over. No, thanks, you can keep your Camel; I'll stick to Bristols. They have some chance."

"You certainly have changed," I said. "The old fire-eater has cooled off and the old war-horse has got stall feet. But why come out at all? Accidents have happened to Bristols. I saw three go down last week on one show. And it was the little Camels that saved the other three. You may draw a dud observer in the back seat, and then what price big eyes and little mouth?"

"Oh, shut up and pass me the champagne and give me the dope on top patrols. We're supposed to look after you little fellows. How high can you get?"

We were at dinner, and the meal was about over. Every one was more or less mellow and jovial, and the next thing in order was a speech from the guest of honor, a colonel.

The colonel began with the usual squadron speech. He announced that the Children's League had petitioned him to substitute malted milk for our issue rum. This was a jab at our major who was not yet twenty-one.

"And I am really in quite a quandary," he went on when the laughter had died down, "over the strange behavior in the Bristol family. Quite a breach of discipline over there. Really quite shocking. One of the Bristol pilots has been seen kissing his observer. This is contrary to all regulations. I have not ascertained whether this was done as sheer force of habit or whether I am missing something and not getting the proper respect as your colonel." There was a terrific uproar at this, and the colonel sat down amid great applause. There were cries of "Speech, speech" directed at Tap who had turned a brilliant scarlet and was trying hard to laugh.

The major arose and introduced Tap as the man who combined business with pleasure, war and peace.

"Mr. President," began Tap, "I know there is no honor among thieves, but my observer, who guards my tail in deadly combat, has been insulted. Neither he nor she, as the case may be, is here to uphold my character. Therefore I am bound to demand satisfaction, and I challenge my accuser to a duel with Very pistols at fifty yards."

There was a cheer at this, and the colonel at once accepted the challenge. Seconds were appointed and we all went out on the airdrome with a large supply of Very pistols. These were large single-barreled affairs which fired different colored signal lights.

The colonel and Tap took their positions and were given twenty-five cartridges each. We retired to a respectful distance, and they opened fire at the signal.

We were beginning to enjoy the fun when there was a terrific explosion just behind us and we were covered with a shower of dirt. Some one shouted, "Lie down, it's a Hun!" But we were already on our faces before the next bomb burst several hundred yards away. A Hun night-bomber had seen the lights from aloft, had shut off his motor, and glided down unheard to drop bombs at close range. Then there was a rattle of machine-gun fire, and we all dashed for the dugout as two more bombs burst nearby.

There were several flesh wounds in the party but no one was seriously hurt. The colonel and Tap declared their honor thoroughly satisfied, and the colonel invited some of us to dine with him the next night.

3

Three weeks later I was leading a high patrol about two hours after sunrise. We had just crossed the lines when I saw a flight of five Bristols about ten miles over. They had apparently been on one of their long reconnaissance trips into Hunland and were now coming back against the wind. There were a number of Fokkers picking at them from above. It was a good fight, but the Fokkers had the advantage of wind and sun and were using it. The Fokkers held their altitude and refused to dogfight. Instead, they were diving on the rear Bristols. This would force the leader to turn and fight and then the lower Fokkers would zoom away while the others dove on the leader. But the Fokkers were single-seaters, which gave the Bristols the advantage at close quarters where two or more of them could fire at the same Fokker.

The Bristols were making little progress and we hurried to join the fight. The Bristols saw us and began to dive at once. This was done so as to bring the Fokkers under us, as well as to get cover. Then the Bristols would pull up and turn and come back to help us. It was a good maneuver and well executed, but one Bristol lagged behind at death grip with a Fokker who was sticking under him for a last shot. As I dove on the Fokker the Bristol slowly turned over and stalled, and then went spinning down in a cloud of smoke—the Fokker pouring in both guns. I lost sight of it as I closed with the Fokker.

That night I learned it was Tap. He was posted dead as his machine was observed from the ground. It spun down all the way and never stopped smoking. I got in touch with the Red Cross headquarters in Paris, and they made inquiries through Switzerland. Word came back that he was dead, and I began to taste the real bitterness of war.

Several weeks later I got a letter from London. It read:

DEAR LIEUTENANT:

I have just come over from America to get the body of my husband. I learned at Headquarters that you were instrumental in packing his effects and arranging the military funeral. I want to express my sincere appreciation of your kind offices. I also wished to thank Lieutenant Johnson, but have been told that he has been killed. Will you please write me if this has been confirmed beyond a doubt? Surely one of you three will be spared, and I will pray for you every night.

Yours,

SARAH WATSON.

I had nightmares for a month. I kept seeing Tap spinning down into the river at Maidenhead and Jim's wife drinking eggnog with the colonel at Ayr.

4

The Armistice found me at Toul where the rest of the British-trained pilots were organized into three squadrons. Most of them were under arrest, and a few more joined them every day. They were all very much fed up and had declared war on the United States Army. We were all ordered to buy new regulation uniforms, and some brilliant staff officer decided that since there were no planes for us to fly, we ought to learn some infantry drill. If this had not been so strenuous it might have been funny. Every morning and afternoon about sixty pilots, hardened by months at the front, would be lined up on the tarmac in front of the hangars, regardless of rank, health or previous experience, and put through the movements of an infantry company by a lieutenant fresh from West Point. It was a question as to which was maddest, the pilots or the West Pointer.

Then some one else decided that our quarters were not properly kept. A tour of inspection by some staff major revealed the fact that our barracks were stuffed with a year's accumulation of equipment, souvenirs, and junk. We were ordered to get rid of all superfluous material and to clean up the barracks. A few earnest souls made a half-hearted attempt to comply with this order, but for the most part the outfit simply packed their voluminous baggage and departed. I have heard strange stories of their adventures and wanderings. Some of them are still in France; one died of pneumonia in a military prison, and one has never been heard of since. But the majority of them managed to get home four or five months later. Three of them actually got to New York without being stopped but were arrested at Hoboken and sent back to France for court-martial.

I heard a piece of news one day: Tap was alive and in Paris. I packed what I could, gave my souvenirs to my sergeant, and went to Paris by the truck route.

I found Tap in the New York Bar. He was a complete wreck and looked worse. He had been shot through the lung and the leg. His observer, also wounded, had been able to get the plane out of the spin and pull the nose up just before it hit the ground. They had crashed and been bent up some more, but were not killed. They were in a Hun field hospital for six weeks, and the observer died. Tap would have died, too, except for a doctor who had once practiced in Chicago and who had him moved to a private hospital. So the Red Cross had never had word of him. He had been back a week now and was supposed to be in a hospital.

He had no news from Maidenhead. He had written and wired. I called his attention to the fact that she had thought him dead for six months and would naturally not leave a forwarding address for him. Where was her home? He didn't know. She would never talk much about herself. He had asked permission to go to London and had been refused. London was out of bounds for all American troops.

"But I am going," he told me, "as soon as I get my back pay. I've got over a thousand dollars due and I can get it to-morrow. I suppose she has been trying to do her bit by cheering up some other poor devil. Probably some naval aviator. I heard London is lousy with them. All over the place! Well, it doesn't make any difference. I must find her. But, my God, to think that for six months . . ."

"Well, what else do you expect?" I asked him. "You can't expect her to sit around and mourn for you forever. Dead men tell no tales, but that is not the only thing they fail to do. There are now two dashing young aviators that have looked upon her in the cool of the evening and then gone far, far away. She has probably brought the same luck to several others by this time. Personally, I'd be afraid to go near her. Cheer up, be a man—those that love so long and so well should stay at home. You don't want to find her. You'd probably be another Enoch Arden!"

"Well, what of it? Will you come to London with me?"

I would cheerfully have gone to the North Pole to get out of France. A million Americans, freshly arrived, were celebrating their victory everywhere, all over France; and arresting each other daily as an evidence of their personal importance. I had nothing to celebrate and I wanted to get away from it all. London, I heard, was mourning for her lost ones and I wanted to go and do likewise. For I was the only one left of those first ten.

Our first attempt to leave Paris ended in a night at the Bastille. We were released from the jail only after considerable argument and much talk of further investigation. So we abandoned the idea of a trip by train. A British colonel that we had once met in London was on his way to Boulogne in a car, and he took us along with him. Once out of the city gates it was easy. We dropped off at Marquis and found an old friend in charge of the ferry pilots. We had no trouble in getting a plane to fly over.

London was indeed in mourning. There had been some celebration the first week of the Armistice, but then the repressed mourning of four years overwhelmed the city. Those who had laughed during the war were now sad, for there was no one that grief had not touched. We saw old friends, but they could talk only of those we missed.

Tap's search was fruitless. I suggested he trace her by the checks. But he had given her no checks. He had never given her any money. No one had seen her. We went to all the head waiters who had served them. They all remembered her, oh, yes—the beautiful lady who would exchange American sugar for meat tickets! But they had not seen her, no, not since the lieutenant had gone away. The proprietor of Skindle's gave us a hint.

"I know nothing," he told us, "but I did hear a rumor. No, I would not repeat it. But if you will find the agent who rerented the house perhaps he may help you."

We located the agent without much difficulty. Yes, he had taken the lease from the beautiful lady. Where had she gone? He regretted to tell us that we had best be discreet. Our acquaintance with the lady might lead to trouble. Well, if we must know, the lady had been arrested and imprisoned as a spy.

Tap was pretty bitter about it. He was very quiet for a while. "I see a lot of things now," he told me later, "that I didn't see before. There was something funny about the whole thing, and I've been puzzling over it. I didn't think it was my face and I didn't think it was my figure and I knew it wasn't the way I danced. I couldn't figure out what that woman saw in me. Well, now I know. It was information! That was why she always loved an aviator. Pretty clever! And as soon as one went West she had to grab another one quick to keep her job. So that's why she wouldn't talk! That's why I couldn't find out anything about her. Well, I am indeed the prize sucker in the big pond. But if you had seen her you would have been a sucker, too. And damn glad to be one! And damn proud to have been one! Well, that's that. Thanks for helping me prove myself a worthy successor to the great saps of the ages. Some day I'll have the laugh on poor old Jim. But maybe she is already with him. Let's go and find out. Lets see the whole show!"

So we went down to Scotland Yard. The officials there were not too cordial. They were more interested in questioning us than in answering our questions. They declined to let us see the files. One of the department chiefs was softened by Tap's tearful pleas and tried to help us out.

"Young man," he said, shuffling through the files, "there's a lot in here about you. Quite a bit. I find that you were held back from the front for observation for a while. Does that interest you? It should. You were suspected. When you did go out we took your correspondence. It seems to have cleared you. But not the lady. When you were reported killed there was no need to delay longer, and she was arrested. She was an alien and could not prove a residence. Her credentials were forged. The other charges against her were dismissed. She was charged with entering the country with false credentials and was deported. There are quite a few of the papers missing, the most important ones, in fact. I find a note here which says they were taken out by the Foreign Office. You can consider yourself very lucky, young man. The story of your iniquity is here, but I can assure you that no one can ever read it. I may have it destroyed. Now that your mind is relieved, will you come out and have lunch with me? I like you Americans. Perhaps you will tell me a story. So jolly, your stories!"

We thanked him profusely but declined the luncheon invitation. Tap was visibly affected.

"Maybe, maybe, maybe," he kept mumbling to himself, "but I'm not sure. But I'm telling you she was the world's greatest actress. That girl used to cry by the hour and I'll never believe she was faking it."

The next day we ran into an officer who was organizing the Polish Air Service and badly in need of experienced pilots. Tap offered his services at once. But when he reported for an examination the doctors laughed. They told him to pick out a nice quiet hospital and save the ambulance fee.

I don't know how it would have ended if Tap had not got pleurisy from the wound in his lung. The house physician at the hotel advised me to get him to a hospital at once. So there was nothing to do but go down to Headquarters and give ourselves up. We were both sent down to Lancaster Gate Hospital. Tap had a hard fight for his life and was still very sick when I was sent home. I had a bad time for a few days with Headquarters and was up for court-martial but managed to get off with a reprimand. I had no trouble getting orders home.

5

I went down to Washington in April to see what was left of Tap. He was in the Walter Reed Hospital and was pretty far gone. An aunt was doing her best to look after him and, as there was nothing I could do to help, I did not stay long. When he got stronger he went out to Arizona and lived on a ranch for eighteen months. He liked being a cowboy, and I had several rather cheerful letters from him.

I went to work in the investment department of a small New York bank and, when Tap came on nearly two years later, I was at the head of a subdepartment. He was looking better than I had ever seen him. His face was bronzed, his frame had filled out, he was really looking quite fit. He wanted a job in New York, and I had no difficulty in arranging to get him one with me. We rented an apartment in the Village and lived the usual life of bond salesmen.

The work suited Tap very well. A bond salesman must be congenial and convivial. Tap was all of that. And there was a party somewhere nearly every night. Every one came to New York that year. At least every one that wasn't there already. Old classmates at college, friends from home, army friends, the chance acquaintances of a lifetime, all greeted us afresh as we speeded the parting guest. And they all demanded high-powered entertainment.

Tap flourished. He broke all records selling bonds. His customers seemed to respect his judgment on account of his indifference. He never cared whether they bought or not. His opinions were unbiased by the desire to make a sale.

And he was always in great demand. He could make excellent gin from strange ingredients and knew all the best bootleggers intimately. He was organizer-in-chief of most of the parties. But they never seemed to satisfy him. He had a wild look in his eyes and was always searching for news of the woman he loved. He kept a sharp lookout for any of the old crowd from London. Under cover of reminiscences he would question them adroitly. Had they ever met a beautiful lady with big eyes and a little mouth? Perhaps they had seen him with her? Yes, that one. Well, had they ever seen her since?

He had found out from a clerk at the American Embassy that she had been turned over to the American authorities because it was an American passport that had been forged. So she had been sent to this country. The clerk knew nothing more.

Nearly every one knew some one who would vaguely answer Tap's requirements. Could they get her address now? Oh, yes. But it was always some one else, some one very different—never the shadow that was cast over Tap's mind. But he was always eagerly optimistic. He went to Buffalo once to see a cabaret singer and another time to Philadelphia to see a nurse. Both were strangers. He joined strange clubs and attended all sorts of reunions and conventions. Always he was searching. He attended various conventions of the American Legion and even went down to Atlantic City for a beauty contest. He resorted to advertising. He tried Washington, but there was no record of her anywhere there.

His ardor was never dampened. Every one who bought a bond had to answer that question, "Did you ever know a girl with big eyes and a little mouth that was once in England?"

"Sometimes," he told me, "I think it is all a dream. It seems to be just part of the funny things I used to see in Germany. But if it isn't, I'm going to find her. And if it is, I'm going to dream some more. Sometimes I do. Spy or no spy, I want her and I'm going to have her! The war is over!"

After such an outburst he would drink too much of his gin and go out to look for some one else to question.

He even tried selling bonds to women in the hope that he might get news of her. But one very comely lady reversed the procedure and wanted to know if he could give her news of her long-lost aviator. Tap could not, but neither could he convince her that he wouldn't do just as well. She would call at the office quite frequently to arrange her investments, and it got to be quite a joke.

Another lady gave him too much real gin and persuaded him to tell her all about the war. Then she made a newspaper article about it that was rather embarrassing. So Tap gave up that method.

And the months dragged on.

6

One of our customers from Boston was in town and asked me to come up to his hotel to discuss some matters in relation to changing a trust fund. I took Tap along to handle the bonds which were involved.

Our customer was an elderly gentleman and a thorough Bostonian. He was so charming and pleasant that we soon got off the subject of investments and wandered far afield. He was quite pleased when he learned we were ex-aviators and asked us many questions about ourselves and the war. He was very interested in Tap's stories and Tap talked more than I had ever heard him. Tap enjoyed entertaining him and even let his imagination make a good story out of everything he told.

"How very interesting, indeed," our customer had remarked approvingly as Tap finished telling him about the night patrol at Stamford; "you must really both stay to lunch. I will send for my daughter. She must know you. She must hear you."

"No," said Tap rather rudely, "I'll feed you all the funny stuff you want if you like it, but I really don't perform for the ladies. They like sob stuff and I usually overdo it. My question answerer is worn out."

The old gentleman was actually wiping his eyes. "My daughter," he said with some dignity, "will never ask you a question about the war, I am quite sure. I only wish she would. I doubt if she will even join us. If she does, you can tell her you are Chinese bandits, if you like. Let us return to the municipal bonds you were advising."

"I am sorry that I spoke," said Tap, with his face blazing. "I beg your pardon, sir. But I love to talk about the war and I talk about it too much. The women try to make a sideshow out of it and make me feel like a fool. They never understand. By the way, did you ever know a girl with big eyes and a little—"

Tap choked, and his eyes bulged. The old gentleman had risen to his feet as a young woman was coming towards us.

Tap grabbed my arm. "It's her," he whispered, "it's Sheila!"

"It can't be," I told him. "Your damn funny gin has affected your sight as well as your brain."

The old gentleman presented us to his daughter. I bowed. Tap took her hand.

"Surely," he said very slowly, "we do not have to be introduced."

"Perhaps not," she told him sweetly, "but I am sorry that I can't place you. Did I meet you at the races or was it in Maine? Were you one of the Yale men on the house-party?"

"Yes," said Tap, "I was all of those." And dropped her hand quickly.

We went in to lunch and it was not a very pleasant affair. The old gentleman was interrupted constantly by his daughter. He was scarcely able to finish a sentence. Tap would not talk at all, and I was not encouraged. Our customer was visibly disappointed. He was unable to control the conversation and finally began talking bonds to me. But he had something else on his mind.

"My daughter," he told me, "had a strange experience during the war. She wanted to nurse abroad, but after she had completed her training they refused to permit her to go because of the objection to relatives of men in service. Her husband was in the air service abroad. She forged some credentials and changed her name and went in spite of this restriction. She was in England for four months nursing and then was detected. They thought she was a spy and actually kept her in jail for some time. It was very distressing and caused a great deal of trouble. But my friend Senator Lodge—"

There was a shuffling of feet under the table, and his daughter interrupted to ask the time.

"We must hurry, father," she told him, "as I must pack at once and I have some things in the room for you to see. Please ask for the check."

"But, my dear," he said in surprise, "you haven't seen the Watsons yet and you really must; you promised, you know."

"Well," she said, "I have changed my mind. We are going home on the three-thirty. I forgot to tell you."

And so our luncheon was over. The old gentleman gave us an order for some securities and promised that we would hear more from him.

Tap and I took a taxi down to the apartment.

"It's her," he kept telling me, "I'd know her anywhere. Did you see her eyes? Did you see that mouth? And she knew me, too. She couldn't take her eyes off this scar. She knew me! Even if my face is a bit messed up. But she didn't want to see me. Well, she needn't. Has to leave town, eh? Afraid I might call on her. Elegant Boston lady! No wonder that accent fooled me! So that's the answer to the works, is it?"

As soon as we reached the apartment he began to make some gin.

"I think," he announced to me, "that I am going to get very drunk. I think it fitting and proper. Will you join me? I need a pacemaker."

I saw that he needed me and gave up all idea of returning to the office, but went out after some oranges instead. Tap was still fuming when I came back.

"She knew me all the time," he told me again as he was filtering his gin. "I found her foot under the table. She kicked my ankle."

"Why didn't you kick her back?"

"I did. Then I got her hand, and she scratched me." He held up the offending hand, which showed a long scratch.

"I must say," I told him, "that you deserve that and considerably more. I had no idea you were such a fool. Jim lived here in New York. His wife came down from Boston to marry him. He met her when he was at Ground School at Teck. Don't you remember? Don't you see it all now?"

"Yes, since lunch. And she's still cuckoo. It's all my fault. But how was I to know? And now a promising young bond salesman is about to resign a very lucrative position and journey on to parts unknown. Here, try this beaker of the golden juice of California and—"

There was a loud knock at the door. It was the old gentleman from Boston. He was quite red in the face and much distressed.

"My daughter sent me," he told us, "and she is acting very queerly. She has changed her mind again, and we are not going to Boston this afternoon. She wishes to see about some investments at once and sent me to find you. Your office said you might be here. She told me to come and wait until you came in. She said you would understand about the investments—some future transaction, I gathered. And I don't understand. Will you please explain it to me?"

"All right," said Tap as he reached for his hat, "you stay here with Mr. Wilson and he will tell you a lot of funny stories and explain the theory of gravitation. And I will run up and see if I can find out what is wrong with your daughter. Maybe I can sell her something."

And he did.

James Warner Bellah

(1899–1976)

James Warner Bellah served in both world wars. In World War I, he enlisted in the Canadian army and was a pilot with the Royal Flying Corps. His war stories appeared in *Sketch Book of a Cadet at Gascony* (1923) and *Gods of Yesterday* (1928). He also wrote the war novel *The Sons of Cain* (1928). Between the wars and after service in World War II, Bellah wrote numerous popular stories and novels, particularly westerns, which became the basis for movies such as *Fort Apache, She Wore a Yellow Ribbon,* and *Rio Grande.* He was also a screenwriter, most known for cowriting *The Man Who Shot Liberty Valance.* First published in the May 28, 1927, *Saturday Evening Post,* "The Great Tradition" anticipates the myth-preserving theme of *The Man Who Shot Liberty Valance,* in which a character declares, "When the legend becomes fact, print the legend."

The Great Tradition

James Warner Bellah

Comstock, the great gangling Texan, was crying softly as he walked across the pounded airdrome in the darkling twilight. The cold of the upper reaches still throbbed sullenly in his feet and hands and played along his raw nerves, like tiny electrical shocks, under the impulse of the returning blood. His face was smudged with oil and the great salt tears that still welled in his smoldering eyes. And as he walked he cursed—earnestly, through tight lips like some ancient Benedictine telling his beads in the shadow of a cloistered shrine. There was something quite terrible about that cursing. It was at once a prayer and a threat—the whining of a whipped dog and the low, sharp challenge of an armed sentry.

He trudged down the path to the darkened village and on through its one shuttered street to the highroad beyond. He was walking now with angry strides and slapping his helmet against his knee, trying to hurt himself in a vain, foolish way. The car that might have taken him to quarters passed him and someone called through the twilight. Comstock didn't answer, nor did he raise his head. He walked on to the stone pillars of the park entrance and turned into the gravel drive of Vieupeyroux.

The great ogling façade of the château frowned down at him presently through the trees. He crossed the grass plot in front of the entryway and went through the open doors into the dark foyer. Far in the rear a light shone from the half-opened door of the squadron mess room. Comstock put his hand on the broad marble balustrade and climbed slowly, wearily up to his room. The little fat Corporal Pau was hunched up on the foot of his cot, reading and puffing huge blue clouds of *tabac naturel* from his short, ancient brier. He looked up as Comstock entered. The Texan stared at him. The corporal met his eye and shrugged and went back to his reading. Comstock flung himself down on his own cot, face to the wall and one arm thrown up across his eyes. Presently the arm and shoulder trembled as the muscles rippled slightly under the Texan's tunic.

Corporal Pau looked up again and then his eyes traveled slowly to the third cot in the room—the empty one—empty save for the hastily packed kit bag, the strapped haversack and the four books that lay piled under a mute fatigue cap. He shrugged again and got up. He was a short roly-poly man of forty-five, Corporal Pau, and his legs were bowed under him in two great arcs. He looked down at them as if he had never seen them before. He wiped his stubby hand across his mouth and crossed the room to Comstock's cot. He laid a hand on Comstock's shoulder.

"Come, my ancient friend," he said. "It is the war. Who can help things? We shall miss the little Jake, of course—just as one shall miss us when we go. It is the way of life. *Pouf!* Tonight we still live and the little Jake does not. Tomorrow—who knows?—perhaps we shall not live either."

"You-all don't seem to understand," said Comstock wearily. "I don't aim to kid myself into believin' I wouldn't've missed him if he'd just sort of been killed regular. But I do say that he'd not've been killed at all if it hadn't been for that ornery coyote Petitjean! Jake was too good a pilot!"

He sat up suddenly and leaned forward with his fists clenched on his knees. "In my country they'd hang a man for less than that! The Eagle of the Skies—the dirty grand-stand player! M'sieur Tac-au-Tac with his medals and his name in the papers and his struttin' about with powdered gals!" Comstock stood up and wiped his hands across his damp face and through his hair.

Pau watched him with his chin up and his fists clasped behind his back. "So?" he said.

"Yes!" said Comstock flatly. "And what can one do—what can one ever do? Petit-jean—the great ace—the great tradition—the lowlife—the dirty scum! I'd like to wring his perfumed neck for him." He raised his arms above his head and let them fall helplessly again.

Pau nodded. "One comprehends," he said.

"One does like hell!" said Comstock. "Not when it costs a pal's life. It's the trick of a yellow-livered skunk. We had those two new lads to break in. We were flying tight and close to the vest. If they want him to do newspaper flying, why don't they detach him? He falls for the stupidest frame-up I ever saw. He shouldn't've led us into a fight at all. But he's got to show off and add up his personal score, so he dives down on two of the boche himself and leaves Jake and me and the two green hands right in the middle of the lousiest dog fight you ever saw. And he never had the decency to come back. How any of us got out alive, I don't know." Comstock shrugged. "The answer is Jake didn't—and we didn't have to come into this man's army, Jake and me." He laid a hand against the kit bag on the empty cot and then turned suddenly to the washbasin. Pau puffed his pipe in silence and paced slowly back and forth in front of the closed door while Comstock scrubbed his face and hands.

The door opened and a face looked in—a thin ascetic face under a rakish cap—Chevagnac. He stood for a moment looking at Pau and then he crossed the room to Comstock.

"It's all right, Chevvy."

"*Non, m'sieur.*" Chevagnac bowed slightly. "It is not, or I would not come to you." With both delicate hands the Frenchman grasped Comstock's elbows in a firm grip. "A thousand pardons," he said softly. "I have heard. In the name of my country—a thousand pardons. Lecour has told me all about it."

Comstock put a hand on his shoulder. "It's all right, Chevvy," he said again awkwardly.

Chevagnac turned away.

Corporal Pau was bent over a bottle, twisting at the cork. It came away with a hollow pop and pale cognac rippled softly into the glasses on the chest top. Comstock buttoned his tunic and hooked his collar. Pau held out the glasses. They turned silently to the empty cot and drank.

Comstock put down the glass on the chest top. "To think we've got to go on living and eating and flying with him, keeping up the great tradition of Mr. One-Two-Three—the conceited little——"

"Sh-h!" said Chevagnac. "It can do no good. It is quite hopeless. We know what we know. He will be alive long after we are all dead. It is written. It is the way of eagles and—peacocks!" He set his cap more firmly on his head. Comstock sloshed his glass half full again and drained it at a gulp.

Corporal Pau looked at him and corked the bottle with a smacking blow of his calloused palm. *"Après!"* he said shortly. "We dine now." Chevagnac opened the door into the dimly lighted upper corridor and stepped out to the stairhead. Pau was holding the door. Comstock slammed his cap on and followed Chevagnac. The liquor burned sullenly in his empty stomach. He pulled a twisted cigarette from his pocket and hunched his great shoulders forward meanwhile he twisted the wheel of his lighter. A door down the hallway slammed sharply and there were quick dapper footsteps on the flagging. Comstock pressed the smudge of his lighter to the cigarette, blew a thin stream of smoke from his nostrils and looked up—into the face of Petitjean. The captain stopped in his tracks and frowned slightly in annoyance. It would be necessary for him to step around the Texan in order to reach the stairhead.

"M'sieur the American wishes something?" he snapped.

Comstock spread his legs insolently and put his great fists upon his hips.

"Name of a name of a dog!" hissed Pau. "Chevagnac—quickly—his other arm—he is drunk!"

Comstock twisted their hands from his wrists and ran his eyes over the little pilot from the tips of his patent-leather dancing shoes to the absurd points of his pomaded mustache.

"Quickly!" snapped Petitjean. "You wish something?"

"Yes," the Texan drawled. "I want to see what a great air fighter looks like."

Petitjean drew himself up and the little enameled crosses on his tunic tinkled faintly.

"Fou!" he snorted. "Step aside!" Comstock grinned foolishly. "Step aside! I wish to pass!" hissed Petitjean. "Do you hear, *bête?"*

Then, his temper flaming, his hand flicked up and smacked sharply across Comstock's cheek. Chevagnac and Pau leaped at the American, but before they could stop him he had the little powdered captain by one shoulder, feet clear of the flagging, shaking him fiercely as a terrier shakes a chipmunk. Medals, teeth and dancing shoes—he shook him till he rattled like a dice box. Pau and Chevagnac wound their arms about Comstock, binding him, pulling him down, but it was some seconds before he let go.

Petitjean stumbled to his knees and sprang up. "You," he said, "I shall have shot!"

"You think you will, but you won't. 'Cause if you do, you'll have to let everyone know I shook you," said Comstock. "Good! I'll enjoy the court, and every minute I stay in the *salle de police!"*

Petitjean looked at him furiously, blind with rage. His lips trembled, but the words fouled one another. He sputtered. He turned and bolted down the great stairway in impotent fury, flinging a filthy phrase at them.

"Now," said Corporal Pau, "one has done a thing."

Comstock raised a hand to the red finger marks on his cheek.

"Come," he growled, *"dîner."*

Chevagnac shrugged elaborately. "It is done," he said. "And who shall say badly done?"

They went slowly down the stairs. In the foyer below they stood for a moment staring out through the darkened entryway, listening to the hooting exhaust of Petitjean's roadster as it raced furiously down the park drive and turned into the Troyes road. Then they went in to dinner.

It was cold in the gray light of early morning and wet mist vapors danced above the chilled soil of the airdrome like drunken dervishes. A mechanician coughed harshly and spat. The tail skid of the last *avion de chasse* scraped in the gravel as the men trundled it out and swung it into line. Corporal Pau grunted and pushed his folded map into the pocket of his flying coat with a cold rustling sound. The Adjutant Lecour came down the line with a paper in his hand.

"Chevagnac—Pau!" he called. *"Ici!"*

Comstock looked up sullenly. Their heads were bent over the paper. He walked slowly over to them.

"The Powder Puff has not returned yet—from last night. We shall go without the swine," said Lecour. Comstock nodded. Chevagnac straightened up and buckled the chin strap of his helmet. Pau was already climbing into his cockpit. Engines commenced to sputter and cough, and the mist beyond the hangars broke suddenly and streamed away into nothingness as the back draft of the propellers caught it. Comstock trudged slowly down to the last Nieuport on the line—his own. His mechanician was fussing still, oiler in hand, and the propeller not yet turning. Chevagnac waved cheerily from the next machine. Lecour was already taxiing slowly out, with Pau after him.

Comstock's mechanician wiped his hands on his overalls and grasped the propeller, waiting. Comstock climbed into the cockpit. Out of the corner of his eye he saw a gray car flash along the misty roadway behind the hangars, turn at the bend and come around, with a retch of brakes, to the tarmac. Petitjean, still in his dancing shoes, climbed out and waved his arms angrily. His mechanician came running to him with his gray fur flying coat and helmet.

Comstock's propeller flashed through an arc, kicked with a loud pop and came to rest again. Chevagnac taxied slowly out to the waiting Lecour. Petitjean, sitting on the step of his roadster, unlaced his patent-leather shoes and stuffed his legs furiously into his flying boots. He stood up and stamped his feet. A mechanician held his coat for him. He shrugged into it and came quickly over to Comstock.

"You could not wait, *hein?* You are impatient?" His pale, pasty face was flushed to a cruel unhealthy vermilion at the cheek bones and the waxed points of his mustache were frayed and untidy. "Tell them to go!" he shouted angrily to a mechanic. "I will meet them. Bring coffee." He crossed in front of Comstock's Nieuport and climbed into his own.

Again Comstock's propeller flashed through its quick arc and his mechanician stumbled back to his haunches as it popped and caught and melted into a roaring circle of light. Comstock revived the engine quickly. A man was running toward Petitjean's machine with the smoke-blackened coffee canister. Lecour, Pau and Chevagnac opened up and moved quickly off across the airdrome for their take-off. Presently as they sang into the air, in a rising swoop, Comstock turned and taxied out onto the 'drome. As he passed he saw Petitjean waving furiously in the cheap anger of stale wine and spitting a thin stream of black coffee from his lips. He pushed at the man who held the canister and shoved him away.

Comstock leaned forward in his cockpit, blipped his engine full on and trailed away after the other three Nieuports. His wheels bumped on the uneven ground as he eased the stick forward and waited. The wheels bumped again, more softly this time. The Nieuport roared down on the line of poplars at the far side of the 'drome and then, in a quick zoom, Comstock pulled back on the stick and swept over their tops in a wide climbing turn. Lecour was circling back, with Pau and Chevagnac behind him. Comstock fell in on their tails. Below him he could see the misty airdrome with Petitjean's avion still standing on the tarmac. Three times Lecour circled, waiting, then he turned deliberately to the eastward and headed out for the front, with Comstock behind, still trailing him, nose slightly down, nursing his sputtering engine. Presently Lecour started to climb again.

Comstock watched him and gave it up. Busses to him were like horses. If one wasn't any good, take another. He had no patience with engines. He kept on behind the patrol, cursing softly and waiting for his engine to cough out entirely. He saw the three others far above him. Too far to catch up with now. He turned in a wide circle and started back to the 'drome, but as he turned the sputtering of his engine died away and left in its wake the even throb of perfect timing. He swept around quickly and climbed into the thin haze that had closed behind the three others.

Presently he warmed his *mitrailleuses* to the higher cold and turned to the northeast to catch Lecour at a tangent. He had ten thousand feet now. Below him the ground was a waxen model etched with mist plumes and faintly yellow with the first light of the pale cloud-filtered sun. He stared at it over the padded rim of his cowling. A long pencil line crossed below him and frayed out into nothingness—a road. Beyond its unraveled end there was a brown jagged belt, pitted and pocked and splashed with the gray smudges of ruined villages. He crossed the line and warmed his guns again. He turned in his cockpit and stared backward and above him. Nothing.

There were clouds ahead and slightly higher. He eased back on his stick and climbed into their lacy fringes. They were gray-bellied snow clouds, piled high in heaped disorder. He climbed through to the creamy gold tops of them and flattened out just above their long serried ruffles. For an hour he skulked in and out, peeking through occasional torn holes at the sullen gray below, but there was nothing interesting and Lecour was gone somewhere else. He squinted at his watch and considered the hunger that was beginning to gnaw at his stomach. He turned again in his cockpit and looked behind and above him from force of habit. For some reason he zoomed, and halfway up looked quickly backward and below his tail, and just as he looked his controls trembled violently and his fuselage vibrated as if a shower of small stones had been hurled against it. He flattened and split-aired and dived upon the other machine. Then suddenly his heart jumped within him and he stopped firing. He pulled back again and flashed above. It was a Nieuport—and Petitjean's. He split-aired again and waved. Lucky thing, that!

Petitjean didn't wave. He Immelmanned deliberately and commenced firing again with the gun on his top plane. The tracers raked Comstock's lower plane and tore up the fabric just inside the V-strut. In amazement, the Texan pulled up and Immelmanned.

Again Petitjean followed and gave him a burst of ten from his guns. The triplex windshield on Comstock's cowling starred into a thousand cracks. He whip-stalled furiously—and then suddenly he knew. The little perfumed monkey hadn't made a mistake. He had followed him to kill him deliberately, alone and above the clouds, where no one could see—to kill him, coldly and easily himself, for the insult.

Comstock stood half up in his cockpit and screamed curses into the pounding bedlam of his engine. Then he hunched forward and dived on Petitjean. The captain slipped under him and came up behind. Comstock swept over in a half loop, but again Petitjean squirmed out of his line of fire. Comstock was flying and firing blindly now in his rage.

For hours, it seemed, they had been ducking and diving for the final burst of shots. Then, quite without warning, the Texan's engine coughed and sputtered miserably, his nose wabbled in the zoom and he stalled off on one wing. He whipped down into a spin, with Petitjean after him, still firing. He could feel the staccato beat of the shots as they raked his tail planes. He tightened his lips and waited meanwhile he tore down upon the golden ruffles of the clouds. "Let me get out of this—let me get out for Jake and myself—for Pau and Chevvy—just one more crack!" he prayed. But he knew in his heart that Petitjean would burn him—follow him down and burn him so that there would be no chance of his living to tell the rotten tale.

Suddenly the soft wet grayness of the clouds closed over him. For minutes he spun through them, waiting, then slowly he ruddered out of the spin and looked at his whirling compass needle. His engine was quite dead now and his controls were loose and wabbly. The needle trembled back and pointed. Nose down in a slow glide, he dived out of the clouds at nine thousand feet and turned westward. "Safe now, if I can only make the line. He won't dare try it where they can see our markings from the ground." His voice rose in an exultant scream. "And I'm alive— I'm going to live! And there will be another time!" Slowly he glided on toward the line. "They'll be after me now—in a minute—with the guns—but I've got to go slowly—keep my height—get in! Got to get in!"

There were shrapnel bursts above him now—bursts that crawled slowly down and lay in the air behind him like the splashed tops of charlotte russes. He clamped his jaws shut and glided on.

Quite plainly he could see the gray stains of ruined villages, sticking up out of the brown mud like disordered piles of shattered skulls. Then, with a swoop and eight hundred feet to spare, he flashed through the rifle fire of the boche trenches, staggered across the French line and piled up behind a slight rise just beyond the support trenches.

It was long after sundown when he reached Vieupeyroux. Four of his teeth were gone—bashed out by the compass—and his right eye was green and blue from the cowling rim, and quite closed. He climbed out of the camion and stalked into the entrance hall.

Le Coq d'Or is the fourth house from the corner where the Rue Maréchal du Plessis runs into the Rue Passy to form that small moth-eaten *place* the name of which no one has yet discovered. The pickets of the low iron fencing that runs round the grass plot of the *place* have roughened tops, where knobs or little molded kings' heads that formerly decorated them have been knocked off for loot or for bullets. Nobody seems to know, nor to care, for people come into the district solely to visit Le Coq d'Or.

Comstock stood for several seconds on the dimly lit landing and straightened the collar of his tunic, rubbing his hand. Then he opened the door and stepped inside. His eyes was bandaged and poulticed against the light and his face was not pleasant to see.

Chevagnac sprang up from the table. "So!" he said. "We heard you were down. You came back?"

Pau grinned. "He always comes back. Not so, my ancient friend?"

"Sure," said Comstock. He looked at the closed door and poured wine into a glass. "They brought me at sundown in a camion. And we meet again. Four nights ago——"

"Sh-h," said Chevagnac. "Let us forget the little Jake." He drained his glass and loosened his collar. "Eh, Marie?"

The girl smiled and patted his arm. Comstock looked at her.

The door opened quickly behind him, and Madame Messeroux, her face pale to the lips, stood upon the threshold. Her black eyes caught Chevagnac's suddenly. "M'sieur!" she panted. They stared at her. "M'sieur"—she raised a beckoning finger—"come, please, quickly—alone."

Chevagnac pushed back his chair, startled. "You wish me, madame?"

"At once!"

He looked at her stupidly and straightened the skirts of his tunic.

Pau laughed mulishly. Comstock shrugged and filled his glass again.

In a moment Chevagnac came back. He closed the door and stood against it with both hands behind him, gripping the knob. He looked first at the girls and raised his eyebrows for them to go. Marie pouted and started to come toward him. He stamped his foot.

"Go!" he shouted. She tossed her head and slammed the other door as she went out. Chevagnac stepped forward and brushed a hand across his forehead.

"*Eh bien,*" he said. "A night's work."

"Have you lost your reason?" Pau was half up in his chair. Comstock looked at them both and waited.

"*Non,*" said Chevagnac. "Upstairs—come."

He led them out onto the darkened landing and started up the rickety stairs. On the floor above, he stopped while they filed silently up behind him.

"What is it?" hissed Pau.

Chevagnac put his hand on the door knob and opened it. Pau went in first, with Comstock after him. Chevagnac closed the door. The latch clicked loudly in the stillness.

It was a smaller room than the one they had come from. There was a table with a white cloth splotched with a stain of red where a wineglass had overturned and spilled its contents. There was a saucer next to the stain—a saucer choked with cigarette ends. Chevagnac turned up the sputtering blue flame at the one gas jet and flooded the room with pale flickering light.

"Name of a——" Pau jumped backward. On the floor under the table edge was Petitjean with his eyes and mouth wide open and his arms sprawled loosely. Pau knelt quickly beside him and felt under the disordered decorations on his tunic. "As dead," he said, "as he'll ever be."

Chevagnac nodded. "I know," he said. He pointed to Petitjean's cheeks, where the black blood was settling under the skin on both sides of his nose. "His neck is broken."

Pau straightened suddenly. "We must go." He turned to the door.

Chevagnac shook his head. "No," he said. "Not to leave him." He raised his hands. "You know what I thought of him as a man—what we all thought. Nevertheless, there is work still to be done. What you see here on the floor belongs to the world. It is a tradition of the ages. It cannot die this way or all history will be worthless." He drew his lips back from his teeth. "Think of the next war, my friends," he sneered. "Where will you get defenders if they learn in the streets and in the Chamber and in the newspaper office that the path of glory leads merely to a broken neck in Le Coq d'Or? Come!" His laugh rang harshly. "We will do a job tonight to be proud of. Madame will not dare speak—for her life. And we shall lock the secret in our own hearts forever." He straightened his shoulders. "Come, Pau, his feet. You, my friend"—he turned to Comstock—"you will help? Good! It is the greatest hoax of all time! You lead the way and keep the passages clear of the curious. We shall return in his roadster to Vieupeyroux."

Carefully they lifted the limp body and moved toward the door. It sagged between them like a half-filled sack of grain. Comstock picked up the cap and turned down the light as Pau and Chevagnac went out to the landing.

Down the creaky stairs they crept with their lolling, ogling burden. On the street floor, Comstock pushed ahead of them and opened the entrance to the alleyway. They trudged out into the wet blackness of the night.

Petitjean's car loomed dimly through the mists. They placed him in the seat and Chevagnac crawled in behind the wheel. "His hands before him, so, and his legs straight out," he whispered. "It will be an hour yet—and who can tell? One stiffens so when one is not alive. You, Pau, you will hold him so." Comstock climbed to the running board and the car purred into life. Chevagnac bent forward over the wheel. Presently they were crawling slowly through the darkened streets toward St.-Parres-les-Vaudes and the open country.

It was perhaps ninety minutes later—a wet, creeping ninety minutes of darkness and mist and silence—that they topped the last rise above Vieupeyroux. Chevagnac turned to the left to circle around the village.

The car bumped and jolted on the rutty back road. Pau cursed once, softly and earnestly, and Chevagnac's arms twisted and writhed mightily about the wheel to keep the crawling roadster from vaulting the cut-back banks and hurtling over into the drain ditches.

"What then?" said Pau.

"The airdrome, of course. You think I brought him this far to put him to bed?"

"Name of——"

"Silence!" hissed Chevagnac.

Pau growled darkly. And because it takes many centuries to become accustomed to the work of the guillotine, he was silent.

Presently Chevagnac stopped the car and climbed stiffly out. "Wait," he said, and stalked off through the darkness.

"Ugh!" said Pau. "A cigarette, my ancient friend. His face is cold. This is devil's work." Comstock gave him a cigarette and the two stood smoking into their cupped hands, waiting.

To the eastward now there was a faint suggestion of grayness. Wind stirred gently in the tree tops and the grass rustled in ghostly whispers about their feet. Pau shivered.

Presently Chevagnac came stumbling toward them. "Quickly now!" he hissed. "There is a light in the quarter of the mechanicians. Carry him and follow me."

He led them tripping and cursing after him. Up over the slight rise they puffed with the thing that had been the Eagle between them. Around the back of the hangars they crept, Chevagnac in the lead. He stopped them just before they bumped into the shadowy outline of the lone Nieuport that stood upon the tarmac.

"Now you see?" said Chevagnac. "He dies as a gentleman dies. Quickly! His arms into his coat—so. His helmet now. Strap it, Comstock—and his goggles. The cap—toss it there upon the ground carelessly. Now then lift him in and hook his belt. Feet upon the rudder bar—tightly. They are stiff enough to hold. You, Pau—the propeller, when I give the word." He leaned forward into the cockpit and pulled the joy stick back until the tail planes came slightly above level. He hooked it in place with Petitjean's stiffened arms and tied a piece of twine about the cold gloved hands. "Now, Pau!"

The motor barked once and came suddenly to life. Pau jumped backward. A moment while Chevagnac warmed the engine, then he waved to the two others to pull out the chocks from the wheels.

The Nieuport trembled and rolled slowly across the ground in the dead still morning air. It gathered speed quickly. Halfway across the 'drome the tail skid left the ground. They could no longer see now because of the mists. But they could hear it.

It was off now in a long low climb. Their ears strained until they knew it had cleared the tree tops. For a moment more they listened as the engine sang down the air into the silence of distance. Then Chevagnac tapped them. "Quickly! Run! We must be in Vieupeyroux asleep before the word spreads. On your honors—silence forever about this! Run!"

It was 9:30. Sprinting feet pounded on the flagging in the corridors of Vieupeyroux. Doors slammed open and shut and men sprang out of bed.

"Petitjean—he is dead! Went up before daylight. His car—they found it behind the hangars. Drunk, he was—again. Crashed at Jouay. His neck—*pouf!*"

Chevagnac pushed open the door. Comstock was alone in the room. He awoke suddenly and sat up on his cot.

"The Eagle is plucked."

Comstock folded his hands, and stared at his swollen knuckles. He nodded.

"Your hand," asked Chevagnac—"it is bad?"

Comstock looked at him closely.

"Last night—you remember—you hit a—lamp-post?"

"How did you know?" the Texan muttered.

"Its jaw was broken as well as its neck. Come, let me fix it. There is only one hand in the world that can hit so. We may need it again. Now that M'sieur Tac-au-Tac is gone, we must be careful of ourselves—look out for each other."

Comstock stood up. "Chevvy," he said, "you are a white man. Shake!"

"*Au contraire,*" said Chevagnac. "A lucky man. You saved me a job. I should have had to shoot—for the sake of the squadron. And Pau, he would have used a knife. Come, *mon ami,*" he said, *"déjeuner."*

Leo V. Jacks
(1896–1972)

Grand Island, Nebraska, native Leo Vincent Jacks graduated from St Mary's College, near Topeka, Kansas, and joined the army in 1917. The diary of his war service with the 119th Field Artillery Regiment in the 32d Division was the basis of the memoir *Service Record of an Artilleryman* published by Scribner's in 1928. After the war, Jacks earned a PhD from the Catholic University of America, in Washington, D.C., and became a classics professor at Creighton University in Omaha. In addition to short stories, Jacks also published the novels *Xenophon, Soldier of Fortune* (1930) and *La Salle* (1931). "One Hundred Per Cent" was first published in *Scribner's Magazine* in November 1928 and was collected in *Great Short Stories of the War* (1930).

One Hundred Per Cent
Leo V. Jacks

Uncle Henry flicked the reins over the black mare, and shifted his quid of Union Leader. "What'd you think of all the speechifyin' at the Crossin'?"

As any dutiful fifteen-year-old nephew would, I said it was good. The Crossing is a town of a thousand inhabitants, and, like many such towns, it takes its Fourth of July undiluted. When there is any Americanism to be dispensed, the Crossing always gulps a liberal dose.

This ideal rural festival had just terminated after a barbecue in the grove, many tubs of pink lemonade, firecrackers till hell wouldn't hold them, and of course some perspiring orators. Now it was sundown, and Uncle Henry and I were on our way home. The yeomen had milled around all day in the hot sun, red-faced, panting, and happy. They enjoyed everything.

The chief speaker was the Honorable J. O. Coughlin, our congressman, and if he didn't twist the British lion's tail, and pull all the feathers out of the Austrian eagle—He gave the French hell for not paying their war debt, and the crowd said he ought to know, for he was there in '18.

He talked at great length about the gallantry of our boys in the war, and he told a story of a very brave Y. secretary who had run out into no man's land, or some place, under the fire of eighty-four machine-guns and several regiments of the Bavarian Guard to rescue some wounded soldier. While this story was being related, I heard Uncle Henry swearing under his breath, and I thought maybe a mosquito had bitten him. Mr. Coughlin told none of his own brave deeds. I suppose he was too bashful.

As I studied him, I couldn't help thinking that he would be a dangerous man in a fight, for he was big and heavy, and he looked strong enough to put an awful push behind a bayonet. Then, too, he had an air of embattled virtue which indicated that when he was roused he could be terrible. It was a mighty good thing for our district that we had such a man to protect the public interests. And, yet, he had an ingratiating way; tall, with a fair, full face, and bright, trusting blue eyes, and a great hand-shake. He dressed very well.

A young boy is a natural-born hero-worshipper. You know how quickly he will construct a heroic character out of any big man he admires, and how badly he feels when he sees the feet of clay. I'll never forget the story of the Chicago White Sox trial, and the newsboy's wail, when Joe Jackson fled from the court-room with his hands over his face: "Say it ain't true, Joe, say it ain't true."

The mayor had introduced Coughlin as a veteran of many battles, who had gone into politics to purify them. I didn't see any medals on him, but he was probably modest and left them at home. The mayor said, anyway, that he had been in some desperate battles, so, like any youngster, I watched the big man with a good deal of admiration and not a little awe. I'd made up my mind that on our way home I'd quiz Uncle Henry about those battles.

Uncle Henry is thin-faced, and always clean-shaved. He has bright gray eyes and a retiring way. He is five feet nine, and he limps a little when he walks. He got a shrapnel bullet in his left foot at the Fond des Meszeires, and didn't go to the hospital.

So, you see, he is an alumnus of the A. E. F., and a clever one, too, and a skilled manipulator of the esteemed soixante-quinze. Now, as we jogged along, he hummed gently over the exploits of the mademoiselle from Bar-le-Duc, and the old farm-wagon rattled. Uncle Henry rolled his quid reflectively and ruminated for a moment. Then he spat accurately at a thirteen-striped gopher that darted out of the rut just in time to escape the encroaching wheels.

"Fourth of July speeches don't mean nothin', kid," he observed. "The politicians—and that goes for Coolidge and Coughlin, and 99 per cent of the men holding offices that they got by votes—they don't care a rap for the common people, or the soldiers either, spite of all they talk about battles, and brave boys, and all that."

"Well, if the politicians don't appreciate what the boys did in France, the people did," I said. "They've elected some of these fighting soldiers to good jobs. There's Mr. Coughlin——"

"Yeah? Well, if the people feel that way, they sure show their appreciation of the fighting man in strange ways.

"Now, I recall a fellow in our battery, and he was—but I'll tell you all about him.

"When our Brigade started up to the Marne in July, the dope had it that there would be a big battle. It came, too. Well, this fellow, a handsome blond with blue eyes and very fair hair, whom you can call Spicks or Sticks, or some such thing, was a cannoneer.

"In the middle of the last night, when we were getting close to the front, and we could hear the guns booming and see the red flashes on the sky-line, it began to rain cats and dogs, and what with all the mud and confusion, and the trampling, and the troops jammed up in the crossroads, and the black darkness, Sticks or Wicks lost his way, and went somewhere else. Damned if we didn't have to go into action without him.

"Our Brigade was in fighting at Fresnes, and Courmont, and the Croix Rouge Farm, and Chamery, and Dravegny, and old Death Valley, where we buried a lot of our good men, and so on, from July 30 to August 24. You'd think, now, wouldn't you, that a rabid patriot who was just yearning to kill him a few Germans would have found his way up to the front, and rejoined his regiment in the course of twenty-six consecutive days of hard fighting?

"But Sticks or Bicks couldn't find his way. By day the thunder of the guns could have guided him somewhat, and at night you could see the sky all lit up like the mouth of hell and fiery red for miles around Hangar Claudin, and Fismes, and Fismettes. But he didn't see or hear. From where we lost him it was only a ten-mile walk to Courmont, and many's the time we hiked thirty miles between sundown and sunrise, so the distance couldn't have bothered him much.

"But, anyway, on August 25 we were pulled out of the Aisne-Marne entertainment, and started elsewhere. And our boys went along feeling pretty chirrupy, because they had it that we were bound for a rest-camp. Soldiers are optimistic cusses. They still think a rest-camp means rest.

"Well, sir, second day on the road we ran right into Ticks or Spicks, and there were tears in his big blue eyes as he told First Lieutenant Finnegan, who happened to be our commanding officer because the captain had been killed by a shell, how hard he'd been hunting for us, and what a rocky time he'd had away from the battery, and, gee! couldn't he have something to eat? He was damn near starved.

"So the Looie rode back to the rolling-kitchen, and he said to the cooks: 'This poor son of something is in an awful fix. Can you give him a little snack?'

"They said they could, and they did.

"For the next three days Spicks or Hicks was one of the most diligent boys I ever laid my two eyes on, and he certainly made some of our prize duty-dodgers look like what they were. He chopped wood for the kitchen, and worked at this and that, and he begged Sergeant Nixon to give him back his old job on the 75.

"On August 27 came a God-awful hike. All day and no let-up. Top speed. Night fell. Some of our men began to get pretty leg-weary. The old horses groaned, and panted, and cursed in horse, and the colonel made every son get down and walk.

"The country we were passing through looked tough. Fields all shell-holes, and the houses in ruins. Besides, you don't go to rest-camps on twenty-four-hour forced marches. Finally, about three in the morning we began to see the old red flashes and hear the guns. We didn't know where we were, but we knew there was a hell of a battle going on, and that was the reason for all the hurry. We were slated for a nice juicy job, probably right in the front row.

"Then it rained. Ye gods, how it rained! But at last our column, blistered and tottering and groaning and cursing and starvation-hungry, pulled up under some trees in a meadow to take a final inventory before we stepped in where the water was deep.

"Then somebody discovered that Sticks was missing. Lost again. By God, that boy had tough luck! He always got lost when there was a battle in the offing.

"The great Oise-Aisne drive is all history now. We had a wild time in company with the First Moroccan Division. They're the greatest soldiers in the world. I take off my hat to those North Africans.

"Our division lost a lot of men, but we took all our objectives, and buried our dead, and, finally, our brigade came out on the 6th of September, after about nine days of real big league battling.

"We were marching down the old sunshiny road toward the Forest of Retz when here came Sticks. Lord! he was a sorry-looking mess, but he was sorrier when Lieutenant Finnegan clapped eyes on him. 'Jesus-God!' Finnegan roared. 'Donner und Blitzen! Sacre nom du chien! Git me a pair of handcuffs quick!'

"And if he didn't grab that Sticks in a hurry, I hope to spit in your mess-kit.

"Believe it or not, Sticks had had a lot of hard luck. Practically all the hard luck in the A. E. F. There were tears in his eyes while he told about it, and Finnegan couldn't make him shut his mouth. And, believe me, he begged hard, and argued.

"For a while nobody really believed that he got lost the second time, but if you keep at a story long enough you can make some people swallow it. And, of course, we didn't have any handcuffs. What'd you do with handcuffs in a regiment of field artillery?

"So Finnegan had to let him go. But the officers were disgusted, and some of the enlisted men that'd had their friends or relatives killed said Spicks should be made an example of, and they talked about court-martial.

"You'd think, maybe, with all that hanging over his head, Picks would have deserted in dead earnest. But he didn't. He wore his air of injured virtue day and night. He was humbler than ever, and more diligent. He cut wood, and he didn't have to be told. He worked hard for the cooks, and he stuck to the battery like a leech. And all the time he protested innocence, and swore his disappearance had been an accident pure and simple. He may have been pure, but he was not so simple.

"We went to a damn rest-camp in the Haute-Marne, where we did everything but rest, and before there was time for a court-martial, before there was time for anything but one or two good drunks, the whole brigade was hustled away to Verdun. The underground telegraph said that all the battles fought up to date would shrink into nursery rhymes alongside what was coming. So we tightened our harness, and oiled the guns, and ate everything we could get. We never let the war interfere with our appetites. And every night we went legging it in thirty-mile hikes up through the Bar-le-Duc country, past Eurville-Bienville, and on to Esnes.

"It rained every night, and lots of the boys fell down by the road just plumb paralyzed, and every morning our column was thinner than the day before. And all day long the cripples would come staggering into camp, and the cooks fed them, and helped them along. We had good cooks.

"On the morning of September 23 we limped into the Bois de Brocourt. The rain stopped, and at six o'clock the sun shone. Lord! that was a beautiful morning. Some birds were singing, and the grass and leaves were sprinkled with rain-drops shining in the light. There were little sunny meadows all around. Lieutenant Finnegan said that when breakfast was over, and the horses fed and groomed and watered, we could sleep all day.

"When we lined up for mess, there was no Sticks at the kitchen. The head cook, Jones, said that Sticks was with them some time during the night, and then again, all of a sudden, he wasn't there. Just like that.

"Lieutenant Finnegan never said a word, but his face got as hard as a steel trap, and I figured it'd be the firing-squad for Sticks if we ever caught him again. So we went on blithely, and from September 26 to November 11 the Meuse-Argonne drive was on, forty-seven days of continuous battling in a country that'd make the Dismal Swamp look like a public playground.

"And our regiment fought in most of that fight, because we saw thirty-nine consecutive days of the fun. When they brought us out at last we could just totter, and that was all. Clothes in rags, equipment busted, guns blown up. Seventy-five per cent of the old horses were dead, 72 per cent of the men killed, wounded, or gassed.

"Nobody laughed, or joked, or talked. They just walked along, glassy-eyed. When it was time to rest, they rested, and when the guides said 'Go,' they got up passively, and went. Thirty-nine days in the Meuse-Argonne without a break. Ask anybody that was there.

"After a week or two we'd hobbled down into the neighborhood of Neuville-sur-Orne, and damned if we didn't walk right on to Private Sticks. And, believe it or not, he got lost on that hike to Verdun. He smiled a wan smile when they took him to the guard-house. He said it was tough treatment for a poor boy who was trying to do his duty, and had had misfortunes. But the M. P. snapped him off, and said that the Y. was also doing its duty, and having misfortunes.

"Our regiment wasn't really a hard-hearted crowd, and nobody hated Sticks, though they all despised him. But you'd think we were a lot of Pontius Pilates from the way he behaved toward us. He got six months in the brig, and the guards cuffed him around a lot, but he was damned lucky he didn't get shot.

"When we finally came back to America, old Finnegan said: 'Turn the blankety-blank son of a skunk loose, and let him go.' So Sticks chirked up immediately. I heard he worked 'em for an honorable discharge."

The plodding team was beginning to descend into the old hollow around grandfather's farm, and we could hear the crows cawing in the woods, and some squirrels barking in the great cottonwoods overhead.

"Gee," I said, "that fellow was a dirty yellow coward, and I wouldn't trust him with anything. What made you think of him, Uncle Henry?"

"Oh, I *saw* him—at the Crossin'."

"You did?" I cried. "Who is he?"

Uncle Henry got rid of his quid of Union Leader, and flicked the reins sharply over the black mare before he answered: "Why, our honorable congressman, J. O. Coughlin."

Mary Borden

(1886–1968)

A Chicago native, Mary Borden Spears served throughout the war as a nurse and medical administrator, establishing at her own expense a mobile surgical hospital near the front. She wrote about her war experience in *The Forbidden Zone* (1929), a collection of sketches, stories, and poems, and in *Journey Down a Blind Alley* (1946), a memoir. In 1918, after the end of her first marriage, she married Edward Spears, who later became an influential English army general and Member of Parliament. Having published fiction before the war as Bridget MacLagen, Borden was highly productive in the 1920s and 1930s, publishing novels, stories, and nonfiction. In 1940, during World War II, she began the Hadfield-Spears ambulance unit, which, after evacuation from occupied France, served in the Middle East, North Africa, and Italy. Of the title of her World War I collection, she wrote: "I have called the collection of fragments 'The Forbidden Zone' because the strip of land immediately behind the zone of fire where I was stationed went by that name in the French Army. We were moved up and down inside it; our hospital unit was shifted from Flanders to the Somme, then to Champagne, and then back again to Belgium, but we never left 'La Zone Interdite.'"[1]

Rosa

Mary Borden

The stretcher bearers staggered under his weight when they brought him along through the sunlight to the operating room. They put him down for a moment on the ground outside the operating hut and wiped the sweat off their old foreheads.

1. Mary Borden, preface to *The Forbidden Zone* (Garden City, N.Y.: Doubleday, Doran, 1929), n.p.

It was a hot summer's day. The sector was quiet. The attack that had filled the hospital two days before had fizzled out. Now only occasional ambulances lurched in at the gate, bringing men who had been missed by the stretcher bearers, left out for a couple of nights on No Man's Land, or been wounded unnecessarily by stray bullets after the big push was over. This man had come up over the horizon alone, a red giant, brought unconscious through the summer afternoon in a battered Ford, and deposited like a log on our doorstep, solitary character of some obscure incident in the aftermath of battle. He lay on the ground like a felled ox, a bull mortally wounded, breathing noisily.

His head was bound with a soiled bandage; his eyes were closed; his bruised mouth was open. Thick tufts of red hair pushed through the head bandage. There was dried blood round his immense rough lips. His huge red face was dark and blurred. He was covered with dust. He looked as if he had been rolling in a dirty field like some farm animal. He was a man of the soil, of the dark earth, with the heavy power of the earth in him. The bright sun shining on his massive unconscious bulk made the darkness of his lost consciousness visible. He seemed to lie deep, distant, withdrawn in a shadowy abyss. His spirit—brother spirit of ox and bullock and all beasts of the field—was deep asleep, in that sleep which is the No Man's Land of the soul, and from which men seldom come back. But his immense body continued, in spite of his absence to hum and drum like a dynamo, like a machine whose tremendous power takes time to run down, and his breath came whistling and spurting through his rough bruised lips like escaping steam.

The old stretcher-bearers lifted him again grunting, and brought him in to us and hoisted him with difficulty on to the narrow white table, in the white room full of glistening bottles and shining basins and silvered instruments, among the white-coated surgeons and nurses. His head hung over one end of the table, and his feet over the other, and his great freckled arms hung helpless and heavy down at either side. Thick curling bunches of red hair, wiry and vigorous, grew out of his enormous chest. We stripped his body. It lay inert, a mountainous mass, with the rough-hewn brick-red face tipped back. His sightless face reminded one of the face of a rock in a sandstone quarry, chiseled with a pick-axe, deeply gashed. His closed eyes were caves under bushy cliffs, his battered mouth a dark shaft leading down into a cavern where a hammer was beating.

Because he was so big, his helplessness was the more helpless. But one could feel life pounding powerfully in his body—senseless life, pounding on, pumping air into his lungs, keeping his heart going. Yes, he would be hard to kill, I thought. Even a bullet in the head hadn't killed him.

I counted his pulse. It was strong and steady.

"Shot through the mouth. Revolver bullet lodged in the brain." Monsieur X was reading the ticket that had been pinned to the man's blanket in the dressing station behind the front line.

But how? I wondered. How queer, I thought. Shot in the mouth—through the roof of the mouth. He must have been asleep in the trench with his mouth open. And I imagined him there, sprawling in the muddy ditch, an exhausted animal with his great stupid mouth open; and I saw a figure crawl in beside him and put the barrel of a revolver between his big yellow teeth. Fool, I thought. You fool—you big hulking brute beast—going to sleep like that in utter careless weariness.

But no, it was impossible. In this war such things didn't happen. Men were killed haphazard—maimed, torn to pieces, scattered by shell fire, plugged full of shrapnel, hit square sometimes by rifle bullets, but not shot neatly through the roof of the mouth with a revolver.

They were whispering as they bent over him. Monsieur X frowned, pinched his lips together, looked down at the great, gentle unconscious carcase sideways.

"But how?" I asked. "Who?"

"Himself. He shot himself through the mouth. It's a suicide."

"Suicide!" I echoed the word vaguely, as if it contained a mystery. There was something queer, out of the ordinary, about it, shocking to the surgeons and orderlies. They were ashamed, worried, rather flustered. "But why suicide?" I asked, suddenly aware of the extraordinary fact that a personal tragedy had lifted its head above the dead level of mass destruction. It was this that shocked them.

He's not young, I thought, cutting the bandage round the rough unconscious head with its shock of matted red hair. A peasant, probably—very stupid—an ox of a man.

"Why suicide?" I asked aloud.

"Panic," answered Monsieur briefly. "Fear—he tried to kill himself from fear of being killed. They do sometimes."

"This one didn't."

"No, he didn't succeed, this big one. He ought to be dead. The bullet is here just under the skull. It's gone clean through his brain. Any other man would be dead. He's strong, this big one."

"You'll extract it?"

"But certainly."

"And he will live?"

"Perhaps."

"And what then?"

"He'll be court-martialed and shot, Madame, for attempted suicide."

They were strapping his iron arms and legs to the narrow table. Someone lifted his heavy head. Someone pulled his great bulk into position and bound him to the table with strong leather bands.

"Don't do it!" I shouted suddenly. "Leave him alone." I was appalled by his immense helplessness.

They went on with their business of getting him ready. They didn't hear me. Perhaps I had not shouted aloud.

"You don't understand," I cried. "You've made a mistake. It wasn't fear. It was something else. He had a reason, a secret. It's locked there in his chest. Leave him alone with it. You can't bring him back now to be shot again."

But they clapped the ether mask over his face, stifling his enormous stentorious breathing, and with that he began to struggle—the dying ox. Life, roused by the menace of the suffocating gas, sprang up in him again—gigantic, furious, suffering a baited bull. It began plunging in him, straining, leaping to get out of his carcase and attack its enemies. A leather thong snapped, a fist shot out, knocking over bottles and basins. There was a crash, a tinkle of broken glass, a scramble of feet, and suddenly through the confusion I heard a thin soft anguished voice cry as if from a great distance, "Rosa, Rosa!" It came from his chest; it sounded like the voice of a man lost in a cave. It came from under his heaving side where the bushy hair grew thick and strong—a hollow heartbroken voice, issuing from his blind unconscious mouth, in a long cry—"Rosa, Rosa!"

Twice again he called Rosa before they could clap the ether mask down again on his face.

It was a neat operation and entirely successful. They took the bullet out of the top of his head, bandaged his head up again, and carried him away through the sunny afternoon to be put to bed.

"He will surely die in the night," I said to myself, and I went again and again in the night to see if, happily, he were dead; but always, standing beside the shadow of his great bulk, I could hear him breathing, and once I thought I heard sighing on his shrouded lips the name of the woman—Rosa.

"He can't live," the night nurse said.

"He can't die," I whispered to myself. "Life is too strong in him, too hard to kill."

He was much better the next day. I found him sitting up in bed in a clean pink flannel night shirt, staring in front of him. He didn't answer when I said "Good morning," or take any notice of me. He hadn't spoken to any one during the day, the nurse told me, but he was very obedient and ate his soup quietly, "as good as gold," she said he was. "A remarkable case," Monsieur X said. "He ought to be dead." But there he was sitting up eating his meals with an excellent appetite.

"So he knows what will happen?" I asked, following the surgeon to the door.

"But certainly. They all know. Everyone in the army knows the penalty."

The suicide did not turn his head or look in my direction. He was still staring straight ahead of him when I came back and stood at the foot of his bed.

Who are you? I wondered, and who is Rosa? And what can I do? How can I help you? And I stood there waiting, miserably spellbound by the patient brute who at last turned on me from his cavernous eyes a look of complete understanding, and then looked heavily away again.

That night when the orderly was dozing and the night nurse was going on her round from hut to hut, he tore the bandage from his head. She found him with his head oozing on the pillow, and scolded him roundly. He didn't answer. He said nothing. He seemed not to notice. Meekly, docile as a friendly trusting dog, he let her bandage him up again, and the next morning I found him again sitting up in his bed in his clean head bandage staring in front of him with that dark look of dumb subhuman suffering. And the next night the same thing happened, and the next, and the next. Every night he tore off his bandage, and then let himself be tied up again.

"If his wound becomes infected he'll die," said Monsieur X, angrily.

"That's what he's trying to do," I answered. "Kill himself again before they can shoot him," I added, "to save them the trouble."

I dared not speak to the man whom I thought of day and night as Rosa, having never learned his name, and he never spoke to me or any one. His eyes, which he now always turned on me when I came in, forbade me to speak to him. They stared into mine with the understanding of a brute mortally wounded, who is not allowed to die, so I went to the General, and, actuated by some hysterical impulse, pleaded for the man's life.

"But, Madame, we have epidemics of suicide in the trenches. Panic seizes the men. They blow their brains out in a panic. Unless the penalty is what it is—to be court-martialed and shot—the thing would spread. We'd find ourselves going over the top with battalions of dead men. The same penalty applies to men who wound themselves. That's the favourite device of a coward. He puts the muzzle of his rifle on his foot and fires."

I argued. I explained that this man was not afraid of being killed, but of not being killed, that his luck was out when the enemy missed him; that he had been kept waiting too long, had shot himself in despair because the Germans wouldn't shoot him; and a woman called Rosa let him down, or perhaps she died. Perhaps he simply wanted to go to her.

"He must have had a letter in the trenches—a letter from Rosa or about her. He's not a young man. He is forty or more—an enormous brute with red hair and hands like hams. A farmer probably. One of those slow plodding gentle brute men, faithful as dogs. His voice was broken-hearted, high and hollow like a child's voice, when he called to her. Like a child that is lost. 'Rosa! Rosa!' If you'd heard him.

"And here you are with your military regulations asking me to save him for you so that you can shoot him. You expect us to tie up his head every night and prevent his dying so that you can march him off to trial and stand him up against a wall."

But what was the good of arguing against army regulations? We were at war. The General could do nothing. The man must be made an example, so that these epidemics of suicide could be kept in check.

I didn't dare go back to Rosa. I went to the door of the hut and called the nurse. Down in the centre of the long row of beds I could see his great shoulders and his huge bandaged head. He looked like a monstrous baby in his white bonnet and pink flannel shirt. But I knew that his big haggard eyes were staring, and I remembered that his face had been a little paler each day, that it was not brick colour any more, but the colour of wax, that his cheek bones stood out like shelves.

He's killing himself in spite of us all, I thought. He's succeeding. It's hard work, it takes patience, but he's doing it. Given a chance, he'll pull it off. Well, he'll have his chance. I almost laughed. I had been a fool to go to the General and plead for his life. That was the last thing he wanted me to do for him. That was just the wrong thing.

I spoke to the nurse who was going on duty for the night.

"When Rosa pulls off his bandage to-night, leave it off," I said abruptly.

She looked at me a minute hesitating. She was highly trained. Her traditions, her professional conscience, the honour of her calling loomed for a moment before her, then her eyes lighted. "All right," she said.

I thought when I stood at the foot of Rosa's bed next morning and found him staring at me that I detected a look of recognition in his eyes, perhaps even a faint look of gratitude, but I could not be sure. His gaze was so sombre, so deep, that I could not read it, but I could see that he was weaker. Perhaps it was his increased pallor that made his eyes so enormously dark and mysterious. Towards evening he grew delirious, but he tore off his bandage all the same, in the middle of the night. He managed to do that. It was his last effort, his last fumbling desperate and determined act. His fixed idea prevailed through his delirium, his will triumphed. It was enough. He was unconscious next morning and he died two days later, calling in his weary abysmal heart for Rosa, though we could not hear him.

Leonard H. Nason

(1895–1970)

As a sergeant with the 76th Field Artillery Regiment, Leonard Hastings Nason was wounded in action in July 1918. After the war he graduated from Norwich University and became a prolific writer of novels and short stories about American soldiers in World War I. He is noted for the novels *Chevrons* (1926), *Sergeant Eadie* (1928), and *A Corporal Once* (1930). His numerous short stories appeared in the *Saturday Evening Post* as well as in the collections *Three Lights from a Match* (1927) and *The Top Kick* (1928). "Among the Trumpets" was first published in the July 27, 1929, *Saturday Evening Post* and was collected in *Great Short Stories of the War* (1930). Nason's interest in horses at war likely stems in part from his service in 1916 with the army's cavalry, and his *Among the Trumpets: Stories of War Horses and Others* appeared in 1932. He also served in the Second World War, achieving the rank of lieutenant colonel. He is buried at Arlington National Cemetery.

Among the Trumpets

Leonard H. Nason

He paweth in the valley, and rejoiceth in his strength: he goeth on to meet the armed men. He mocketh at fear. . . . He saith among the trumpets, Ha, ha; and he smelleth the battle afar off, the thunder of the captains, and the shouting. The glory of his nostrils is terrible.
—*The Book of Job*, xxxix, 21–25, 20.

The morning was well advanced—that is to say, it was some time after nine o'clock. Westward the high-banked clouds that were the remnants of those that had deluged the countryside with rain the night before were still black and menacing, but eastward the sky was blue, and the sun already gave promise of unpleasant heat later on.

From the black woods on the right, gloomy and sinister beneath the clouds, to the rolling hills of the horizon stretched a wavy band of newly plowed earth. It was wide, it was irregular, it ran up and down hill and squirmed along the side of crests as if the man that had furrowed it had been either drunk or blind. That wavy band of earth, though made with steel, had not been plowed. It marked the German front line in front of Richecourt; it showed where the defense system that the French had crowned with such names as the Trench of the Goths, Trench of the Vandals, and Trench of the Barbarians had once frowned on Seicheprey and Jury Wood. The system was no more. Parapet and parados had been flattened into one uneven heap of mangled earth, the wire had been plucked up by shells, tossed about, rolled up, and flattened again by the passage of tanks. Dugouts and strong points that had defied assault for four years had gone as the snows of yesteryear.

The American attack that had begun at dawn had crossed this band of plowed ground in one jump, found no resistance and had gone on across the fields to the north, where they were already out of range.

The American artillery, most of its guns outranged, and the others unable to direct the barrage at such a distance from the target, had ceased firing. The Germans, their guns abandoned or in retreat, had done likewise. Deep silence had fallen where so short a time before thunderbolts had crashed and the ground had trembled with the recoil of a thousand guns. Where all had been smoke and shouts and frantic rockets, were now only peaceful fields and quiet, shady woods, except for that long, waving, sinister gash that was like a wound that had killed this countryside.

From a hollow suddenly appeared a group of horsemen. They drew rein before their silhouettes cut the skyline and hurriedly examined the ground to the right flank with their field glasses. The fields through a field glass were not at all deserted.

The leader of the horsemen, a captain of United States cavalry, could see men stringing telephone wire, prisoners in groups of three and four coming back, ambulances being loaded with wounded, and far away northward, white puffs of smoke that came from bursting grenades, and that showed where the American advance was bombing its way toward an objective it had not hoped to reach until the morrow.

"We're through the first line," said the captain decisively. "The road will be about there." He pointed to his left front, then looked curiously at Mont Sec, a sugarloaf hill that rose abruptly a thousand feet from the surrounding plain. Its summit was crowned with smoke, from which came the continuous flash of bursting shells. "I doubt if any boche up there can see us," said the captain. "We'll assume not. Can you make out the road, lieutenant? We'd better locate it before we start across."

The officer addressed wore the blue of the French army. He had a round bullethead and mustaches that were much too long.

He polished his field glasses with a white handkerchief, breathing upon them, wiping them carefully, and holding them to the light to see if they were clean.

The captain tightened his lips impatiently. Behind him he heard the stamping of a horse and, turning about, saw a sergeant who had just ridden up.

"Where have you been?" barked the captain.

"Sir, I had to come in from the extreme left, and this horse ain't much of a horse."

The sergeant panted slightly. It was apparent from his flushed countenance that he had been having difficulties with his mount.

"Well, if you can't ride him, turn him in!" snapped the captain, and turned back to the French officer trying to locate the road.

An enlisted man, his legs seemingly lost behind the high pommel of his packed saddle, under slicker, gun boot, saber, saddle pockets, blanket roll, and two days' grain ration, moved his horse over next to the sergeant's. "Hey, gold brick," he whispered, "where yuh been?"

The sergeant turned. "Hey, Mac!" he cried. He suddenly paused. He noted that the other wore a trumpet slung across his shoulders, and on the sleeve of his blouse, plainly discernible, was the scar of recently removed chevrons.

"You been busted?" went on the sergeant. "Huh? Drunk? A. W. O. loose? A guy with your service! Yuh oughta know better!"

"Naw, naw," grinned the trumpeter. "I got caught with a pair o' leather putts on. 'N' by the corps commander, too—no less. Don't worry. I got a better job blowin' a horn. Why di'n' yuh join up with us at Mandrees? Where yuh been, anyway, the last three months?"

"At Besançon, learnin' machine rifle. I'm commandin' the machine-gun troop. How come else I got invited to a council of war? Whaddyuh think, kid? See any other sergeants around?"

The trumpeter grinned a slow grin, then ejected tobacco juice.

"Machine-gun troop, huh? You an' them two machine rifles! Well, if you get from here to them woods with 'em I'll buy yuh a drink!"

"You think that's the entrance, then?" The captain's voice came clearly in the silence that followed. "Very well, I think I'll move them across there in echelon of double columns. I don't think we'll meet any resistance yet. The infantry would never have got by the woods if there were any squareheads in a fighting mood there. . . . Troop commanders! You will cross the open space by troops, in echelon of platoons in double column. You will regulate the gait according to the nature of the ground and the circumstances, without attempting to maintain the regularity of the squadron formation. On arriving at the woods we'll again resume column formation. I will be with H Troop's first platoon. Understand? Posts!"

"Boy," whispered the trumpeter, "if any o' them take up the gallop the captain won't have a man left in the saddle."

"How come?" demanded the sergeant. "What yuh been doin' all summer?"

"Diggin' a sewer for the Q. M. corps at Gievres!" grinned the trumpeter. "Ninety per cent o' this here raggedy-pants-cadet outfit ain't never been on a horse before in their lives!"

"No kiddin'!"

"No kiddin'. If we meet up with any boche that's on the peck any, there'll be a hot time in the old town; now, what I mean!"

"Sergeant Lee!"

"Sir!"

"Where are your machine rifles?"

"In rear of H Troops, sir!"

"Good. Ride with me so that I can give you orders for their employment. Off we go!"

The troop commanders—there were but two, and one of them a lieutenant—rejoined their troops; there was an arm signal, a few moaning whistle blasts; then the squadron, in a formation very similar to that which old-timers used to style "column of bunches," topped the sky line and hurriedly descending into the hollow beyond, proceeded at a fast trot toward the distant woods. A fast trot. Too fast, for the slower horses began to canter, whereat the faster ones, hearing tremendous clatter and thumping of hoofs, wanted to canter, too, and here and there a bolter began to go from rear to front of a platoon column, to the accompaniment of squeals and kicks from the other horses, and untrammeled language from the riders who had received a blow from a rifle butt on the thigh, a cinch ring on the knee, or who had been nearly torn from the saddle by the impetuous rush of the bolting horse.

"They'll get over that!" observed the trumpeter sagely. "They been fillin' 'em with oats! They won't prance very long under them full packs!"

"They didn't waste any oats on mine!" panted the sergeant. He had, by dint of voice, heel, and a club he carried, urged his horse into a shambling trot.

"Nor on that Frog looey's either!"

The French officer's horse was one of those who are averse to traveling alone and who will not leave ranks or picket line for any persuasion. This steed was proceeding at a sort of drifting gait, going sideways like a yacht with no centerboard, and making always toward H Troop's second platoon. The French officer kept the horse's head firmly toward the woods, so that the steed could not see his companions, but he knew they were there, and ever kept an ear turned in their direction.

Spur and whip prevailed for a time, but the moment the lieutenant stopped to draw breath or rest his tired leg, the drifting began again, accompanied by head tossing and lightninglike thrusts of the neck, which attempts had the effect each time of nearly unseating the French officer.

"That's a nice horse for an officer to ride!" observed the sergeant. "You'd think he'd know better than to bring a goat like that with him!"

"We give it to him. It's an H Troop horse. Sidewinder, they call him. He's like Coke Gillis. He ain't gone straight since he was born!"

"We give it to him!" protested the sergeant. "That's a great way to treat a officer and a Ally! Give him a star-gazin' goat like that!"

"Huh!" grunted the trumpeter, helping himself to another chew. "The French give him to us in the first place. Let 'em see now how they like their own horses!"

They arrived, finally, at the edge of the woods. No sign of life. Not a shot fired. There was a narrow field there, along the edge of which ran a rough track, an old cart path, but now beaten flat by many feet. Beyond, across the field, were more woods, into which this cart path led. There was a trench along the edge of the woods, but empty, and the hurdle that barred the road where it went through the wire had been so hastily put in place that the advance guard had been able to unwire it and drag it clear before the main body had come up.

Across the field went the squadron, skirting a communication trench; then the advance guard was seen to halt, troopers galloped out to left and right, and some indecision was manifested.

"What's the matter?" demanded the captain, riding up.

"There's four roads here!" replied one of the troopers of the advance guard.

"Which road, lieutenant?"

The French officer pulled up his horse and dragged forward his map case.

"You're not going to look at a map, are you?" demanded the captain. "I can look at a map myself. I thought you knew this country! Do you realize I've got a squadron of horse standing here in a field that runs from Apremont halfway to Metz? Do you suppose the boche are going to sit down and wait for us to cut them off? They're running so fast now we won't catch up with them before night!"

"The other end of this field is held by French troops," replied the French lieutenant. "They won't fire, because they have been warned not to. There will be plenty of boche very soon, don't worry." He bent over his map.

"Very well," snapped the captain, "I'll make my own decision!"

"If you do," replied the other, lifting his long mustache in a sneer, "you are liable to come into an area that is under our own artillery preparation, in which case the responsibility will be yours!"

The captain flushed, but said nothing. After all, this French officer had been sent for just that purpose—to keep this squadron out of areas that the French were pounding. It would not advance the situation to have the squadron destroyed by friendly artillery fire.

The French officer put away his map, took out a cigarette case, extracted one, and lighted it.

"The road to the right," said he.

The trumpeter tossed his chin meaningly in the direction of the French officer.

"Ah, don't worry about him," replied Sergeant Lee. "The French are probably just as proud of him as we are of some of the mail-order wonders we got! Boy, they got 'em in all armies, like coots!"

Thick trees, but no underbrush, huts, scattered gray overcoats; then, suddenly, long lines of wagons and empty picket lines. Loose horses, many of them wounded, could be seen among the trees, some trotting and whinnying at the sight of the advancing troops, others bounding away, and one or two limping in their direction, as if to ask for help from others of their kind.

Suddenly, at an alley that crossed the main track, the Americans saw men. The captain, the trumpeter, an orderly, and Sergeant Lee saw them almost simultaneously. There was a group of ten or fifteen that had probably heard the advance guard thud by and had come out of their holes to see what it was all about.

The captain swung his horse, whipped out his pistol and charged. H Troop's leading platoon followed him. Pistols barked, and Sergeant Lee's horse, that up until that time had given but the faintest signs of life, bolted, and having got a firm grip of the bit before the sergeant had recovered himself, was well away into the trees.

It was impossible to circle the runaway in the trees, but the sergeant saw before him an opening in the woods, into which the horse presently tore. Here was the place to reach out, seize the headstall, and by main strength drag the horse's head around so that he must run in a circle and eventually stop.

Bark!

"Cut out shooting, you fool!" shouted the sergeant. "Can't you see this horse——"

Bark-bark!

There was another man there, on a black horse. Flame spat form his hand. It was a German. Lee whipped out his saber, and instantly stopping all attempts to control his horse, let him go headlong for the black. The black, however, did not wait for the attack, but leaped aside, and its rider shot at Lee, as he tore by, at point-blank range.

But Lee had pinked him with the saber. Not badly, he knew, but he had felt resistance as he had lunged out. If only now he could pull this goat down—but they had crossed the glade and were again amidst the trees.

Bark! Again! The man on the black was pursuing him! Swiftly through the sergeant's mind passed the realization that he was very probably drawing his last breath. The German was behind, hence Lee would either have to sheathe his saber—impossible at that gait—let it hang by the saber knot while he drew his pistol—impossible because he had not put his hand through the wrist loop when he had drawn it—throw it away and then engage in a pistol combat with the German—impossible because if he turned around, the horse would undoubtedly dash headlong into the first tree—or just lay on the horse's neck, say a prayer, and pour the hooks into him.

How many shots? The German's gun must be nearly empty now! Ah, no, the German pistol held ten.

Before him suddenly loomed wire—a parapet—would the horse jump it? He was done now, anyway.

The horse bucked to a halt. Lee dropped his saber, tore out his pistol, and swinging around in the saddle, had one wild shot with it anyway. He shouted and fired again, more shouts, crashing, then the black horse tore by, saddle empty, and came to a rearing halt at the belt of wire, like a horse that has thrown his rider before the barrier in a riding hall.

There were Americans there—the trumpeter, pistol in hand, two privates of the advance guard.

"Hey, Lee!" cried the trumpeter. "We come down the road! I got that guy on the black!"

He and the two privates rode back to look at the German. He was on his face, but when one had dismounted and turned him over, they saw that he was dead. He was a private, with the black medal that indicates one wound, and the light blue and yellow shoulder straps of a Jäger zu Pferde, or mounted rifleman.

"Striker, probably," decided the trumpeter, "because this here horse looks like an officer's!"

"I'll say!" agreed Sergeant Lee. He had ridden over and taken the black's bridle, and then led him back to the others.

"Well, let's go!" said the others hurriedly. "This ain't no place to match pennies. These woods are full o' boche!"

"Right!" agreed Lee. "Where's the rest of 'em?"

"On the road. Whachuh dismountin' for?"

"I'm goin' to mount up on this black horse."

"You are?" cried the trumpeter. "Why, if anyone mounts him, I do! I knocked the guy off his back with a .45!"

"How do you know?" demanded the sergeant, picking up the saber he had dropped. "I had two or three shots at him myself!"

"No, it was the trumpeter got him!" said one of the privates, looking nervously about him. "We better be gettin' back. I see the captain out there. . . . No, the trumpeter got that kraut! I seen it!"

"Well, this horse is mine," said Sergeant Lee, mounting, "because I'm rankest man! What's the good of having three stripes if you can't rank somebody out of a bunk or a horse or something?"

"What are you men doing in there—see anything?" called a voice from behind the trees.

All wheeled their horses and went out. The alley down which they had charged curved, and the captain with the rest of the platoon had halted there.

"The trumpeter shot a German, sir," said Sergeant Lee. "He was chasing me. I've captured his horse."

"Nice horse, that," remarked the captain. "Better change saddles the first chance you get! We'll be able to use all the extra horses we can get before we're through. Trumpeter, ride back and tell Lieutenant Bennett to push a patrol forward on the road. I'm going to prospect around in here a little to see what we've run onto, to see if there is any sign of a force here—if this is just a bunch of wagoners and stable orderlies that we've run into. See that the French officer knows what's going on. . . . Corporal Petersen, take your squad and see if there are any Germans left in those huts. Write down any regimental numbers you see on the wagons. . . . Sergeant Lee, take a set of fours and follow along that trench to see what you find. When you hear three blasts of the whistle, rejoin."

He blew a short blast on his whistle. "Foragers, ho-o-oh!" The platoon, in line of foragers, at "raise pistol" moved off among the trees.

Sergeant Lee, riding the black and leading his own horse, led his four men along the line of the trench that had stopped the runaway rush of his horse. The trench was shallow, and had been newly dug. They found, shortly after, a small house, a sort of shelter for foresters or shepherds, very strongly built of stone. The trench was evidently part of an attempt to make a strong point out of this house; to prevent, perhaps, the flanking of positions farther back in the woods by attack from the road. The house, however, seemed to be abandoned, for its door hung open.

Sergeant Lee, his pistol ready, rode up, but there was nothing in the interior but scattered bedclothing and the disorder of boots, belts and equipment that told of hasty flight.

"Number One," said the sergeant, "take this horse. Don't turn him loose whatever happens, because he's got everything I own on him. I'm going to ride on a little. Listen for the three whistles and repeat them if you hear them."

He turned over his own horse and, being now free, could enjoy the feel of riding the black. The horse was a thoroughbred. Lee had never been on one like him before. It was like sitting on a dynamo. He could feel beneath him the nervous energy and the power of those steel muscles running up and down. A touch of the spur, a flection of the wrist, and the black was cantering. A turn of the shoulder, a shift of the left leg, and the black had changed leads. What a horse! Schooled, intelligent, powerful. Lee, without pressure on the reins, closed his legs and leaned slightly back. The horse slowed his gait. He leaned farther back. The black halted.

"Ah, boy! That's a horse!" breathed the sergeant to himself. What couldn't a man do with a mount like that? He saw himself leading a charge, outstripping lieutenants, captain, everyone, hurling himself upon the enemy, capturing their commander, their flags, raging about among them on that black horse.

"Hey, sergeant! Three whistles!"

There was, alas, a war on. The sergeant, taking one last look about him, moved his hand ever so slightly to the left, and the black, coming around beautifully, cantered back to the others. The sun, higher, began to glitter through the trees. No sign of the enemy, no crash of shell, no crackle of machine gun.

"Come on with that set of fours!" called someone faintly. "Rejoin! Rally! Ral-le-e-e!"

Lee gathered his four men, and trotting through the underbrush, rejoined the platoon, which the captain was leading back in the direction of the road they had left. They came out, in a minute or two, into the sunlight, and found there the head of the column, the trumpeter and the French lieutenant.

"What did you see, sergeant—anything?" demanded the captain.

"No, sir; only blankets and stuff lying around. That trench hadn't even been finished."

"We're losing time," said the captain quickly. "There was no force in there. We'll probably be seeing stragglers and orderlies and first-aid men and all sorts of gold bricks running loose in these woods, but that's not what we're here for. Now, then, we'll push forward vigorously. Pass the word back that if any isolated enemy are seen, to shoot at them, but not to delay the advance to try to capture them. Leave that for the doughboys. That agree with your thoughts, lieutenant?"

The French officer nodded. "Quite right, captain," said he. He did not turn his face, however, in the captain's direction. His eyes were upon the black horse that Sergeant Lee rode. "Captain," he went on, "I think I shall have to ask you to give me that horse that man is riding!"

"Huh? Give you that horse? That's a German horse! He captured it."

"I see that by the equipment, but it is a much better horse than mine. I want it."

"Perhaps you do," said the captain, gathering his reins, "but we don't take horses away from noncommissioned officers in this man's army!"

"Do you mean to say, sir," cried the French officer, "that you will not give an officer of an Allied army a captured horse simply because some soldier found it first? Which is the most important for the success of our mission—that he should be well mounted, or that I, who am the guide and the officer of liaison and the interpreter, should have the best horse? I think that higher authority would not take very long to decide the question!"

It was in the captain's mind to make no reply, but to order the advance to be resumed. But then this French officer would make a report of it when he returned, which report would come drifting down from corps headquarters, gathering indorsements and bitterness like a descending snowball, until it came into the hands of the squadron commander's immediate superiors. He would get Hades. And he would get no more details to command provisional squadrons.

"Give him the horse, sergeant," ordered the captain.

The sergeant's face hardened, and for just a second his blazing eyes met the captain's, whereat that officer's jaw muscles stood out like cords.

"Dismount!" he barked.

The sergeant obeyed, as well as some half dozen troopers who thought that the captain had meant them too. In the slight confusion attendant on these men being cursed back into their saddles by their respective corporals, Sergeant Lee was able to turn over the black, go to Number One and get his own horse, and mount. The column moved forward again at a rapid trot.

Sergeant Lee and the trumpeter were once more side by side, Lee muttering under his breath his opinion of some nameless person. His language was picturesque, for he decorated it with idioms learned in barroom, barrack and camp, from Jolo in the days of the Sultan of Sulu to the Camp de Valdahon at the present moment.

"You talkin' about that French looey?" inquired the trumpeter.

"Well, who the hell else would you think?" demanded Lee.

The trumpeter spat expertly between his horse's ears. "Well, I dunno. You ain't got any kick against him. He was just rankest man! What's the use o' bein' rankest man if you can't rank someone out of a bunk or a horse or somethin'?"

The sergeant's reply was horrible, whereat the trumpeter grinned so widely that he lost his chew.

There were signs, now, of distress from the squadron. The gait of the head of the column was too fast for that of the rear, so that the last third was at a slow gallop. The smothered admonitions of platoon leader, sergeant and corporal to "Keep that horse back!" or "Four feet from head to croup, you. You know what that means?" or "Tully! You ridin' that horse or is he ridin' you? Git him into ranks!" were becoming louder and more frequent.

The pack of a man in the second set of fours had come undone, so that the shelter half trailed behind him like an old-fashioned caparison, and his blankets he was carrying over his free arm in a most unsoldierly manner. Finally a poorly cinched saddle turned, the rider was thrown, and the horse, the saddle under its belly, went the length of the column, kicking and squealing, until it caught one foot in the trailing stirrup, fell, and had two men hurl themselves from their saddles and sit on its head. The column perforce halted, for one of the men was the acting troop commander of H Troop and the other Sergeant Lee.

"And the rest of the dash-blanked Johns sitting in their saddles looking at us!" exclaimed Lee.

"Get the saddle off him!" ordered the squadron commander. "Whose horse is it? Take his name, sergeant. Give him a month in the kitchen and all the spare horses to saddle up. Maybe he'll learn to cinch properly. Have H Troop dismount and look over their equipment. When they've finished, have I Troop do the same. This will be your last chance. I'm not going to stop again until I run into the enemy. Time flies. They'll all be in Berlin if we don't show more progress than this!"

Sergeant Lee took the opportunity to have a look at his machine rifles, riding in rear of H Troop. He met, on his way there, the French lieutenant, prancing along on the black horse. Lee ground his teeth. He had not ridden a McClellan saddle for a long time, and stirrup buckle and gun boot were beginning to rub sores on his unaccustomed shins.

How much more pleasure he would have had riding the officer's beautiful saddle on that black! Saddle! That wasn't the half of it! He would have ridden that horse bareback! It grinds a man to have his horse taken away from him. The mildest man will fly into a murderous rage. Lee thought of a man he had known with a clear record during three enlistments that had deserted because his horse had been taken for the polo team. Well, that bird had the right idea! When the march was resumed Lee still thought of him. He, Lee, would go "over the hill." He would find an outfit where a guy was appreciated.

"Forget it!" said the trumpeter finally, wearied of Lee's silence. "Don't worry about it no more. The Frog's gone, an' good riddance!"

"He's not gone!" replied Lee, spurring his horse savagely. "He's riding with I Troop."

"What for?"

"How should I know?"

"Well, cheer up, anyway. Maybe we'll run into somebody that'll rank that horse away from him!"

They continued the march through the silent woods. They passed collections of huts, then a rustic village built about a tiny lake, that was obviously a recreation center, a narrow-gauge railway yard, more wagons, more loose horses, and one or two isolated wandering men that took to their heels pursued by random pistol bullets as soon as they had identified the nationality of the horsemen.

The column crossed hurriedly a surfaced road that cut through the forest from east to west. At one end, in the hazy distance, they could see the roofs and steeple of a town, and to the west against the foot of the forest-covered hills, another. But in between all was deserted. Across this road they found fewer huts; then, after a while, nothing. The brush grew thicker on both sides.

The captain suddenly reined up his horse. Lee, startled out of his black thoughts, raised his head. The advance guard had halted where the road came to the edge of the woods. It was only a grove, because Lee could see the trees where the road entered the forest again farther on. But two of the advance guard had dismounted, and one was wildly pumping his rifle up and down above his head in the old army signal that means, "Enemy in large numbers."

"Hold the squadron in readiness!" ordered the captain hurriedly. "Trumpeter, Sergeant Lee, follow me!"

The three of them went down to the advance guard as swiftly as their horses could carry them. They did not need to have the enemy pointed out to them.

There was a wide, circular cut in the woods here, made by an open field, across which the road they were on took its way, to enter the forest once more. This field sloped sharply down on the right, and at the bottom of the slope was another road, wide and surfaced, with a narrow-gauge track running along.

On this road was a column of infantry—perhaps a battalion—marching steadily along in good order, and with their rifles slung German fashion across their breasts. In front were two mounted officers. Behind the infantry, rapidly approaching, was a truck column, eight, ten, perhaps more—they could not see the end of them. There were eight hundred Germans there at least, and they were not to be charged with one-quarter that number.

"Bring up the auto rifles, trumpeter," whispered the captain, "and fast! Everyone dismount. Put the led horses in the brush! Now, sergeant, where shall we put the guns?"

"They've got to be fired prone," said the sergeant hurriedly. "The grass—now that will be all right!" He threw himself on the ground. "You can't see over the slope here," he decided. "They'll have to be moved downhill—maybe along the edge of the woods! I'll have a look!"

"Don't let any of those squareheads spot you! Don't waste too much time now!"

The German infantry continued to advance, unsuspecting. They had no advance guard out, no flankers. The captain's heart swelled. The classic role of the cavalrymen was to be his—to drive far behind the enemy's lines and fall upon unsuspecting troops. That truck column should be his, too, and the smoke of its burning would spread terror and alarm! On the heels of this panic the squadron would be on to Vigneulles, destroy the railway station there, and cut off the retreat of all the mass of troops along the heights of the Meuse. But first, destroy this infantry.

"Hold the rifles here!" ordered the captain, as the gunners with their ammunition bearers appeared. "There's no rush. We'll site them together, let the column pass, and then each gun take half with traversing fire. Now damn those trucks! They'll get here at just the wrong time!"

The trucks, however, did not pass the infantry, but halted. Perhaps the road was too narrow, perhaps those trucks contained the battalion's baggage. The Germans came on, while the Americans watched with beating hearts, holding their breath so that the enemy would not hear them. The Germans would pass at less than a hundred yards!

"When I give the signal," hissed the captain, "rush out, flop, set up the guns, and turn loose!"

The column drew near, and the dismounted Americans flattened themselves in the brush.

The enemy marched by, boots slumping, bayonets rattling, the harsh coughing of the men coming clearly to the ears of the watchers. Wagons creaked past, one of the drivers idly cracking his whip. Then the second company.

There was a thud of hoofs from behind the Americans. The captain swung around. Who was this that had left the squadron without permission? It was the French officer, on the shining black, galloping up from I Troop to see what the halt was about.

"Get off that horse!" husked the captain. "Get him back out of sight!"

The black halted. He was alone. Far behind him the squadron waited impatiently. The black tossed his head. He smelled the concealed horses of the advance guard and the machine-rifle men in the brush, or did he see an old stable fellow down there on the road? Did he smell his countrymen? He tossed his head again, then neighed shrilly. The horses in the brush and another in the squadron answered him.

White faces from the marching troops looked up the hill, curious at the sound. Not many, but enough. The captain, wordless, but thinking many things, rose out of the bush and leaped for the black's head. The black, like all Thoroughbreds, was nervous. The sudden rush of the officer from the bushes frightened him. He reared and bolted, and in two jumps was in the meadow. His rider flung himself clear, but too late. The Germans below, open-mouthed, had first heard horses neigh in those woods, and had then seen, clearly against the dark background, a figure in the horizon-blue uniform of the French army hurl itself from the saddle and run back into the woods again.

"Out with the guns!" shouted the captain. "Action front! At enemy in road! Fire at will!"

The guns spat, but the road was already half empty. Two seconds more and the whole column had taken refuge in the ditch on the other side. Wagons, mounted officers, all disappeared.

But the blast of firing that had begun could not have come from the machine rifles alone! The air crackled, the eardrums rang with the sudden pound of heavy firing. Astonished, the captain turned about. From the alley in the woods came a thunder of hoofs. Horses reared, others were down and kicking. Dismounted men ran about. There was smoke and the flash of pistols, but the noise was so great that the captain could not hear the bark of the .45's.

He looked behind him at the road below. The machine rifles roared, but the road was empty. There were packs there, and bundles that the marching troops had dropped in their haste to get to cover, but the captain could see no bodies.

The German infantry were now in position behind the road. The only thing for two troops of cavalry in front of a battalion of intrenched infantry is to withdraw. The squadron seemed to have already made up its mind to this.

In just the three seconds that the captain had spent in looking at the road, his men had stampeded. They were going, tails high, saddle bags flying, hell for leather down the road. Even as he watched, dark figures in bucket-shaped helmets appeared from the woods, shot down a dismounted trooper, and began to plunder the saddle pockets of the dead horses.

There still remained to him, however, the auto rifles. He leaped back, threw himself down beside the gunners and shouted in their ears:

"Cease firing!"

The gunners heard and complied. With the roar of the auto rifles stilled, a sudden hush seemed to fall.

"You! Number One gun! Action rear. Searching, in those woods, two clips! Commence firing! Number Two gun——" He stopped.

Below and to the left, in the center of that white road, head high, tail outstretched like a plume, stood the black horse. Rifles cracked, men shouted, machine guns roared, but the horse paid no attention. He pawed the ground, and the captain could have sworn that he neighed again the shrill proud shriek that had alerted the Germans and ruined the squadron. That was the horse that had been frightened by the captain's rising from the brush? Never! He had bolted purposely! He was a German horse; he had known!

"Number Two gun!" ordered the captain. "Get me that horse on the road, blast his black soul!"

He was not himself, for he had seen his men butchered from ambush, his squadron destroyed, and he knew that the span of his own life could be measured in minutes.

The muzzle of the gun shifted ever so slightly, and the gunner's body thumped the ground as he wiggled himself into his new position. The gun roared. The horse tossed his head quickly, for he must have heard bullets crack by. A German dashed from the shelter of the ditch to seize the trailing bridle, but he seemed to slip in the mud, and then fall, a flat, shapeless, motionless heap.

"The horse!" cried the captain. "Never mind the men! Get the horse!"

Another burst. Tchk! Silence. "Gimme another clip!" panted the gunner.

"Hey, bring up that other gun!" shouted Sergeant Lee. "We got an opening here!"

"Take up your rifle!" ordered the captain. "Fall back and report to Sergeant Lee!"

Then the captain, drawing his pistol, dropped on one knee and, supporting his right hand on his left arm, took aim at the black horse.

"Hey, captain!"

The shout in his ear disturbed the officer's aim and the bullet went skyward.

"What is the matter with you?" he snarled. But it was Sergeant Lee.

"They had machine guns in the brush!" panted the sergeant. "We put one of 'em down! They don't seem to be firin' now. If we're ever gonna get out of here, we better go!"

From the road below came a deep shout: "Hoch!"

On the heels of it a thin line of the enemy leaped up and, crossing the road, took shelter in the grass at the lower edge of the field.

The captain emptied his pistol at them, then rose and reloaded. The Germans saw him, for fire crackled along their line.

"Let's get the hell out of here!" said the captain.

The black horse had turned and, trotting down the road, now faced the German infantry, as though he carried on his back an officer who urged his men on. The captain would have taken one more shot at him, but bullets whispered about his ears or cracked overhead like whips. At the edge of the woods the men had already mounted. The captain, stifling a curse, rejoined them.

Poorly fed horses in full pack, even when stampeded, will not run far, and the captain, riding off down the woods with his chin on his breast, like Napoleon retreating from Moscow, found the squadron at the crossroads whence they had been able to see the two towns.

It had been a rear or flank guard that had ambushed them, and there had been no pursuit. Noncommissioned officers were already displaying their vocabularies, saddles were being transferred from wounded horses to well ones, men were binding up one another's wounds or refilling empty pistol clips.

Into this scene arrived the captain like an avenging angel. He was a man of few words, but those to whom he addressed himself would remember his remarks to their dying day.

Sergeant Lee, having the care of his auto rifles first in mind, withdrew them to one side, questioned the gunners, overhauled the ammunition supply and inspected the horses. His own mount was nearly foundered. Seeing at a little distance a man holding three horses, he went in his direction, thinking he might make an exchange. The other man was the trumpeter, ruefully examining his trumpet, that had been punctured by a bullet.

"It'll blow," said the trumpeter, as Lee approached, "but I have to keep my finger over the hole. It don't look military to blow a trumpet that way!"

"How's chances on one o' those horses?" demanded Lee. "Mine's about outta breath."

"Naw. One's mine, one's the skipper's, and one's for the Frog lootenant. He's goin' back."

"Yuh. The Old Man says to him, 'What was the grand idea to gallop out in front where all the boche would see you? Want them to admire your horsemanship or something?' And the looey says, 'We rode into an ambush. We went too far without reconnaissance. We haven't lost any ground because this here is the Heudicourt-Nonsard road that we're on now, and we weren't supposed to be here for half an hour yet!' 'Awright,' says the skipper, 'you know the country so well, you go back and report our progress and where we run into the enemy!' 'But I'm your guide!' says the looey. 'Well, we'll try to struggle along without you!' bites the Old Man. So then——Psst!"

The French officer, his bullet-shaped face like a thundercloud, strode toward the two men. They paid not the slightest attention as he took his old horse, mounted and rode off.

"You mighta held his stirrup for him, at least," observed the trumpeter.

"Who was his dog robber last year? Anyway, I'm a sergeant. I don't hold nobody's stirrup."

The trumpeter hitched his pistol belt higher and tilted his helmet just a little farther over his left eye.

"John Lee," said he, "did it ever occur to you you owe that looey a whole lot? Suppos'n' he hadn't ranked you off that black horse. Wouldn't he nickered just the same and give us away to the boche?"

"Hey?" gasped the sergeant.

Wouldn't the horse have nickered with him? Oh, man! Yes, he would have. And then what would the skipper have done to Lee? He was not an officer, but a buck sergeant. He choked at the thought. If it had been his horse that had nickered—well, the least they would have done would have been to hang him. His name would have been a mock and a disgrace throughout the mounted arm of the United States Army from that day forth. Gone would be his stripes! Gone his pistol and saber! He would wield nothing but a dishrag for the rest of his military career!

"Naw," said he to the trumpeter, "that black wouldn't have done it with me. I'd ha' ridden him!"

"Uh-huh!" remarked the trumpeter. "Well, if you're lookin' for a horse, try Corporal Scully's. Scully's hit. That's a good horse for a sergeant."

"No," said the sergeant, "I guess I'll stick to the one I got. He ain't much on looks, but he's no nickerer!"

Victor R. Daly

(1895–1986)

Victor R. Daly grew up in New York City. When America entered the First World War, he left Cornell University for the army and trained at the camp for black officers at Fort Des Moines in Iowa. Commissioned a first lieutenant, he joined the 367th Infantry Regiment and saw combat as part of the American offensive in the Argonne forest. For their valor, his regiment was awarded the Croix de Guerre. After the war he earned his university degree and served for thirty-two years with the U.S. Department of Labor, where he became a spokesman for African American civil rights. In addition to essays and three short stories, he published *Not Only War* (1932), "the only World War I novel written by an African American veteran."[1] "Private Walker Goes Patrolling" was published in the *Crisis* in June 1930. It also appears, along with his novel and other stories, in *Not Only War: A Story of Two Great Conflicts* (2010) edited by David A. Davis.

Private Walker Goes Patrolling

Victor R. Daly

Jerry Walker did not know what it was all about. He made no secret of that. To him, the war was somebody's else business—and he had always been told to mind his own. He had a very remote idea that somewhere across the river and out beyond Memphis, somebody was having a war. He would have none of it. He hated a fight.

---

1. David A. Davis, introduction to *Not Only War: A Story of Two Great Conflicts*, by Victor Daly (Charlottesville: Univ. of Virginia Press, 2010), vii.

But the man at the Court House in Cotton Plant thought differently. With a heavy heart and a heavier foot Jerry Walker dragged himself into Camp Pike. Elijah couldn't have been any more bewildered when he landed in Heaven. The rows and rows of little wooden barracks awed him. Marching soldiers and barking non-coms terrified him. Hustle, bustle, everywhere. Jerry was just plumb scared to death.

The next chapter in Jerry's life might have been entitled "Six Weeks" or "From Farm-hand to Dough-boy." Jerry made a bum soldier. Naturally as aggressive as the family cow, one other factor contributed to his unhappy lot—the top-sergeant.

"Memphis Bill," otherwise known as First Sergeant William Dade, was a born soldier, if soldiering meant the love of a fight. Memphis Bill was known to pack a punch. Beale Street could testify to that. Six foot four in his stocking feet, arms dangling to his knees, voice sounding like a brass horn—thundering, threatening, cursin', what a top-sergeant he did make. Bill was a man among men. He also thought that he was a man among women, too. As a matter of fact, Bill had only one real weakness, women. He was even more proud of his charm and grace among women, than he was of his strength and prowess among the men of his acquaintance.

Memphis Bill had taken a hearty dislike to Jerry Walker at first sight. Deep in his subconscious mind, Bill had the feeling that somewhere before he had met this same Jerry—and there was something peculiarly distasteful to Bill about the thought. He felt that he knew this "aukard, lazy, good-fer-nothin' stiff" as he characterized Jerry, but for the life of him, he couldn't figure out why or how or where he had ever "met up wid de laks of sich trash befor'."

"Whar yo' frum, sojer?" he had roared at Jerry on the occasion of their first meeting in the mess hall.

"Awk'nsaw," was Jerry's laconic reply, and from then on Bill knew that he disliked Jerry.

Not long after, Bill had suddenly jumped up from a huge boulder on which he had been resting by the side of the road and marched straight over to Jerry, who had seized the few minutes of rest on his first practice hike, to remove his shoes.

"Sojer, yo' ever been'n Memfis?" he had demanded of Jerry.

"Once't," came the meager, disinterested response, and Bill had walked back slowly to his boulder shaking his head and mumbling to himself.

The top-sergeant's dislike for Jerry showed itself in many forms. Poor Jerry found himself a member of every disagreeable detail. There was no end of kitchen police for him. When stumps on the drill ground had to be grubbed, his was the first name called. He never was assigned to guard duty in the middle of the week, only on Saturdays and Sundays, when the rest of the outfit was off duty. Sergeant William Dade was relentless in his petty persecution of Private Jerry Walker.

Jerry, on the other hand, didn't exactly fall in love with the top-sergeant at first sight, either. But for that matter he didn't like the lieutenants, or the captain, or the army, or the war. He hated a fight, although he was no coward. He kept repeating to himself that the war was none of his affair, and he detested everything connected with it. And because he hated the war and the army and the officers and the details, most of the top-sergeant's persecution was absolutely lost on Jerry. Since he was there against his will anyhow, what difference did it make what he was called upon to do. Kitchen police was no more disagreeable than marching for hours up and down the dusty old drill ground, and never going anywhere. Just marching, marching, marching—and never arriving! Grubbing stumps was a pleasure compared to the ridiculous tactics of flopping down on your stomach behind the stumps and stupidly clicking the trigger on your gun as though you were shooting at somebody. And guard duty was no trouble—it was a relief—a relief to get away from everybody, and be by himself in some lonely patch of woods down by the railroad station, or way out by the highway gate where only a few stragglers would pass all day.

So most of Memphis Bill's scheming hostility to Jerry went for naught. The sergeant listened in vain for the first word of complaint or the first sign of dissatisfaction on the part of his victim—and Jerry's total indifference just further infuriated him.

"I wish he'd open his mouf, so I could mash it," Bill would sigh to himself. But Jerry never opened it.

"Sergeant, I want you to take a detail of four men and explore the abandoned communication trench running out in front of the Company sector. Wait until it gets dark. Don't go too far; but go far enough to contact the enemy barbed wire."

"Yas suh, Cap'n," spoke up Sergeant Bill Dade, and saluting, turned on his heel and strode thoughtfully away.

"Detail, detail," he kept mumbling to himself, "hyar's whar I fixes dat pol'cat frum Awk'nsaw."

"Co'pral, git me two o' yo' men right quick, an' hav'em repo't to mah dugout at once't," commanded the top-sergeant to the first corporal he could find.

"Hey, yo', sojer!" roared Bill a few minutes later, stepping up behind Private Jerry Walker who leaned absently against the parapet of a trench, looking out into space, wondering what it was all about.

"Git yo'self t'gidder an' cum 'long wid me—stanin' dar lak Ston'all Jackson! What yo' starin' at, anyhow?"

"Nothin'," drawled Jerry, looking up from his reverie, and glaring into the scowling face above him.

Bill's brow darkened, and he glowered at Jerry with an evil eye. That crushing right fist itched nervously. "Not now," he mumbled to himself, "mah time'll cum."

"Sta'k dem rifles hyar in dis dugout! Whar yo' alls t'inks yo' alls gwine—Berlin?" shouted Sergeant Dade, as he lined up his patrol for final instructions and inspection.

The sun had dropped hazily behind the wooded peaks of the Vosges several hours before, and a cloudy sky gave promise of one of those inky, pitch-black nights that this sector was noted for. Nights that seemed to be hewn from ebony itself. Nights on which it was impossible to distinguish friend from foe. Nights on which it was just as dangerous to move around behind your own lines as it was behind the enemy's.

"Hurry, 'em along, Sergeant, it's getting late, and it's black as Hell out here," came a voice down the steps of the dugout. "Yas suh, Lootenan', cumin'," sang out Bill from the depths below. His spirits were rising now. He sniffed a fight. His huge hob-nailed feet literally pawed the ground. Memphis Bill was rarin' to go.

"Now Co'pral, yo' an' yo' two sojers will git into dat trencht as soon as we gits pas' our wire. Mak' yo' alls way ahaid in singl' file tru de trencht 'till yo' all gits to de Boshes wire, an' den wait dar fo' me. Me an' Big Boy hyar frum Awk'nsaw'll crawl along each side o' de trencht, an' ef we sees any trubl' ahaid, we'll signal to yo' all down in de trencht fer to stop. Git me?" And with that he cast a triumphant glance in the direction of Private Jerry Walker. But as usual, the glance was lost for want of a receiver. Jerry wasn't even looking. He was barely listening. Certainly he wasn't thinking. He was just there, no more, no less. It wasn't his war—and he hated a fight.

"No shootin'," was the sergeant's final order, "ef we meets up wid any Boshes use yer fistes, and dem trencht knifes o' yourn. Shootin' never did nobody no good, nohow. Use yer fistes!" With that he led the way up out of the dugout into the inky blackness of the night.

"Feld," a muffled voice whispered in a strange tone not three feet from where Memphis Bill lay flat on his stomach out there in the ebony night.

"Maus," came back the other half of the pass word from out of the blackness. Bill's big heart was bumping against the ground as his eyes searched in vain for the enemy patrol that he knew was passing through them.

If he could only see. If he only knew where the rest of his patrol had gone to. Where was that big stiff from Arkansas hiding? Where was the trench? If he only knew what time it was. Gee he'd hate to go back and face the Captain and the Lieutenant—and the men. How they'd snicker and laugh behind his back. He, Memphis Bill, world-beater, lost—hopelessly, helplessly lost. His patrol lost. Maybe captured by now. Hell! What a big bum they'd call him. It must be nearly daybreak. How long had be been groping around out there in that black tomb? Which way was forward and which way was backward. These and a million similar thoughts were torturing the mind of that big hulk as it lay there helpless in the pitch dark.

Bill was beaten. Just once before in his life he had been beaten, and there was nothing to do but take it. He would have to stay where he was until morning. "Dam' sich nights," he swore under his breath.

Suddenly the sergeant became aware of a movement near him. He strained his eyes in vain. He strained every nerve to pierce the mystery of that veil of night. He lay perfectly still—motionless. He was tense. Bill was on guard, ready to spring at a split-second notice, just like a big black panther. Was it the enemy patrol returning? Was it one of his own men? Was he still in No-Man's Land, or was he actually within the enemy lines?

"Whar d'Hell am I?" he kept asking himself.

But nothing appeared out of the darkness for him to spring upon, and gradually the sergeant relaxed to await the coming of dawn. The rest of the night passed quietly.

Gradually, Sergeant Dade began to recognize objects about him. Carefully, quietly, he reconnoitered his position. Quickly he realized that he couldn't stay where he was much longer. He found himself perched on top of a grassy knoll that was plainly visible from the surrounding hills, some of which were less than two hundred yards away. But the factor that bothered the patrol leader most at that moment, was which way led to safety. Now that it was getting light and he could see, he was ready to go, but he had no place to go.

In that particular sector in the Vosges, battle-lines were not clearly defined. Both sides had entrenched themselves at strategic points throughout the heavily wooded hills, and were satisfied to adopt a policy of watchful waiting. It was known as a quiet sector. New troops were sent there by both sides to learn the art of war under the most favorable circumstances. Patrolling was the most active form of encounter. In some places the mythical lines were a half a mile apart, at other points they came as close as one hundred and fifty yards, depending solely on the nature of the terrain.

That's why Bill Dade was so completely lost. He couldn't tell one hill from another: "Why doan dey hang out a flag or sumptin' so a guy c'n tell whar he's at," thought Bill as the hopelessness of his situation dawned upon him with the morning light. He failed to recognize a single landmark that would give him the slightest clue to his whereabouts. But he had to get off that knoll.

In one direction the knoll sloped gently to a large open field that evidently had been used as pasture land before the war. For Bill to venture forth into that open field would have been disastrous if any of the surrounding hills were occupied by the Boche. Snipers, who were constantly on the lookout high up in the tree-tops, would spot him as soon as the morning haze lifted from the valley. You never could tell in those hills and woods when snipers were taking aim on you—and since it was a one-shot game, they rarely missed. In the opposite direction the knoll sloped much more abruptly, and was practically covered by a growth of young pine. This side of the hill had at one time or another been under shell fire, as a number of broken trees and ragged shell-holes testified. At the foot of the slope about a hundred feet distant was the dried bed of a brook, from which the steep sides of another thickly wooded hill arose. The sergeant saw that this dried stream bed at the foot of both slopes, offered him the best shelter for the present. Gathering his six foot four together, Bill set out on his hands and knees, moving cautiously and silently. When he reached the foot of the slope his eye fell upon a small section of the bank that had been undercut by the force of the water years ago. Exposed roots of overhanging tree in front of this section of the bank furnished ideal support for the honeysuckle and other vines that formed a perfect mesh across the opening of the undercut bank. Here was a perfectly screened cave. Sergeant Dade felt for the first time in many hours that luck had come his way. He would keep watch from this hiding place until dusk, hoping that by then something would happen to give him some idea of where he was in respect to the war.

Once more he resumed his crawling tactics. Finally he reached the vines hanging in front of the cave. Just as he was about to part them and peer in, he was struck by the sound of a familiar voice from within.

"Cum in befo' yo' brings de whole army wid yo'." There sat Private Jerry Walker of Arkansas, atop a huge round stone.

"Fer cryin' in de sink!" was Bill's hushed exclamation.

"Whar's de Co'pral?" he excitedly continued.

"I dunno."

"Whar's dem sojers o' his'n?"

"I dunno."

"Whar's dat ar trencht we cum out in?"

"I dunno."

"Yo' doan know much, does yo'?" Bill added sarcastically.

"No, but I ain't los'."

At that moment the dull roar of a squadron of planes overhead brought both men sharply to the realization that this was neither the time nor the place for argument.

"What I wants t' know mos'," continued the sergeant, some minutes later, in an almost friendly manner, "is which one o' dem hills is de one we cum over las' night?"

"Dar it stan's," nodded Jerry decisively, in the direction of a sparsely covered hill about a couple of hundred yards across the valley.

"How yo' know?" eagerly spoke up the gent from Memphis, parting the vines and peering out enthusiastically.

"Cuz I staid up atop o' it all night, 'till I crawls down hyar dis mornin'."

"Well, fool, whatcher cum dis way fo'; why yo' didn't crawl back d'udder way whar we cums frum?"

"Cuz I seen one o' dem Boshes wand'rin' roun' out dar—look lak t' me he was los', too—an' cuz I wasn't after gittin' mix'd up wid 'im, I cums on dis way 'till it gits dark, den I'se gwine ba'k."

This was the longest speech that Jerry Walker had made since he joined the armed forces of his Uncle Samuel. It seemed to leave him exhausted for he lapsed into a grave-like silence. The sergeant, satisfied now that he would be able to make his way back to his outfit soon after dark, stretched himself out at full length on the ground, and gradually went off to sleep. The day wore on uneventfully. Bill slept off and on, while Jerry kept watch.

Finally, refreshed by several hours of sleep and a little water from his canteen, Memphis Bill aroused himself. He was in better spirits now. He cast his gaze in the direction of his roommate who was as motionless as the stone on which he sat. Bill felt grateful. He knew that he owed his chance of getting back safely to his outfit, to this same soldier for whom he had developed such a strong dislike.

"After all," thought Bill, "he ain't never done nuthin' t'me."

"When we gits ba'k to de States," said the sergeant in the friendliest voice, "I wants yo' to stop off wid me in Memfis an' meet sum o' mah gals."

"I doan lak Memfis," replied Jerry breaking his long silence.

"Watcher know 'bout Memfis?" queried Bill, his voice still friendly, and his eyes sparkling at the thought of the figure he'd cut when he returned to Beale Street in his First Sergeant's uniform and his swagger stick.

"Been dar once't, an' gits into a fite. Ain' never gwine dar no mo'!"

"Tell me 'bout it, Big Boy," pleaded Bill sympathetically.

And then Jerry, in a low voice, after some hesitation, told the story of his one trip to Memphis. And Bill sat there on the floor of their cave looking up at him in wide-eyed amazement.

Jerry told how he had gone to Memphis on an excursion boat, one Sunday about a year before the war. How he had wandered about the big city most of the day, sight-seeing, and finally wound up late in the afternoon in a Beale Street cafe. The place had been crowded with hungry excursionists, who were trying to get something to eat before the boat started back on its trip down the river. Seated atop a high stool at the lunch counter, Jerry was suddenly startled by the shrill scream of a woman, followed by the sound of blows to the accompaniment of curses and shouts. Looking about him in dismay, he realized that a fight had started at a table in the corner and was rapidly progressing in his direction. As the crowd of non-combatants gave way before the approach of the fighters, Jerry from his perch on the stool, could see that three of the excursionists appeared to be battling with a huge man, who seemed to be getting the better of the scrap, in spite of the odds against him. Jerry's heart had been made sick by this desecration of the Sabbath— and he hated a fight anyhow. The huge man kept his opponents at bay as he slowly backed his way toward the door. Both fists were lashing out skull-crushing blows, and his opponents continued their attacks from a respectful distance. Finally the battlers had reached a place near where Jerry was perched at the counter. The huge fighter's back was almost touching Jerry. He made a terrific lunge at his nearest assailant and floored him with a hay-making right uppercut. But in so doing he lost his own footing on the greasy floor and slipped to his knees, almost under Jerry's stool. Then Jerry told how he had been seized with a sudden, mad frenzy to end this disgusting fight. Looking about him, he grabbed with both hands a huge earthen crock half full of waffle batter and brought it down with all his force upon the head of the massive fighter, who was just about to rise off one knee.

Momentarily dazed by this sudden attack from a new quarter, and partially blinded by the messy batter that engulfed him from the broken crock, the giant fighter was easily subdued by his remaining two opponents who were still on their feet. Once inside of that deadly right, they flung their combined weight against him and thrashed him within an inch of his life. When Jerry left the cafe several minutes later, they were loading this Colossus of Clout into a hospital ambulance.

"'Twasn't dat I had anyt'ing agin' dat man," Jerry concluded, "I never seen him befo' nor sence, but I jest naterally hates a fite, an' I wanted fer to stop dem frum fitin'."

Sergeant William Dade sat through this recital absolutely speechless. He seemed to be drinking in every word that fell from Jerry's lips. Toward the end, he sat rigid and fixed, like a bird in the charm of a snake. That clenched, crushing right fist itched nervously. He remembered that fight perfectly. He could taste that batter yet!

Suddenly there was a sound just outside their hiding place. Yes—another and another. They could hear the breaking of small twigs, but they couldn't see anything. Inside the cave was the stillness of death. Neither man dared move. Jerry sat on the edge of his stone. Bill was on his hands and knees, ready to spring—like a wild cat. He was afraid that the thumping of his heart would give them away. He tried to see through the labyrinth of vines, but there was nothing to see. He was just about to speak when a huge frame darkened the front of their cave. From his place on the ground Sergeant Dade could see the shoes and the leggings of the man standing not two feet away from him. He was a Boche.

One second's reflection was all that Memphis Bill needed. He would carry that Boche back alive to his outfit if he had to whip the whole German army one by one. It would absolve him from his sin of getting lost on patrol. It would restore his standing with the Lieutenant, with the Captain, and above all, with the men. It would make him a hero instead of a goat.

So without the slightest consideration for his companion, Bill made up his mind. He waited a moment until the solider moved away from the cave entrance, and then he suddenly emerged from his hiding. As he straightened up he was confronted with the biggest man that he had ever seen in his life. The German was dumbfounded. He was also unarmed. And as his enemy made no effort to draw the automatic that dangled from his belt, the Teuton saw that he had a chance, and he cleared for action. Quick as a flash he sized up his opponent; he realized from Bill's bulk and the determined look in his eyes that this was no mean adversary. So he was prepared for the terrific right uppercut that just missed his chin by an eyelash. Like lightning itself, he whipped over a left hook that caught the astounded Bill flush on the jaw. The gent from Memphis shook the cob-webs from his brain as it slowly dawned upon him that he had met more than his match. So there they stood in that quiet, peaceful valley, in the gathering dusk, toe to toe, the Bavarian butcher and the stevedore from Memphis, trading punches, blow for blow. Bill realized that the Boche could take it and the Boche could give it, too. The German wondered what kind of animal this was that could kick like a mule with his right arm and grin like an ape at the hardest blows. The battle raged in front of the cave, and Jerry crouched behind the vines. He hated a fight.

Bill was giving ground now. One eye was partially closed, and he was bleeding profusely from the nose. His adversary realized this and was trying desperately for a knockout. He shot a wicked left to Bill's chin that sent him reeling and groggy, but the German slipped on the treacherous gravel in front of the cave. He went down on one knee almost under the stone on which Jerry was sitting behind the vines.

Private Jerry Walker was suddenly seized with a mad frenzy to end this disgusting fight. Quick as a flash he thrust his arm through the vines and came down with all his force upon the unprotected Bavarian skull with the butt end of an army automatic. The huge frame crumpled in a heap. Jerry had stopped the fight.

"Well, Big Boy, I gess we's quits," was Sergeant Dade's only comment. As usual, this was lost on Jerry.

Shortly after dark the news spread like wildfire through the Company sector—battalion headquarters heard it—even regimental headquarters, five miles back got it—Sergeant "Memphis Bill" Dade had stayed all night and all day in the German lines, and had just returned, dragging a two hundred and fifty pound Boche with him. But to every proffered congratulation, Bill had only the one laconic reply, "Giv' it to muh buddie hyar from Awk'nsaw!"

William March

(1893–1954)

William March was the pen name for William Edward March Campbell. Born in Alabama, March enlisted in the United States Marine Corps. Twice wounded in combat, he was awarded the Distinguished Service Cross, the Navy Cross, and the Croix de Guerre. He based the novel *Company K* (1933) on his war experiences; a number of previously published short stories were incorporated into this novel, including the controversial "Nine Prisoners," which depicts the shooting of German prisoners of war by a squad of American soldiers. The story generated letters of protest. In response, March defended the story on the grounds of its "universal . . . implications" and stated the facts of his war record before concluding: "It is futile and it is hopeless for any man who has actually served on the line to attempt to make well-meaning, romantic folk share his knowledge; there is, simply, no common denominator."[1] "To the Rear" was originally published in *Midland: A Magazine of the Middle West,* in April 1931 and was reprinted in *Trial Balance: The Collected Short Stories of William March* (1945). March's biographer Roy S. Simmonds writes admiringly of this story: "Without introducing any scenes of actual combat, it seems to encapsulate the whole ethos of life in a fighting unit, vividly illustrating the way in which war brings out the best and the worst in man."[2]

1. Quoted in Steven Trout, "William March," in *American Prose Writers of World War I: A Documentary Volume,* vol. 316 of *Dictionary of Literary Biography,* ed. Steven Trout (Detroit: Thomson Gale, 2005), 269.

2. Roy S. Simmonds, *The Two Worlds of William March* (Tuscaloosa: Univ. of Alabama Press, 1984), 105–6.

To the Rear

William March

The company was going to the rear for ten days and the men were in high spirits. They sat waiting for the relief troops to arrive, their packs rolled and their equipment stacked.

Lying flat on one of the wire bunks in the dugout was a boy with an eager, undeveloped face, and weak eyes that were habitually narrowed against sunlight, whose ears crinkled and bent forward like the leaf of a geranium and whose shoulders were high and thin with the sparseness of immaturity. He was Private Ernest Lunham, and before his enlistment he had worked as a soda dispenser in a drug store in Erie, Pa. He was coughing steadily into a soiled handkerchief, his face the color of biscuit dough dusted with ashes. At intervals he would shiver, as if cold, and then he would catch his breath with a surprised, wheezing sound. He had been gassed that afternoon while he and Private Overstreet were gathering firewood for the officers' dugout.

Jimmy Reagan, corporal of the squad, came over to him: "What did the doctor say, Ernie? . . . Why didn't he send you to the hospital?"

Lunham sat up and stared around him, as if unable to remember exactly where he was. Then he began to talk: "When I went in the sick bay, the doctor looked me over and listened to my heart . . . 'So you claim you got gassed?' he asked in an amused voice. 'Yes, sir,' I said. 'How do you explain that when the Germans haven't thrown over any gas for a week?' . . . 'I don't know,' I said. 'I'll tell you how you got gassed,' said the doctor, 'you dipped a cigarette in iodine and smoked it. Did you think I'd fall for anything like that?' I didn't say anything—it wasn't any use to say anything."

Lunham lay back on the wire bunk, as if exhausted, and breathed heavily. There were red splotches coming on the backs of his hands and on his forearm. His weak eyes pained him. It was with difficulty that he held them open.

"*That's* a bright son of a bitch for you!" said Joe Birmingham; "why didn't you ask him where you'd get a cigarette to put iodine on?"

"I didn't say anything at all," said Lunham, "I just came on out."

Corporal Reagan called Buckner, LaBella and Davey and they whispered quietly. Then he conferred with Birmingham and Overstreet. At last he approached the bunk where Lunham lay.

"You don't have to worry about carrying the clip bags or taking your turn on the *chauchat*," he said. "You don't have to carry anything but your pack."

Max Tolan, the last member of the squad, came off watch and entered the dug-out. He was a powerful man, with a nose that flattened to a triangle and nostrils that splayed widely. His lips were thick and calm: they seemed made of a substance somewhat harder, and somewhat less flexible than flesh. For a moment he stared at Lunham quietly. Then, somehow, his lips managed to open: "He don't have to carry that. I'll carry his pack for him," he said.

A little later Lloyd Buckner approached the bed, a package in his hand: "Here are some malted milk tablets I've been saving. You'd better eat them, Ernie—they'll do you good."

Lunham nodded his head, but he did not speak. He wanted more than anything to thank Buckner and Max Tolan and the rest of the men for their kindness, but he was afraid he would start crying and make a fool of himself if he tried to say anything.

At six o'clock the relief troops came and the men moved in single file down the communication trenches that led to the rear.

The trenches widened after awhile and became less deep. On either side were the charred remnants of a grove of trees. Many of the trees had been uprooted in past barrages and lay flat on the ground; many, with dead limbs trailing the parent stem, had split asunder in the shelling, or snapped halfway up their trunk; but a few of the trees, sapless and black, stood upright in the field, inflexible now in the March wind. The terrain hereabouts was pitted with great shell holes from which the roots of the fallen trees protruded, dry and seasoned.

Overstreet became very excited: "That's the place where Ernie got gassed!" he said. The men stared about them curiously. "That's the very place!" continued Overstreet. " . . . I wanted to go farther back, around Mandray Farm, for the wood; but Ernie thought that this would be as good a place as any; so I said all right, it suited me, if it suited him."

Overstreet hunched his shoulders and scratched his armpits vigorously. Then he started whistling *La Golondrina* through his teeth. He was a stocky lad, with a neck so short and a chest so thick and rounded that people were surprised, upon regarding him so closely, to discover that he was not a hunchback. His teeth were infantile and irregular and they grew together in a V shape. His voice, a counter-tenor, was high with a quality of tremulous, penetrating sweetness in it.

"How did Lunham happen to get gassed?" asked Buckner.

"Well, it was this way," said Overstreet. "Ernie thought the dry roots in the shell holes would make good firewood, so he jumped down and began chopping them off. I sat outside and took the roots that he handed up and cut them small enough for the dugout stove." Overstreet was conscious that the whole squad was listening to him attentively.

. . . "Well, sir, while we were working there, a French soldier came run-ning toward us. He was waving his arms about and shouting—You know how these Frogs act . . . ?" Overstreet turned to his companions. "Sure!" they said. . . ."Well, I put down my axe and I said to Ernie: 'What's wrong with him, do you suppose?' and Ernie said: 'He's sore because we're taking this firewood!' . . . Ain't that right, Ernie?" said Overstreet suddenly. Lunham nodded his head, but he did not answer: he was saving his breath for the long march.

"Well," continued Overstreet, "when the Frenchman reached us, he began to talk excitedly and make gestures, but Ernie and me didn't know what it was all about; so finally this Frenchman catches hold of Ernie's arms and tries to drag him out of the shell hole; but Ernie gives him a shove in the face and the Frenchman falls backward into a mud puddle. Ernie and me were laughing like everything by that time, but the Frog kept staring at us in a peculiar way. Finally he seemed to see the joke, because he began laughing too. He made a low bow to Ernie and me and as he turned to go, he blew us each a kiss . . ."

The communicating trench was only waist high now and the men could see the barren fields that stretched interminably on either side. It was seven o'clock, but it was not entirely dark. Then, after a time, the trenches ended in a road that was roofed carefully with a framework of wire netting, over which burlap sacking, painted brown and green, had been thrown.

"What happened after the Frenchman left?" asked Wilbur Davey.

Overstreet, feeling his importance as a narrator, waited a moment before re-suming . . . "Well, Ernie went on cutting roots and I went on chopping them up; but after awhile he said to me: 'Say, Al, did that monkeymeat at dinner make you sick?' and I said, 'No, why?' . . . 'Nothing,' said Ernie, 'except I keep tasting it.' Then, about five minutes later, he said to me: 'Al, I'm beginning to feel funny.' 'What's the matter with you?' I asked. 'I don't know,' said Ernie . . . 'I'm going to heave, I think.' I looked down and saw that he had dropped his axe and was leaning against the side of the hole. His face had got gray and his forehead and his lips were sweating like he had a fever . . . 'You better come up here and lay down,' I said; but he didn't answer me . . . 'Listen, Ernie,' I said, 'come on up here with me!'"

Overstreet paused a moment. "When Ernie didn't answer me, I jumped down and lifted him out of the hole. He tried to stand up, but he couldn't make it. "I'm dizzy, Al . . . dizzy as hell,' he said. Then he fell down and began to heave . . . Well, as we lay there, who should come back but the French soldier. He had a Frog civilian with him this time who spoke English. He told us that the terrain around Verdun had been shelled so many times that the ground was full of old gas. It was dangerous to dig in shell holes, he said, because a man could be gassed before he knew what was happening to him."

Overstreet began to laugh in his high, tremulous voice. "The joke sure was on Ernie and me—There he was heaving at the top of his voice; and all I could think of to say was: 'We're much obliged to you fellows for telling us.'"

The camouflaged strip ended at last and the troops came out upon the Verdun road. Darkness had settled, and the faces of the men were no longer visible. Joe Birmingham was talking about his hoped-for leave. Birmingham was bright eyed and sudden with an alert, intelligent face. His straight hair, parted in the middle, hung upon his forehead like yellow curtains imperfectly drawn. His teeth were strong and brilliantly white and as he talked he moved his hands with quick, nervous gestures. He could read print that was not too difficult and he could sign his name to the pay roll, but that was about all . . .

"And when I get to Paris, the first thing I do will be to round up a dozen of the best looking ladies in town: four blondes, four brunettes and four red heads."

"I wouldn't be caught short if I were you; I wouldn't cut down on women that way!"

Joe paid no attention to Overstreet. "One of the blondes is going to be dressed in purple silk and have on violet perfume. The best looking brunette is going to wear a red dress with pearls sewed down the front of it and be scented up with carnation. The red heads will all wear green dresses with Jockey Club and have lots of lace on their drawers."

"How about a blonde flavored with vanilla?" laughed LaBella.

"I'll take a red head," said Lloyd Buckner, "but, she'll have to wash off the Jockey Club, by God!"

Reagan spoke then: "Don't let them kid you, Joe. If there's anybody in this squad who's particular, it hasn't been brought to my attention."

"Oh, we'll come to your party all right," interposed LaBella; "you can bank on all of us accepting."

Birmingham gave him a friendly shove. "You will like hell come to my party!— If one of my girls got a look at you dirty bums they'd—they'd—" Birmingham paused, groping for the appropriate word.

"Swoon?" suggested Buckner helpfully.

Birmingham looked up mildly: "For Christ sake, Buck! . . . Can't you ever get that off your mind?"

Reagan smiled broadly, but Buckner and LaBella began to shout with laughter. Sergeant Stokes came toward them angrily. "What's going on here?" he demanded; "do you want the Germans to start shelling this road?" . . . LaBella interrupted him. "All right, Doc; all right," he said quietly.

Lunham walked in silence. He was standing the hike better than he had thought possible. He looked at his pack, riding high on Tolan's shoulders, and at Tolan walking firmly, with no sign of fatigue. It was white of Max to carry the extra pack, particularly since his feet blistered easily, as every one knew, and long marches were difficult for him . . . "The fellows sure have been white to me," whispered Lunham softly to himself. He began to feel feverish and from time to time he took a mouthful of water from his canteen.

The men continued to laugh and joke, but they were careful not to raise their voices. Then, after a time, when their muscles were cramped and tired with the burdens they carried, they became silent, one by one, and settled down in earnest for the long march.

The road bent again and ran north and east, and a late moon rose slowly behind a burned farm-house. To the west Very lights and colored flares were ascending, hanging motionless for a time, and then drifting toward nothingness with a hesitant, languid motion. There came a sound resembling iron wheels jolting over a bridge of unnailed, wooden planks; there was the constant flash of guns along the horizon and the muffled sound of exploding shells.

Birmingham unbuttoned his cartridge belt: "Give 'em hell!" he said excitedly: "I wish I was with you to give the bastards hell!"

"Do you think we're really going back for a rest?" asked Davey.

"That's the dope they're putting out."

Tolan made a gesture of disbelief with his heavy, wooden lips: "That's all bunk about getting a rest."

Eddie LaBella spoke up: "We'll get a rest, all right—in a hick burg with a dozen manure piles and one dirty cafe."

"It might be all right at that," said Birmingham. "Some of these Frog women ain't bad!" He brushed his yellow hair out of his eyes and licked his lips in an exaggerated, sensual way. "Baby! . . . I'll say they're not bad!" Lloyd Buckner stared at him with sudden unconcealed distaste. He seemed on the point of saying something, but changed his mind. He turned his head away.

"The next time they have a war, they'll have to come after me with a machine gun," said Reagan laughingly.

"Some of these Frog women ain't bad," insisted Birmingham; "I'll bet we have just as good a time as we had in Chatillon. I'll bet—"

Buckner whispered something to LaBella behind his hand. LaBella laughed and in turn whispered to Reagan; but Reagan shook his head. "Let him say it!" said Birmingham; "what do I care what he says!"

The early exuberance of the men had disappeared. They were tired now and becoming irritable. Lunham, walking painfully, realized that. He took no part in the conversation. His nausea had returned and he clutched at his belly. "I won't heave again," he kept repeating miserably; "I'll put my mind on something else! . . . I won't heave again!" He hugged his thin ribs with his elbows and rocked back and forth beside the road. Then he began to retch shrilly. He slipped to the side of the road and pressed his face into a heap of dead leaves that had drifted against a log. When his nausea had passed he felt somewhat stronger. He rose to his feet and stood there swaying. He tried to laugh: "There went Buck's malted milk tablets!" he gasped.

The moon had detached itself from the burned farm-house and swung now swollen and yellow and low in the sky. The sound of the iron wheels became fainter and at last a turn in the road hid the flashes of the guns from view.

"How long have we been on the road, Jimmy?"

Reagan looked at his watch: "A little better than five hours," he said.

The road rose gradually. The men were feeling the march in earnest now. They shifted their packs and strapped them higher on their shoulders. A rhythmic whirring of motors was heard overhead. Then the sound of the motors ceased and across the face of the moon the bombing plane floated and listened. Sergeant Stokes came running down the road. "Fall out in the fields and lie down!" He stood there swearing excitedly at the men who were slow in obeying: "Don't bunch up like sheep! . . . Spread out and lie down!"

The men stared up at the plane drifting silently above them. "He's got guts flying so low on a bright night," said LaBella. At that moment there came the sharp, quick bark of an anti-aircraft gun, and two flashlights began to play crosswise in the sky. "They'll never get him," said Reagan, "they're firing too high."

Birmingham lifted his quick, excited face: "Shoot hell out of him!" he said. He moved his hands excitedly and bared his white, perfect teeth . . . "Give the bastard hell!"

The plane with motors whirring again was zigzagging up the sky, the gunners firing impotently. In a moment he was lost in the clouds and the guns became silent again, but the flashlights moved across the sky for a long time, crossing each other and uncrossing with a jerking, mathematical precision.

"They let him get away," wailed Birmingham; "I could shoot that good with a rifle . . . Christ!—They let him get away!"

Buckner could hide his dislike no longer. "You're quite a fire eater when you're safe behind the lines, aren't you?"

Birmingham looked up resentfully. "I've stood enough of your cracks—who the hell are you, anyway? You act like you were Jesus Christ or somebody!"

Before Buckner could answer, Reagan stopped him. Buckner spat in the road. "I can't help it, Jimmy. I've got a belly full of that common little boor, and he might as well know it."

"Who the hell are you?" shouted Birmingham excitedly; "I don't see no bars on your shoulders!"

Overstreet began to laugh in his high, penetrating voice: "That's the idea, Joe. Don't let him get away with that stuff."

"What I said goes for you too!" said Buckner coldly.

LaBella narrowed his eyes and pursed up his lips, as if denying beforehand the malice in his purposed remark: "At least Buckner can read and write. He didn't have to get the drill corporal to recite General Orders out loud until he memorized them."

Birmingham's alert little face twisted suddenly. He was eternally conscious of his illiteracy, and ashamed of it.

Wilbur Davey, who spoke rarely, spoke now: "That was a dirty crack to make, LaBella."

Reagan turned, his customary good nature gone: "Pipe down, all of you, or I'll report the whole squad when we get in." But the men paid little attention to him. They continued to quarrel for a long time.

Presently the column turned from the main road and took a road to the left. The ground was rising sharply now, and the hills of Verdun were imminent and threatening ahead. Lunham raised his canteen and drank the last of his water. Then, as he returned the canteen to its cover and adjusted his belt, he noticed that Tolan had begun to limp. A feeling of despair came over him. In terror he leaned forward and touched Tolan's arm: "We'll get paid when we get to the rear, Max, and I got four months coming." Tolan turned, a slight frown on his primitive features, but he did not answer. "I won't forget about you carrying my pack," he continued, "you can be sure of that." But Tolan continued to limp painfully, giving no sign that he heard. "I won't forget about you being so white, Max. We'll go out pay night and spend every franc of that money." Lunham paused, his face frightened and abject. "What do you say, Max?—What do you say to that?" Tolan regarded him in silence, steadily. His round blue eyes were interested and bright. Then he sighed and shook his head doubtfully.

The company was falling out beside an abandoned village and a young officer, on horseback, came clattering down the road. "There's running water in the wash house to the left of the square, if you want to fill your canteens," he said, as if he were reading from a book. It was apparent that speaking to men made him nervous and self-conscious. Overstreet made a derisive, sucking sound with his lips and repeated a strong phrase. The young officer's blush could almost be felt. He ignored the remark and a moment later he could be heard delivering his message farther down the line.

Tolan had swung Lunham's pack to the ground and sat regarding it stolidly . . . "Honest to God! Max, we'll spend every franc of that money. We'll have a fine time, all right!" Tolan seemed to be turning the matter over in his mind. His heavy lips opened once or twice, but no words came from them. Then he picked up the pack and laid it regretfully in front of Lunham. "My feet hurt too bad," he said.

The load on Lunham's shoulders was a hand, heavy and insistent, to tug at his breath and draw him gradually backward. His heart began to pump alarmingly and the veins in his neck were taut and swollen . . . "Christ! . . . Christ!" he gasped.

After that he lost all feeling of time, all idea of direction and all sense of his individual identity. He was aware only of feet moving over the surface of the road in an irregular pattern and of men quarreling continuously. He seemed detached and no longer a part of his surroundings, and gradually he possessed the power to stand outside his body and to survey himself and his companions impersonally: There was Reagan shuffling doggedly, his dreamy, impractical eyes tired and serious; there was Max Tolan with ankles turned outward, flinching each time his feet touched the road; LaBella, cheap and flashy, his theatric prettiness caked with dirt and streaked with sweat. He saw Overstreet, his triangular mouth open and his infantile teeth displayed; and Lloyd Buckner's deeply curved nose thrust forward, his light eyes cold and sullen. Only Davey walked with dignity and only Birmingham's wiry body seemed impervious to the weight he carried or the steady tug of the miles.

Without warning Lunham staggered and lurched forward. Somebody shoved him into his proper place. He righted himself with difficulty, confused . . . uncertain. "My mouth tastes salty . . ." he said in a frightened voice. Reagan regarded him closely: "You've started bleeding," he said. Lunham pressed the back of his hand against his mouth and then withdrew it. "You're bleeding, all right," said Buckner . . . The feet of the men were hardly clearing the roadbed. They shuffled in a monotonous rhythm, while the moon hung low in the sky, near to setting, and from the west there came the smell of fresh water.

" . . . Why can't he take his turn carrying the clip bags?"

"He's sick, Eddie. You wouldn't ask him to do that when he's sick . . ." Reagan's voice seemed to come from a great distance.

Davey made one of his rare speeches: "I guess he's no sicker than anybody else."

" . . . If he was gassed, why didn't they send him to a hospital?"

The knowledge that his comrades were discussing him gradually penetrated Lunham's consciousness. He realized now that they had been talking about him for a long time . . . Birmingham laughed: "He might fool us, but he didn't fool that doctor at the sick bay none."

The road curved to the right and circled the base of a hill. The young liaison officer came galloping down the road again. The moon had set and there was an indefinite feeling of day break in the air. "Fall out for fifteen minutes before you start climbing the hill," he said. He repeated the order firmly. If the men tried to razz him this time, they'd find out very quickly who he was. But the men remained silent, perversely ignoring him. They fell to the ground gratefully. Tolan took off his shoes and began to pour water on his blistered feet. Davey was already asleep and snoring softly, but Birmingham and Buckner continued their quarrel. The liaison officer rode away regretfully.

Lunham lay on his back and stared at the sky turning faintly gray toward the east. An imperative drowsiness was overpowering him, but some impulse made him struggle against it. With eyes closed, and lips half parted, his thin face and wilting ears seemed doubly immature and pathetic.

The men were talking again, their voices coming from a distance remote and blurred . . . "Why can't Lunham take his turn on the clip bags?" LaBella's voice was flat and toneless . . . And Overstreet, petulant: "By God! he's no sicker than anybody else." There came a thud on the earth beside him and Lunham knew that the clip bags lay before him. He began to laugh suddenly. "I never heard anything so silly," he thought; "I can't lift those bags, let alone carry them up the hill . . ."

He turned on his face and pressed his body against the cool, damp earth. The feel of the soil against his cheek steadied him and gave him strength and gradually the cloudiness that had obscured his mind disappeared. He was conscious of his body paining him unbearably. He drew up his arms and pressed his hands against his burning lungs. He began to think, against his will, of many things: of his enlistment, his eagerness, his romantic thoughts concerning noble deaths and imperishable ideas. Then, in justification of himself, he tried to recall one noble thing that he had seen or done since his enlistment, but he could remember nothing except pain, filth, and servile degradation . . . "By God, they sold me out!" he thought . . . "The things they said were all lies!" . . . He lay trembling at his discovery, his eyes closed, his lips opening and shutting silently. Then an unbearable sense of disgust came over him. He reached for the rifle that lay beside him, surprised to realize that the thought had been in his mind for a long time, and stood bending forward clumsily, his mouth swaying above the barrel as he tried patiently to spring the trigger with his foot.

Joe Birmingham was coming toward him shouting a warning. "Look out!— Look out!" he cried. The two men struggling for the rifle stumbled back and forth beside the road. The entire squad was on its feet now, but it was Wilbur Davey who wrenched the rifle from Lunham's weak hands and flung it far into the valley below. Then he slapped Lunham smartly on both cheeks. He said: "What the hell? What you trying to pull off? . . . Do you want to get court martialed?"

Lunham had fallen to the road and lay with his face pressed into the dirt, but the men paid no further attention to him. He beat the earth with his fists and cried in a weak childish voice. "Oh Christ! . . . Oh Christ almighty!" . . . he said over and over.

The first light, new and hard, came over the tops of the hills and cast strange shadows on the faces of the men. In a farmyard, somewhere, a cock crew, and below in the valley mist hung above the fields. Word came down the line for the men to fall in. They rose stiffly and put on their equipment. Lunham did not rise. He lay limp and relaxed, his arms outstretched, and as he lay there he could hear his comrades climbing the hill: he heard their hard breathing and their grumbling voices. He heard the irregular shuffle of their feet, the clink of a canteen and the creaking of a leather strap . . . but after awhile even these sounds became faint and vanished, and he was alone.

Presently a peasant woman carrying a wicker basket strapped to her back and leading a she-goat with a distended udder, paused on her way to market and stood regarding Lunham with uncertainty. The she-goat, feeling the rope slacken, approached cautiously and nibbled his uniform, twitching her sensitive muzzle and baring her yellow teeth, but the woman jerked the cord and the goat moved away. Lunham turned and lifted his head heavily. He was still bleeding—a thin, insistent stream that would not stop—and where his mouth had rested there was a pool of blood that the earth had not entirely absorbed.

From her basket the woman took a metal cup and got down upon her knees, the she-goat spreading her hindquarters obediently. When the cup was full, the woman lifted Lunham's head and held it to his lips, but the milk was tepid, with a rank smell, and after he had swallowed a portion of it, he rose suddenly to his knees and swayed dizzily from side to side, his face white and dead, his hands splayed like the claws of a hawk. Then he tried desperately to stand upright, but his knees collapsed under him and he fell flat on his face and vomited with a hoarse, screaming sound.

The woman stretched out her arms and raised them slowly sidewise with a gesture singularly frustrate, and as she raised her arms the handle of the cup turned on her finger and the milk ran over its edge and spilled into the road . . . but Lunham lay stretched on his back, his face and hands covered with sweat, his thin body trembling . . . "Let me alone," he said . . . "let me alone, for Christ's sake." . . . The woman had risen and stood regarding him with stupid, compassionate eyes. She shook her head sadly. "*Je ne comprends pas!*" she said.

In the valley a farm-boy shouted to his team, a dog barked on a high, pure note and a flock of rooks, flying swiftly, dropped silently into a field.

Langston Hughes

(1902–1967)

A major American poet, Langston Hughes was also an editor, essayist, playwright, librettist, children's book author, and fiction writer. His first two books of poetry, *The Weary Blues* (1926) and *Fine Clothes to the Jew* (1927), established him as a leading light in the Harlem Renaissance and demonstrated his interest in the voices and characters of lower-class African American society. *Not Without Laughter* (1930), his first novel, is the story of black family life in the Midwest. His first collection of stories, *The Ways of White Folks* (1934), presents a pessimistic view of race relations in the United States and reflects Hughes's allegiance to leftist politics. During World War II he began a column for the *Chicago Defender* in which he introduced the character of Simple, or Jesse B. Semple, a plainspoken folk hero who comments incisively on American racism. This character became his most popular fictional creation, appearing for twenty years in the *Defender* and in five subsequent collections. "Poor Little Black Fellow" was published first in the *American Mercury* in November 1933 and later in *The Ways of White Folks*.

Poor Little Black Fellow

Langston Hughes

Amanda Lee had been a perfect servant. And her husband Arnold likewise. That the Lord had taken them both so soon was a little beyond understanding. But then, of course, the Lord was just. And He had left the Pembertons poor little black Arnie as their Christian duty. There was no other way to consider the little colored boy whom they were raising as their own, *their very own*, except as a Christian duty. After all, they were white. It was no easy thing to raise a white child, even when it belonged to one, whereas this child was black, and had belonged to their servants, Amanda and Arnold.

But the Pembertons were never known to shirk a duty. They were one of New England's oldest families, one of the finest. They were wealthy. They had a family tree. They had a house in a charming maple-shaded town a few hours from Boston, a cottage at the beach, and four servants. On Tuesdays and Fridays Mr. Pemberton went to town. He had an office of some sort there. But the ladies, Grace Pemberton and her sister, sat on the wide porch at home and crocheted. Or maybe let James take them for a drive in the car. One of them sang in the choir.

Sometimes they spoke about the two beautiful Negro servants they once had, Amanda and Arnold. They liked to tell poor little Arnie how faithful and lovely his parents had been in life. It would encourage the boy. At present, of course, all their servants were white. Negroes were getting so unsteady. You couldn't keep them in the villages any more. In fact, there were none in Mapleton now. They all went running off to Boston or New York, sporting their money away in the towns. Well, Amanda and Arnold were never like that. They had been simple, true, honest, hard-working. Their qualities had caused the Pembertons to give, over a space of time, more than ten thousand dollars to a school for Negroes at Hampton, Va. Because they thought they saw in Amanda and Arnold the real qualities of an humble and gentle race. That, too, was why they had decided to keep Arnie, poor little black fellow.

The Pembertons had lost nobody in the war except Arnold, their black stable man, but it had been almost like a personal loss. Indeed, after his death, they had kept horses no longer. And the stable had been turned into a garage.

Amanda, his wife, had grieved terribly, too. She had been all wrapped up in Arnold, and in her work with the Pembertons (she was their housekeeper) and in her little dark baby, Arnold, Junior. The child was five when his father went to war; and six when Amanda died of pneumonia a few weeks after they learned Arnold had been killed in the Argonne. The Pembertons were proud of him. A Negro who died for his country. But when that awful Winter of 1919 ended (the Pembertons judged it must have been awful from what they read), when that Winter ended the family was minus two perfect servants who could never come back. And they had on their hands an orphan.

"Poor little black fellow," said Grace Pemberton to her husband and her sister. "In memory of Arnold and Amanda, I think it is our Christian duty to keep it, and raise it up in the way it should go." Somehow, for a long time she called Arnie "it."

"We can raise it, without keeping it," said her husband. "Why not send it to Hampton?"

"Too young for that," said Emily, Mrs. Pemberton's sister. "I have been to Hampton, and they don't take them under twelve there."

So it was decided to keep the little black boy right in Mapleton, to send him to the village school, and to raise him up a good Christian and a good worker. And, it must be admitted, things went pretty well for some years. The white servants were kind to Arnie. The new housekeeper, a big-bosomed Irish woman who came after Amanda's death, treated him as though he were her very own, washed him and fed him. Indeed, they all treated him as if he were their very own.

II

Mr. Pemberton took Arnie to Boston once a season and bought him clothes. On his birthday, they gave him a party—on the lawn—because, after all, his birthday came in the Spring, and there was no need of filling the living-room with children. There was much more room on the lawn. In Summer Arnie went to the sea-shore with the rest of the family.

And Arnie, dark as he was, thrived. He grew up. He did well in his classes. He did well at home, helped with the chores about the house, raked the yard in the Fall, and shoveled snow when the long Winters set in. On Sundays he went to church with the family, listened to a dry and intelligent sermon, chanted the long hymns, and loved the anthems in which Miss Emily sang the solo parts.

Arnie, in church, a little black spot in a forest of white heads above stiff pews. Arnie, out of church, a symbol of how Christian charity should really be administered in the true spirit of the human brotherhood.

The church and the Pembertons were really a little proud of Arnie. Did they not all accept him as their own? And did they not go out of their way to be nice to him—a poor little black fellow whom they, through Christ, had taken in? Throughout the years the whole of Mapleton began to preen itself on its charity and kindness to Arnie. One would think that nobody in the town need ever again do a good deed: that this acceptance of a black boy was quite enough.

Arnie realized how they felt, but he didn't know what to do about it. He kept himself quiet and inconspicuous, and studied hard. He was very grateful, and very lonely. There were no other colored children in the town. But all the grown-up white people made their children be very nice to him, always very nice. "Poor little black boy," they said. "An orphan, and colored. And the Pembertons are so good to him. You be nice to him, too, do you hear? Share your lunch with him. And don't fight him. Or hurt his feelings. He's only a poor little Negro who has no parents." So even the children were over-kind to Arnie.

Everything might have been all right forever had not Arnie begun to grow up. The other children began to grow up, too. Adolescence. The boys had girls. They played kissing games, and learned to dance. There were parties to which Arnie was not invited—really couldn't be invited—with the girls and all. And after generations of peace the village of Mapleton, and the Pembertons, found themselves beset with a Negro problem. Everyone was a little baffled and a little ashamed.

To tell the truth, everybody had got so used to Arnie that nobody really thought of him as a Negro—until he put on long trousers and went to high-school. Now they noticed that he was truly very black. And his voice suddenly became deep and mannish, even before the white boys in Arnie's class talked in the cracks and squeaks of coming manhood.

Then there had arisen that problem of the Boy Scouts. When Arnie was sixteen the Pembertons applied for him to be admitted to a Summer camp for the Scouts at Barrow Beach, and the camp had refused. In a personal letter to Mr. Pemberton, they said they simply could not admit Negroes. Too many parents would object. So several of Arnie's friends and classmates went off to camp in June, and Arnie could not go. The village of Mapleton and the Pembertons felt awfully apologetic for American democracy's attitude to Arnie, whose father had died in the War. But, after all, they couldn't control the Boy Scout Camp. It was a semi-private institution. They were extra nice to Arnie, though—everybody.

That Summer, the Pembertons bought him a bicycle. And toward the end of the Summer (because they thought it was dull for him at the bungalow) they sent him to a Negro charity camp near Boston. It would be nice for him to come to know some of his own people. But Arnie hated it. He stayed a week and came home. The charity camp was full of black kids from the slums of Boston who cussed and fought and made fun of him because he didn't know how to play the dozens. So Arnie, to whom Negroes were a new nation, even if he was black, was amazed and bewildered, and came home. The Pembertons were embarrassed to find him alone in his attic room in the big empty house when they and the servants returned from the beach.

But they wanted so to be nice to him. They asked him if he'd met any friends he'd like to ask down for a week-end. They thought they would give him the whole top floor of the garage that year for a little apartment of his own and he could have his colored friends there. But Arnie hadn't met anyone he wanted to have. He had no colored friends.

The Pembertons knew that he couldn't move in the social world of Mapleton much longer. He was too big. But, really, what could they do? Grace Pemberton prayed. Emily talked it over with the mission board at church, and Mr. Pemberton spoke to the Urban League in Boston. Why not send him to Hampton now?

Arnie had only one more year in the high-school. Then, of course, he would go to college. But to one of the nicer Negro colleges like Fisk, they decided, where those dear Jubilee singers sang so beautifully, and where he would be with his own people, and wouldn't be embarrassed. No, Fisk wasn't as good as Harvard, they knew, but then Arnie had to find his own world after all. They'd have to let him go, poor black fellow! Certainly, he was their very own! But in Mapleton, what could he do, how could he live, whom could he marry? The Pembertons were a bit worried, even, about this one more year. So they decided to be extra nice to him. Indeed, everybody in Mapleton decided to be extra nice to him.

The two rooms over the garage made a fine apartment for a growing boy. His pennants and books and skis were there. Sometimes the white boys came in the evenings and played checkers and smoked forbidden cigarettes. Sometimes they walked out and met the girls at the soda-fountain in Dr. Jourdain's drug-store, and Arnie had a soda with the group. But he always came away alone, while the others went off in pairs. When the Christmas parties were being given, many of the girls were lovely in dresses that looked almost like real evening gowns, but Arnie wasn't invited anywhere but to the Allens'. (And they really didn't count in Mapleton—they were very poor white folks.)

The Pembertons were awfully sorry, of course. They were one of New England's oldest families, and they were raising Arnie as their son. But he was an African, a nice Christian African, and he ought to move among his own people. There he could be a good influence and have a place. The Pembertons couldn't help it that there were no Negroes in Mapleton. Once there had been some, but now they had all moved away. It was more fashionable to have white help. And even as a servant in Mapleton, Arnie would have been a little out of place. But he was smart in school, and a good clean boy. He sang well. (All Negroes were musical.) He skated and swam and played ball. He loved and obeyed the Pembertons. They wanted him to find his place in the world, poor fine little black fellow. Poor dear Arnie.

So it was decided that he would go to Fisk next year. When Arnie agreed, the Pembertons breathed a sort of sigh of joy. They thought he might remember the camp at Boston, and not want to go to a Negro college.

III

And now the Summer presented itself, the last Summer before they let Arnie go away—the boy whom they'd raised as their own. They didn't want that last Summer spoiled for him. Or for them. They wanted no such incidents as the Boy Scout business. The Pembertons were kind people. They wanted Arnie to remember with pleasure his life with them.

Maybe it would be nice to take him to Europe. They themselves had not been abroad for a long time. Arnie could see Paris and his father's grave and the Tower of London. The Pembertons would enjoy the trip, too. And on their return, Arnie could go directly to Fisk, where his life at college, and in the grown-up world, would begin. Maybe he'd marry one of those lovely brown girls who sang spirituals so beautifully, and live a good Christian man—occasionally visiting the Pembertons, and telling them about his influence on the poor black people of the South.

Graduation came. Arnie took high honors in the class, and spoke on the program. He went to the senior prom, but he didn't dance with any of the girls. He just sort of stood around the punch-bowl, and joked with the fellows. So nobody was embarrassed, and everyone was glad to see him there. The one dark spot in a world of whiteness. It was too bad he didn't have a partner to stand with him when they sang the Alma Mater after the final dance. But he was a lucky chap to be going to Europe. Not many youngsters from Mapleton had been. The Pembertons were doing well by him, everybody said aloud, and the church board had got him into Fisk.

But with all their careful planning, things weren't going so well about the European trip. When the steamship company saw the passports, they cancelled the cabin that had been engaged for Arnie. Servants always went second class, they wrote. That Arnie wasn't a servant, it was revealed ultimately, made no difference. He was a Negro, wasn't he?

So it ended with the Pembertons going first, and Arnie second class on the same boat. They would have all gone second, out of sympathy for Arnie, except that accommodations in that class had been completely booked for months ahead. Only as a great favor to first-class passengers had the steam-ship company managed to find a place for Arnie at all. The Pembertons and their boy had a cross to bear, but they bore it like Christians. At Cherbourg they met the little black fellow again on an equal footing. The evening found them in Paris.

Paris, loveliest of cities, where at dusk the lights are a great necklace among the trees of the Champs Elysées. Paris, song-city of the world. Paris, with the lips of a lovely woman kissing without fear. June, in Paris.

The Pembertons stopped at one of the best hotels. They had a suite which included a room for Arnie. Everything was very nice. The Louvre and the Eiffel Tower and the Café de la Paix were very nice. All with Arnie. Very nice. Everything would have gone on perfectly, surely; and there would have been no story, and Arnie and the Pembertons would have continued in Christian love forever—Arnie at Fisk, of course, and the Pembertons at Mapleton, then Arnie married and the Pembertons growing old, and so on and on—had not Claudina Lawrence moved into the very hotel where the Pembertons were staying. Claudina Lawrence! My God!

True, they had all seen dark faces on the boulevards, and a Negro quartet at the Olympia, but only very good Americans and very high English people were staying at this hotel with the Pembertons. Then Claudina Lawrence moved in—the Claudina who had come from Atlanta, Georgia, to startle the Old World with the new beauty of brown flesh behind footlights. That Claudina who sang divinely and danced like a dryad and had amassed a terrible amount of fame and money in five years. Even the Pembertons had heard of Claudina Lawrence in the quiet and sedate village of Mapleton. Even Arnie had heard of her. And Arnie had been a little bit proud. She was a Negro.

But why did she have to move next door to the Pembertons in this hotel? "Why, Lord, oh, why?" said Grace Pemberton. "For the sake of Arnie, why?" But here the tale begins.

IV

A lot of young Negroes, men and women, shiny and well-dressed, with good and sophisticated manners, came at all hours to see Claudina. Arnie and the Pembertons would meet them in the hall. They were a little too well dressed to suit the Pembertons. They came with white people among them, too—very pretty French girls. And they were terribly lively and gay and didn't seem dependent on anybody. Their music floated out of the windows on the Summer night. The Pembertons hoped they wouldn't get hold of Arnie. They would be a bad influence.

But they did get hold of Arnie.

One morning, as he came out to descend to the lobby to buy post-cards, Claudina herself stepped into the hall at the same time. They met at the elevator. She was the loveliest creature Arnie had ever seen. In pink, all tan and glowing. And she was colored.

"Hello," she said to the young black boy who looked old enough to be less shy. "You look like a home-towner."

"I'm from Mapleton," Arnie stuttered.

"You sound like you're from London," said Claudina, noting his New England accent and confusing it with Mayfair. "But your face says Alabama."

"Oh, I'm colored all right," said Arnie, happy to be recognized by one of his own. "And I'm glad to know you."

"Having a good time?" asked Claudina, as the elevator came.

"No," Arnie said, suddenly truthful. "I don't know anybody."

"Jesus!" said Claudina, sincerely. "That's a shame. A lot of boys and girls are always gathering in my place. Knock on the door some time. I can't see one of my down-home boys getting the blues in Paris. Some of the fellows in my band'll take you around a bit, maybe. They know all the holes and corners. Come in later."

"Thanks awfully," said Arnie.

Claudina left him half-dazed in the lobby. He saw her get into her car at the curb, saw the chauffeur tip his hat, and then drive away. For the first time in his life Arnie was really happy. Somebody had offered him something without charity, without condescension, without prayer, without distance, and without being nice.

All the pictures in the Luxembourg blurred before his eyes that afternoon, and Miss Emily's explanations went in one ear and out the other. He was thinking about Claudina and the friends he might meet in her rooms, the gay and well-dressed Negroes he had seen in the hall, the Paris they could show him, the girls they would be sure to know.

That night he went to see Claudina. He told the Pembertons he didn't care about going to the Odéon, so they went without him, a little reluctantly—because they didn't care about going either, really. They had been sticking rather strenuously to their program of cultural Paris. They were tired. Still, the Pembertons went to the Odéon—it was a play they really should see—and Arnie went next door to Claudina's. But only after he was sure the Pembertons were sitting in the theatre.

Claudina was playing whist. A young Englishman was her partner. Two sleek young colored men were their opponents. "Sit down, honey," Claudina said as if she had known Arnie for years. "You can take a hand in a minute, if you'd like to play. Meet Mr. So and so and so. . . ." She introduced him to the group. "It's kinda early yet. Most of our gang are at work. The theatres aren't out. . . . Marie, bring him a drink." And the French maid poured a cocktail.

A knock, and a rather portly brown-skinned woman, beautifully dressed, entered. "Hello! Who's holding all the trump cards? Glad to meet you, Mr. Arnie. From Boston, you say? My old stamping-ground. Do you know the Roundtrees there?"

"No'm," Arnie said.

"Well, I used to study at the Conservatory and knew all the big shots," the brown-skin woman went on. "Did you just come over? Tourist, heh? Well, what's new in the States now? I haven't been home for three years. Don't intend to go soon. The color-line's a little too much for me. What are they dancing now-a-days? You must've brought a few of the latest steps with you. Can you do the Lindy Hop?"

"No'm," said Arnie.

"Well, I'm gonna see," said the brown-skin lady. She put a record on the victrola, and took Arnie in her arms. Even if he couldn't do the Lindy Hop, he enjoyed dancing with her and they got along famously. Several more people came in, a swell-looking yellow girl, some rather elderly musicians, in spats, and a young colored art student named Harry Jones. Cocktails went around.

"I'm from Chicago," Harry said eventually. "Been over here about a year and like it a hell of a lot. You will, too, soon as you get to know a few folks."

Gradually the room took on the life and gaiety of a party. Somebody sat down at a piano in the alcove, and started a liquid ripple of jazz. Three or four couples began to dance. Arnie and the lovely yellow girl got together. They danced a long time, and then they drank cocktails. Arnie forgot about the clock. It was long after midnight.

Somebody suggested that they all go to the opening of a new Martinique ballroom where a native orchestra would play rattles and drums.

"Come on, Arnie." Harry Jones said. "You might as well make a night of it. To-morrow's Sunday."

"I start rehearsals tomorrow," Claudina said, "so I can't go. But listen here," she warned. "Don't you-all take Arnie out of here and lose him. Some of these little French girls are liable to put him in their pockets, crazy as they are about chocolate."

Arnie hoped he wouldn't meet the Pembertons in the hall. He didn't. They were long since in bed. And when Arnie came in at dawn, his head was swimming with the grandest night he'd ever known.

At the Martinique ball he'd met dozens of nice girls: white girls and brown girls, and yellow girls, artists and students and dancers and models and tourists. Harry knew everybody. And everybody was gay and friendly. Paris and music and cocktails made you forget what color people were—and what color you were yourself. Here it didn't matter—color.

Arnie went to sleep dreaming about a little Rumanian girl named Vivi. Harry said she was a music student. But Arnie didn't care what she was, she had such soft black hair and bright grey eyes. How she could dance! And she knew quite a little English. He'd taken her address. Tomorrow he would go to see her. Aw, hell, tomorrow the Pembertons wanted to go to Versailles!

V

When Arnie woke up it was three o'clock. This time Grace Pemberton had actually banged on the door. Arnie was frightened. He'd never slept so late before. What would the Pembertons think?

"What ever is the matter, Arnold?" Mrs. Pemberton called. Only when she was put out did she call him Arnold.

"Up late reading," Arnie muttered through the closed door. "I was up late reading." And then was promptly ashamed of himself for having lied.

"Well, hurry up," Mrs. Pemberton said. "We're about to start for Versailles."

"I don't want to go," said Arnie.

"What ever is the matter with you, boy?" gasped Grace Pemberton.

Arnie had slipped on a bathrobe, so he opened the door.

"Good morning," he said. "I've met some friends. I want to go out with them." The contrariness of late adolescence was asserting itself. He felt stubborn and mean.

"Friends?" said Grace Pemberton. "What friends, may I ask?"

"A colored student and some others."

"Where did you meet them?"

"Next door, at Miss Lawrence's."

Grace Pemberton stiffened like a bolt. "Get ready, young man," she said, "and come with us to Versailles." She left the room. The young man got ready.

Arnie pouted, but he went with the Pembertons. The sun gave him a headache, and he didn't give a damn about Versailles. That evening, after a private lecture by Mr. Pemberton on the evils of Paris (Grace and Emily had spoken about the beauty of the city), he went to bed feeling very black and sick.

For several days, he wasn't himself at all, what with constant excursions to museums and villages and chateaux, when he wanted to be with Vivi and Harry and Claudina. (Once he did sneak away with Harry to meet Vivi.) Meanwhile, the Pembertons lectured him on his surliness. They were inclined to be dignified and distant to the poor little black fellow now. After all, it had cost them quite a lot to bring him to Paris. Didn't he appreciate what they were doing for him? They had raised him. Had they then no right to forbid him going about with a crowd of Negroes from the theatres?

"He's a black devil," said Mr. Pemberton.

"Poor little fellow," said Grace. She was a little sorry for him.

"After all, he doesn't know. He's young. Let us just try loving him, and being very nice to him."

So once again the Pembertons turned loose on Arnie their niceness. They took him to the races, and they bought him half a dozen French ties from a good shop, and they treated him better than if he were their own.

But Arnie was worse than ever. He stayed out all night one night. Grace knew, because she knocked on his door at two o'clock. And the Negroes next door, how they laughed! How they danced! How the music drifted through the windows. It seemed as if the actual Devil had got into Arnie. Was he going to the dogs before their very eyes? Grace Pemberton was worried. After all, he *was* the nearest thing she'd ever had to a son. She was really fond of him.

As for Arnie, it wasn't the Devil at all that had got him. It wasn't even Claudina. It was Vivi, the little girl he'd met through Harry at the Martinique ball. The girl who played Chopin on the piano, and had grey eyes and black hair and came from Rumania. By himself, Arnie had managed to find, from the address she had given him, the tall house near the Parc Monceau where she lived in an attic room. Up six flights of stairs he walked. He found her with big books on theory in front of her and blank music pages, working out some sort of exercise in harmony. Her little face was very white, her grey eyes very big, and her black hair all fluffy around her head. Arnie didn't know why he had come to see her except that he liked her very much.

They talked all afternoon and Arnie told her about his life at home, how white people had raised him, and how hard it was to be black in America. Vivi said it didn't make any difference in Rumania, or in Paris either, about being black.

"Here it's only hard to be poor," Vivi said.

But Arnie thought he wouldn't mind being poor in a land where it didn't matter what color you were.

"Yes, you would mind," Vivi said.

"Being poor's not easy anywhere. But then," and her eyes grew bigger, "by and by the Revolution will come. In Rumania the Revolution will come. In France, too. Everywhere poor people are tired of being poor."

"What Revolution?" Arnie asked, for he hadn't heard about it in Mapleton. Vivi told him.

"Where we live, it's quiet," he said. "My folks come from Massachusetts."

VI

And then the devil whispered to Arnie. Maybe Vivi would like to meet some real Americans. Anyway, he would like the Pembertons to meet her. He'd like to show them that there actually was a young white girl in the world who didn't care about color. They were always educating him. He would educate them a bit. So Arnie invited Vivi to dinner at the hotel that very night.

The Pembertons had finished their soup when he entered the sparkling dining-room of the hotel. He made straight for their table. The orchestra was playing Strauss. Gentlemen in evening clothes and ladies in diamonds scanned a long and expensive menu. The Pembertons looked up and saw Arnie coming, guiding Vivi by the hand. Grace Pemberton gasped and put her spoon back in the soup. Emily went pale. Mr. Pemberton's mouth opened. All the Americans stared. Such a white, white girl and such a black, black boy coming across the dining-room floor! The girl had a red mouth and grey eyes.

The Pembertons had been waiting for Arnie since four o'clock. Today a charming Indian mystic, Nadjuti, had come to tea with them, especially to see the young Negro student they had raised in America. The Pembertons were not pleased that Arnie had not been there.

"This is my friend," Arnie said. "I've brought her to dinner."

Vivi smiled and held out her hand, but the Pembertons bowed in their stiffest fashion. Nobody noticed her hand.

"I'm sorry," said Grace Pemberton, "but there's room for only four at our table."

"Oh," said Arnie. He hadn't thought they'd be rude. Polite and formal, maybe, but not rude. "Oh!" Don't mind us then. Come on, Vivi." His eyes were red as he led her away to a vacant table by the fountain. A waiter came and took their orders with the same deference he showed everyone else. The Pembertons looked and could not eat.

"Where ever did he get her?" whispered Emily in her thin New England voice, as her cheeks burned. "Is she a woman from the streets?" The Pembertons couldn't imagine that so lovely a white girl would go out with a strange Negro unless she were a prostitute. They were terribly mortified. What would he do next?

"But maybe he doesn't know. Did you warn him, John?" Grace Pemberton addressed her husband.

"I did," replied Mr. Pemberton shortly.

"A scarlet woman," said Emily faintly. "A scarlet . . . I think I shall go to my room. All the Americans in the dining-room must have seen." She was white as she rose. "We've been talked about enough as it is—travelling with a colored boy. For our sakes he might have been careful."

The Pembertons left the dining-room. But Grace Pemberton was afraid for Arnie. Near the door, she turned and came over to the table by the fountain.

"Please, Arnold, come to my room before you go."

"Yes, Miss Grace, I'll come," he said.

"You mustn't mind." Vivi patted his arm. The orchestra was playing "The Song of India." "All old people are the same."

As they ate, Vivi and Arnie talked about parents. Vivi told him how her folks hadn't allowed her to come away to study music, how they'd even tried to stop her at the station. "Most elderly people are terrible," she said, "especially parents."

"But they're not my parents," Arnie said. "They are white people."

When he took Vivi home, he kissed her. Then he came back and knocked on the living-room door.

VII

"Come in," Grace Pemberton said. "Come in, Arnie, I want to talk to you." She was sitting there alone, very straight with her iron-grey hair low on her neck. "Poor little black fellow," she said, as though Arnie had done a great and careless wrong. "Come here."

When Arnie saw her pale white face from the door, he was a little sad and ashamed that he might have done something to hurt her. But when she began to pity him, "poor little black fellow," a sudden anger shook him from head to foot. His eyes grew sultry and red, his spirit stubborn.

"Arnold," she said, "I think we'd better go home, back to America."

"I don't want to go," he replied.

"But you don't seem to appreciate what we are doing for you here," she said, "at all."

"I don't," Arnie answered.

"You don't!" Grace Pemberton's throat went dry. "You don't? We're showing you the best of Paris, and you don't? Why, we've done all we could for you always, Arnie boy. We've raised you as our own. And we want to do more. We're going to send you to college, of course, to Fisk this Fall."

"I don't want to go to Fisk," Arnie said.

"What?"

"No," said Arnie. "I don't want to go. It'll be like that camp in Boston. Everything in America's like that camp in Boston." His eyes grew redder. "Separate, segregated, shut-off! Black people kept away from everybody else. I go to Fisk; my classmates, Harvard and Amherst and Yale. . . . I sleep in the garage, you sleep in the house."

"Oh," Grace Pemberton said. "We didn't mean it like that!"

Arnie was being cruel, just cruel. She began, in spite of herself, to cry.

"I don't want to go back home," Arnie went on. "I hate America."

"But your father *died* for America," Grace Pemberton cried.

"I guess he was a fool," said Arnie.

The hall door opened. Mr. Pemberton and his sister-in-law came in from a walk through the park.

They saw Mrs. Pemberton's eyes wet, and Arnie's sultry face. Mrs. Pemberton told them what he'd said.

"So you want to stay here," said Mr. Pemberton, trying to hold his temper. "Well, stay. Take your things and stay. Stay now. Get out! Go!"

Anger possessed him, fury against this ungrateful black boy who made his wife cry. Grace Pemberton never cried over anything Mr. Pemberton did. And now, she was crying over this . . . this . . . In the back of his mind was the word *nigger.* Arnold felt it.

"I want to go," said Arnie. "I've always wanted to go."

"You little black fool!" said Emily.

"Where will you go?" Grace Pemberton asked. Why, oh why, didn't Arnie say he was sorry, beg their pardon, and stay? He knew he could if he wanted to.

"I'll go to Vivi," Arnie said.

"Vivi?" a weak voice gasped.

"Yes, marry Vivi!"

"Marry white, eh?" said Mr. Pemberton. Emily laughed drily. But Grace Pemberton fainted.

Next door, just then, the piano was louder than ever. Somebody was doing a tap dance. The dancing and the music floated through the windows on the soft Paris air. Outside, the lights were a necklace of gold over the Champs Elysées. Autos honked. Trees rustled. People passed.

Arnie went out.

Kay Boyle

(1902–1992)

A writer of both novels and stories, Kay Boyle is praised by critics for the artistry and psychological insight of her short fiction. Born in St. Paul, Minnesota, Boyle lived in Europe, mostly in France and Austria, from 1923 to 1941, writing about both the aftermath of World War I and the German occupation of France during World War II. In this period, notable modernist writers admired her work and she won two O. Henry Awards. After the Second World War she covered occupied Germany for the *New Yorker* before returning to the United States permanently in the early 1950s. She was later active in the anti–Vietnam War protests, and she taught creative writing for seventeen years at San Francisco State University. Her collections include *Wedding Day and Other Stories* (1930), *The First Lover and Other Stories* (1933), and *White Horses of Vienna and Other Stories* (1936), in which "Count Lothar's Heart" appeared.

Count Lothar's Heart

Kay Boyle

Elsa was twenty-four the year the Count went off to war, and the Count was twenty-two. She remembered very well how he looked the day he left: the light hair brushed back from the point of his forehead, and color high on his cheeks because he had come fast through the chill of the September afternoon. All the manly, bodily things came alive in his blood when he walked and rang aloud until the echo was heard in every woman's heart that he passed. He had broken the black branches from the trees as they walked that day and carried them back to dress up the *Schloss* before he went away. On the other side of the Traunsee stood the mountains Elsa and Count

Lothar had climbed all their childhood together, rising almost straight from the water and the crests, unwooded and faintly blue with height.

The *Schloss* had no beauty or comfort to offer, belonging as it did to other centuries and people with a grimness no woman or season could subdue. The flagstones in the entryway were wide enough to mark a grave, and the carpets Count Lothar's mother had set down in the halls and the reception rooms were as good as nothing. There was nothing strong enough to defeat the hard, cold living of the ancestors: their cellars and their earth beneath the house were present in every room, imbuing, invading, destroying with a damp, chill, deathly breath.

The old Countess was sitting with her velvet boots on by the fire, and the old Count reading his newspaper there. It was nearly dark, but the lamps were still unlighted. Everything that came into the house and everything that went out of it was counted so there would never be any want for the people who came after. There was only a little wood in the chimney, burning slowly, scarcely enough to give a heart of warmth to the tall, gray-windowed, sepulchral room.

Elsa and Count Lothar came in through the arch of the door and put down their branches of leaves on the piano. The leaves hung yellow and thin as silk from the ebony stems of the boughs. The old Countess looked up at once at Elsa, and took her hand from the pocket of her gown. It might have been that she had been waiting for them, her thoughts going sharp and lean with venom, gathering her bitterness close to give it to them when they came through the door.

"Here's the ring, Elsa," she said. Her face was set in dry and violent old age against the blast of evening they brought in. "You may as well have it now as long as Lothar has taken it into his head to die."

Lothar stepped toward the fire, smiling, rubbing his fair, strong hands over and over before the wan, fluttering wings of flame.

"I'm not going to die, Mother," he said with patience.

No one said anything about the war, except these other things that were said of it, but in a little while he would be on a train going toward it with a quiver of exaltation in his blood. He was so young that he was in haste to make for himself an unconquerable, a manly past, and come back with the power of that as well in the look that he gave a woman on the street. He squatted there on the hearth on his fine, strong thighs, reaching out with his hands for the fire that was nearer to death than life. And Elsa sat down near the old Count, and opened her coat at the neck.

"There's your engagement ring," said the old Countess sharply, and she leaned forward from the other side and tossed the ring into Elsa's lap.

"Whom am I engaged to?" said Elsa, and she picked it up from her dress and laughed. She sat in her dark suit in the chair, looking with laughter in her eyes at the two old people, and at their son, who did not turn from the flame.

"If Lothar hasn't asked you yet," said the old Countess, lighting a cigarette, "then I'm sorry for you. Love and courtship, thank God, were entirely different when I was young. My husband fought two duels for me in the afternoon and we waltzed the whole night together after he had won me."

The old Count started up gently, as if from sleep, folded his newspaper over, and smoothed out his white soft mustaches with his delicate, shaking hand.

"I forgot about it," said Lothar, without turning on his heels. "It's all right with you, isn't it, Elsa?"

They had known each other so long, the same mountains and lakes, heard the same music, the same words over and over, all since they were children, but there had been no talk of love. But somehow, and without passion, it had been known between them; it had been understood, and Elsa's face was warm and brimming now as she held the fine ring closed inside her hand.

"Yes, Lothar. Yes, it is all right," she said softly, but the old woman cried out: "Kiss her! Kiss her!"

Count Lothar stood up and turned his back to the fireplace and walked to the chair where Elsa sat. She saw his face, clear and youthful, coming closer, bending to her, his eyes confused, his color rising. And suddenly she leaped up laughing.

"No, no, Lothar, not now!" she said. "It's really silly to do it now, isn't it? It doesn't matter! We'll do it some other time," she said.

"I never met 'another time' coming toward me," said the old Countess, and she snapped the end of her cigarette into the scarcely flickering fire. "They were always going the other way and they always will be."

The old Count cleared his throat and took out his watch in the palm of his hand.

"The train goes in half an hour," he said, peering into the face of it in the gathering dark.

"I'm going to the station with you," said Elsa softly, and Count Lothar said: "I'm going to drive the horses myself," and his eyes were glowing.

The old Countess watched her son sharply a moment, and then she stood up and faced him, holding fast to the back of her chair.

"If you come back," she said, "I hope you have some of the rot licked out of you. War has nothing to do with courage. You won't hear me out when I try to tell you. You and your father here, you take every word from the papers. Neither one or the other of you has ever had a thought of his own. When I was a girl there weren't any politics, the men were too good for it. But you were born too late in my life, and you're the worse for it. You kept hemming and hawing around and taking your time, and when I was near forty you made up your mind to appear. War has nothing to do with gentlemen!" she cried out. "Anyone with good blood in him and some sense has better things to do!"

Her hand was shaking on the high, carved head of her chair, and her face was lifted, white and strongly boned, with the skin drawn over it like lace.

"Lothar will be going in five minutes now," said the old Count as if in apology to them all.

"Upstarts!" said the old lady fiercely. "Pot-wallopers like Napoleon! War was good enough for them, just as harlots were good enough for them to marry." She stood with her two hands clasping the head of the chair, the empty folds of her soft cheeks quivering, the beak of her high nose thin as a blade. Her lids were stretched across her marble eyes, like curtains fallen, and she looking mightily and brazenly up from under their frayed hems. And suddenly Lothar crossed the space between them, dropped his head, and with his lips embraced her hands which did not falter. She stood holding to the strong, elaborate carving while Lothar followed the old Count from the room.

"You mustn't worry. It will be all right," said Elsa softly.

And "Worry?" cried out the old lady. The sound of the horses and the carriage could be heard on the drive. "My dear girl," said the old Countess, "you have my sympathy." She stood tall and immobile, staring without emotion beyond the sight of Elsa buttoning her warm coat over. "Your fiancé is a man of no particular talents, neither studious nor musical, gifted nor ambitious. He could never keep a single date of history in his head. He is stubborn as a mule, and I frequently wonder where he gets it from." Elsa pulled on her gloves, and from the hall they could hear the sound of his box being carried down. The old Countess drew her mouth in, close and bloodless in her sagging face. "He has no more idea why he is going to war than those horses out there, tearing the ground up with their feet, know why they're being driven to the station."

Elsa went quickly to the old lady and touched her hand. Her eyes had filled with tears before the old lady's dry, unswerving gaze.

"Say good-by to him then," she said softly. "Say good-by to him before he goes."

"Good-by won't enlighten him," said the old Countess tartly. She stood quite motionless, her hands holding fast to the chair back as Elsa too went out into the hall. The dark was gathering in the window behind her and blotting out entirely the day.

II

Count Lothar had been gone six years, and now it was the end of the summer again and the war a long time over. The old Countess was dead, and the old Count lived to himself, alone in the castle among the ravaged trees. In the spring of each year since Count Lothar had been gone, the trees had been cut down for fuel, and the *Schloss* was no longer now a place of mystery and darkness. It could be seen clearly from the road and from the water, towering in solitude over the gaps and the destruction where the bitten trunks stood.

No one had thought to see him again, for everything that had to do with his youth had dwindled and dimmed and it was almost certain that he had died as well. The whole country had fallen into poverty, and if he were alive somewhere, why should he return? Elsa wore the ring on her finger still, but she wore it in dignity and resignation, as an old lady might who had known the things of love and sorrow as they came: year after year the births and deaths and the altering of the spirit, the despair and the renunciation. If he comes back, was written in Elsa's face but she never spoke it out, he will come back because there is nowhere else to go.

There had been letters from him from Siberia, where he worked in the prison camp, and letters from China when they wrote him that his mother had died. But no one ever thought to see him back again, for so many of the prisoners had stayed and made a new life where they were, or else they had perished; but Count Lothar came back one day at the tail end of summer. He had only a rucksack to carry on his shoulders, so when he came through the gate at the station he started at once down the road. His boots were heavy and caked with earth and his topcoat was graying with a mist of use and age. He was still a thick-set fairish man with a small nose, fresh color running under his skin, and a look of gravity and willfulness in his eyes. His face was marked with weariness, and in weariness he took the first path into the woods, packed thick with the rotting leaves as it was under foot, and followed it as if from habit.

At the side of the water he halted and watched the boats curving out under their single canvas wings. He thought of his own sloop lying, still belly-up doubtless, as he had left it in the boat shed near the mouth of the stream. The swift, lovely boats were blowing across the Traunsee's shining breast, and he remembered the leap of his own boat's perilous giving and the rope running quick as water through his hands. He stood there a little, watching the single petals of the masts unfurling, now to the right in the wind and now to the left. The mountains on the other side had looked mighty and barren to him when he went away, and he saw with surprise now what had happened to them in his sight: they seemed to have lost their wildness and their power, and they were as pretty and mild as any pastureland.

Near to the town where the moored boats and the little white steamer rode on the water, the swans were floating still as they had floated every summer of his life. He had put his rucksack down on the gravel and with his arms crossed on the railing he watched these things, dimly, dimly, as a man in a dream might see profoundly, yet scarcely see. And, watching so, he saw the swans rise suddenly and of one accord from the water where they drifted and fly in great, strong, eager flight above the lake. Their necks were stretched out hungering and thirsting before them as they went, and the mighty flap of their wings was as good as a clear wind blowing. The blood ran up into Count Lothar's face, and he cried aloud:

"My God, I'd forgotten the swans flying!"

They were not near to him, but still he could feel on his flesh the strength of the pure white pinions stroking the quiet air. They might have passed close to him, so well could he feel the power and love of their bodies as they went. They were not like birds in flight, for the masterful wings seemed to raise strong, stallionlike, white bodies from their natural place and fling them headlong in egression into space. White horses might have flown like this, their vulnerable, soft breasts pressed sweet with flesh upon the current. The sight of the swans in flight across the Traunsee was a thing that made Count Lothar's heart rouse suddenly in anguish.

The birds had settled again on the water, and Count Lothar was standing so by the rail when Elsa came down the walk. Her head was lowered, her face ageless, colorless, and she was walking toward the streets of Gmunden with her shopping bag over her arm. There was nothing of youth left to her, nothing there that he might remember. She went past him in her high-laced, black shoes, and he looked back at the swans which were drifting at ease far out on the water. How ugly and shabby this woman and all the other women were, he thought, going down the walk past the lake and into town.

"Your mother was very sorry to go without seeing you again," said the old Count after they had eaten together. He looked from Lothar's face to Elsa's, apologizing because the old Countess had died. "She was very sorry at the end."

"What did she say?" asked Count Lothar, sitting with his legs stretched out and his eye and his heart quite dry.

"She didn't say anything," said the old Count, smoothing in his fingers what was left of his mustaches. "But she turned your photograph around so that it faced her. She had turned it to the wall the day you went away."

In a little while the old Count went out of the room, leaving Count Lothar and Elsa together, and the afternoon light came through the windows and fell on the dust on the floor and the ashes in the fireplace. There was white in Elsa's hair: it ran back from her brow in a dull, wide avenue of resignation, and Count Lothar turned his face from one side to the other. He looked at the rug worn thin on the floor, and at the light in the window. He did not want to see her face or to hear what she would say.

"You'll take a rest for a while, won't you, Lothar?" she said at last.

"What's that?" he said, and he started at the sound of her voice.

"You'll take a rest here," she repeated, "and then I suppose you'll go to Vienna?"

"To Vienna?" said Count Lothar in true surprise.

"There isn't anywhere else to make a living, is there? said Elsa, and she opened her hands out quietly in her lap.

"Oh, no," said Lothar. "I forgot. That's true."

"What do you think you want to do?" said Elsa gently after a moment.

"Do?" asked Count Lothar, and the look in his face might easily have been taken for stupidity. He had no sharpness and no subterfuge, but all that he felt in his flesh he felt so deeply that it moved him one way or the other of its own accord. All the years were put away behind him in confusion, and he was back amongst his people in confusion. He sat quite still, looking at the rug at his feet and the dust that had gathered on it, his gaze threshing from the table to the window, away from Elsa in despair.

After tea they walked down to the lake and past it out over the pathway of wooden bridges that followed the overflow of the Traunsee where it fell in a fast-running stream. Here the water poured out of the lake and went off down the mountains, and here where they walked above it, it was dammed in a staircase of smooth sliding falls. On the edge of these the swans had gathered; they were standing clear of the falling water on the brink, their webbed feet spread in the fernlike slime that rippled with the current, their legs as black as leather in the startling clarity of the quivering stream.

Count Lothar and Elsa stopped on the bridge, and the birds below them were preening their immaculate breasts and opening their wings out one by one, stretching them stark white against the water.

"How wonderful their necks are!" Count Lothar said, and suddenly a tremor of wonder ran through his blood and he had to steady himself by taking the wooden rail of the bridgeway in his hands.

"Do you remember?" said Elsa softly, holding his arm in hers. "We used to come here so often—"

He saw her face beside him, distasteful as a stranger's face, the lip of it trembling, and the bar of gray like a warning in her hair. And he turned his eyes back, slowly, in dumb confusion to the sight of the birds on the edge of slipping water. Some of them had thrust the long stalks of their throats down into the deeper places before the falls and were seeking for refuse along the bottom. Nothing remained but the soft, flickering, short peaks of their clean rumps and their leathery black elbows with the down blowing soft at the ebony bone. In such ecstasies of beauty were they seeking in the filth of lemon rinds and shells and garbage that had drifted from the town, prodding the leaves and branches apart with their dark, lustful mouths.

"Lothar," said Elsa, and then she stopped speaking. "I thought—" she began again, and suddenly she slipped the ring off her finger and put it in his hand. "I don't want you to feel bound to me, Lothar," she said. "It's been so long. I don't want to hold you to anything you don't want. I know there may be someone else. I understand that very well."

Count Lothar looked at the ring lying in the palm of his hand, and then he gave it back to her.

"No," he said. "There is nobody else. I'll make some money, I'm sure I shall find something to do, and then we can get married."

And then he burst out laughing at what was left of the swans above the water: the white, beautiful rumps wagging and flickering and seeming to hark to the sudden burst of sound. Elsa put the ring back upon her finger and she spoke his name softly, but he was laughing aloud in delight and he did not hear her. He scarcely knew she was there, for he was watching the strong, greedy beaks and the weaving of the swans' necks under water.

So he took the habit of coming to see the swans every afternoon, no matter what the weather. He would come down past the Traunsee and stand on the bridgeway, watching the swans. When the fine mountain rain of the autumn was falling, the great birds would go under the beams, under the rotting pillars of the pier, and he could see them interwinding the long, white vines of their throats, one with the other. He could stand so on the boards over the shallow stream, leaning with his arms crossed on the railing, and watch the swans forever. They were a deep caress to his wandering spirit, they were a soft call in the darkness to his heart. He did not know what he thought of them, but there he stood hour after hour, watching the writhing necks of the white birds uncoiling and bridling suavely in embrace.

"I hope the snow doesn't come early this year," Count Lothar said to his father one afternoon, for he was thinking of what might become of the birds once the cold of the winter set in.

But the old Count said: "Perhaps you'll be in Salzburg by that time."

Count Lothar was thinking of the swans, and for a moment he did not seem to hear. He could not remember well the things of his youth and he did not know any more if the birds stayed here or if they went to warmer places. But suddenly he lifted his head.

"Why should I be in Salzburg?" he said.

The old man had begun to tremble as if in fear of some echo of his dead wife's wrath which might now sound out of his son's mouth. He raised his failing, gentlemanly hand and from where they walked on the road he pointed back through the mutilated tress.

"There's the *Schloss*," he said, and his voice was shaking. "I would like to give it to you when you marry. I would like to see you and Elsa live in it together, while I am still here. Elsa and I have been trying here and there, and there's a bank in Salzburg where they've offered you a place. You could come back here with your wife to the *Schloss* for the summers. It would be nice for your children to grow up here," he said.

"That's true," said Count Lothar, but he spoke as if he had scarcely heard. "Do the swans migrate or do they stay the winter here?" he asked after a little while.

In the night the moon was out and Count Lothar put his coat on after supper. The old Count woke up in his chair where he had been sleeping by the fire, and looked with his small, pink eyes at his son.

"Are you going to see Elsa?" he asked, and his voice was faint with hope on his lips. Count Lothar nodded, and at once the tears sprang from the old man's eyes.

But Count Lothar's heart was as dry as a dead leaf blowing down the driveway. He went past the gleaming edge of the lake, and walked through the town, and so out over the bridges that carried the wooden pathway down the shining stream. The moon was high and perfect in the sky, and the swarming light of it gave the land a single dimension of cold, exalted purity. The waters below him were slipping down the stony bed, warbling and calling softly to each other, hollow and sweet as flute notes sounding. Count Lothar stopped on the bridgeway and looked back at the lake that lay behind: the moon's light was riding, white as ice, on the dark waves that murmured in through the stones.

As the Count stood watching the nightly, muted world, a stirring of life sounded out across the water: it began at the end of the lake that was far from him, and it moved like a wind on the water. It came as strong as a foehn wind over the lake, gathering throb by throb until the sky and the land were filled with the sound of passage. Count Lothar held fast to the rail of the bridge, and the blood was shaking in his body, and his ears and his mouth were filled with music like those of a drowning man. There was no longer any earth on which to stand, no air to breathe, no human sound to hear. The elements had become one in the great wind that filled the rushing heavens, drawing with it, long and slow and mighty, the power of spread, gigantic wings.

"Is it the swans? Is it the swans indeed?" Count Lothar cried out in madness, for it seemed to him that a thousand birds had risen on the current and were passing above him, their necks outstretched, their rich, majestic bodies flowing with the deep, ardent pulsing of their monstrous wings. "Is it the swans?" he cried into the thunder of their flight, and the air itself was passing, lashed fast as pinion feathers to the curved and reaching bone.

As he listened now, he could hear the young Cossacks coming, riding six abreast, the sound of their horses as they galloped. He could see their young faces, as beautiful as women's, and he could hear them singing in the wild, high, boyish voices, galloping, with their coats gone white as swans under the falling snow, galloping, galloping, galloping as they crossed the heavens. Elsa had come onto the bridgeway and was standing there beside him, and he seized her arm in his fingers and began calling out to her of what he saw. He could hear the young Cossacks coming, he could see them riding six abreast, coming into the camp as young and rich as stallions.

"Listen to me now, Elsa," he said. "Listen to me."

He saw the women well who came to the prison camp, and were given to the men as rations were given, with no youth or beauty or gusto left in their flesh. He saw their hard, long, riddled faces, and the look of greed they had under the scars left there by hunger and pox and cold. He held Elsa's arm like a man gone mad, and he told her what he saw, telling her these things, talking fast. There were the women offered them, and over the snow rode the Cossacks, galloping, galloping six abreast. They came into the camp, elegant in their good furs, stamping and chattering and dancing like lively women as they warmed their fingers by the stove.

"In some men and women there are conflicting cells," said Count Lothar, talking wildly as they walked. "There are the male and the female cells. We're near the beginning of life still and there is still the conflict of the two physical demands in us. We're near to the worms and the snails, and they are both male and female in themselves."

He saw them laying their coats off, the wide bear coats that went down to their heels. He heard them asking that wine be brought, and the youth in their bodies was thundering, thundering, like the blood that thunders aloud in the ears.

"They never looked at the women," he said. "Some of the women were so strong that they carried wounded men for miles on their backs. And some of the strongest, youngest men turned in loneliness to one another."

He could see their faces clearly, and their eyes turned up like Oriental women's, tilted with lust under their silky brows.

"In some men," Count Lothar was saying wildly, "there are more of the female cells, and only in need they discover this. . . . And in need we turned to one another. . . ."

They had suddenly come to the road, and Elsa was holding fast to him, looking up into his face. At last, at last, was her silence saying softly, at last. He is speaking, and I am to know a little of what became of his youth and what became of the things he had in the years he has been away. At last, at last. . . .

"In Siberia," Count Lothar said, and then his throat seemed to close in despair and he could say no more. Elsa pressed his arm in gentleness.

"Tell me, tell me," she said. "It is very beautiful . . . it is friendship . . . tell me, do."

Count Lothar saw that the road lights were burning at intervals beneath the hanging boughs along the road, and that people were walking back from the *Kino* that was just over in the town.

"There is nothing to tell," he said in a low voice. "No, I have said it all. There is nothing more to tell," he said, and they never spoke of it again, neither in Salzburg, where he worked in the bank in the winter, or in the *Schloss,* where they came every summertime.

Katherine Anne Porter

(1890–1980)

An influential writer of short fiction, Katherine Anne Porter began publishing stories in literary journals in the 1920s. Her first collection, *Flowering Judas,* appeared in 1930 and was expanded in 1935 as *Flowering Judas and Other Stories.* Born and educated in Texas, Porter developed artistically while working as an actress in Chicago, a newspaper reporter in Fort Worth and Denver, and an editor and arts educator in Mexico. Living in Germany and Paris in the 1930s she witnessed the ascent of Nazism. Porter was popular with readers in her time, and critics now see her as a master of the short story genre, placing her in the company of Anton Chekov and James Joyce. In addition to *Flowering Judas and Other Stories, Pale Horse, Pale Rider: Three Short Novels* (1939) and *The Leaning Tower and Other Stories* (1944) contain much of her best fiction. In 1962 she published *Ship of Fools,* a novel that dramatizes the international scene on the eve of Hitler's rise to power.

Pale Horse, Pale Rider

Katherine Anne Porter

In sleep she knew she was in her bed, but not the bed she had lain down in a few hours since, and the room was not the same but it was a room she had known somewhere. Her heart was a stone lying upon her breast outside of her; her pulses lagged and paused, and she knew that something strange was going to happen, even as the early morning winds were cool through the lattice, the streaks of light were dark blue and the whole house was snoring in its sleep.

Now I must get up and go while they are all quiet. Where are my things? Things have a will of their own in this place and hide where they like. Daylight will strike a sudden blow on the roof startling them all up to their feet; faces will beam asking, Where are you going, What are you doing, What are you thinking, How do you feel, Why do you say such things, What do you mean? No more sleep. Where are my boots and what horse shall I ride? Fiddler or Graylie or Miss Lucy with the long nose and the wicked eye? How I have loved this house in the morning before we are all awake and tangled together like badly cast fishing lines. Too many people have been born here, and have wept too much here, and have laughed too much, and have been too angry and outrageous with each other here. Too many have died in this bed already, there are far too many ancestral bones propped up on the mantel-pieces, there have been too damned many antimacassars in this house, she said loudly, and oh, what accumulation of storied dust never allowed to settle in peace for one moment.

And the stranger? Where is that lank greenish stranger I remember hanging about the place, welcomed by my grandfather, my great-aunt, my five times removed cousin, my decrepit hound and my silver kitten? Why did they take to him, I wonder? And where are they now? Yet I saw him pass the window in the evening. What else besides them did I have in the world? Nothing. Nothing is mine, I have only nothing but it is enough, it is beautiful and it is all mine. Do I even walk about in my own skin or is it something I have borrowed to spare my modesty? Now what horse shall I borrow for this journey I do not mean to take, Graylie or Miss Lucy or Fiddler who can jump ditches in the dark and knows how to get the bit between his teeth? Early morning is best for me because trees are trees in one stroke, stones are stones set in shades known to be grass, there are no false shapes or surmises, the road is still asleep with the crust of dew unbroken. I'll take Graylie because he is not afraid of bridges.

Come now, Graylie, she said, taking his bridle, we must outrun Death and the Devil. You are no good for it, she told the other horses standing saddled before the stable gate, among them the horse of the stranger, gray also, with tarnished nose and ears. The stranger swung into his saddle beside her, leaned far towards her and regarded her without meaning, the blank still stare of mindless malice that makes no threats and can bide its time. She drew Graylie around sharply, urged him to run. He leaped the low rose hedge and the narrow ditch beyond, and the dust of the lane flew heavily under his beating hoofs. The stranger rode beside her, easily, lightly, his reins loose in his half-closed hand, straight and elegant in dark shabby garments that flapped upon his bones; his pale face smiled in an evil trance, he did not glance at her. Ah, I have seen this fellow before, I know this man if I could place him. He is no stranger to me.

She pulled Graylie up, rose in her stirrups and shouted, I'm not going with you this time—ride on! Without pausing or turning his head the stranger rode on. Graylie's ribs heaved under her, her own ribs rose and fell, Oh, why am I so tired,

I must wake up. "But let me get a fine yawn first," she said, opening her eyes and stretching, "a slap of cold water in my face, for I've been talking in my sleep again, I heard myself but what was I saying?"

Slowly, unwillingly, Miranda drew herself up inch by inch out of the pit of sleep, waited in a daze for life to begin again. A single word struck in her mind, a gong of warning, reminding her for the day long what she forgot happily in sleep, and only in sleep. The war, said the gong, and she shook her head. Dangling her feet idly with their slippers hanging, she was reminded of the way all sorts of persons sat upon her desk at the newspaper office. Every day she found someone there, sitting upon her desk instead of the chair provided, dangling his legs, eyes roving, full of his important affairs, waiting to pounce about something or other. "*Why* won't they sit in the chair? Should I put a sign on it, saying, 'For God's sake, sit here'?"

Far from putting up a sign, she did not even frown at her visitors. Usually she did not notice them at all until their determination to be seen was greater than her determination not to see them. Saturday, she thought, lying comfortably in her tub of hot water, will be pay day, as always. Or I hope always. Her thoughts roved hazily in a continual effort to bring together and unite firmly the disturbing oppositions in her day-to-day existence, where survival, she could see clearly, had become a series of feats of sleight of hand. I owe—let me see, I wish I had pencil and paper—well, suppose I *did* pay five dollars now on a Liberty Bond, I couldn't possibly keep it up. Or maybe. Eighteen dollars a week. So much for rent, so much for food, and I mean to have a few things besides. About five dollars' worth. Will leave me twenty-seven cents. I suppose I can make it. I suppose I should be worried. I am worried. Very well, now I am worried and what next? Twenty-seven cents. That's not so bad. Pure profit, really. Imagine if they should suddenly raise me to twenty I should then have two dollars and twenty-seven cents left over. But they aren't going to raise me to twenty. They are in fact going to throw me out if I don't buy a Liberty Bond. I hardly believe that. I'll ask Bill. (Bill was the city editor.) I wonder if a threat like that isn't a kind of blackmail. I don't believe even a Lusk Committeeman can get away with that.

Yesterday there had been two pairs of legs dangling, on either side of her typewriter, both pairs stuffed thickly into funnels of dark expensive-looking material. She noticed at a distance that one of them was oldish and one was youngish, and they both of them had a stale air of borrowed importance which apparently they had got from the same source. They were both much too well nourished and the younger one wore a square little mustache. Being what they were, no matter what their business was it would be something unpleasant. Miranda had nodded at them, pulled out her chair and without removing her cap or gloves had reached into a pile of letters and sheets from the copy desk as if she had not a moment to spare. They did not move, or take off their hats. At last she had said "Good morning" to them, and asked if they were, perhaps, waiting for her?

The two men slid off the desk, leaving some of her papers rumpled, and the oldish man had inquired why she had not bought a Liberty Bond. Miranda had looked at him then, and got a poor impression. He was a pursy-faced man, gross-mouthed, with little lightless eyes, and Miranda wondered why nearly all of those selected to do the war work at home were of his sort. He might be anything at all, she thought; advance agent for a road show, promoter of a wildcat oil company, a former saloon keeper announcing the opening of a new cabaret, an automobile salesman—any follower of any one of the crafty, haphazard callings. But he was now all Patriot, working for the government. "Look here," he asked her, "do you know there's a war, or don't you?"

Did he expect an answer to that? Be quiet, Miranda told herself, this was bound to happen. Sooner or later it happens. Keep your head. The man wagged his finger at her, "Do you?" he persisted, as if he were prompting an obstinate child.

"Oh, the war," Miranda had echoed on a rising note and she almost smiled at him. It was habitual, automatic, to give that solemn, mystically uplifted grin when you spoke the words or heard them spoken. *"C'est la guerre,"* whether you could pronounce it or not, was even better, and always, always, you shrugged.

"Yeah," said the younger man in a nasty way, "the war." Miranda, startled by the tone, met his eye; his stare was really stony, really viciously cold, the kind of thing you might expect to meet behind a pistol on a deserted corner. This expression gave temporary meaning to a set of features otherwise nondescript, the face of those men who have no business of their own. "We're having a war, and some people are buying Liberty Bonds and others just don't seem to get around to it," he said. "That's what we mean."

Miranda frowned with nervousness, the sharp beginnings of fear. "Are you selling them?" she asked, taking the cover off her typewriter and putting it back again.

"No, we're not selling them," said the older man. "We're just asking you why you haven't bought one." The voice was persuasive and ominous.

Miranda began to explain that she had no money, and did not know where to find any, when the older man interrupted: "That's no excuse, no excuse at all, and you know it, with the Huns overrunning martyred Belgium."

"With our American boys fighting and dying in Belleau Wood," said the younger man, "anybody can raise fifty dollars to help beat the Boche."

Miranda said hastily, "I have eighteen dollars a week and not another cent in the world. I simply cannot buy anything."

"You can pay for it five dollars a week," said the older man (they had stood there cawing back and forth over her head), "like a lot of other people in this office, and a lot of other offices besides are doing."

Miranda, desperately silent, had thought, "Suppose I were not a coward, but said what I really thought? Supposed I said to hell with this filthy war? Suppose I asked that little thug, What's the matter with you, why aren't you rotting in Belleau Wood? I wish you were . . ."

She began to arrange her letters and notes, her fingers refusing to pick up things properly. The older man went on making his little set speech. It was hard, of course. Everybody was suffering, naturally. Everybody had to do his share. But as to that, a Liberty Bond was the safest investment you could make. It was just like having the money in the bank. Of course. The government was back of it and where better could you invest?

"I agree with you about that," said Miranda, "but I haven't any money to invest."

And of course, the man had gone on, it wasn't so much her fifty dollars that was going to make any difference. It was just a pledge of good faith on her part. A pledge of good faith that she was a loyal American doing her duty. And the thing was safe as a church. Why, if he had a million dollars he'd be glad to put every last cent of it in these Bonds. . . . "You can't lose by it," he said, almost benevolently, "and you can lose a lot if you don't. Think it over. You're the only one in this whole newspaper office that hasn't come in. And every firm in this city has come in one hundred per cent. Over at the *Daily Clarion* nobody had to be asked twice."

"They pay better over there," said Miranda. "But next week, if I can. Not now, next week."

"See that you do," said the younger man. "This ain't any laughing matter." They lolled away, past the Society Editor's desk, past Bill the City Editor's desk, past the long copy desk where old man Gibbons sat all night shouting at intervals, "Jarge! Jarge!" and the copy boy would come flying. "Never say *people* when you mean *persons*," old man Gibbons had instructed Miranda, "and never say *practically*, say *virtually*, and don't for God's sake ever so long as I am at this desk use the barbarism *inasmuch* under any circumstances whatsoever. Now you're educated, you may go." At the head of the stairs her inquisitors had stopped in their fussy pride and vainglory, lighting cigars and wedging their hats more firmly over their eyes.

Miranda turned over in the soothing water, and wished she might fall asleep there, to wake up only when it was time to sleep again. She had a burning slow headache, and noticed it now, remembering she had waked up with it and it had in fact begun the evening before. While she dressed she tried to trace the insidious career of her headache, and it seemed reasonable to suppose it had started with the war. "It's been a headache, all right, but not quite like this." After the Committeemen had left, yesterday, she had gone to the cloakroom and had found Mary Townsend, the Society Editor, quietly hysterical about something. She was perched on the edge of the shabby wicker couch with ridges down the center, knitting on something rose-colored. Now and then she would put down her knitting, seize her head with both hands and rock, saying, "My *God,*" in a surprised, inquiring voice. Her column was called Ye Towne Gossyp, so of course everybody called her Towney. Miranda and Towney had a great deal in common, and liked each other. They had both been real reporters once, and had been sent together to "cover" a scandalous elopement, in which no marriage had taken place, after all, and the recaptured girl, her face swollen, had sat with her mother, who was moaning steadily under a mound of blankets. They had both wept painfully and implored the young reporters to suppress the worst of the story. They had suppressed it, and the rival newspaper printed it all the next day. Miranda and Towney had then taken their punishment together, and had been degraded publicly to routine female jobs, one to the the-aters, the other to society. They had this in common, that neither of them could see what else they could possibly have done, and they knew they were considered fools by the rest of the staff—nice girls, but fools. At sight of Miranda, Towney had broken out in a rage. "I can't do it, I'll never be able to raise the money, I told them, I can't, I can't, but they wouldn't listen."

Miranda said, "I knew I wasn't the only person in this office who couldn't raise five dollars. I told them I couldn't, too, and I can't."

"My *God,*" said Towney, in the same voice, "they told me I'd lose my job—"

"I'm going to ask Bill," Miranda said; "I don't believe Bill would do that."

"It's not up to Bill," said Towney. "He'd have to if they got after him. Do you suppose they could put us in jail?"

"I don't know," said Miranda. "If they do, we won't be lonesome." She sat down beside Towney and held her own head. "What kind of soldier are you knitting that for? It's a sprightly color, it ought to cheer him up."

"Like hell," said Towney, her needles going again. "I'm making this for myself. That's that."

"Well," said Miranda, "we won't be lonesome and we'll catch up on our sleep." She washed her face and put on fresh make-up. Taking clean gray gloves out of her pocket she went out to join a group of young women fresh from the country club dances, the morning bridge, the charity bazaar, the Red Cross workrooms, who were wallowing in good works. They gave tea dances and raised money, and with the money they bought quantities of sweets, fruit, cigarettes, and magazines for the men in the cantonment hospitals. With this loot they were now setting out, a gay procession of high-powered cars and brightly tinted faces to cheer the brave boys who already, you might very well say, had fallen in defense of their country. It must be frightfully hard on them, the dears, to be floored like this when they're all crazy to get overseas and into the trenches as quickly as possible. Yes, and some of them are the cutest things you ever saw, I didn't know there were so many good-looking men in this country, good heavens, I said, where do they come from? Well, my dear, you may ask yourself that question, who knows where they did come from? You're quite right, the way I feel about it is this, we must do everything we can to make them contented, but I draw the line at talking to them. I told the chaperons at those dances for enlisted men, I'll dance with them, every dumbbell who asks me, but I will NOT talk to them, I said, even if there is a war. So I danced hundred of miles without opening my mouth except to say, Please keep your knees to yourself. I'm glad we gave those dances up. Yes, and the men stopped coming, anyway. But listen, I've heard that a great many of the enlisted men come from very good families; I'm not good at catching names, and those I did catch I'd never heard before, so I don't know . . . but it seems to me if they were from good families, you'd know it, wouldn't you? I mean, if a man is well bred he doesn't step on your feet, does he? At least not that. I used to have a pair of sandals ruined at every one of those dances. Well, I think any kind of social life is in very poor taste just now, I think we should all put on our Red Cross head dresses and wear them for the duration of the war—

Miranda, carrying her basket and her flowers, moved in among the young women, who scattered out and rushed upon the ward uttering girlish laughter meant to be refreshingly gay, but there was a grim determined clang in it calculated to freeze the blood. Miserably embarrassed at the idiocy of her errand, she walked rapidly between the long rows of high beds, set foot to foot with a narrow aisle between. The men, a selected presentable lot, sheets drawn up to their chins, not seriously ill, were bored and restless, most of them willing to be amused at anything. They were for the most part picturesquely bandaged as to arm or head, and those who were not visibly wounded invariably replied "Rheumatism" if some tactless girl, who had been solemnly warned never to ask this question, still forgot and asked a man what his illness was. The good-natured, eager ones, laughing and calling out from their hard narrow beds, were soon surrounded. Miranda, with her wilting bouquet and her basket of sweets and cigarettes, looking about, caught the unfriendly bitter eye of a young fellow lying on his back, his right leg in a cast and pulley. She stopped at the foot of his bed and continued to look at him, and he looked back with an unchanged, hostile face. Not having any, thank you and be damned to the whole business, his eyes said plainly to her, and will you be so good as to take your trash off my bed? For Miranda had set it down, leaning over to place it where he might be able to reach it if he would. Having set it down, she was incapable of taking it up again, but hurried away, her face burning, down the long aisle and out into the cool October sunshine, where the dreary raw barracks swarmed and worked with an aimless life of scurrying, dun-colored insects; and going around to a window near where he lay, she looked in, spying upon her soldier. He was lying with his eyes closed, his eyebrows in a sad bitter frown. She could not place him at all, she could not imagine where he came from nor what sort of being he might have been "in life," she said to herself. His face was young and the features sharp and plain, the hands were not laborer's hands but not well-cared-for hands either. They were good useful properly shaped hands, lying there on the coverlet. It occurred to her that it would be her luck to find him, instead of a jolly hungry puppy glad of a bite to eat and a little chatter. It is like turning a corner absorbed in your painful thoughts and meeting your state of mind embodied, face to face, she said. "My own feelings about this whole thing, made flesh. Never again will I come here, this is no sort of thing to be doing. This is disgusting," she told herself plainly. "Of course I would pick him out," she thought, getting into the back seat of the car she came in, "serves me right, I know better."

Another girl came out looking very tired and climbed in beside her. After a short silence, the girl said in a puzzled way, "I don't know what good it does, really. Some of them wouldn't take anything at all. I don't like this, do you?"

"I hate it," said Miranda.

"I suppose it's all right, though," said the girl, cautiously.

"Perhaps," said Miranda, turning cautious also.

That was for yesterday. At this point Miranda decided there was no good in thinking of yesterday, except for the hour after midnight she had spent dancing with Adam. He was in her mind so much, she hardly knew when she was thinking about him directly. His image was simply always present in more or less degree, he was sometimes nearer the surface of her thoughts, the pleasantest, the only really pleasant thought she had. She examined her face in the mirror between the windows and decided that her uneasiness was not all imagination. For three days at least she had felt odd and her expression was unfamiliar. She would have to raise that fifty dollars somehow, she supposed, or who knows what can happen? She was hardened to stories of personal disaster, of outrageous accusations and extraordinarily bitter penalties that had grown monstrously out of incidents very little more important than her failure—her refusal—to buy a Bond. No, she did not find herself a pleasing sight, flushed and shiny, and even her hair felt as if it had decided to grow in the other direction. I must do something about this, I can't let Adam see me like this, she told herself, knowing that even now at that moment he was listening for the turn of her door knob, and he would be in the hallway, or on the porch when she came out, as if by sheerest coincidence. The noon sunlight cast cold slanting shadows in the room where, she said, I suppose I live, and this day is beginning badly, but they all do now, for one reason or another. In a drowse, she sprayed perfume on her hair, put on her moleskin cap and jacket, now in their second winter, but still good, still nice to wear, again being glad she had paid a frightening price for them. She had enjoyed them all this time, and in no case would she have had the money now. Maybe she could manage for that Bond. She could not find the lock without leaning to search for it, then stood undecided a moment possessed by the notion that she had forgotten something she would miss seriously later on.

Adam was in the hallway, a step outside his own door; he swung about as if quite startled to see her, and said, "Hello. I don't have to go back to camp today after all—isn't that luck?"

Miranda smiled at him gaily because she was always delighted at the sight of him. He was wearing his new uniform, and he was all olive and tan and tawny, hay colored and sand colored from hair to boots. She half noticed again that he always began by smiling at her; that his smile faded gradually; that his eyes became fixed and thoughtful as if he were reading in a poor light.

They walked out together into the fine fall day, scuffling bright ragged leaves under their feet, turning their faces up to a generous sky really blue and spotless. At the first corner they waited for a funeral to pass, the mourners seated straight and firm as if proud in their sorrow.

"I imagine I'm late," said Miranda, "as usual. What time is it?"

"Nearly half past one," he said, slipping back his sleeve with an exaggerated thrust of his arm upward. The young soldiers were still self-conscious about their wrist watches. Such of them as Miranda knew were boys form southern and southwestern towns, far off the Atlantic seaboard, and they had always believed that only sissies wore wrist watches. "I'll slap you on the wrist watch," one vaudeville comedian would simper to another, and it was always a good joke, never stale.

"I think it's a most sensible way to carry a watch," said Miranda. "You needn't blush."

"I'm nearly used to it," said Adam, who was from Texas. "We've been told time and again how all the he-manly regular army men wear them. It's the horrors of war," he said; "are we downhearted? I'll say we are."

It was the kind of patter going the rounds. "You look it," said Miranda.

He was tall and heavily muscled in the shoulders, narrow in the waist and flanks, and he was infinitely buttoned, strapped, harnessed into a uniform as tough and unyielding in cut as a strait jacket, though the cloth was fine and supple. He had his uniforms made by the best tailor he could find, he confided to Miranda one day when she told him how squish he was looking in his new solider suit. "Hard enough to make anything of the outfit, anyhow," he told her. "It's the least I can do for my beloved country, not to go around looking like a tramp." He was twenty-four years old and a Second Lieutenant in an Engineers Corps, on leave because his outfit expected to be sent over shortly. "Came in to make my will," he told Miranda, "and get a supply of toothbrushes and razor blades. By what gorgeous luck do you suppose," he asked her, "I happened to pick on your rooming house? How did I know you were there?"

Strolling, keeping step, his stout polished well-made boots setting themselves down firmly beside her thin-soled black suède, they put off as long as they could the end of their moment together, and kept up as well as they could their small talk that flew back and forth over little grooves worn in the thin upper surface of the brain, things you could say and hear clink reassuringly at once without disturbing the radiance which played and darted about the simple and lovely miracle of being two persons named Adam and Miranda, twenty-four years old each, alive and on the earth at the same moment: "Are you in the mood for dancing, Miranda?" and "I'm always in the mood for dancing, Adam!" but there were things in the way, the day that ended with dancing was a long way to go.

He really did look, Miranda thought, like a fine healthy apple this morning. One time or another in their talking, he had boasted that he had never had a pain in his life that he could remember. Instead of being horrified at this monster, she approved his monstrous uniqueness. As for herself, she had had too many pains to mention, so she did not mention them. After working for three years on a morning newspaper she had an illusion of maturity and experience; but it was fatigue merely, she decided, from keeping what she had been brought up to believe were unnatural hours, eating casually at dirty little restaurants, drinking bad coffee all night, and smoking too much. When she said something of her way of living to Adam, he studied her face a few seconds as if he had never seen it before, and said in a forthright way, "Why, it hasn't hurt you a bit, I think you're beautiful," and left her dangling there, wondering if he had thought she wished to be praised. She did wish to be praised, but not at that moment. Adam kept unwholesome hours too, or had in the ten days they had known each other, staying awake until one o'clock to take her out for supper; he smoked also continually, though if she did not stop him he was apt to explain to her exactly what smoking did to the lungs. "But," he said, "does it matter so much if you're going to war, anyway?"

"No," said Miranda, "and it matters even less if you're staying at home knitting socks. Give me a cigarette, will you?" They paused at another corner, under a half-foliaged maple, and hardly glanced at a funeral procession approaching. His eyes were pale tan with orange flecks in them, and his hair was the color of a haystack when you turn the weathered top back to the clear straw beneath. He fished out his cigarette case and snapped his silver lighter at her, snapped it several times in his own face, and they moved on, smoking.

"I can see you knitting socks," he said. "That would be just your speed. You know perfectly well you can't knit."

"I do worse," she said, soberly; "I write pieces advising other young women to knit and roll bandages and do without sugar and help win the war."

"Oh, well," said Adam; with the easy masculine morals in such questions, "that's merely your job, that doesn't count."

"I wonder," said Miranda. "How did you manage to get an extension of leave?"

"They just gave it," said Adam, "for no reason. The men are dying like flies out there, anyway. This funny new disease. Simply knocks you into a cocked hat."

"It seems to be a plague," said Miranda, "something out of the Middle Ages. Did you ever see so many funerals, ever?"

"Never did. Well, let's be strong minded and not have any of it. I've got four days more straight from the blue and not a blade of grass must grow under our feet. What about tonight?"

"Same thing," she told him, "but make it about half past one. I've got a special job beside my usual run of the mill."

"What a job you've got," said Adam, "nothing to do but run from one dizzy amusement to another and then write a piece about it."

"Yes, it's too dizzy for words," said Miranda. They stood while a funeral passed and this time they watched it in silence. Miranda pulled her cap to an angle and winked in the sunlight, her head swimming slowly "like goldfish," she told Adam, "my head swims. I'm only half awake, I must have some coffee."

They lounged on their elbows over the counter of a drug store. "No more cream for the stay-at-homes," she said, "and only one lump of sugar. I'll have two or none; that's the kind of martyr I'm being. I mean to live on boiled cabbage and wear shoddy from now on and get in good shape for the next round. No war is going to sneak up on me again."

"Oh, there won't be any more wars, don't you read the newspapers?" asked Adam. "We're going to mop 'em up this time, and they're going to stay mopped, and this is going to be all."

"So they told me," said Miranda, tasting her bitter lukewarm brew and making a rueful face. Their smiles approved of each other, they felt they had got the right tone, they were taking the war properly. Above all, thought Miranda, no tooth-gnashing, no hair-tearing, it's noisy and unbecoming and it doesn't get you anywhere.

"Swill," said Adam rudely, pushing back his cup. "Is that all you're having for breakfast?"

"It's more than I want," said Miranda.

"I had buckwheat cakes, with sausage and maple syrup, and two bananas, and two cups of coffee, at eight o'clock, and right now, again, I feel like a famished orphan left in the ashcan. I'm all set," said Adam, "for broiled steak and fried potatoes and—"

"Don't go on with it," said Miranda, "it sounds delirious to me. Do all that after I'm gone." She slipped from the high seat, leaned against it slightly, glanced at her face in her round mirror, rubbed rouge on her lips and decided that she was past praying for.

"There's something terribly wrong," she told Adam. "I feel too rotten. It can't just be the weather, and the war."

"The weather is perfect," said Adam, "and the war is simply too good to be true. But since when? You were all right yesterday."

"I don't know," she said slowly, her voice sounding small and thin. They stopped as always at the open door before the flight of littered steps leading up to the newspaper loft. Miranda listened for a moment to the rattle of typewriters above, the steady rumble of presses below. "I wish we were going to spend the whole afternoon on a park bench," she said, "or drive to the mountains."

"I do too," he said; "let's do that tomorrow."

"Yes, tomorrow, unless something else happens. I'd like to run away," she told him; "let's both."

"Me?" said Adam. "Where I'm going there's no running to speak of. You mostly crawl about on your stomach here and there among the debris. You know, barbed wire and such stuff. It's going to be the kind of thing that happens once in a lifetime." He reflected a moment, and went on, "I don't know a darned thing about it, really, but they make it sound awfully messy. I've heard so much about it I feel as if I had been there and back. It's going to be an anticlimax," he said, "like seeing the pictures of a place so often you can't see it at all when you actually get there. Seems to me I've been in the army all my life."

Six months, he meant. Eternity. He looked so clear and fresh, and he had never had a pain in his life. She had seen them when they had been there and back and they never looked like this again. "Already the returned hero," she said, "and don't I wish you were."

"When I learned the use of the bayonet in my first training camp," said Adam, "I gouged the vitals out of more sandbags and sacks of hay than I could keep track of. They kept bawling at us, 'Get him, get that Boche, stick him before he sticks you'—and we'd go for those sandbags like wildfire, and honestly, sometimes I felt a perfect fool for getting so worked up when I saw the sand trickling out. I used to wake up in the night sometimes feeling silly about it."

"I can imagine," said Miranda. "It's perfect nonsense." They lingered, unwilling to say good-by. After a little pause, Adam, as if keeping up the conversation, asked,

"Do you know what the average life expectation of a sapping party is after it hits the job?"

"Something speedy, I suppose."

"Just nine minutes," said Adam; "I read that in your own newspaper not a week ago."

"Make it ten and I'll come along," said Miranda.

"Not another second," said Adam, "exactly nine minutes, take it or leave it."

"Stop bragging," said Miranda. "Who figured that out?"

"A noncombatant," said Adam, "a fellow with rickets."

This seemed very comic, they laughed and leaned towards each other and Miranda heard herself being a little shrill. She wiped the tears from her eyes. "My, it's a funny war," she said; "isn't it? I laugh every time I think about it."

Adam took her hand in both of his and pulled a little at the tips of her gloves and sniffed them. "What nice perfume you have," he said, "and such a lot of it, too. I like a lot of perfume on gloves and hair," he said, sniffing again.

"I've got probably too much," she said. "I can't smell or see or hear today. I must have a fearful cold."

"Don't catch cold," said Adam; "my leave is nearly up and it will be the last, the very last." She moved her fingers in her gloves as he pulled at the fingers and turned her hands as if they were something new and curious and of great value, and she turned shy and quiet. She liked him, she liked him, and there was more than this but it was no good even imagining, because he was not for her nor for any woman, being beyond experience already, committed without any knowledge or act of his own to death. She took back her hands. "Good-by," she said finally, "until tonight."

She ran upstairs and looked back from the top. He was still watching her, and raised his hand without smiling. Miranda hardly ever saw anyone look back after he had said good-by. She could not help turning sometimes for one glimpse more of the person she had been talking with, as if that would save too rude and too sudden a snapping of even the lightest bond. But people hurried away, their faces already changed, fixed, in their straining towards their next stopping place, already absorbed in planning their next act or encounter. Adam was waiting as if he expected her to turn, and under his brows fixed in a strained frown, his eyes were very black.

At her desk she sat without taking off jacket or cap, slitting envelopes and pretending to read the letters. Only Chuck Rouncivale, the sports reporter, and Ye Towne Gossyp were sitting on her desk today, and them she liked having there. She sat on theirs when she pleased. Towney and Chuck were talking and they went on with it.

"They say," said Towney, "that it is really caused by germs brought by a German ship to Boston, a camouflaged ship, naturally, it didn't come in under its own colors. Isn't that ridiculous?"

"Maybe it was a submarine," said Chuck, "sneaking in from the bottom of the sea in the dead of night. Now that sounds better."

"Yes, it does," said Towney; "they always slip up somewhere in these details . . . and they think the germs were sprayed over the city—it started in Boston, you know—and somebody reported seeing a strange, thick, greasy-looking cloud float up out of Boston Harbor and spread slowly all over that end of town. I think it was an old woman who saw it."

"Should have been," said Chuck.

"I read it in a New York newspaper," said Towney; "so it's bound to be true."

Chuck and Miranda laughed so loudly at this that Bill stood up and glared at them. "Towney still reads the newspapers," explained Chuck.

"Well, what's funny about that?" asked Bill, sitting down again and frowning into the clutter before him.

"It was a noncombatant saw that cloud," said Miranda.

"Naturally," said Towney.

"Member of the Lusk Committee, maybe," said Miranda.

"The Angel of Mons," said Chuck, "or a dollar-a-year man."

Miranda wished to stop hearing, and talking, she wished to think for just five minutes of her own about Adam, really to think about him, but there was no time. She had seen him first ten days ago, and since then they had been crossing streets together, darting between trucks and limousines and pushcarts and farm wagons; he had waited for her in doorways and in little restaurants that smelled of stale frying fat; they had eaten and danced to the urgent whine and bray of jazz orchestras, they had sat in dull theaters because Miranda was there to write a piece about the play. Once they had gone to the mountains and, leaving the car, had climbed a stony trail, and had come out on a ledge upon a flat stone, where they sat and watched the lights change on a valley landscape that was, no doubt, Miranda said, quite apocryphal—"We need not believe it, but it is fine poetry," she told him; they had leaned their shoulders together there, and had sat quite still, watching. On two Sundays they had gone to the geological museum, and had pored in shared fascination over bits of meteors, rock formations, fossilized tusks and trees, Indian arrows, grottoes from the silver and gold lodes. "Think of those old miners washing out their fortunes in little pans beside the streams," said Adam, "and inside the earth there was this—" and he had told her he liked better those things that took long to make; he loved airplanes too, all sorts of machinery, things carved out of wood or stone.

He knew nothing much about them, but he recognized them when he saw them. He had confessed that he simply could not get through a book, any kind of book except textbooks on engineering; reading bored him to crumbs; he regretted now he hadn't brought his roadster, but he hadn't thought he would need a car; he loved driving, he wouldn't expect her to believe how many hundreds of miles he could get over in a day . . . he had showed her snapshots of himself at the wheel of his roadster; of himself sailing a boat, looking very free and windblown, all angles, hauling on the ropes; he would have joined the air force, but his mother had hysterics every time he mentioned it. She didn't seem to realize that dog fighting in the air was a good deal safer than sapping parties on the ground at night. But he hadn't argued, because of course she did not realize about sapping parties. And here he was, stuck, on a plateau a mile high with no water for a boat and his car at home, otherwise they could really have had a good time. Miranda knew he was trying to tell her what kind of person he was when he had his machinery with him. She felt she knew pretty well what kind of person he was, and would have liked to tell him that if he thought he had left himself at home in a boat or an automobile, he was much mistaken. The telephones were ringing, Bill was shouting at somebody who kept saying, "Well, but listen, well, but listen—" but nobody was going to listen, of course, nobody. Old man Gibbons bellowed in despair, "Jarge, Jarge—"

"Just the same," Towney was saying in her most complacent patriotic voice. "Hut Service is a fine idea, and we should all volunteer even if they don't want us." Towney does well at this, thought Miranda, look at her; remembering the rose-colored sweater and the tight rebellious face in the cloakroom. Towney was now all open-faced glory and goodness, willing to sacrifice herself for her country. "After all," said Towney, "I *can* sing and dance well enough for the Little Theater, and I could write their letters for them, and at a pinch I might drive an ambulance. I have driven a Ford for years."

Miranda joined in: "Well, I can sing and dance too, but who's going to do the bed-making and the scrubbing up? Those huts are hard to keep, and it would be a dirty job and we'd be perfectly miserable; and as I've got a hard dirty job and am perfectly miserable, I'm going to stay at home."

"I think the women should keep out of it," said Chuck Rouncivale. "They just add skirts to the horrors of war." Chuck had bad lungs and fretted a good deal about missing the show. "I could have been there and back with a leg off by now; it would have served the old man right. Then he'd either have to buy his own hooch or sober up."

Miranda had seen Chuck on pay day giving the old man money for hooch. He was a good-humored ingratiating old scoundrel, too, that was the worst of him.

He slapped his son on the back and beamed upon him with the bleared eye of paternal affection while he took his last nickel.

"It was Florence Nightingale ruined wars," Chuck went on. "What's the idea of petting soldiers and binding up their wounds and soothing their fevered brows? That's not war. Let 'em perish where they fall. That's what they're there for."

"You can talk," said Towney, with a slantwise glint at him.

"What's the idea?" asked Chuck, flushing and hunching his shoulders. "You know I've got this lung, or maybe half of it anyway by now."

"You're much too sensitive," said Towney. "I didn't mean a thing."

Bill had been raging about, chewing his half-smoked cigar, his hair standing up in a brush, his eyes soft and lambent but wild, like a stag's. He would never, thought Miranda, be more than fourteen years old if he lived for a century, which he would not, at the rate he was going. He behaved exactly like city editors in the moving pictures, even to the chewed cigar. Had he formed his style on the films, or had scenario writers seized once for all on the type Bill in its inarguable purity? Bill was shouting to Chuck: *"And if he comes back here take him up the alley and saw his head off by hand!"*

Chuck said, "He'll be back, don't worry." Bill said mildly, already off on another track, "Well, saw him off." Towney went to her own desk, but Chuck sat waiting amiably to be taken to the new vaudeville show. Miranda, with two tickets, always invited one of the reporters to go with her on Monday. Chuck was lavishly hardboiled and professional in his sports writing, but he had told Miranda that he didn't give a damn about sports, really; the job kept him out in the open, and paid him enough to buy the old man's hooch. He preferred shows and didn't see why women always had the job.

"Who does Bill want sawed today?" asked Miranda.

"That hoofer you panned in this morning's," said Chuck. "He was up here bright and early asking for the guy that writes up show business. He said he was going to take the goof who wrote that piece up the alley and bop him in the nose. He said . . ."

"I hope he's gone," said Miranda; "I do hope he had to catch a train."

Chuck stood up and arranged his maroon-colored turtle-necked sweater, glanced down at the peasoup tweed plus fours and the hobnailed tan boots which he hoped would help to disguise the fact that he had a bad lung and didn't care for sports, and said, "He's long gone by now, don't worry. Let's get going; you're late as usual."

Miranda, facing about, almost stepped on the toes of a little drab man in a derby hat. He might have been a pretty fellow once, but now his mouth drooped where he had lost his side teeth, and his sad red-rimmed eyes had given up coquetry. A thin brown wave of hair was combed out with brilliantine and curled against the rim of the derby. He didn't move his feet, but stood planted with a kind of inert resistance, and asked Miranda: "Are you the so-called dramatic critic on this hick newspaper?"

"I'm afraid I am," said Miranda.

"Well," said the little man, "I'm just asking for one minute of your valuable time." His underlip shot out, he began with shaking hands to fish about in his waistcoat pocket. "I just hate to let you get away with it, that's all." He riffled through a collection of shabby newspaper clippings. "Just give these the once-over, will you? And then let me ask you if you think I'm gonna stand for being knocked by a tanktown critic," he said, in a toneless voice; "look here, here's Buffalo, Chicago, Saint Looey, Philadelphia, Frisco, besides New York. Here's the best publications in the business, *Variety*, the *Billboard*, they all broke down and admitted that Danny Dickerson knows his stuff. So you don't think so, hey? That's all I wanta ask you."

"No, I don't," said Miranda, as bluntly as she could, "and I can't stop to talk about it."

The little man leaned nearer, his voice shook as if he had been nervous for a long time. "Look here, what was there you didn't like about me? Tell me that."

Miranda said, "You shouldn't pay any attention at all. What does it matter what I think?"

"I don't care what you think, it ain't that," said the little man, "but these things get round and booking agencies back East don't know how it is out here. We get panned in the sticks and they think it's the same as getting panned in Chicago, see? They don't know the difference. They don't know that the more high class an act is the more the hick critics pan it. But I've been called the best in the business by the best in the business and I wanta know what you think is wrong with me."

Chuck said, "Come on, Miranda, curtain's going up." Miranda handed the little man his clippings, they were mostly ten years old, and tried to edge past him. He stepped before her again and said without much conviction, "If you was a man I'd knock your block off." Chuck got up at that and lounged over, taking his hands out of his pockets, and said, "Now you've done your song and dance you'd better get out. Get the hell out now before I throw you downstairs."

The little man pulled at the top of his tie, a small blue tie with red polka dots, slightly frayed at the knot. He pulled it straight and repeated as if he had rehearsed it, "Come out in the alley." The tears filled his thickened red lids. Chuck said, "Ah, shut up," and followed Miranda, who was running towards the stairs. He overtook her on the sidewalk. "I left him sniveling and shuffling his publicity trying to find the joker," said Chuck, "the poor old heel."

Miranda said, "There's too much of everything in this world just now. I'd like to sit down here on the curb, Chuck, and die, and never again see—I wish I could lose my memory and forget my own name . . . I wish—"

Chuck said, "Toughen up, Miranda. This is no time to cave in. Forget that fellow. For every hundred people in show business, there are ninety-nine like him. But you don't manage right, anyway. You bring it on yourself. All you have to do is play up the headliners, and you needn't even mention the also-rans. Try to keep in mind that Rypinsky has got show business cornered in this town; please Rypinsky and you'll please the advertising department, please them and you'll get a raise. Hand-in-glove, my poor dumb child, will you never learn?"

"I seem to keep learning all the wrong things," said Miranda, hopelessly.

"You do for a fact," Chuck told her cheerfully. "You are as good at it as I ever saw. Now do you feel better?"

"This is a rotten show you've invited me to," said Chuck. "Now what are you going to do about it? If I were writing it up, I'd—"

"Do write it up," said Miranda. "You write it up this time. I'm getting ready to leave, anyway, but don't tell anybody yet."

"You mean it? All my life," said Chuck, "I've yearned to be a so-called dramatic critic on a hick newspaper, and this is positively my first chance."

"Better take it," Miranda told him. "It may be your last." She thought, This is the beginning of the end of something. Something terrible is going to happen to me. I shan't need bread and butter where I'm going. I'll will it to Chuck, he has a venerable father to buy hooch for. I hope they let him have it. Oh, Adam, I hope I see you once more before I go under with whatever is the matter with me. "I wish the war were over," she said to Chuck, as if they had been talking about that. "I wish it were over and I wish it had never begun."

Chuck had got out his pad and pencil and was already writing his review. What she had said seemed safe enough but how would he take it? "I don't care how it started or when it ends," said Chuck, scribbling away, "I'm not going to be there."

All the rejected men talked like that, thought Miranda. War was the one thing they wanted, now they couldn't have it. Maybe they had wanted badly to go, some of them. All of them had a sidelong eye for the women they talked with about it, a guarded resentment which said, "Don't pin a white feather on me, you bloodthirsty female. I've offered my meat to the crows and they won't have it." The worst thing about war for the stay-at-homes is there isn't anyone to talk to any more. The Lusk Committee will get you if you don't watch out. Bread will win the war. Work will win, sugar will win, peach pits will win the war. Nonsense. *Not* nonsense, I tell you, there's some kind of valuable high explosive to be got out of peach pits. So all the happy housewives hurry during the canning season to lay their baskets of peach pits on the altar of their country. It keeps them busy and makes them feel useful, and all these women running wild with the men away are dangerous, if they aren't given something to keep their little minds out of mischief. So rows of young girls, the intact cradles of the future, with their pure serious faces framed becomingly in Red Cross wimples, roll cockeyed bandages that will never reach a base hospital, and knit sweaters that will never warm a manly chest, their minds dwelling lovingly on all the blood and mud and the next dance at the Acanthus Club for the officers of the flying corps. Keeping still and quiet will win the war.

"I'm simply not going to be there," said Chuck, absorbed in his review. No, Adam will be there, thought Miranda. She slipped down in the chair and leaned her head against the dusty plush, closed her eyes and faced for one instant that was a lifetime the certain, the overwhelming and awful knowledge that there was nothing at all ahead for Adam and for her. Nothing. She opened her eyes and held her hands together palms up, gazing at them and trying to understand oblivion.

"Now look at this," said Chuck, for the lights had come on and the audience was rustling and talking again. "I've got it all done, even before the headliner comes on. It's old Stella Mayhew, and she's always good, she's been good for forty years, and she's going to sing 'O the blues ain't nothin' but the easy-going heart disease.' That's all you need to know about her. Now just glance over this. Would you be willing to sign it?"

Miranda took the pages and stared at them conscientiously, turning them over, she hoped, at the right moment, and gave them back. "Yes, Chuck, yes, I'd sign that. But I won't. We must tell Bill you wrote it, because it's your start, maybe."

"You don't half appreciate it," said Chuck. "You read it too fast. Here, listen to this—" and he began to mutter excitedly. While he was reading she watched his face. It was a pleasant face with some kind of spark of life in it, and a good severity in the modeling of the brow above the nose. For the first time since she had known him she wondered what Chuck was thinking about. He looked preoccupied and unhappy, he wasn't so frivolous as he sounded. The people were crowding into the aisle, bringing out their cigarette cases ready to strike a match the instant they reached the lobby; women with waved hair clutched at their wraps, men stretched their chins to east them of their stiff collars, and Chuck said, "We might as well go now." Miranda, buttoning her jacket, stepped into the moving crowd, thinking, What did I ever know about them? There must be a great many of them here who think as I do, and we dare not say a word to each other of our desperation, we are speechless animals letting ourselves be destroyed, and why? Does anybody here believe the things we say to each other?

Stretched in unease on the ridge of the wicker couch in the cloakroom, Miranda waited for time to pass and leave Adam with her. Time seemed to proceed with more than usual eccentricity, leaving twilight gaps in her mind for thirty minutes which seemed like a second, and then hard flashes of light that shone clearly on her watch proving that three minutes is an intolerable stretch of waiting, as if she were hanging by her thumbs. At last it was reasonable to imagine Adam stepping out of the house in the early darkness into the blue mist that might soon be rain, he would be on the way, and there was nothing to think about him, after all. There was only the wish to see him and the fear, the present threat, of not seeing him again; for every step they took towards each other seemed perilous, drawing them apart instead of together, as a swimmer in spite of his most determined strokes is yet drawn slowly backward by the tide. "I don't want to love," she would think in spite of herself, "not Adam, there is no time and we are not ready for it and yet this is all we have—"

And there he was on the sidewalk, with his foot on the first step, and Miranda almost ran down to meet him. Adam, holding her hands, asked, "Do you feel well now? Are you hungry? Are you tired? Will you feel like dancing after the show?"

"Yes to everything," said Miranda, "yes, yes. . . ." Her head was like a feather, and she steadied herself on his arm. The mist was still mist that might be rain later, and though the air was sharp and clean in her mouth, it did not, she decided, make breathing any easier. "I hope the show is good, or at least funny," she told him, "but I promise nothing."

It was a long, dreary play, but Adam and Miranda sat very quietly together waiting patiently for it to be over. Adam carefully and seriously pulled off her glove and held her hand as if he were accustomed to holding her hand in theaters. Once they turned and their eyes met, but only once, and the two pairs of eyes were equally steady and noncommittal. A deep tremor set up in Miranda, and she set about resisting herself methodically as if she were closing windows and doors and fastening down curtains against a rising storm. Adam sat watching the monotonous play with a strange shining excitement, his face quite fixed and still.

When the curtain rose for the third act, the third act did not take place at once. There was instead disclosed a backdrop almost covered with an American flag improperly and disrespectfully exposed, nailed at each upper corner, gathered in the middle and nailed again, sagging dustily. Before it posed a local dollar-a-year man, now doing his bit as a Liberty Bond salesman. He was an ordinary man past middle life, with a neat little melon buttoned into his trousers and waistcoat, an opinion-ated tight mouth, a face and figure in which nothing could be read save the inept sensual record of fifty years. But for once in his life he was an important fellow in an impressive situation, and he reveled, rolling his words in an actorish tone.

"Looks like a penguin," said Adam. They moved, smiled at each other, Miranda reclaimed her hand, Adam folded his together and they prepared to wear their way again through the same old moldy speech with the same old dusty backdrop. Miranda tried not to listen, but she heard. These vile Huns—glorious Belleau Wood—our keyword is Sacrifice—Martyred Belgium—give till it hurts—our noble boys Over There—Big Berthas—the death of civilization—the Boche—

"My head aches," whispered Miranda. "Oh, why won't he hush?"

"He won't," whispered Adam. "I'll get you some aspirin."

"In Flanders Field the poppies grow, Between the crosses row on row"—"He's getting into the home stretch," whispered Adam—atrocities, innocent babes hoisted on Boche bayonets—your child and my child—if our children are spared these things, then let us say with all reverence that these dead have not died in vain—the war, the *war,* the WAR to end WAR, war for Democracy, for humanity, a safe world forever and ever—and to prove our faith in Democracy to each other, and to the world, let everybody get together and buy Liberty Bonds and do without sugar and wool socks—was that it? Miranda asked herself, Say that over, I didn't catch the last line. Did you mention Adam? If you didn't I'm not interested. What about Adam, you little pig? And what are we going to sing this time, "Tipperary" or "There's a Long, Long Trail"? Oh, please do let the show go on and get over with. I must write a piece about it before I can go dancing with Adam and we have no time. Coal, oil, iron, gold, international finance, why don't you tell us about them, you little liar?

The audience rose and sang, "There's a Long, Long Trail A-winding," their opened mouths black and faces pallid in the reflected footlights; some of the faces grimaced and wept and had shining streaks like snail's tracks on them. Adam and Miranda joined in at the tops of their voices, grinning shamefacedly at each other once or twice.

In the street, they lit their cigarettes and walked slowly as always. "Just another nasty old man who would like to see the young ones killed," said Miranda in a low voice; "the tom-cats try to eat the little tom-kittens, you know. They don't fool you really, do they, Adam?"

The young people were talking like that about the business by then. They felt they were seeing pretty clearly through that game. She went on, "I hate these potbellied baldheads, too fat, too old, too cowardly, to go to war themselves, they know they're safe; it's you they are sending instead—"

Adam turned eyes of genuine surprise on her. "Oh *that* one," he said. "Now what could the poor sap do if they did take him? It's not his fault," he explained, "he can't do anything but talk." His pride in his youth, his forbearance and tolerance and contempt for that unlucky being breathed out of his very pores as he strolled, straight and relaxed in his strength. "What *could* you expect of him, Miranda?"

She spoke his name often, and he spoke hers rarely. The little shock of pleasure the sound of her name in his mouth gave her stopped her answer. For a moment she hesitated, and began at another point of attack. "Adam," she said, "the worst of war is the fear and suspicion and the awful expression in all the eyes you meet . . . as if they had pulled down the shutters over their minds and their hearts and were peering out at you, ready to leap if you make one gesture or say one word they do not understand instantly. It frightens me; I live in fear too, and no one should have to live in fear. It's the skulking about, and the lying. It's what war does to the mind and the heart, Adam, and you can't separate these two—what it does to them is worse than what it can do to the body."

Adam said soberly, after a moment, "Oh, yes, but suppose one comes back whole? The mind and the heart sometimes get another chance, but if anything happens to the poor old human frame, why, it's just out of luck, that's all."

"Oh, yes," mimicked Miranda. "It's just out of luck, that's all."

"If I didn't go," said Adam, in a matter-of-fact voice, "I couldn't look myself in the face."

So that's all settled. With her fingers flattened on his arm, Miranda was silent, thinking about Adam. No, there was no resentment or revolt in him. Pure, she thought, all the way through, flawless, complete, as the sacrificial lamb must be. The sacrificial lamb strode along casually, accommodating his long pace to hers, keeping her on the inside of the walk in the good American style, helping her across street corners as if she were a cripple—"I hope we don't come to a mud puddle, he'll carry me over it"—giving off whiffs of tobacco smoke, a manly smell of scentless soap, freshly cleaned leather and freshly washed skin, breathing through his nose and carrying his chest easily. He threw back his head and smiled into the sky which still misted, promising rain. "Oh, boy," he said, "what a night. Can't you hurry that review of yours so we can get started?"

He waited for her before a cup of coffee in the restaurant next to the pressroom, nicknamed The Greasy Spoon. When she came down at last, freshly washed and combed and powdered, she saw Adam first, sitting near the dingy big window, face turned to the street, but looking down. It was an extraordinary face, smooth and fine and golden in the shabby light, but not set in a blind melancholy, a look of pained suspense and disillusion. For just one split second she got a glimpse of

Adam when he would have been older, the face of the man he would not live to be. He saw her then, rose, and the bright glow was there.

Adam pulled their chairs together at their table; they drank hot tea and listened to the orchestra jazzing "Pack Up Your Troubles."

"In an old kit bag, and smoil, smoil, smoil," shouted half a dozen boys under the draft age, gathered around a table near the orchestra. They yelled incoherently, laughed in great hysterical bursts of something that appeared to be merriment, and passed around under the tablecloth flat bottles containing a clear liquid—for in this western city founded and built by roaring drunken miners, no one was allowed to take his alcohol openly—splashed it into their tumblers of ginger ale, and went on singing, "It's a Long Way to Tipperary." When the tune changed to "Madelon," Adam said, "Let's dance." It was a tawdry little place, crowded and hot and full of smoke, but there was nothing better. The music was gay; and life is completely crazy anyway, thought Miranda, so what does it matter? This is what we have, Adam and I, this is all we're going to get, this is the way it is with us. She wanted to say, "Adam, come out of your dream and listen to me. I have pains in my chest and my head and my heart and they're real. I am in pain all over, and you are in such danger as I can't bear to think about, and why can we not save each other?" When her hand tightened on his shoulder his arm tightened about her waist instantly, and stayed there, holding firmly. They said nothing but smiled continually at each other, odd changing smiles as though they had found a new language. Miranda, her face near Adam's shoulder, noticed a dark young pair sitting at a corner table, each with an arm around the waist of the other, their heads together, their eyes staring at the same thing, whatever it was, that hovered in space before them. Her right hand lay on the table, his hand over it, and her face was a blur with weeping. Now and then he raised her hand and kissed it, and set it down and held it, and her eyes would fill again. They were not shameless, they had merely forgotten where they were, or they had no other place to go, perhaps. They said not a word, and the small pantomime repeated itself, like a melancholy short film running monotonously over and over again. Miranda envied them. She envied that girl. At least she can weep if that helps, and he does not even have to ask, What is the matter? Tell me. They had cups of coffee before them, and after a long while—Miranda and Adam had danced and sat down again twice—when the coffee was quite cold, they drank it suddenly, then embraced as before, without a word and scarcely a glance at each other. Something was done and settled between them, at least; it was enviable, enviable, that they could sit quietly together and have the same expression on their faces while they looked into the hell they shared, no matter what kind of hell, it was theirs, they were together.

At the table nearest Adam and Miranda a young woman was leaning on her elbow, telling her young man a story. "And I don't like him because he's too fresh. He kept on asking me to take a drink and I kept telling him, I don't drink and he said, Now look here, I want a drink the worst way and I think it's mean of you not to drink with me, I can't sit up here and drink by myself, he said. I told him, You're not by yourself in the first place; I like that, I said, and if you want a drink go ahead and have it, I told him, why drag *me* in? So he called the waiter and ordered ginger ale and two glasses and I drank straight ginger ale like I always do but he poured a shot of hooch in his. He was awfully proud of that hooch, said he made it himself out of potatoes. Nice homemade likker, warm from the pipe, he told me, three drops of this and your ginger ale will taste like Mumm's Extry. But I said, No, and I mean no, can't you get that through your bean? He took another drink and said, Ah, come on, honey, don't be so stubborn, this'll make your shimmy shake. So I just got tired of the argument, and I said, I don't need to drink, to shake my shimmy, I can strut my stuff on tea, I said. Well, why don't you then, he wanted to know, and I just told him—"

She knew she had been asleep for a long time when all at once without even a warning footstep or creak of the door hinge, Adam was in the room turning on the light, and she knew it was he, though at first she was blinded and turned her head away. He came over at once and sat on the side of the bed and began to talk as if he were going on with something they had been talking about before. He crumpled a square of paper and tossed it in the fireplace.

"You didn't get my note," he said. "I left it under the door. I was called back suddenly to camp for a lot of inoculations. They kept me longer than I expected, I was late. I called the office and they told me you were not coming in today. I called Miss Hobbe here and she said you were in bed and couldn't come to the telephone. Did she give you my message?"

"No," said Miranda drowsily, "but I think I have been asleep all day. Oh, I do remember. There was a doctor here. Bill sent him. I was at the telephone once, for Bill told me he would send an ambulance and have me taken to the hospital. The doctor tapped my chest and left a prescription and said he would be back, but he hasn't come."

"Where is it, the prescription?" asked Adam.

"I don't know. He left it, though, I saw him."

Adam moved about searching the tables and the mantelpiece. "Here it is," he said. "I'll be back in a few minutes. I must look for an all-night drug store. It's after one o'clock. Good-by."

Good-by, good-by. Miranda watched the door where he had disappeared for quite a while, then closed her eyes, and thought, When I am not here I cannot remember anything about this room where I have lived for nearly a year, except that the curtains are too thin and there was never any way of shutting out the morning light. Miss Hobbe had promised heavier curtains, but they had never appeared. When Miranda in her dressing gown had been at the telephone that morning, Miss Hobbe had passed through, carrying a tray. She was a little red-haired nervously friendly creature, and her manner said all too plainly that the place was not paying and she was on the ragged edge.

"My dear *child*," she said sharply, with a glance at Miranda's attire, "what is the matter?"

Miranda, with the receiver to her ear, said, "Influenza, I think."

"*Horrors*," said Miss Hobbe, in a whisper, and the tray wavered in her hands. "Go back to bed at once . . . go at *once!*"

"I must talk to Bill first," Miranda had told her, and Miss Hobbe had hurried on and had not returned. Bill had shouted directions at her, promising everything, doctor, nurse, ambulance, hospital, her check every week as usual, everything, but she was to get back to bed and stay there. She dropped into bed, thinking that Bill was the only person she had ever seen who actually tore his own hair when he was excited enough . . . I suppose I should ask to be sent home, she thought, it's a respectable old custom to inflict your death on the family if you can manage it. No, I'll stay here, this is my business, but not in this room, I hope . . . I wish I were in the cold mountains in the snow, that's what I should like best; and all about her rose the measured ranges of the Rockies wearing their perpetual snow, their majestic blue laurels of cloud, chilling her to the bone with their sharp breath. Oh, no, I must have warmth—and her memory turned and roved after another place she had known first and loved best, that now she could see only in drifting fragments of palm and cedar, dark shadows and a sky that warmed without dazzling, as this strange sky had dazzled without warming her; there was the long slow wavering of gray moss in the drowsy oak shade, the spacious hovering of buzzards overhead, the smell of crushed water herbs along a bank, and without warning a broad tranquil river into which flowed all the rivers she had known. The walls shelved away in one deliberate silent movement on either side, and a tall sailing ship was moored near by, with a gangplank weathered to blackness touching the foot of her bed. Back of the ship was jungle, and even as it appeared before her, she knew it was all she had ever read or had been told or felt or thought about jungles; a writhing terribly alive and secret place of death, creeping with tangles of spotted serpents, rainbow-colored birds with malign eyes, leopards with humanly wise faces and extravagantly crested lions; screaming long-armed monkeys tumbling among broad fleshy leaves that glowed with sulphur-colored light and exuded the ichor of death, and rotting trunks of unfamiliar trees sprawled in crawling slime. Without surprise, watching from her pillow, she saw herself run swiftly down this gangplank to the slanting deck, and standing there, she leaned on the rail and waved gaily to herself in bed, and the slender ship spread its wings and sailed away into the jungle. The air trembled with the shattering scream and the hoarse bellow of voices all crying together, rolling and colliding above her like ragged storm-clouds, and the words became two words only rising and falling and clamoring about her head. Danger, danger, danger, the voices said, and War, war, war. There was her door half open, Adam standing with his hand on the knob, and Miss Hobbe with her face all out of shape with terror was crying shrilly, "I tell you, they must come for her *now*, or I'll put her on the sidewalk. . . . I tell you, this is a plague, a plague, my God, and I've got a houseful of people to think about!"

Adam said, "I know that. They'll come for her tomorrow morning."

"Tomorrow morning, my God, they'd better come now!"

"They can't get an ambulance," said Adam, "and there aren't any beds. And we can't find a doctor or a nurse. They're all busy. That's all there is to it. You stay out of the room, and I'll look after her."

"Yes, you'll look after her, I can see that," said Miss Hobbe, in a particularly unpleasant tone.

"Yes, that's what I said," answered Adam, drily, "and you keep out."

He closed the door carefully. He was carrying an assortment of misshapen packages, and his face was astonishingly impassive.

"Did you hear that?" he asked, leaning over and speaking very quietly.

"Most of it," said Miranda, "it's a nice prospect, isn't it?"

"I've got your medicine," said Adam, "and you're to begin with it this minute. She can't put you out."

"So it's really as bad as that," said Miranda.

"It's as bad as anything can be," said Adam, "all the theaters and nearly all the shops and restaurants are closed, and the streets have been full of funerals all day and ambulances all night—"

"But not one for me," said Miranda, feeling hilarious and light-headed. She sat up and beat her pillow into shape and reached for her robe. "I'm glad you're here, I've been having a nightmare. Give me a cigarette, will you, and light one for yourself and open all the windows and sit near one of them. You're running a risk," she told him, "don't you know that? Why do you do it?"

"Never mind," said Adam, "take your medicine," and offered her two large cherry-colored pills. She swallowed them promptly and instantly vomited them up. "*Do* excuse me," she said, beginning to laugh. "I'm so sorry." Adam without a word and with a very concerned expression washed her face with a wet towel, gave her some cracked ice from one of the packages, and firmly offered her two more pills. "That's what they always did at home," she explained to him, "and it worked." Crushed with humiliation, she put her hands over her face and laughed again, painfully.

"There are two more kinds yet," said Adam, pulling her hands from her face and lifting her chin. "You've hardly begun. And I've got other things, like orange juice and ice cream—they told me to feed you ice cream—and coffee in a thermos bottle, and a thermometer. You have to work through the whole lot so you'd better take it easy."

"This time last night we were dancing," said Miranda, and drank something from a spoon. Her eyes followed him about the room, as he did things for her with an absent-minded face, like a man alone; now and again he would come back, and slipping his hand under her head, would hold a cup or a tumbler to her mouth, and she drank, and followed him with her eyes again, without a clear notion of what was happening.

"Adam," she said, "I've just thought of something. Maybe they forgot St. Luke's Hospital. Call the sisters there and ask them not to be so selfish with their silly old rooms. Tell them I only want a very small dark ugly one for three days, or less. Do try them, Adam."

He believed, apparently, that she was still more or less in her right mind, for she heard him at the telephone explaining in his deliberate voice. He was back again almost at once, saying, "This seems to be my day for getting mixed up with peevish old maids. The sister said that even if they had a room you couldn't have it without doctor's orders. But they didn't have one, anyway. She was pretty sour about it."

"Well," said Miranda in a thick voice, "I think that's abominably rude and mean, don't you?" She sat up with a wild gesture of both arms, and began to retch again, violently.

"Hold it, as you were," called Adam, fetching the basin. He held her head, washed her face and hands with ice water, put her head straight on the pillow, and went over and looked out of the window. "Well," he said at last, sitting beside her again, "they haven't got a room. They haven't got a bed. They haven't even got a baby crib, the way she talked. So I think that's straight enough, and we may as well dig in."

"Isn't the ambulance coming?"

"Tomorrow, maybe."

He took off his tunic and hung it on the back of a chair. Kneeling before the fireplace, he began carefully to set kindling sticks in the shape of an Indian tepee, with a little paper in the center for them to lean upon. He lighted this and placed other sticks upon them, and larger bits of wood. When they were going nicely he added still heavier wood, and coal a few lumps at a time, until there was a good blaze, and a fire that would not need rekindling. He rose and dusted his hands together, the fire illuminated him from the back and his hair shone.

"Adam," said Miranda, "I think you're very beautiful." He laughed out at this, and shook his head at her. "What a hell of a word," he said, "for me." "It was the first that occurred to me," she said, drawing up on her elbow to catch the warmth of the blaze. "That's a good job, that fire."

He sat on the bed again, dragging up a chair and putting his feet on the rungs. They smiled at each other for the first time since he had come in that night. "How do you feel now?" he asked.

"Better, much better," she told him. "Let's talk. Let's tell each other what we meant to do."

"You tell me first," said Adam. "I want to know about you."

"You'd get the notion I had a very sad life," she said, "and perhaps it was, but I'd be glad enough to have it now. If I could have it back, it would be easy to be happy about almost anything at all. That's not true, but that's the way I feel now." After a pause, she said, "There's nothing to tell, after all, if it ends now, for all this time I was getting ready for something that was going to happen later, when the time came. So now it's nothing much."

"But it must have been worth having until now, wasn't it?" he asked seriously as if it were something important to know.

"Not if this is all," she repeated obstinately.

"Weren't you ever—happy?" asked Adam, and he was plainly afraid of the word; he was shy of it as he was of the word *love,* he seemed never to have spoken it before, and was uncertain of its sound or meaning.

"I don't know," she said, "I just lived and never thought about it. I remember things I liked, though, and things I hoped for."

"I was going to be an electrical engineer," said Adam. He stopped short. "And I shall finish up when I get back," he added, after a moment.

"Don't you love being alive?" asked Miranda. "Don't you love weather and the colors at different times of the day, and all the sounds and noises like children screaming in the next lot, and automobile horns and little bands playing in the street and the smell of food cooking?"

"I love to swim, too," said Adam.

"So do I," said Miranda; "we never did swim together."

"Do you remember any prayers?" she asked him suddenly. "Did you ever learn anything at Sunday School?"

"Not much," confessed Adam without contrition. "Well, the Lord's Prayer."

"Yes, and there's Hail Mary," she said, "and the really useful one beginning, I confess to Almighty God and to blessed Mary ever virgin and to the holy Apostles Peter and Paul—"

"Catholic," he commented.

"Prayers just the same, you big Methodist. I'll bet you *are* a Methodist."

"No, Presbyterian."

"Well, what others do you remember?"

"Now I lay me down to sleep—" said Adam.

"Yes, that one, and Blessed Jesus meek and mild—you see that my religious education wasn't neglected either. I even know a prayer beginning O Apollo. Want to hear it?"

"No," said Adam, "you're making fun."

"I'm not," said Miranda, "I'm trying to keep from going to sleep. I'm afraid to go to sleep, I may not wake up. Don't let me go to sleep, Adam. Do you know Matthew, Mark, Luke and John? Bless the bed I lie upon?"

"If I should die before I wake, I pray the Lord my soul to take. Is that it?" asked Adam. "It doesn't sound right, somehow."

"Light me a cigarette, please, and move over and sit near the window. We keep forgetting about fresh air. You must have it." He lighted the cigarette and held it to her lips. She took it between her fingers and dropped it under the edge of her pillow. He found it and crushed it out in the saucer under the water tumbler. Her head swam in darkness for an instant, cleared, and she sat up in panic, throwing off the covers and breaking into a sweat. Adam leaped up with an alarmed face, and almost at once was holding a cup of hot coffee to her mouth.

"You must have some too," she told him, quiet again, and they sat huddled together on the edge of the bed, drinking coffee in silence.

Adam said, "You must lie down again. You're awake now."

"Let's sing," said Miranda. "I know an old spiritual, I can remember some of the words." She spoke in a natural voice. "I'm fine now." She began in a hoarse whisper, "'Pale horse, pale rider, done taken my lover away . . .' Do you know that song?"

"Yes," said Adam, "I heard Negroes in Texas sing it, in an oil field."

"I heard them sing it in a cotton field," she said; "it's a good song."

They sang that line together. "But I can't remember what comes next," said Adam.

"'Pale horse, pale rider,'" said Miranda, "(We really need a good banjo) 'done taken my lover away—'" Her voice cleared and she said, "But we ought to get on with it. What's the next line?"

"There's a lot more to it than that," said Adam, "about forty verses, the rider done taken away mammy, pappy, brother, sister, the whole family besides the lover—"

"But not the singer, not yet," said Miranda. "Death always leaves one singer to mourn. 'Death,'" she sang, "'oh, leave one singer to mourn—'"

"'Pale horse, pale rider,'" chanted Adam, coming in on the beat, "'done taken my lover away!' (I think we're good, I think we ought to get up an act—)"

"Go in Hut Service," said Miranda, "entertain the poor defenseless heroes Over There."

"We'll play banjos," said Adam; "I always wanted to play the banjo."

Miranda sighed, and lay back on the pillow and thought, I must give up, I can't hold out any longer. There was only that pain, only that room, and only Adam. There were no longer any multiple planes of living, no tough filaments of memory and hope pulling taut backwards and forwards holding her upright between them. There was only this one moment and it was a dream of time, and Adam's face, very near hers, eyes still and intent, was a shadow, and there was to be nothing more. . . .

"Adam," she said out of the heavy soft darkness that drew her down, down, "I love you, and I was hoping you would say that to me, too."

He lay down beside her with his arm under her shoulder, and pressed his smooth face against hers, his mouth moved towards her mouth and stopped. "Can you hear what I am saying? . . . What do you think I have been trying to tell you all this time?"

She turned towards him, the cloud cleared and she saw his face for an instant. He pulled the covers about her and held her, and said, "Go to sleep, darling, darling, if you will go to sleep now for one hour I will wake you up and bring you hot coffee and tomorrow we will find somebody to help. I love you, go to sleep—"

Almost with no warning at all, she floated into the darkness, holding his hand, in sleep that was not sleep but clear evening light in a small green wood, and angry dangerous wood full of inhuman concealed voices singing sharply like the whine of arrows and she saw Adam transfixed by a flight of these singing arrows that struck him in the heart and passed shrilly cutting their path through the leaves. Adam fell straight back before her eyes, and rose again unwounded and alive; another flight of arrows loosed from the invisible bow struck him again and he fell, and yet he was there before her untouched in a perpetual death and resurrection. She threw herself before him, angrily and selfishly she interposed between him and the track of the arrow, crying, No, no, like a child cheated in a game, It's my turn now, why must you always be the one to die? and the arrows struck her cleanly through the heart and through his body and he lay dead, and she still lived, and the wood whistled and sang and shouted, every branch and leaf and blade of grass had its own terrible accusing voice. She ran then, and Adam caught her in the middle of the room, running, and said, "Darling, I must have been asleep too. What happened, you screamed terribly?"

After he had helped her to settle again, she sat with her knees drawn up under her chin, resting her head on her folded arms and began carefully searching for her words because it was important to explain clearly. "It was a very odd sort of dream, I don't know why it could have frightened me. There was something about an old-fashioned valentine. There were two hearts carved on a tree, pierced by the same arrow—you know, Adam—"

"Yes, I know, honey," he said in the gentlest sort of way, and sat kissing her on the cheek and forehead with a kind of accustomedness, as if he had been kissing her for years, "one of those lace paper things."

"Yes, and yet they were alive, and were us, you understand—this doesn't seem to be quite the way it was, but it was something like that. It was in a wood—"

"Yes," said Adam. He got up and put on his tunic and gathered up the thermos bottle. "I'm going back to that little stand and get us some ice cream and hot coffee," he told her, "and I'll be back in five minutes, and you keep quiet. Good-by for five minutes," he said, holding her chin in the palm of his hand and trying to catch her eye, "and you be very quiet."

"Good-by," she said. "I'm awake again." But she was not, and the two alert young internes from the County hospital who had arrived, after frantic urgings from the noisy city editor of the Blue Mountain *News*, to carry her away in a police ambulance, decided that they had better go down and get the stretcher. Their voices roused her, she sat up, got out of bed at once and stood glancing about brightly. "Why, you're all right," said the darker and stouter of the two young men, both extremely fit and competent-looking in their white clothes, each with a flower in his buttonhole. "I'll just carry you." He unfolded a white blanket and wrapped it around her. She gathered up the folds and asked, "But where is Adam?" taking hold of the doctor's arm. He laid a hand on her drenched forehead, shook his head, and gave her a shrewd look. "Adam?"

"Yes," Miranda told him, lowering her voice confidentially, "he was here and now he is gone."

"Oh, he'll be back," the interne told her easily, "he's just gone round the block to get cigarettes. Don't worry about Adam. He's the least of your troubles."

"Will he know where to find me?" she asked, still holding back.

"We'll leave him a note," said the interne. "Come now, it's time we got out of here."

He lifted and swung her up to his shoulder. "I feel very badly," she told him; "I don't know why."

"I'll bet you do," said he, stepping out carefully, the other doctor going before them, and feeling for the first step of the stairs. "Put your arms around my neck," he instructed her. "It won't do you any harm and it's a great help to me."

"What's your name?" Miranda asked as the other doctor opened the front door and they stepped out into the frosty sweet air.

"Hildesheim," he said, in the tone of one humoring a child.

"Well, Dr. Hildesheim, aren't we in a pretty mess?"

"We certainly are," said Dr. Hildesheim.

The second young interne, still quite fresh and dapper in his white coat, though his carnation was withering at the edges, was leaning over listening to her breathing through a stethoscope, whistling thinly, "There's a Long, Long Trail—" From time to time he tapped her ribs smartly with two fingers, whistling. Miranda observed him for a few moments until she fixed his bright busy hazel eye not four inches from hers. "I'm not unconscious," she explained, "I know what I want to say." Then to her horror she heard herself babbling nonsense, knowing it was nonsense though she could not hear what she was saying. The flicker of attention in the eye near her vanished, the second interne went on tapping and listening, hissing softly under his breath.

"I wish you'd stop whistling," she said clearly. The sound stopped. "It's a beastly tune," she added. Anything, anything at all to keep her small hold on the life of human beings, a clear line of communication, no matter what, between her and the receding world. "Please let me see Dr. Hildesheim," she said, "I have something important to say to him. I must say it now." The second interne vanished. He did not walk away, he fled into the air without a sound, and Dr. Hildesheim's face appeared in his stead.

"Dr. Hildesheim, I want to ask you about Adam."

"That young man? He's been here, and left you a note, and has gone again," said Dr. Hildesheim, "and he'll be back tomorrow and the day after." His tone was altogether too merry and flippant.

"I don't believe you," said Miranda, bitterly, closing her lips and eyes and hoping she might not weep.

"Miss Tanner," called the doctor, "have you got that note?"

Miss Tanner appeared beside her, handed her an unsealed envelope, took it back, unfolded the note and gave it to her.

"I can't see it," said Miranda, after a pained search of the page full of hasty scratches in black ink.

"Here, I'll read it," said Miss Tanner. "It says, 'They came and took you while I was away and now they will not let me see you. Maybe tomorrow they will, with my love, Adam,'" read Miss Tanner in a firm dry voice, pronouncing the words distinctly. "Now, do you see?" she asked soothingly.

Miranda, hearing the words one by one, forgot them one by one. "Oh, read it again, what does it say?" she called out over the silence that pressed upon her, reaching towards the dancing words that just escaped as she almost touched them. "That will do," said Dr. Hildesheim, calmly authoritarian. "Where is that bed?"

"There is no bed yet," said Miss Tanner, as if she said, We are short of oranges. Dr. Hildesheim said, "Well, we'll manage something," and Miss Tanner drew the narrow trestle with bright crossed metal supports and small rubbery wheels into a deep jut of the corridor, out of the way of the swift white figures darting about, whirling and skimming like water flies all in silence. The white walls rose sheer as cliffs, a dozen frosted moons followed each other in perfect self-possession down a white lane and dropped mutely one by one into a snowy abyss.

What is this whiteness and silence but the absence of pain? Miranda lay lifting the nap of her white blanket softly between eased fingers, watching a dance of tall deliberate shadows moving behind a wide screen of sheets spread upon a frame. It was there, near her, on her side of the wall where she could see it clearly and enjoy it, and it was so beautiful she had no curiosity as to its meaning. Two dark figures nodded, bent, curtsied to each other, retreated and bowed again, lifted long arms and spread great hands against the white shadow of the screen; then with a single round movement, the sheets were folded back, disclosing two speechless men in white, standing, and another speechless man in white, lying on the bare springs of a white iron bed. The man on the springs was swathed smoothly from head to foot in white, with folded bands across the face, and a large stiff bow like merry rabbit ears dangled at the crown of his head.

The two living men lifted a mattress standing hunched against the wall, spread it tenderly and exactly over the dead man. Wordless and white they vanished down the corridor, pushing the wheeled bed before them. It had been an entrancing and leisurely spectacle, but now it was over. A pallid white fog rose in their wake insinuatingly and floated before Miranda's eyes, a fog in which was concealed all terror and all weariness, all the wrung faces and twisted backs and broken feet of abused, outraged living things, all the shapes of their confused pain and their estranged hearts; the fog might part at any moment and loose the horde of human torments. She put up her hands and said, Not yet, not yet, but it was too late. The fog parted and two executioners, white clad, moved towards her pushing between them with marvelously deft and practiced hands the misshapen figure of an old man in filthy rags whose scanty beard waggled under his opened mouth as he bowed his back and braced his feet to resist and delay the fate they had prepared for him. In a high weeping voice he was trying to explain to them that the crime of which he was accused did not merit the punishment he was about to receive; and except for this whining cry there was silence as they advanced. The soiled cracked bowls of the old man's hands were held before him beseechingly as a beggar's as he said, "Before God I am not guilty," but they held his arms and drew him onward, passed, and were gone.

The road to death is a long march beset with all evils, and the heart fails little by little at each new terror, the bones rebel at each step, the mind sets up its own bitter resistance and to what end? The barriers sink one by one, and no covering of the eyes shuts out the landscape of disaster, nor the sight of crimes committed there. Across the field came Dr. Hildesheim, his face a skull beneath his German helmet, carrying a naked infant writhing on the point of his bayonet, and a huge stone pot marked Poison in Gothic letters. He stopped before the well that Miranda remembered in a pasture on her father's farm, a well once dry but now bubbling with living water, and into its pure depths he threw the child and the poison, and the violated water sank back soundlessly into the earth. Miranda, screaming, ran with her arms above her head; her voice echoed and came back to her like a wolf's howl, Hildesheim is a Boche, a spy, a Hun, kill him, kill him before he kills you. . . . She woke howling, she heard the foul words accusing Dr. Hildesheim tumbling from her mouth; opened her eyes and knew she was in a bed in a small white room, with Dr. Hildesheim sitting beside her, two firm fingers on her pulse. His hair was brushed sleekly and his buttonhole flower was fresh. Stars gleamed through the window, and Dr. Hildesheim seemed to be gazing at them with no particular expression, his stethoscope dangling around his neck. Miss Tanner stood at the foot of the bed writing something on a chart.

"Hello," said Dr. Hildesheim, "at least you take it out in shouting. You don't try to get out of bed and go running around." Miranda held her eyes open with a terrible effort, saw his rather heavy, patient face clearly even as her mind tottered and slithered again, broke from its foundation and spun like a cast wheel in a ditch. "I didn't mean it, I never believed it, Dr. Hildesheim, you musn't remember it—" and was gone again, not being able to wait for an answer.

The wrong she had done followed her and haunted her dream: this wrong took vague shapes of horror she could not recognize or name, though her heart cringed at sight of them. Her mind, split in two, acknowledged and denied what she saw in the one instant, for across an abyss of complaining darkness her reasoning coherent self watched the strange frenzy of the other coldly, reluctant to admit the truth of its visions, its tenacious remorses and despairs.

"I know those are your hands," she told Miss Tanner, "I know it, but to me they are white tarantulas, don't touch me."

"Shut your eyes," said Miss Tanner.

"Oh, no," said Miranda, "for then I see worse things," but her eyes closed in spite of her will, and the midnight of her internal torment closed about her.

Oblivion, thought Miranda, her mind feeling among her memories of words she had been taught to describe the unseen, the unknowable, is a whirlpool of gray water turning upon itself for all eternity . . . eternity is perhaps more than the distance to the farthest star. She lay on a narrow ledge over a pit that she knew to be bottom-less, though she could not comprehend it; the ledge was her childhood dream of danger, and she strained back against a reassuring wall of granite at her shoulders, staring into the pit, thinking, There it is, there it is at last, it is very simple; and soft carefully shaped words like oblivion and eternity are curtains hung before nothing at all. I shall not know when it happens, I shall not feel or remember, why can't I consent now, I am lost, there is no hope for me. Look, she told herself, there it is, that is death and there is nothing to fear. But she could not consent, still shrinking stiffly against the granite wall that was her childhood dream of safety, breathing slowly for fear of squandering breath, saying desperately, Look, don't be afraid, it is nothing, it is only eternity.

Granite walls, whirlpools, stars are things. None of them is death, nor the image of it. Death is death, said Miranda, and for the dead it has no attributes. Silenced she sank easily through deeps under deeps of darkness until she lay like a stone at the farthest bottom of life, knowing herself to be blind, deaf, speechless, no longer aware of the members of her own body, entirely withdrawn from all human con-cerns, yet alive with a peculiar lucidity and coherence; all notions of the mind, the reasonable inquiries of doubt, all ties of blood and the desires of the heart, dissolved and fell away from her, and there remained of her only a minute fiercely burning particle of being that knew itself alone, that relied upon nothing beyond itself for its strength; not susceptible to any appeal or inducement, being itself composed entirely of one single motive, the stubborn will to live. This fiery motionless particle set itself unaided to resist destruction, to survive and to be in its own madness of being, motiveless and planless beyond that one essential end. Trust me, the hard unwinking angry point of light said. Trust me. I stay.

At once it grew, flattened, thinned to a fine radiance, spread like a great fan and curved out into a rainbow through which Miranda, enchanted, altogether believ-ing, looked upon a deep clear landscape of sea and sand, of soft meadow and sky, freshly washed and glistening with transparencies of blue. Why, of course, of course, said Miranda, without surprise but with serene rapture as if some promise made to her had been kept long after she had ceased to hope for it. She rose from her narrow ledge and ran lightly through the tall portals of the great bow that arched in its splendor over the burning blue of the sea and the cool green of the meadow on either hand.

The small waves rolled in and over unhurriedly, lapped upon the sand in silence and retreated; the grasses flurried before a breeze that made no sound. Moving towards her leisurely as clouds through the shimmering air came a great company of human beings, and Miranda saw in an amazement of joy that they were all the living she had known. Their faces were transfigured, each in its own beauty, beyond what she remembered of them, their eyes were clear and untroubled as good weather, and they cast no shadows. They were pure identities and she knew them every one without calling their names or remembering what relation she bore to them. They surrounded her smoothly on silent feet, then turned their entranced faces again towards the sea, and she moved among them easily as a wave among waves. The drifting circle widened, separated, and each figure was alone but not solitary; Miranda, alone too, questioning nothing, desiring nothing, in the quietude of her ecstasy, stayed where she was, eyes fixed on the overwhelming deep sky where it was always morning.

Lying at ease, arms under her head, in the prodigal warmth which flowed evenly from sea and sky and meadow, within touch but not touching the serenely smiling familiar beings about her, Miranda felt without warning a vague tremor of apprehension, some small flick of distrust in her joy; a thin frost touched the edges of this confident tranquility; something, somebody, was missing, she had lost something, she had left something valuable in another country, oh, what could it be? There are no trees, no trees here, she said in fright, I have left something unfinished. A thought struggled at the back of her mind, came clearly as a voice in her ear. Where are the dead? We have forgotten the dead, oh, the dead, where are they? At once as if a curtain had fallen, the bright landscape faded, she was alone in a strange stony place of bitter cold, picking her way along a steep path of slippery snow, calling out, Oh, I must go back! But in what direction? Pain returned, a terrible compelling pain running through her veins like heavy fire, the stench of corruption filled her nostrils, the sweetish sickening smell of rotting flesh and pus; she opened her eyes and saw pale light through a coarse white cloth over her face, knew that the smell of death was in her own body, and struggled to lift her hand. The cloth was drawn away; she saw Miss Tanner filling a hypodermic needle in her methodical expert way, and heard Dr. Hildesheim saying, "I think that will do the trick. Try another." Miss Tanner plucked firmly at Miranda's arm near the shoulder, and the unbelievable current of agony ran burning through her veins again. She struggled to cry out, saying, Let me go, let me go; but heard only incoherent sounds of animal suffering. She saw doctor and nurse glance at each other with the glance of initiates at a mystery, nodding in silence, their eyes alive with knowledgeable pride. They looked briefly at their handiwork and hurried away.

Bells screamed all off key, wrangling together as they collided in mid air, horns and whistles mingled shrilly with cries of human distress; sulphur-colored light exploded through the black window pane and flashed away in darkness. Miranda waking from a dreamless sleep asked without expecting an answer, "What is happening?" for there was a bustle of voices and footsteps in the corridor, and a sharpness in the air; the far clamor went on, a furious exasperated shrieking like a mob in revolt.

The light came on, and Miss Tanner said in a furry voice, "Hear that? They're celebrating. It's the Armistice. The war is over, my dear." Her hands trembled. She rattled a spoon in a cup, stopped to listen, held the cup out to Miranda. From the ward for old bedridden women down the hall floated a ragged chorus of cracked voices singing, "My country, 'tis of thee . . ."

Sweet land . . . oh, terrible land of this bitter world where the sound of rejoicing was a clamor of pain, where ragged tuneless old women, sitting up waiting for their evening bowl of cocoa, were singing, "Sweet land of Liberty—"

"Oh, say, can you see?" their hopeless voices were asking next, the hammer strokes of metal tongues drowning them out. "The war is over," said Miss Tanner, her underlip held firmly, her eyes blurred. Miranda said, "Please open the window, please, I smell death in here."

Now if real daylight such as I remember having seen in this world would only come again, but it is always twilight or just before morning, a promise of day that is never kept. What has become of the sun? That was the longest and loneliest night and yet it will not end and let the day come. Shall I ever see light again?

Sitting in a long chair, near a window, it was in itself a melancholy wonder to see the colorless sunlight slanting on the snow, under a sky drained of its blue. "Can this be my face?" Miranda asked her mirror. "Are these my own hands?" she asked Miss Tanner, holding them up to show the yellow tint like melted wax glimmering between the closed fingers. The body is a curious monster, no place to live in, how could anyone feel at home there? Is it possible I can ever accustom myself to this place? she asked herself. The human faces around her seemed dulled and tired, with no radiance of skin and eyes as Miranda remembered radiance; the once white walls of her room were now a soiled gray. Breathing slowly, falling asleep and waking again, feeling the splash of water on her flesh, taking food, talking in bare phrases with Dr. Hildesheim and Miss Tanner, Miranda looked about her with the covertly hostile eyes of an alien who does not like the country in which he finds himself, does not understand the language nor wish to learn it, does not mean to live there and yet is helpless, unable to leave it at his will.

"It is morning," Miss Tanner would say, with a sigh, for she had grown old and weary once for all in the past month, "morning again, my dear," showing Miranda the same monotonous landscape of dulled evergreens and leaden snow. She would rustle about in her starched skirts, her face bravely powdered, her spirit unbreakable as good steel, saying, "Look, my dear, what a heavenly morning, like a crystal," for she had an affection for the salvaged creature before her, the silent ungrateful human being whom she, Cornelia Tanner, a nurse who knew her business, had snatched back from death with her own hands. "Nursing is nine-tenths, just the same," Miss Tanner would tell the other nurses; "keep that in mind." Even the sunshine was Miss Tanner's own prescription for the further recovery of Miranda, this patient the doctors had given up for lost, and who yet sat here, visible proof of Miss Tanner's theory. She said, "Look at the sunshine, now," as she might be saying, "I ordered this for you, my dear, do sit up and take it."

"It's beautiful," Miranda would answer, even turning her head to look, thanking Miss Tanner for her goodness, most of all her goodness about the weather, "beautiful, I always loved it." And I might love it again if I saw it, she thought, but truth was, she could not see it. There was no light, there might never be light again, compared as it must always be with the light she had seen beside the blue sea that lay so tranquilly along the shore of her paradise. That was a child's dream of the heavenly meadow, the vision of repose that comes to a tired body in sleep, she thought, but I have seen it when I did not know it was a dream. Closing her eyes she would rest for a moment remembering that bliss which had repaid all the pain of the journey to reach it; opening them again she saw with a new anguish the dull world to which she was condemned, where the light seemed filmed over with cobwebs, all the bright surfaces corroded, the sharp planes melted and formless, all objects and beings meaningless, ah, dead and withered things that believed themselves alive!

At night, after the long effort of lying in her chair, in her extremity of grief for what she had so briefly won, she folded her painful body together and wept silently, shamelessly, in pity for herself and her lost rapture. There was no escape. Dr. Hildesheim, Miss Tanner, the nurses in the diet kitchen, the chemist, the surgeon, the precise machine of the hospital, the whole humane conviction and custom of society, conspired to pull her inseparable rack of bones and wasted flesh to its feet, to put in order her disordered mind, and to set her once more safely in the road that would lead her again to death.

Chuck Rouncivale and Mary Townsend came to see her, bringing her a bundle of letters they had guarded for her. They brought a basket of delicate small hothouse flowers, lilies of the valley with sweet peas and feathery fern, and above these blooms their faces were merry and haggard.

Mary said, "You *have* had a tussle, haven't you?" and Chuck said, "Well, you made it back, didn't you?" Then after an uneasy pause, they told her that everybody was waiting to see her again at her desk. "They've put me back on sports already, Miranda," said Chuck. For ten minutes Miranda smiled and told them how gay and what a pleasant surprise it was to find herself alive. For it will not do to betray the conspiracy and tamper with the courage of the living; there is nothing better than to be alive, everyone has agreed on that; it is past argument, and who attempts to deny it is justly outlawed. "I'll be back in no time at all," she said; "this is almost over."

Her letters lay in a heap in her lap and beside her chair. Now and then she turned one over to read the inscription, recognized this handwriting or that, examined the blotted stamps and the postmarks, and let them drop again. For two or three days they lay upon the table beside her, and she continued to shrink from them. "They will all be telling me again how good it is to be alive, they will say again they love me, they are glad I am living too, and what can I answer to that?" and her hardened, indifferent heart shuddered in despair at itself, because before it had been tender and capable of love.

Dr. Hildesheim said, "What, all these letters not opened yet?" and Miss Tanner said, "Read your letters, my dear, I'll open them for you." Standing beside the bed, she slit them cleanly with a paper knife. Miranda, cornered, picked and chose until she found a thin one in an unfamiliar handwriting. "Oh, no, now," said Miss Tanner, "take them as they come. Here, I'll hand them to you." She sat down, prepared to be helpful to the end.

What a victory, what triumph, what happiness to be alive, sang the letters in a chorus. The names were signed with flourishes like the circles in air of bugle notes, and they were the names of those she had loved best; some of those she had known well and pleasantly; and a few who meant nothing to her, then or now. Then thin letter in the unfamiliar handwriting was from a strange man at the camp where Adam had been, telling her that Adam had died of influenza in the camp hospital. Adam had asked him, in case anything happened, to be sure to let her know.

If anything happened. To be sure to let her know. If anything happened. "Your friend, Adam Barclay," wrote the strange man. It had happened—she looked at the date—more than a month ago.

"I've been here a long time, haven't I?" she asked Miss Tanner, who was folding letters and putting them back in their proper envelopes.

"Oh, quite a while," said Miss Tanner, "but you'll be ready to go soon now. But you must be careful of yourself and not overdo, and you should come back now and then and let us look at you, because sometimes the aftereffects are very—"

Miranda, sitting up before the mirror, wrote carefully: "One lipstick, medium, one ounce flask Bois d'Hiver perfume, one pair of gray suède gauntlets without straps, two pairs gray sheer stockings without clocks—"

Towney, reading after her, said, "Everything without something so that it will be almost impossible to get?"

"Try it, though," said Miranda, "they're nicer without. One walking stick of silvery wood with a silver knob."

"That's going to be expensive," warned Towney. "Walking is hardly worth it."

"You're right," said Miranda, and wrote in the margin, "a nice one to match my other things. Ask Chuck to look for this, Mary. Good looking and not too heavy."

Lazarus, come forth. Not unless you bring me my top hat and stick. Stay where you are then, you snob. Not at all. I'm coming forth. "A jar of cold cream," wrote Miranda, "a box of apricot powder—and, Mary, I don't need eye shadow, do I?" She glanced at her face in the mirror and away again. "Still, no one need pity this corpse if we look properly to the art of the thing."

Mary Townsend said, "You won't recognize yourself in a week."

"Do you suppose, Mary," asked Miranda, "I could have my old room back again?"

"That should be easy," said Mary. "We stored away all your things there with Miss Hobbe." Miranda wondered again at the time and trouble the living took to be helpful to the dead. But not quite dead now, she reassured herself, one foot in either world now; soon I shall cross back and be at home again. The light will seem real and I shall be glad when I hear that someone I know has escaped from death. I shall visit the escaped ones and help them dress and tell them how lucky they are, and how lucky I am still to have them. Mary will be back soon with my gloves and my walking stick, I must go now, I must begin saying good-by to Miss Tanner and Dr. Hildesheim. Adam, she said, now you need not die again, but still I wish you were here; I wish you had come back, what do you think I came back for, Adam, to be deceived like this?

At once he was there beside her, invisible but urgently present, a ghost but more alive than she was, the last intolerable cheat of her heart; for knowing it was false she still clung to the lie, the unpardonable lie of her bitter desire. She said, "I love you," and stood up trembling, trying by the mere act of her will to bring him to sight before her. If I could call you up from the grave I would, she said, if I could see your ghost I would say, I believe . . . "I believe," she said aloud. "Oh, let me see you once more." The room was silent, empty, the shade was gone from it, struck away by the sudden violence of her rising and speaking aloud. She came to herself as if out of sleep. Oh, no, that is not the way, I must never do that, she warned herself. Miss Tanner said, "Your taxicab is waiting, my dear," and there was Mary. Ready to go.

No more war, no more plague, only the dazed silence that follows the ceasing of the heavy guns; noiseless houses with the shades drawn, empty streets, the dead cold light of tomorrow. Now there would be time for everything.

Hervey Allen

(1889–1949)

Hervey Allen served in France with the 111th Infantry Regiment, a unit of the Pennsylvania National Guard, fighting in the Second Battle of the Marne in July 1918. These experiences were the basis for *Toward the Flame* (1926) a highly praised memoir that remained in print throughout the 1930s. In his later career, Allen was a successful historical novelist most known for *Anthony Adverse* (1933), which is set during the Napoleonic Wars. "Blood Lust" appeared along with "Report to Major Roberts" in *It Was Like This: Two Stories of the Great War* (1940). Published before the United States entered the Second World War, these stories sought to answer questions for a new generation of young men soon to see combat, questions such as "'What is war like? Not war over the radio, or in the headlines, but real war, fighting? How would I, and how do American soldiers, act and react in modern battles?'" Of "Blood Lust," Allen wrote: "The attack on the machine-gun nest, the death of the captain, and the murder of the German sentry by cutting off his head in a trench, were told to me by a corporal in my own company, whom I afterward talked to in the hospital. Those incidents are almost literally described; including the giving of dope to the prisoners by the German surgeon."[1]

1. Hervey Allen, introduction to *It Was Like This: Two Stories of the Great War* (New York: Farrar & Rinehart, 1940), 4, 8.

Blood Lust

Hervey Allen

GENERAL FACTS BEHIND THE STORY OF "BLOOD LUST"

The main scene of this story is laid, in so far as the fighting is concerned, on the east bank of the river Vesle, on a steep hillside above the small town of Fismette. The Allied lines, at this point occupied by the Americans, had advanced as far as the Vesle in early August, 1918. The town of Fismes had been occupied, after bitter fighting, by the Americans. Fismette, just across the river from Fismes, was the bridgehead, and as such was the prize for which the French Staff—the Americans were then incorporated with the French army—was willing to gamble a great many men. For a time the Americans in the little town of Fismette were cut off. The units sent to hold the town were fighting "the whole German army" on the hill above it. Attack after attack was made by the Americans, and repulsed. The casualty rate was terrific. It was in one of these attacks that Corporal Virgin managed to reach a German trench, was taken prisoner, and later escaped, as recounted in the story.

BLOOD LUST

1

It is a nice question whether the essential, underlying human passions are ever fundamentally changed. Perhaps the objects of desire vary from age to age, for the opportunities and the incentives for various passions to display themselves go, like so many other things, in a vague cycle of fashions usually unpredictable. Yet given the opportunity, or better still the necessity, and the most "unfashionable" passions will emerge and be displayed in action in all their pristine simplicity.

Take blood lust, for instance. Probably a manifestation of fear, it usually transmits itself into "bravery" or even into bravado. The metamorphosis is often subtle and swift. You do not suspect the presence of blood lust in most of your acquaintances, particularly the mild ones who look at you through heavy spectacles. Certainly just now blood lust is not "fashionable" and yet, and yet . . . ! Here, anyway, is the true story of one of the mildest of men. The opportunity, perhaps the necessity, for his metamorphosis came when the world suddenly shifted from a state of intermittent peace to one of wholesale war. That was only a few years ago, you may remember. Fashions sometimes return, however.

His name was William Henry Virgin, and the army when he first joined it called him "baby-face." Perhaps it would have gone on calling him baby-face to the bitter end—and bitter enough it would have been for him, for he was a tall, willowy, sensitive boy with a large, innocent, and indescribably mild countenance—if his comrades at arms had not found that the babe in arms in their midst was actually named "Virgin."

It seemed too good to be true. Accident so seldom co-operates. But Virgin he was and Virgin he remained from the time of the first company roll call when he was forced to answer up to his name.

The Virgin had overstated his age when he volunteered, among the first to rush to the defense of his country. Afterward a paternal War Department forced his captain to get his mamma's permission, which was easily had, for she proved to be an all but hysterically patriotic mother. She might be said to have been matriotic. Probably a descendant of Herod to judge by her conversation on her visits to camp, like the War Horse of Scripture she, too, clothed her fat neck with thunder—and sniffed the battle from afar. It must have been a mystery to her why the army insisted that enlisted men should at least have reached the age of puberty. There were, it appeared, two other vicarious sacrifices ready at home, so she said, "to shoulder arms against the Hun." Mr. Virgin never appeared to confirm this; either he was nonexistent or unnecessary, we gathered. A few of us thought of this afterward when William Henry returned to parade among the survivors. To some of us it seemed as though Mrs. Virgin's natural joy at the return of her son was slightly misted over. Blown upon, as it were, when she looked at the flag-draped stand where the "gold-star mothers" sat. Ten thousand dollars apiece. And when the government sent them to France afterward! But perhaps we were mistaken; for, after all, Mrs. Virgin was a maternal soul, easily moved to tears, and mild. Very mild-looking.

It was this same smoothness and mildness in her son which at first kept him perpetually in hot water. That mildness combined with his name caused him to move in a constant atmosphere of more or less suppressed laughter. It was the training camp of a hard-boiled National Guard division where he eventually found himself. They were being rapidly and relentlessly prepared for the front, and the life of William Henry Virgin was a troubled one.

He was homesick, and he found no friends. His name prevented it. All his comrades were older. Even those who secretly felt some commiseration for him dared not show it. No one cared to share in his lonely ridicule and no one wanted to be known as the solitary friend of the Virgin. Even in the squad tent, where a certain ease and friendliness usually prevails, where sometimes a sign "God Bless Our Home" appeared until the first inspection abolished it—even his tent was no refuge for him. He was the butt of all the wits of his squad, seven of them. But most devastating of all, they took to dumping him at night. The cot crashed regularly, and with it his nervous system. Even at night William Henry slept tensely. Huddled up and hunched, the skin on his face drawn tight. If it had not been for his mother, he might have gone "over the hill," back home. Relief when it did come was overdue, almost too late. It just saved him.

Yet an important hardening process had already set in. Innocent when he had first joined, the constant ringing of the changes and fundamental innuendoes on his name, the tremendous stories which it evoked, had inadvertently presented him with a fund of sorry biological information regarding some of the more curious habits of man that Rabelais himself might have envied. In this process his entire company, officers excepted, had collaborated. And even his own squad admitted that he had taken it on the chin like a man. They were even a little proud of him and began to regard him with a certain amount of complacence tinged with pride.

So the tent became a little less sinister to him. He began to discover that amused indifference was a good defense. Presently his indifference to what might be called the manuring process became real. He even began to take a certain dim pleasure in it himself. After a while he collaborated.

Out of the mouth of this suckling came stories that were arresting, startling even to the old soldiers. With his baby face behind them they produced even upon the callous the novel and forgotten effect of a shock. It is certain now that they led not indirectly to the death of three men later on. For manuring is good for gardens, but if you catch a flower on its stem in the process and hold it down with dirt something happens to the flower. In the case of a rosebush the stem frequently goes in for bigger and better thorns. So something like thorns sprouted, thickening on the soul of William Henry just as his chin now began to break out in fluffy stubble. But before all this happened Captain Ward had stepped in, and no small part of the metamorphosis of the Virgin was due to Captain Ward.

Captain Ward was an ex-cavalryman, a noncom of the old regular establishment of long and varied experience, who had been given a temporary commission to help train the new levy in mass. Almost any instrument which is perfect in itself is admirable, and without mincing words Captain Ward was simply splendid.

Outwardly he was a sheerly clean-cut man, with brown eyes of great brilliance, a precision of glance which his clear, straight features made quietly piercing. He wore his stiff campaign hat tilted just a little to the right and forward. The strap of it traced a precise leather border along the semicircular edge of his cavalry haircut behind. The hat was calculated to stay on in a charge and a high wind. He never lost it. It was like his presence of mind. This is not the story of Captain Ward and yet in a way it is, for it was his personality that welded the company haply committed to his charge into the army. He was the adequate cause of a necessary effect. William Henry Virgin—like most of us—was made over by him, temporarily at least.

When Ward joined the outfit he appeared first at reveille roll call in the place of the fatherly old National Guard captain whom a Medical Board had wisely but reluctantly dismissed. The military column of the new captain's neck and body ran down into a basic semicircle of legs that had grown around a horse. Set on the shining posts of his puttees he addressed the infantry that fate had delivered over to him body and soul.

"Men," said he, "your commanding officer may be a gentleman but I am not. I'm just a poor son of a bitch with more experience in the army than you will ever live to get. There is only one difference between you and me. I happen to have a commission signed by the President of the United States that makes me your captain. What I say happens, when I say it. Listen! I never mean more and I never mean less than just what I say. Dismissed."

And from that time on the Virgin, along with the rest of us, was in the army. Reality descended like a meat cleaver upon umbilical and ectoplasmic cords, upon the golden and the iron links and the mystic threads that bound us to the past. Things began to happen in the present.

Only two days after Captain Ward's inaugural address that officer happened to notice William Henry while he was filling his canteen at the company faucet preparatory to a long march. His hands trembled.

"What's the matter with that man—boy?" said the captain, his eyes narrowing. "Got the palsy?"

"His name's Virgin, sir," replied the lieutenant at whom the question had been hurled.

"Is that the answer?" insisted Ward.

"Yes, sir, yes, *sir*," said the lieutenant; "now that I come to think of it, I guess it is." The captain's glance followed the disconsolate progress of William Henry down the company street until he turned in woefully with drooping shoulders at his tent.

"Number Seven tent," noted the captain mentally.

Half an hour later he remarked to the lieutenant as they finished some paper work together in the company office, "Virgin is a name that comes under 'V' on the payroll. That is all there is to that, lieutenant. Get me?"

"Yes, sir."

"You have an old soldier, Maginn, in your platoon, haven't you?" continued Ward.

"Yes, sir, a good man. He sings a lot of Irish songs and makes the boys sad but keeps them happy. But they say, sir, in fact, it's on the records, that he did a couple of years at Leavenworth for—"

"Send him to me," interrupted Ward. The lieutenant saluted and left.

A few minutes later a rather chubby but spotlessly neat soldier, with a touch of iron-gray about his temples, stood at rigid attention before the company commander's tent.

"Private Maginn reportin', sor."

Ward shifted his hat back and looked the man over carefully. "What outfit?" he said laconically.

"The owld Sivinth Infantry. Three enlistmints"—the man hesitated a moment—"and two years at—"

"Never mind that," said Ward. "This is another war."

The man's face had grown stolid. It came to life again.

"I hear they call you 'pap.' Is that right?"

"Yis, sor."

"Come in," said the captain, "and sit down."

For ten minutes the company clerk strained his ears uselessly trying to overhear a low murmur of conversation in the captain's tent. Only the word "virgin," a short bark of a laugh from Captain Ward and Pap Maginn's chuckle rewarded him. That occasion was the first and almost the last time that the company clerk ever heard the captain laugh.

" . . . an' so," said Maginn, finally emerging from the tent and talking to the captain as though he were an old buddy, "all the bhoys was lined up for physological tists an' made to do all koinds of monkey tricks. Howld yer hands the-gither an' clowse yer eyes an' say ef ye can shtill shtand shteady, an' a' that. An' the little Jew major-man, he says to me, 'In what shtate was you born?' An' I give him the answer from the catechism. 'I don't mean that,' says he. 'I mane in what shtate of the American Union was you born?' An' I says, 'In Antrim, sor, but I shpint the innocent years of me childhood in Delaware, U.S.A.' 'An' how many years was that?' 'Ownly about five,' says I. 'Ye see, I was four whin me parents landed—an' the factory girls at Wilmington . . . ' 'Niver moind that,' says he, lookin' a little fussed, but beginnin' to grin at last. 'An' who thin is the governor of the shtate iv Delaware?' he shouts at me. 'Ah, now, major,' says I, 'shurely ye wouldn't expect a sane man to know that,' I says. And so he just turned to the clerk and says, 'Mark him Highly Intilligint.'

"But nixt day I met him on lave goin' into the Pat-ridge Inn downtown and he calls out to me, 'Come on in.' An' thin he shtands me to a tall drink of double-whisky at the bar. So there I was shtandin' up drinkin' with a circumscribed major and loikin' it."

Ward's shoulders moved silently while he returned Maginn's salute. He watched him do about-face and cross the street to the mess sergeant's tent.

"A swig of limon exthract, ye domned grafter," said Maginn to the sergeant.

"Me breath was that heavy with yer vanilla while I was talkin' to the owld man, all I needed was candles in me two hands to be taken for a child's birthday cake."

Two days later the unhappy canvas home of William Henry Virgin was disturbed and astonished by the arrival of Lance Corporal Maginn, clothed with authority, a kind of dangerous geniality, and the prestige of having once been the trainer of a noted prize fighter. A big lout of a fellow who had plagued William Henry nearly to death was transferred to another squad tent to make room for the lance corporal. Maginn permitted himself to be addressed as "Pap," but an incipient attempt to undermine his authority by calling him "papa" met with a painful repulse in the form of an army boot thrown with a loud laugh. The evening was devoted to a cleansing of rifles and equipment that even "an inspictor of the owld sivinth" would have passed with a gold star. And the Eye-talian of the squad bathed. "For," said Pap Maginn, "if there's anything oi dislike more than dumpin' cots it's owld prespiration an' I'll moider a cot dumper." All this was borne in the silence that sneaks about a tyrant's throne. "An'," said the czar of Tent Seven, just as taps sounded, with the air of a Romanoff dictating a ukase, "whiniver anybody in this squad says 'Vargin' thir to cross thimsilves three toimes, fir'rst."

On the cot nearest the door the form of William Henry Virgin relaxed, comfortable for the first time in several weeks. He turned over with a sigh and settled himself for an untroubled sleep . . .

Six months later the division entrained, ordered to France.

2

Meanwhile much had happened. The division was no longer a mere aggregation of organized but bewildered citizens. It was a giant unit of an even larger machine called the army, a machine that moved with a deadly precision and required a smooth reciprocal motion in all its parts. The function of the eight men who slept in Tent Seven on a certain company street was like that of a small spring in a great mechanism, minor but essential when its turn should come to act. They were bombers and William Henry Virgin was now corporal of the squad.

Pap Maginn's reign as lance corporal had been salutary but brief. Like many other reformers, he failed to last. His skid from grace was via a half case of lemon extract and a night of tremulous tenor ditties that advertised his condition to the world. It was impossible, under the circumstances, for Captain Ward to confirm Maginn in his corporalship. The captain had made the Virgin leader because he had become the most promising soldier in the squad, the best shot, the neatest, and the most intelligent. Ward's choice of noncoms was always the despair of his lieutenants and the captain was always right.

No one, except Ward, suspected just how hard-boiled the Virgin had become. He was still mild-eyed and rosy in countenance but long months of patient practice, grueling marches, the well-ordered and well-fed life of the soldier under forced training in the open had turned him into a powerful youth. He was already broad-shouldered and deep-voiced. A short pipe, which he smoked only semioccasionally, and a shorter but none the less genuine mustache served at once to disguise him as a man and to advertise his self-confidence. The last had been greatly advanced by a fine little course in boxing under the tutelage of Pap Maginn. Fights, and a pair of muscular arms made ironlike by months of lobbing heavy dummy bombs at longer and longer distances, had completed the physical metamorphosis of the Virgin. Add to this that he now swore awful, and that his stories were green with adolescent decay. In fact, for the rest of his life his humor was bound to be of the fungus variety.

Only once was the progress of the Virgin toward the accolade of his blooding as a full-fledged veteran endangered or impeded. It was his mother who almost lost him the necessary prestige that must surround even a corporal and he remembered it against her. It was the final severing of the umbilical cord and it was done by an umbrella.

Mrs. Virgin visited camp, bringing with her a gift of pies, cigarettes—these reluctantly—overshoes, and an umbrella. The overshoes were rejected by William Henry himself. They were too small to begin with, his old school size, so she returned with them in her bag. The umbrella had also been spurned. Its ineptitude for military service was tactfully explained to her by Pap Maginn. Nevertheless, feeling that she knew better by maternal instinct, and that it would help keep her boy dry when it rained at the front, she hid it under his cot before she departed.

Next day there was a general inspection. One of the General Staff arrived from Washington to report on the division's fitness for the front. He and the major general of the division saw everything. They could even see, as though by clairvoyance, where garbage had been buried, hastily, and green potatoes sprouting at the bottom of kitchen bins. Some of Captain Ward's potatoes had sprouted. That was the only cloud on an otherwise perfect company until the major general found the umbrella.

"What," said the major general, his voice like a bronchial foghorn, as he and the General Staff, the colonel, and the captain entered Tent Seven, "what in hell is that?" He made a sort of dive and retrieved the most domestic of all things, save one, from under the corporal's cot. "Good God," cried the major general, shaking and turning purple, "it's an umbrella!" Homeric laughter ensued. Even the squad joined in. "You might have it camouflaged as a mushroom and use it as an observation post when you get to the front, captain," said the general, still rather weakly. "Yes, sir," said Captain Ward, even more weakly. He felt his career crashing.

"What's your name, corporal?" said the major general. An adjutant took out his notebook and stood with his pencil poised. "Virgin, sir," gulped William Henry, turning green, and his voice broke.

"Virgin?" roared the major general. "Virgin!" He could be heard on the next company street. "By God, I knew it!" The officers erupted from the tent trying not to beat each other on the back.

William Henry stood stunned, at attention. Not since the day when the janitor had found him and young Maggie Crispin together in the big ventilator at high school had he felt so undone.

"You've a fine outfit, sarge—I mean Captain Ward," said the General Staff as they left the company street. "But!" he nodded toward Tent Seven.

"I know, sir," said Ward as they left him.

"Get rid of that umbrella, corporal," said Ward as he passed the tent. And that was all he ever did say. But the story went all over the division.

William Henry got rid of the umbrella. He threw it down a latrine and that got him into trouble again. Finally he buried it but it would not stay down. It haunted him in his dreams. He brooded over the incident. He even thought of suicide now that he was the joke of the division. It cost him two fights to keep his squad in order and maintain his stripes. He won the fights and felt better. But he ended by hating his mother as nearly as any American boy can.

At last she came to bid him good-bye, with a flag and his two younger brothers. "They'll be joining you soon, Bill," she screamed, patting the tallest as the train pulled out. She meant to encourage the corporal. But William Henry Virgin leaned out of the car window and roared, "Keep them poor little bastards back home, ma." The car howled approval and good-bye. Just for one moment she stopped waving her flag. But then she was sure she couldn't have heard him right. No, it was impossible. He must have said something else. "Yes, that was it!" She remembered what he had said now. Something noble and fine. The flag waved again frantically. Every man in the regiment saw it and waved his hat back at her. It was thrilling. Good-bye, good-bye.

She pasted a star in her front window at home when she returned. Her bit.

In his own mind and determination Corporal Virgin was the bitterest and hardest-boiled soul on the transport. They pulled into Saint-Nazaire on a beautiful Sunday afternoon in April with a French blimp overhead and the Y.M.C.A. service going on on the fo'c'sle, the congregation lining the rails and rigging. The Y.M.C.A. "chaplain" stood on the capstan for a pulpit and as the ship neared the green coast of France exhorted the "magnificent specimens of manhood before me to abstain from wine and tobacco in all forms," but a cigarette especially. Next to a woman a cigarette, it seemed, was the cunningest snare of the Prince of Evil. It was incredible but true. The sermon's peroration mentioned "virginity." Unfortunately. For at the word a whole package of cigarettes descended upon the exhorter's head from somewhere and broke in a wide shower about him. It was a good bomber's shot and it broke up the meeting amid delighted roars. It also reinstated Corporal Virgin in his own opinion and in the minds of the little group of atheists, scoffers, and hard-boiled shirts, who cheered his action and claimed him as their own. In every way it was a fortunate hit for William Henry. By it he became not only the corporal but the actual leader of his squad, and Pap Maginn's hopeful affection now turned to paternal pride.

During the usual trip to the front in the men-and-cattle cars William Henry first became acquainted with the comparative advantages and afflictions of cognac versus water in his canteen.

Six weeks later there were only three of the original squad left—Corporal Virgin, Maginn, and one Rutherford. Their survival was not altogether due to luck. In the heavy fighting between the Marne and the Vesle they had learned much about the saving merits of small dips in the ground scarcely visible to amateurs. They had, in fact, become a team of remarkable Indian fighters. Like Napoleon's army, but for different reasons, they moved almost exclusively upon the belly. "A battle is gamble enough," Pap Maginn would say hopefully, to each batch of replacements. There had been two batches so far. "Thir's no need for takin' extra personal risks. Keep yer tail down. Wiggle. Wiggle's the way to Berlin. If ye act like a hound diggin' out a fox, ye'll die from behoind."

And most of them did die that way. Machine guns shot their sterns off. Others believed what they had been taught at training camp and attempted to rush in with the bayonet and "treat 'em ruff." "'Twas the favor-ite form of suicide for thim bhoys from Camp Meade," remarked Pap as the three of them held a reunion after a desperate day in the Forêt de Fère. He looked over the five new replacements they received from a western division a few days later and sniffed. He and the Virgin and Rutherford now took it for granted they would be the only survivors.

Their particular job was to cut out machine gun nests. Disregarding the rest of the squad who were supposed to act as riflemen and help rush in at the end, the three of them acted as a team. Rutherford had been a hot-spot pitcher on a nine that had once been champions of the upper Susquehanna valley and he handled his bombs like a baseball. Through long practice he learned to "pitch" from an almost prone position and he had remarkable control and even a fantastic curve to his ball. For that reason he affected a small French citron bomb that looked like and handled like a baseball rather than the heavy pineapple, English Mills. All this was not in the books on tactics but it worked. They had been facing Bavarians most of the "way up," and several of the boys from Munich had been surprised into oblivion by a citron which came apparently out of the nowhere into the here, sizzling. It was thrown from a distance that French bombers could not have imagined.

When Rutherford got his citron home on the machine gun emplacement they were working on, the recruit replacements nearly always rushed in—and were cut down by the other machine gun invariably on their flank. The replacements never lived long enough to learn not to do this. By good luck the Trinity had learned the first time.

"Thir's always two and sometimes three guns," said Maginn, as he and the Virgin collected the identification tags from the casualties later. It got to be a part of a ghastly routine. The little Irishman also had four gold watches, only one was German.

War, of course, had not been what they expected it to be. There were no trenches, and they had been trained for trench warfare almost exclusively. But the kind of open fighting they engaged in was that most natural to their own country. It resembled a series of Indian stalks. They moved forward through an endless flat plateau of gloomy woods west of the Marne, littered with the grotesque debris of advancing and retreating armies. There were vast abandoned piles of shells in wicker cases, huge guns that on half-cloudy nights seemed to be baying the moon sullenly. Villages of subterranean huts in glades where a sinister sunlight played over the mustard gas on the brown leaves and scorched grass. On the low crests stood the skeletons of châteaux shelled intermittently. There were wired paths that led to ambuscades now silent; bloated animals; and here and there, constantly and continually, the gray-faced and greenish dead decomposing in a silence that seemed to mock those who still continued the deadly activities of life around them. And over all this land, as they advanced slowly and painfully through it, hung the silence of a terror broken only by the constant, distant mutter of cannon by night and infernal fires flickering along the horizon. By day the voice of this fear, which kept them living to the very last tip of their nerve fibers, was the sudden shattering chatter of a machine gun which they disturbed in its nest like some antediluvian monster guarding its eggs, and which it was their mission to kill.

They had in their own minds given up hope of surviving and their psychology was unconsciously that of sentenced men to whom every day was a reprieve. It was this feeling which made them live more vividly than they had lived before or would ever live again. Across this sensation of vividness gradually gathered the cloud of fatigue. Supplies slowly grew slimmer as they grew more and more tired. Tobacco was their only solace and a little warmth in the sun when they rested, always, or whenever possible, behind a bank or in a dry shell hole. And yet all this was only "a rear-guard action," a perfunctory and delaying gesture on the part of the army in retreat.

About the middle of August they came to a river where the enemy had decided to hold and consolidate his lines. Resistance blazed up and fighting became continuous. They were shelled long and frequently. Their own guns moved up and blasted constantly over their heads. Sleep was impossible. The ground and air shivered. And then suddenly one night they went into the full tide of fire in the furnace of battle.

They had received another batch of replacements. But this time Corporal Virgin, Pap Maginn, and Rutherford were too tired to pay any attention to them at all. More important was a draught of hot coffee, a plate of steaming beans, received just before their rolling kitchen was hit, their first hot food in five days. They felt briefly better and then . . .

The staff of the French army corps commander had decided to take and hold the bridgehead, a little village on the other side of the river.

The place was, for large military reasons, worth gambling for, and the staff was prepared to bet a large number of lives on it with a fair, although not a bright, prospect of winning the prize. The pawns immediately chosen for sacrifice were the battalion in which Corporal Virgin's squad belonged. Captain Ward was now in command of the battalion by process of survival. When the lieutenants mustered his company, including the new replacements, there were just forty-six. About two o'clock in the morning, they crawled over the wreck of what had once been a bridge and entered the street of the little village that had all the bright welcoming illumination of a furnace door. A few minutes later the enemy's artillery completed the wreck of the bridge. It was fight now or die, and it was fight and die.

The murderous rush that left a fringe of gasping wounded behind it took the first house, nearest the bridgehead. From it a machine gun had been murdering them whenever they moved, stabbing red fire through a plank door. A bomb explosion, shrieks and jibbering, were followed by silence. Corporal Virgin emerged from the door with two prisoners.

"Rutherford and Maginn found 'em hiding on the third floor," said he to his lieutenant. "But look, they're just babies." And, indeed, they were.

The enemy had called up his last class of reserves. The two shivering and quivering prisoners were mere "boy scouts," messengers, perhaps, but just china-faced German boys with purple-ringed blue eyes and grimy, tear-streaked faces. One of them stood whimpering, the other occasionally bleated a weak-chinned "*Kamerad.*"

"I'll comrade you," said the Virgin, in the intense silence between shells, making a threatening move. Both boys shrieked.

"Don't do that," said the lieutenant nervously; "take them down to Sergeant Kirk by the riverbank. He's got some reserve ammunition down there under guard and can take care of them."

The Virgin started the two boys ahead of him like cattle. One of them looked back, caught the glint of a bayonet, and fled like a crazed calf. He was running directly toward the American lines on the other side of the river. The Virgin raised his rifle and brought the running figure flat with one shot. The boy fell sprawling and didn't even crumple. It was easy. The German lad hadn't got beyond battle sight. The lip of Corporal Virgin curled up in a kind of drawn, automatic smile. The crash of shells falling about the bridge and along the riverbank was now so constant that the whole scene lay bare in a kind of alternating glare. You couldn't hear anything but the cannon and screaming shells. The rifle had made only a faint crack. Virgin was surprised that he had even felt its kick, and he was also surprised at the result. For a second he stood dazed. The other German lad came half crawling toward him. He grabbed William Henry about his puttees and made a kind of pathetic O movement with his mouth. No sound could be heard.

It was the round mouth, the round hat, ridiculous on a shock of wiry flaxen hair, and round staring eyes that did it. It was all this silly roundness and a great shell that exploded like a star going to pieces in cosmic murk with detonating thunder, so close that a geyser of dirt collapsed on them. Virgin had never seen a boy who looked like that, and something which the shell personified was trying to kill him. He didn't reason but he felt it all as one thing. The strangeness, the terror, and the infernal night going to pieces about him like an exploding furnace. That and months of stabbing at bags with a bayonet—all ended in a lunge at the thing before him. There was a shriek beyond repair, and an indescribable moment trying to get his bayonet out. The damn rifle sight caught in the thing's tunic and ripped it half off. The thin, starved ribs stood out, and it was only then that Corporal Virgin saw and understood that it was a white boy like himself that he had killed. He got his rifle loose and ran.

3

The barrage closed down. A series of Minenwerfer shells dropped down and along the village street with breath-taking swiftness. There must have been a whole battery playing on the bridge. The Germans were wise to the attack now. Virgin and the lieutenant dived like frogs into the black window of the house where the machine gun had been, and lay flat on the floor. Fragments of paving drove through the gaping windows and rattled about them. An insane glare lit the street and the place rocked. For some moments they existed at the heart of thunder. Then there was a sudden swift silence while the darkness was lit with a blue wink of sloping shadows of Very lights and rockets. The black house seemed full of dead, and there were a good many there. Presently some not so dead began to come to life and stir about. The barrage seemed to be over. Corporal Virgin found himself lying next to Pap Maginn. He knew him from the noise his throat made swallowing liquid.

"Are y'all right?" he said, putting his hand out.

"Aye. Have a drink?" He forced his canteen into the corporal's hands. The fiery draught of cognac swept into William Henry's midriff. He sighed.

"Christ, what I done!" said Corporal Virgin.

"Whativer it is, niver moind it," replied Maginn. "It's nothin' to what's ahead."

Suddenly William Henry Virgin felt boastful. He began to recount the attempted escape of the prisoners in a loud voice.

"Shut up, you bastard," said someone and threw a rock at him out of the darkness. It caromed off his tin hat. Some of the wounded moaned.

"Get up out of here," suddenly said the still all-compelling voice of Captain Ward through a window. "Are you still there, Lieutenant Brice?"

"Yes, sir."

"Get your men out in the rear of this house and form up along the old stone wall there. We're going to attack. That's the orders. Straight up the hill. Follow me and don't bunch."

It was quite a job getting the men out and formed along the old stone wall, since some of them were dead and the others unenthusiastic. It was about half an hour later, when the remnant of the company was finally strung along the low ridge with a few loose stones along it that Ward had called a wall. There were only thirty-one of them counting officers, the lieutenant noted.

The men lay along the wall with rifles ready and bayonets fixed. Some of them were strung with bandoliers of cartridges. Some of the bombers still had pear-shaped objects and little bags of citrons hung over them. Rutherford who had been hit in the left arm, but was still there, had a string of his "baseballs" about his waist. Maginn's prophecy had come true. He and Corporal Virgin and Rutherford were once again, and for the third time, the survivors of the squad.

It was near dawn. They were waiting for the light. It was true that the enemy could then see them, but they could also see the enemy when dawn came. Otherwise they would just wander out into the darkness toward the top of a hill somewhere high above them whence now and again a parachute light or a flare smoldered up, out, and down. The darkness slowly grayed.

Before them a steep hillside began to define itself. Against the sky was a long cliff of black hillcrest with a notch in it like the spine of some animal killed by an ax. To the left was a wrecked orchard. The trees stuck up like scorched hands out of a grave. In the center was a small draw or drain, an almost imperceptible depression of the drainage of ancient fields—and to the left was a haystack alone and single, with a wrecked house eyeless and collapsing into its own cellar.

In all the lonely fields before them, that gradually widened and grew vast in the glow of morning, not a soul was to be seen. But from somewhere above a machine gun began to chatter and to rake the wall. All of them knew it was their zero hour without having been told. The German army was up there on the hill and there were only thirty-one of them with orders to attack. The reason they were actually going to get up and go forward into all that was Captain Ward, and the United States government.

Ward and the two lieutenants lay a little behind the line and below it. The occasional fanfare of bullets poured over the wall and plunged into the houses beyond. Slate slithered off the roofs. Presently a bullet ricocheted and struck one of the lieutenants in the throat. Ward and the other lieutenant tried to help him. But the man choked to death in his own blood. He pointed to his pocket and Ward took out a letter. He fell back then. Ward had probably delayed too long. Full day came suddenly. He put his whistle to his lips . . .

Meanwhile Corporal Virgin and his teammates had been figuring it out. They both saw the draw just in front of them. A rat fled up it, making the grass wave. "Don't get up, slither into that drain," said the Virgin, "and keep on crawlin'." He looked at the stains on his bayonet and felt as hard as any human being can ever feel. He wasn't afraid. Neither was Maginn nor Rutherford. They were too tired. And it was old stuff now, old stuff!

Just then Captain Ward's whistle blew.

Ward rose and darted forward. The line followed him. Virgin, Maginn, and Rutherford dived into the shallow little valley made by the drain. They began to crawl up it trying to keep up with the line. At first nothing happened.

"Come on," said Rutherford. He was going to get up and try to overtake the line. Maginn hung on to him, cursing. Just then a whole college of riveters turned loose.

The three lay flat. Over their heads the tops of the long grasses fell off, cut clean. The line went down like a chine of grain at which a harvester has taken a long swing with a scythe. The guns chattered on for a while searching the ground. Then there was silence. Miles away the three survivors in the swale of ground heard the *br-ump br-ump* of heavy shells falling somewhere across the river. After half an hour they began to crawl forward again, trying not to wave the grass. The swale made a wide swing to the right. That was the reason it had not been raked by machine guns. One of its banks grew a little higher. They dared to peer through the grass a little. Presently to the left they saw Captain Ward. There were two halves of him. He had been cut in two by machine guns. His hat was still on. They crawled a little farther and stopped in a basinlike space near the roots of a tree stump. The tree had also been cut in two and lay over the drain. They hid under the shelter of its branches and drank the remnants of their water and cognac. They opened a can of salmon ration, their last, and ate it. Then they slept like the dead through the heat of the day in the high hilltop meadow with the grass waving about them.

An airplane with a black cross on it came snooping low, saw the three figures under the tree in a little depression. But the aviator thought they were dead and drifted back over the crest into the German lines.

They awoke about four o'clock. There was firing. It was their own machine guns chattering behind them, combined with scattered artillery fire. The barrage came searching up the hill and some of the shells began to fall along the little depression in which they lay. They crawled on and up again around the curve. The curve saved them again.

Presently the little drain grew shallower and threatened to flatten out into the field above. Their backs were now almost as high as the tops of the grasses. They peered ahead through the grass with some wisps of it wrapped about their heads, and saw just before them, a few yards to the left, the haystack.

It was a very convincing haystack. Farther up the hill somewhere a machine gun was turning loose—to judge by the racket. They looked for it carefully but there was nothing but open meadow there, apparently clear to the crest. Either the gun was in a pit sodded over, or it was in the haystack. There was no other cover.

Locate it they must. Going back was impossible now. Their own artillery and machine guns were searching the hill above the village against a counter-attack. And the fire was slowly moving up. Besides, it was their business to get enemy machine guns. All this was self-evident and needed no discussion.

A thin blue haze from the middle of the haystack and the sound of a gun, apparently still up on the hill, gave the enemy's trick away. It was the echo of a gun they heard. The gun itself was in the haystack. As they looked closely a black mark in the hay showed where the emplacement was. The gun was firing at the village. But from where they lay the haystack was too far to reach by a bomb pitched from the ground. And there was no cover just ahead. They discussed that, whispering.

"I'll have to get up to pitch," said Rutherford. "Maybe I'll last for two balls."

"If ye don't git wan in over the plate," said Pap Maginn, "we'll all strike out the-gither."

"An' they'll get me, anyway," said Rutherford. The Virgin nodded. He was not going to give orders to Rutherford to stand up. They were all silent for nearly ten minutes. Then the gun burst out again with an irritating chatter.

"I'll do it," whispered Rutherford, as though the sound of the riveting had got on his nerves. He took two citrons out of the bag about his waist. Just then the gun stopped and they waited again. The silence seemed tremendous.

"Here's for you guys!" Rutherford exclaimed suddenly. He hit the citrons on his tin hat, one after the other (to start the fuse), and laid one on the ground, sizzling. He rose with the other and hurled it at the stack.

He missed.

The angles looked different when he stood up. The bomb curved into the side of the stack, and lay smoking. The gun burst out chattering like a monkey that has had a stone shied at it. Rutherford swooped down, seized the other bomb and sent it home into the middle of the hay. Then he rushed forward for about twenty yards.

A burst of bullets caught him across the waist. He disappeared in a great white blaze of fire, even brighter than the sunlight, in a thunderclap of all his bombs at once. The others lay still. A few seconds later there were two distinct explosions at the haystack. The first lifted the hay off and showed the concrete emplacement underneath. Then the top of the emplacement itself lifted off, and lay smoking. Rutherford's last bomb must have been hurled directly into the emplacement.

Something was still squealing inside like a pig in a fire when the Virgin and Maginn passed the haystack, racing. They were bent on a hollow just ahead of them in the field. They could see it now since they were on their feet. There was no use pausing at the haystack, all was over there.

They gained about thirty yards, dived for the hollow, slid and fell headlong over the edge into something deep. It was a six-foot drop into a concealed trench. And before they could move, a company of Germans fell on them like one man.

The Germans started to kick them to death and hammer them with whatever objects were handy. One of the bombs went off accidentally and killed three of the Germans. The rest fled. Why they were not both killed and why the rest of the bombs they had been carrying didn't go off they could never understand. They were both stunned either by the explosion or by the beating they had sustained.

When they came to they were propped up against a piece of duckboard in some deeper part of the trench opposite a dugout. The dugout was evidently a command post and had glass windows and a gas curtain. Before it a Prussian officer was eating supper from an exceedingly neat iron folding table. His boots and eyeglasses glittered. The table was laid with an embroidered cloth and served by an orderly from a wicker basket with a silver coat of arms on its clasp. Hot food, bottles of wine, and a jellied chicken emerged from it and were placed on the table to a heel-clicking by the orderly that sounded like castanets.

To William Henry, who was just emerging painfully from the stupor of having been knocked out by a blow on the head, the scene had all the irrational reality and crazy unexpectedness of a child's dream. After a while he noticed that Pap was sitting beside him, still unconscious, and bleeding at the mouth. He bubbled a little when he breathed. Just then the officer caught William Henry's eye. His spectacles flashed at him over a plate of salad.

"You're lucky to be here, my boy," said the officer, without a trace of accent. It was good American, not English.

"Yep?" said William Henry. There was a considerable pause while the officer finished his salad.

"It's a long way from Pennsylvania, isn't it?" remarked the officer, pushing his glasses aside.

"'S a long way," agreed Henry.

"Pittsburgh?" queried the Prussian carelessly. There was no answer, but the officer persisted. "How would you like to stroll down Fifth Avenue from the Court House and drop in to Reymer's for a chocolate sundae?"

"God, I'd like it!" said Henry. "I ain't eat nothing but some aspirin and a mouthful of goldfish for about a week, it seems."

"Have some chicken?"

"Chicken!" exclaimed Henry. "Golly!" They both laughed.

But chicken he had, hot from the basket, fed to him by the orderly. Trying to eat it, he discovered that his left arm must be broken. He was so sore all over that he hadn't noticed it before. The arm wouldn't work, yet he felt better. So much better! The Germans weren't so bad, after all. At least one of them wasn't. He seemed to know all about William Henry's home town.

He and the officer got along famously. All he had to do was answer questions now and then. Suddenly he felt weak and dizzy. He fell back against the side of the trench. The officer shouted something in German. A doctor with a Red Cross brassard came and gave him and Pap a shot in the arm. Presently Henry felt much better. His bruises stopped hurting. He became quite cheerful and started to talk to the officer again. He told him a lot of interesting things. And then the dream—he always thought of that part of the day as a dream—dissolved.

A telephone buzzed in the dugout. A runner dashed down the trench with a message. The officer read it and began to bark commands. Everybody in the dugout, and there had been quite a crowd in it, rushed out past William Henry and Pap and scattered up the trench. The officer went, with a big dog tearing after him. The dog came out of the dugout too. The orderly folded the table, seized the basket, spilling most of the contents, and fled after the others.

Five minutes later the barrage fell.

Their own guns came searching up the hill again. William Henry wondered how the Germans knew this in advance. Somehow, he didn't care now. Even a bombardment left him confident. He felt unaccountably cheerful and strong again.

Pap came to and looked about him. Almost instantly he was talking. He seemed to regard the spitting of blood as a humorous pastime. In the midst of his jocular and bloody remarks about being shelled by their own artillery they were joined by a German sentry. Either he had just appeared or they had not noticed him before. Whatever the medical man had injected into them it was a wonderful pickup. Their pains became far-off, unimportant, their minds clear and gay. Consequences no longer existed for them. Maginn, who was dying, had never felt better in his life. Loss of blood only made him lightheaded. He felt on a glorious drunk. He hailed the little German sentry joyfully.

During the worst of the shelling the man came and stood opposite them, next to the door of the dugout, as though for human company. He was an inconsequential little fellow with gray hair and a round cap with a small button on it.

"I onced knew a tin peddler who looked just loike him," wheezed Maginn.

The little old man, who had no weapon but a pistol in a holster, shivered and shook as the shells fell about them. The glass behind him in the silly dugout window rattled and clicked. The prisoners laughed at him like men in a fever. The range shifted and went higher up the hill. The earth began to boil and dissolve in claps of thunder behind them instead of before. The trench had been skipped.

"Maybe they're just bracketin'," said Maginn. "In a few minutes they'll git us." He seemed to regard this as a splendid joke. He took a box and stepped up on it and boldly looked over the edge of the trench.

Through the drifting haze and dust down the hillside he saw the little village they had left that morning. It was more wrecked now, but from the darker upper windows here and there still came the flash of rifle fire. He was surprised to see it was only a quarter of a mile away. Crawling had made the distance seem much longer.

"Glory be, the bhoys are still howlin' out! Thir's some of the battalion still lift! What's to privint us from shtrollin' home? Ownly wan thing. The little tin peddler thir," and he pointed at the man derisively.

Their conversation soon became highly excited. The drug which the doctor had administered was now taking full effect. They talked in shrill, hysterical tones and with violent gestures that brought more and more blood to Pap's mouth. He was now half covered with it down the front of his blouse, and a terrific sight. "Thim divils did for me insides" was his only comment. He jumped up on the box and looked at the village again. A rifle bullet sang by his ear. The sentry, who plainly regarded them as demented, now became alarmed and forced them back to their seat before the dugout with a drawn pistol. The barrage ceased as suddenly as it began.

"Damn him," said the Virgin. "The others will be back soon, now the barrage is over. I wonder how they knew it was coming."

"Ye'd better fix the little peddler man now," said Pap. The Virgin did not reply.

"I fixed two of them this morning," he said after thinking it over.

They sat quietly for a minute or two more.

"I knew a man that moidered a peddler onced," suggested Pap.

"Only onced?" countered the Virgin. They laughed till a rush of blood choked Pap. The smallest joke seemed enormous. Everything seemed enormous. The distance and the vista of the trench itself grew vast and clear.

It was just then that the Virgin saw the sickle. It was an old rusty sickle with a bright keen edge as though someone had recently been sharpening it; just an old farm implement some of the riflemen had been using to clear away the grass for a better place to sight from along the edge of the trench. The handle seemed to present itself to the Virgin in a kind of accentuated perspective with the butt larger than the end which ran into the blade. He pointed it out to Pap. The little Irishman's eyes popped.

"Take it an' cut off the peddler's head," he remarked casually.

"You do it," replied the corporal, "I fixed two of them this morning."

"Shure and I'm too wake, me chist is gone intirely."

Automatically William Henry picked up the sickle, when the sentry wasn't looking, and hid it behind him with his good right arm.

The little German was tramping up and down the trench now, stopping occasionally before the dugout. He felt relieved that his prisoners now seemed to be more quiet.

"He's got a thin neck," said Pap. They argued for some time about this.

"Even if it's a thick one I could do it," said the Virgin, who was becoming exasperated.

All during this time the little sentry continued to plod up and down his short traverse oblivious to the discussion of his own death in loud tones but in a foreign tongue.

"And yet I'd hate to cut off his head," said the corporal as the man passed him again.

"Afther ye do it," replied Maginn, "we'll just shinny out of this trench an' down into the drain the same way we come. We can crawl back to the village afther dark, and the sun's goin' down now. Hit him whin he passes nixt."

But the Virgin let the man pass him three times.

"O God," sobbed Maginn, "ef oi only had me shtrength!" His tears ran down into the bloody lower part of his face. "Ye damned mamma's bhoy, I'll go an' fetch the umbrella to keep the dew off ye tonight."

The Virgin was so angry he could not reply. He sat and shook.

The sentry at the end of the trench turned and came back again. He paid no attention to the indescribable mess of the hysterical little prisoner and his sullen companion sitting by the wall. They seemed helpless and all in. The red rays of the level sun spilled over the parapet. The German stopped, took off his thick-lensed glasses and started to wipe them with a red handkerchief. In the sunset, and without his spectacles, he looked to be the helpless and smooth little grocer's clerk that he actually was. He breathed on the lenses, wiped them again thoroughly, and was just . . .

When his head was cut off.

It had all been quite simple. William Henry had merely risen, taken one step, and made a tremendous swing at the sentry from behind. The German stood for an instant, a little fountain coming out of his neck. Then he sat down with a crash, doubling up like a jackknife in the place where the Virgin had just been sitting.

Pap jumped up hastily, not liking his company. They both stood staring for an instant.

"Come on!" cried William Henry, at last. He threw the sickle into the grass outside the trench. "They might find us here!"

"That's what the man that moidered the peddler said," wheezed Maginn.

"Come on, you old fool!" roared the Virgin and plucked Pap after him up over the edge of the trench. They wriggled off down the hillside, past the haystack that was still smoking a little. It was twilight and no one on either side saw them. They made the mouth of the little valleylike drain and lay panting.

"Oh," said Maginn. "Oh, oh!"

"What's the matter now?" demanded William Henry.

"I'm just dyin'," bubbled Pap. He began to cough great gouts of blood and lay still.

"Pap," whispered the Virgin and shook him. "Pap!" There was no answer.

The Virgin lay there till deep night came and the Very lights began to sail up along the trench behind him. Evidently the Germans had come back there again. A paralyzing terror gripped him. He couldn't go back and he was afraid to go forward for fear his own comrades, sniping from the village below, would get him. So he was stopped, partly by the fact and partly by his own conception of his situation.

Then the drug died out in him, suddenly, returning him to a state of exhaustion that was all but complete. Part of his exhaustion was a sense of vast outer and inner degradation that made all effort seem futile. He could not be more miserable than he was. His body was being made into carrion. What he had done was against his own mind. He did not remember in detail what he had done. He was not filled with remorse. He simply suffered the effect total. Some small remnant of physical energy made him crawl forward little by little for about half an hour as though by instinct. Then, as a flare went up, he found himself face to face with half of Captain Ward.

The expression on Captain Ward's face was not describable. It was the expression which only Captain Ward's face could assume, given the circumstances under which he had died. It was not the same as any other expression. Death had fixed it, and the glare of the flares seemed to photograph it. William Henry had acted on the will power of Pap Maginn and Captain Ward for some months past. They had substituted for him. Now they were both gone. To the Virgin the meaning of the expression on Captain Ward's dead face, and he saw it repeatedly as the flares rose, was: "Sheer determination is not enough." Captain Ward looked surprised.

That was the reason the Virgin resigned himself to die. He crawled on only far enough to get past Captain Ward. Then he lay still among the other dead and gave up. He passed out, exhausted inside and out. He slept like the dead.

Except for one thing. His heart went on.

4

His first sensation when he revived in the cold morning hours before dawn was an inner one. He felt his heart inside him laboring on. By it he took up the count of time as though he had returned from eternity. Whatever made his heart go on, he knew now he had nothing to do with it. He was here in spite of himself. It was in effect like being born again, but being conscious of it. And like most infants, as he gained a little strength and continued to survive, he felt sorry for himself and began to whimper. Also he began to remember something of past time and of the future. So with his toes and right arm, for the other arm was now stiff and useless, he began to inch himself down toward the village where the American troops might still be. After a while he knew they were still there. He disturbed a small slide of stones and they began to snipe at him. He edged over into the drain from which he had wandered.

William Henry was now only about a hundred yards out from his own lines. The night breeze occasionally brought him snatches of conversation in his own language. It was the tones of the voices that he recognized. The dark village before him was still full of his friends.

So he lay still for another hour.

Sorrow for himself now filled the world. "Poor Bill, poor little William Henry." He was almost home but he was going to die. He needed a mother. Not *his* mother. A mother. Something he had missed. His mind wandered a little and he began to sing. "I want a girl just like the girl that married dear old Dad . . ."

"Poor Dad, and poor, poor William Henry." No, no, no, no, he didn't want a mother like that. What he wanted was what he had missed. He knew what it was now.

It was the mother in the Little Gray Home in the West. Oh, how he had missed her, needed her! But better still, yes, much better, Mother Machree.

"Yes, that was her name. Mother Machree!"

About four o'clock in the morning a machine gunner in the American lines by the name of Mandolino heard somebody out on the corpse-strewn field before the village singing "Mother Machree."

"Listen," said Mandolino. They all listened. "By God, it's the Virgin!" cried Mandy. They shouted to him. The singing stopped.

In a short while it began again. But it was so eerie that some of them were afraid to try to get an answer.

"I *know* it's the Virgin," insisted Mandolino. "Hi, Virgin, hi!" he called into the night. "It's Mandolino, crawl this way."

"Mandy, Mandy, don't you shoot," called the Virgin. "I'm coming! I'm coming in!"

And then at last they saw him inching home.

One of them crawled out and helped drag him in.

He managed to tell them his story before the sergeant sent him off to the base hospital. A shattered arm, mustard gas, and exhaustion. Next day they made a general advance and found Captain Ward, Pap, and the headless German, just as the Virgin had said.

William Henry got the D.S.C., and the Croix de Guerre from the French government later on. He wore them in parades at home.

The medals were one thing that almost reconciled Mrs. Virgin to her son's return. But they weren't hers, of course. And after a while she began to realize that her son hadn't really come back. It was somebody else with the same name.

Richard Brautigan

(1935–1984)

Best known for his widely popular novels *Trout Fishing in America* (1967) and *In Watermelon Sugar* (1968), Richard Brautigan was also a poet and short-story writer. Although his literary reputation was long seen as beholden to the counterculture of the 1960s and its links to the Beat Movement of the previous decade, more recently Brautigan has been praised for his participation in an American frontier philosophy and for his postmodern experimentation in style and subject matter. The experimental fiction in *Revenge of the Lawn: Stories, 1962–1970* (1971) stretches the traditional form of the short story while providing early examples of what is now known as sudden or flash fiction. "The World War I Los Angeles Airplane," the final story in this collection, is based on the life of his first wife's father. Of the story's central theme, critic David Galloway concludes: "If war makes heroes, both life and death unmake them."[1] "The World War I Los Angeles Airplane" was originally published in *New American Review* in 1971.

The World War I Los Angeles Airplane

Richard Brautigan

He was found lying dead near the television set on the front room floor of a small rented house in Los Angeles. My wife had gone to the store to get some ice cream. It was an early-in-the-night-just-a-few-blocks-away store. We were in an ice-cream

---

1. David Galloway, "Richard Brautigan, 'The World War I Los Angeles Airplane' (1971)," *Die amerikanische Short Story der Gegenwart: Interpretationen,* ed. Peter Freese (Berlin: Erich Schmidt Verlag, 1976), 337.

mood. The telephone rang. It was her brother to say that her father had died that afternoon. He was seventy. I waited for her to come home with the ice cream. I tried to think of the best way to tell her that her father was dead with the least amount of pain but you cannot camouflage death with words. Always at the end of the words somebody is dead.

She was very happy when she came back from the store.

"What's wrong?" she said.

"Your brother just called from Los Angeles," I said.

"What happened?" she said.

"Your father died this afternoon."

That was in 1960 and now it's just a few weeks away from 1970. He has been dead for almost ten years and I've done a lot of thinking about what his death means to all of us.

1. He was born from German blood and raised on a farm in South Dakota. His grandfather was a terrible tyrant who completely destroyed his three grown sons by treating them exactly the way he treated them when they were children. They never grew up in his eyes and they never grew up in their own eyes. He made sure of that. They never left the farm. They of course got married but he handled all of their domestic matters except for the siring of his grandchildren. He never allowed them to discipline their own children. He took care of that for them. Her father thought of his father as another brother who was always trying to escape the never-relenting wrath of their grandfather.

2. He was smart, so he became a schoolteacher when he was eighteen and he left the farm which was an act of revolution against his grandfather who from that day forth considered him dead. He didn't want to end up like his father, hiding behind the barn. He taught school for three years in the Midwest and then he worked as an automobile salesman in the pioneer days of car selling.

3. There was an early marriage followed by an early divorce with feelings afterward that left the marriage hanging like a skeleton in her family's closet because he tried to keep it a secret. He probably had been very much in love.

4. There was a horrible automobile accident just before the First World War in which everybody was killed except him. It was one of those automobile accidents that leave deep spiritual scars like historical landmarks on the family and friends of the dead.

5. When America went into the First World War in 1917, he decided that he wanted to be a pilot, though he was in his late twenties. He was told that it would be impossible because he was too old but he projected so much energy into his desire to fly that he was accepted for pilot training and went to Florida and became a pilot.

In 1918 he went to France and flew a De Havilland and bombed a railroad station in France and one day he was flying over the German lines when little clouds began appearing around him and he thought that they were beautiful and flew for a long time before he realized that they were German antiaircraft guns trying to shoot him down.

Another time he was flying over France and a rainbow appeared behind the tail of his plane and every turn that the plane made, the rainbow also made the same turn and it followed after him through the skies of France for part of an afternoon in 1918.

6. When the war was over he got out a captain and he was travelling on a train through Texas when the middle-aged man sitting next to him and with whom he had been talking for about three hundred miles said, "If I was a young man like you and had a little extra cash, I'd go up to Idaho and start a bank. There's a good future in Idaho banking."

7. That's what her father did.

8. He went to Idaho and started a bank which soon led to three more banks and a large ranch. It was by now 1926 and everything was going all right.

9. He married a schoolteacher who was sixteen years his junior and for their honeymoon they took a train to Philadelphia and spent a week there.

10. When the stock market crashed in 1929 he was hit hard by it and had to give up his banks and a grocery store that he had picked up along the way, but he still had the ranch, though he had to put a mortgage on it.

11. He decided to go into sheep raising in 1931 and got a big flock and was very good to his sheepherders. He was so good to them that it was a subject of gossip in his part of Idaho. The sheep got some kind of horrible sheep disease and all died.

12. He got another big flock of sheep in 1933 and added more fuel to the gossip by continuing to be so good to his men. The sheep got some kind of horrible sheep disease and all died in 1934.

13. He gave his men a big bonus and went out of the sheep business.

14. He had just enough money left over after selling the ranch to pay off all his debts and buy a brand-new Chevrolet which he put his family into and he drove off to California to start all over again.

15. He was forty-four, had a twenty-eight-year-old wife and an infant daughter.

16. He didn't know anyone in California and it was the Depression.

17. His wife worked for a while in a prune shed and he parked cars at a lot in Hollywood.

18. He got a job as a bookkeeper for a small construction company.

19. His wife gave birth to a son.

20. In 1940 he went briefly into California real estate, but then decided not to

pursue it any further and went back to work for the construction company as a bookkeeper.

21. His wife got a job as a checker in a grocery store where she worked for eight years and then an assistant manager quit and opened his own store and she went to work for him and she still works there.

22. She has worked twenty-three years now as a grocery checker for the same store.

23. She was very pretty until she was forty.

24. The construction company laid him off. They said he was too old to take care of the books. "It's time for you to go out to pasture," they joked. He was fifty-nine.

25. They rented the same house they lived in for twenty-five years, though they could have bought it at one time with no down payment and monthly payments of fifty dollars.

26. When his daughter was going to high school he was working there as the school janitor. She saw him in the halls. His working as a janitor was a subject that was very seldom discussed at home.

27. Her mother would make lunches for both of them.

28. He retired when he was sixty-five and became a very careful sweet wine alcoholic. He liked to drink whiskey but they couldn't afford to keep him in it. He stayed in the house most of the time and started drinking about ten o'clock, a few hours after his wife had gone off to work at the grocery store.

29. He would get quietly drunk during the course of the day. He always kept his wine bottles hidden in a kitchen cabinet and would secretly drink from them, though he was alone.

He very seldom made any bad scenes and the house was always clean when his wife got home from work. He did though after a while take on that meticulous manner of walking that alcoholics have when they are trying very carefully to act as if they aren't drunk.

30. He used sweet wine in place of life because he didn't have any more life to use.

31. He watched afternoon television.

32. Once he had been followed by a rainbow across the skies of France while flying a World War I airplane carrying bombs and machine guns.

33. "Your father died this afternoon."

Historical Timeline with Literary, Cultural, and Political Events (1914–1940)

1914

United States population: 99,111,000.

Construction begins on the Lincoln Memorial.

Colorado National Guard members fire on striking coal miners in Ludlow, killing eighteen people, including women and children.

The U.S. navy and Marines occupy Veracruz, Mexico.

June 28: Archduke Franz Ferdinand is assassinated.

August 1: Germany declares war on Russia.

August 3: Germany declares war on France.

August 4: Germany declares war on Belgium. Britain declares war on Germany. The United States declares neutrality.

The Panama Canal opens.

September 5: The Battle of the Marne begins.

October 19: The First Battle of Ypres is fought.

Robert Frost publishes *North of Boston*.

The *Little Review* is founded in Chicago.

Marsden Hartley paints *Portrait of a German Officer*.

1915

January 3: The Germans are the first to use poison gas.

The Woman's Peace Party forms, with Jane Addams as chair.

A telephone line links New York and San Francisco.

The Birth of a Nation, D. W. Griffith's epic Civil War film, premieres.

April 15: The Allies land on Gallipoli.

April 22: The Second Battle of Ypres begins.

May 7: A German submarine sinks the ocean liner *Lusitania*. Among the 1,198 dead are 128 Americans.

May 23: Italy declares war on Austria-Hungary.

Edgar Lee Masters publishes his *Spoon River Anthology*.

Henry James becomes a British citizen, in part to protest America's refusal to enter the war.

Banks in the United States loan Britain and France $500 million to finance the war.

The Ku Klux Klan is reorganized by William J. Simmons at Stone Mountain, Georgia, on Thanksgiving night.

1916

Louis Brandeis is appointed to the U.S. Supreme Court.

The Battle of Verdun lasts from February to December.

U.S. troops enter Mexico in pursuit of Poncho Villa.

Marcus Garvey moves to New York City and begins the Back to Africa movement.

The Easter Rising occurs in Ireland.

May 31: British and German navies clash in the Battle of Jutland.

Mary Pickford receives a $1 million contract.

July 1: The Battle of the Somme begins.

Coca-Cola's contour bottle debuts.

Ring Lardner publishes *You Know Me, Al.*

The National Park Service is formed.

Woodrow Wilson is reelected president, running on the slogan "He kept us out of war."

1917

January 31: The United States is informed of the German decision to resume unrestricted submarine warfare.

Tsar Nicholas II abdicates.

April 6: The United States declares war.

John Joseph Pershing is appointed commander of the American Expeditionary Forces.

April 28: Congress authorizes a draft of five hundred thousand men. In the next two years, almost 24 million American men will be registered in drafts and almost 2 million American soldiers will serve in Europe.

July 31: The Third Battle of Ypres (Passchendaele) begins.

T. S. Eliot publishes "The Love Song of J. Alfred Prufrock" in *Prufrock and Other Observations.*

The Espionage Act is passed, prohibiting the mailing of publications deemed "seditious."

Alfred Stieglitz closes 291, his New York gallery for avant-garde art.

The 17th Provisional Training Regiment at Fort Des Moines, Iowa, graduates 639 African Americans, who are commissioned as captains or lieutenants.

The U.S. government takes control of the nation's railroads.

The first Americans in U.S. combat units are killed on the Western Front.

November 7: Bolsheviks overthrow the provisional Russian government.

1918

President Wilson presents his "Fourteen Points" for postwar Europe, including the formation of a League of Nations.

An influenza pandemic erupts, eventually claiming an estimated 50 million lives, including those of 675,000 Americans.

June 1–26: Americans fight at Belleau Wood.

September 12: The American offensive on the St. Mihiel salient begins

September 26: The American offensive in the Meuse-Argonne begins.

At the front, John Singer Sargent sketches and paints the war's wreckage.
The cookbook *Foods That Will Win the War and How to Cook Them* is published.
Edith Wharton publishes *The Marne.*
Willa Cather publishes *My Ántonia.*
November 11: Germany accepts the terms of Armistice, and the war ends.
America incurs 323,018 casualties (killed, wounded, and missing).

1919

In February, the 369th Infantry Regiment, an African American unit that the French dub
the "Hell Fighters," marches up 5th Avenue through Manhattan to Harlem.
Sherwood Anderson publishes *Winesburg, Ohio.*
The Eighteenth Amendment, which prohibits liquor, becomes law.
The American Legion is founded.
The Communist Party USA is established.
June 28: Germany signs the Treaty of Versailles.
The Thompson submachine gun is invented.
Race riots erupt in twenty-five American cities.
More than seventy black people are lynched, including some in army uniforms.
A Red Scare leads to the arrest and deportation of Americans deemed radical.

1920

Sinclair Lewis publishes *Main Street.*
F. Scott Fitzgerald publishes *This Side of Paradise.*
Beyond the Horizon, by Eugene O'Neill, wins the Pulitzer Prize for drama.
The Nineteenth Amendment is ratified, and women gain the right to vote in all U.S. elections.
Eight Chicago White Sox players are indicted for conspiring with gamblers to throw the
1919 World Series.
Station KDKA in Pittsburgh broadcasts the returns for the presidential election, inaugurat-
ing radio as a commercial enterprise in the United States.
Warren G. Harding is elected president, running on the slogan "Return to normalcy."
Eugene V. Debs, running from prison as the Socialist party candidate for president, wins
nearly a million votes.
Ernest Moore Viquesney patents his statue *The Spirit of the American Doughboy;* in the ensu-
ing two decades replications are erected in hundreds of American towns.

1921

John Dos Passos publishes *Three Soldiers.*
Edith Wharton's *The Age of Innocence* receives the Pulitzer Prize for the Novel.
Margaret Sanger founds the American Birth Control League.
The Federal Highway Act is passed and increases funding for paved roads.

The first transcontinental airmail flight links New York City with San Francisco.

Congress enacts immigration quotas.

Wonder Bread and *Wheaties* are invented.

On November 11, President Harding presides at the burial of an American soldier in the Tomb of the Unknown Soldier at Arlington National Cemetery.

The Sheik, a film starring Italian actor Rudolph Valentino, debuts; it grosses $1 million in its first year.

1922

Reader's Digest begins publication.

T. S. Eliot publishes *The Waste Land.*

e. e. cummings publishes *The Enormous Room.*

Willa Cather publishes *One of Ours,* which is awarded the Pulitzer Prize for the Novel the next year.

Suspected of being a Bolshevik agent, dancer Isadora Duncan is detained in New York City.

International Harvester introduces a power takeoff device that enables tractors to directly power farm implements.

Secretary of the Interior Albert Fall comes under investigation for accepting bribes to lease the government oil reserves held at Teapot Dome.

1923

Time magazine begins publication.

Upside down in New York City, Harry Houdini frees himself from a straightjacket.

Jean Toomer publishes *Cane.*

Edith Wharton publishes *A Son at the Front.*

D. H. Lawrence publishes *Studies in Classic American Literature.*

The Hollywoodland sign is erected on the hills above Los Angeles.

The Ten Commandments, directed by Cecil B. DeMille, premieres.

Warren G. Harding dies; Calvin Coolidge becomes president.

1924

Rhapsody in Blue, by George Gershwin, is first played in concert.

Calvin Coolidge delivers the first presidential radio address.

The Broadway play *What Price Glory,* by Maxwell Anderson and Laurence Stallings debuts.

Billy Budd, by Herman Melville, is published.

Nathan F. Leopold and Richard A. Loeb confess to murdering fourteen-year-old Robert Franks.

Congress passes the Indian Citizenship Act, which grants citizenship to Native Americans born in the United States.

Rogers Hornsby of the St. Louis Cardinals hits .424.

Rand McNally's first road atlas is published.

The Betty Crocker School of the Air, America's first cooking show, debuts.

J. Edgar Hoover is appointed FBI director.

The Statue of Liberty is declared a national monument.

Calvin Coolidge is elected president, running on the slogan "Keep cool and keep Coolidge."

1925

Air conditioning is installed at the Rivoli movie theater in New York City.

Clarence Birdseye and the General Seafood Corporation launch the frozen food industry.

The *New Yorker* begins publication.

Theodore Dreiser publishes *An American Tragedy.*

Willa Cather publishes *The Professor's House.*

F. Scott Fitzgerald publishes *The Great Gatsby.*

Ernest Hemingway publishes *In Our Time.*

John Dos Passos publishes *Manhattan Transfer.*

Sinclair Lewis publishes *Arrowsmith.*

Anita Loos publishes *Gentlemen Prefer Blondes.*

Guggenheim Fellowships are established.

Louis Armstrong records his first songs with his own group, His Hot Five.

In Dayton, Tennessee, John Thomas Scopes is tried for teaching evolution in high school.

Two hundred thousand Ku Klux Klan members march in Washington, D.C.

1926

The Book of the Month Club is founded.

Ernest Hemingway publishes *The Sun Also Rises.*

Langston Hughes publishes *The Weary Blues.*

William Faulkner publishes *Soldiers' Pay.*

Carl Sandburg publishes *Abraham Lincoln: The Prairie Years.*

The Railway Labor Act is passed.

U.S. Army Air Corps is created.

The National Broadcasting Company is formed.

Before a crowd of 135,000, Gene Tunney defeats reigning champion Jack Dempsey for
boxing's heavyweight title.

1927

Upton Sinclair publishes *Oil!*

Charles and Mary Beard publish *The Rise of American Civilization.*

Charles A. Lindbergh completes the first solo airplane flight across the Atlantic Ocean.

The Ford Motor Company produces the last Model T. In the previous nineteen years, more
than 15 million Model T automobiles were manufactured.

Nicola Sacco and Bartolomeo Vanzetti, avowed anarchists, are executed in the electric chair,
six years after being found guilty of robbery and murder.

The Jazz Singer, starring Al Jolson, opens, signaling the rise of movie "talkies."

Duke Ellington's orchestra becomes the house band at the Cotton Club in Harlem.

Show Boat, by Jerome Kern and Oscar Hammerstein II and based on a novel by Edna Ferber, premieres at the Ziegfeld Theatre on Broadway.

1928

Paris premieres on Broadway and features Cole Porter's *Let's Do It, Let's Fall in Love.*

Claude McKay publishes *Home to Harlem.*

Mickey Mouse debuts, in *Steamboat Willie.*

The Federal Radio Commission grants the first license for an experimental television station.

Eugene O'Neill's *Strange Interlude* is staged.

John Brown's Body, an epic of the Civil War by Stephen Vincent Benet, is published and receives the Pulitzer Prize for Poetry the next year.

Herbert Hoover is elected president, running on the slogan "A chicken in every pot and a car in every garage."

George Gershwin's *An American in Paris* premieres.

1929

Wings, an epic about World War I aviators directed by William Wellman, wins the Academy Award for Best Picture.

Ernest Hemingway publishes *A Farewell to Arms.*

William Faulkner publishes *The Sound and the Fury.*

Astronomer Edwin Hubble demonstrates the expansion of the universe.

Frigidaire manufactures its millionth home refrigerator.

The Museum of Modern Art opens in New York City.

The U.S. Stock Market collapses, and the Great Depression begins.

1930

John Dos Passos publishes *The 42nd Parallel.*

Mike Gold publishes *Jews Without Money.*

Sinclair Lewis receives the Nobel Prize for Literature.

The Veterans Administration is established.

American Gothic, a painting by Grant Wood, is first exhibited at the Art Institute of Chicago.

All Quiet on the Western Front, directed by Lewis Milestone and based on the novel by Erich Maria Remarque, wins the Academy Award for Best Picture.

1931

A white posse stops a train in Paint Rock, Alabama, and takes custody of nine black men who are soon accused of rape. Twelve days later, these "Scottsboro boys" are convicted and sentenced to death.

The "Star-Spangled Banner" is declared the national anthem.

Eugene O'Neill stages *Mourning Becomes Electra.*

The Empire State Building is completed.

Of Thee I Sing opens on Broadway and becomes the first musical comedy to win the Pulitzer Prize.

Jane Addams is awarded the Nobel Peace Prize (jointly with Nicholas Murray Butler).

1932

John Dos Passos publishes *1919.*

William Faulkner publishes *Light in August.*

Charles A. Lindbergh Jr. is kidnapped and murdered.

Al Capone, convicted of tax evasion, enters prison.

With bayonets and tear gas, troops under Douglas MacArthur forcefully remove the Bonus Army of World War I veterans from Washington, D.C.

Franklin D. Roosevelt is elected president, running on the promise of a "New Deal."

1933

Gertrude Stein publishes *The Autobiography of Alice B. Toklas.*

Edgar Ansel Mowrer of the *Chicago Daily News* wins the Pulitzer Prize for reporting on the rise of the Nazis.

The Tennessee Valley Authority is established.

Billie Holiday makes her recording debut, singing two songs with Benny Goodman's orchestra.

December 5: Prohibition ends when Utah provides the deciding vote for the Twenty-first Amendment, which repeals the Eighteenth Amendment.

1934

Alcatraz becomes a federal prison.

The Federal Deposit Insurance Corporation is activated.

For two days in May, a dust storm sweeps across the Great Plains.

F. Scott Fitzgerald publishes *Tender Is the Night.*

The Securities and Exchange Commission is created.

In Chicago, John Dillinger is shot and killed by FBI agents.

Anything Goes, with music and lyrics by Cole Porter, opens on Broadway.

The first 33⅓ rpm record is released.

1935

Sinclair Lewis publishes *It Can't Happen Here.*

Clifford Odets's *Waiting for Lefty* and *Awake and Sing* are staged.

James T. Farrell publishes *Judgment Day,* the final novel in the Studs Lonigan trilogy.

The Federal Writers' Project begins.

The Social Security Act passes.

The Works Progress Administration gets underway.

The Rural Electrification Administration is established.

Huey Long is assassinated in Baton Rouge, Louisiana.

President Roosevelt dedicates the Boulder Dam (later Hoover Dam).

Porgy and Bess premieres, with a cast of African American singers.

1936

John Dos Passos publishes *The Big Money.*

William Faulkner publishes *Absalom! Absalom!*

Joe DiMaggio debuts with the New York Yankees.

Babe Ruth hits his last homerun, number 714, at Forbes Field in Pittsburgh.

At the Eleventh Olympics, in Berlin, Jesse Owens wins four gold medals.

Franklin D. Roosevelt is reelected president, running on the slogan "Remember Hoover."

Eugene O'Neill receives the Nobel Prize for Literature.

1937

The German airship *Hindenburg* catches fire in Lakehurst, New Jersey, killing thirty-five
people.

John Steinbeck publishes *Of Mice and Men* and *The Red Pony.*

The Golden Gate Bridge opens.

Amelia Earhart and Fred Noonan disappear on a flight over the Pacific Ocean.

The Pullman Company formally recognizes the Brotherhood of Sleeping Car Porters.

Ernest Hemingway publishes *To Have and Have Not.*

1938

Babe Didrikson plays in the Los Angeles Open, a men's Professional Golf Association
tournament.

Our Town, by Thornton Wilder, is staged.

The House Committee on Un-American Activities is established.

In two minutes and four seconds, Joe Louis defeats Max Schmeling, a German touted by
the Nazis for his Aryan heritage, to retain boxing's heavyweight title.

A federal law establishes the minimum wage at forty cents an hour.

Nylon is introduced.

Orson Welles broadcasts *War of the Worlds.*

Seabiscuit outraces War Admiral in a thoroughbred match of the century.

Pearl S. Buck receives the Nobel Prize for Literature.

1939

Little Foxes, by Lillian Hellman, is staged.

The New York World's Fair opens, with the theme "Building the World of Tomorrow."

Pablo Picasso's *Guernica* travels to the United States as a fund-raiser for refugees from the Spanish Civil War.

John Steinbeck publishes *The Grapes of Wrath,* winner of the Pulitzer Prize the next year.

Nathanael West publishes *The Day of the Locust.*

Robert Frost publishes *Collected Poems.*

Carl Sandburg publishes *Abraham Lincoln: The War Years.*

The Time of Your Life, by William Saroyan, is staged.

Glenn Miller and His Orchestra record "Tuxedo Junction."

1940

Gone with the Wind, directed by Victor Fleming and based on a novel by Margaret Mitchell, wins the Academy Award for Best Picture.

Richard Wright publishes *Native Son.*

Ernest Hemingway publishes *For Whom the Bell Tolls.*

Charlie Chaplin stars in *The Great Dictator.*

The Selective Service and Training Act is passed, instituting a peacetime draft.

Franklin D. Roosevelt is reelected president, running on the slogan "Better a third term than a third-rater."

December 21: F. Scott Fitzgerald dies.

United States population: 132,122,446.

Selected Bibliography

COLLECTED STORIES

Allen, Hervey. "Blood Lust." *It Was Like This: Two Stories of the Great War*, 105–53. New York: Farrar & Rinehart, 1940.

Bellah, James Warner. "The Great Tradition." *Gods of Yesterday*, 209–35. New York: D. Appleton, 1928.

Borden, Mary. "Rosa." *The Forbidden Zone*, 98–111. Garden City, N.Y.: Doubleday, Doran, 1929.

Boyd, Thomas. "The Kentucky Boy." *Points of Honor*, 35–64. New York: Charles Scribner's Sons, 1925.

Boyle, Kay. "Count Lothar's Heart." *White Horses of Vienna and Other Stories*, 125–44. New York: Harcourt, Brace, 1936.

Brautigan, Richard. "The World War I Los Angeles Airplane." *Revenge of the Lawn: Stories, 1962–1970*, 170–74. New York: Simon & Schuster, 1971.

Canfield, Dorothy. "The Permissionaire." *Home Fires in France*, 27–59. New York: Henry Holt, 1918.

Cather, Willa Sibert. "The Namesake." *McClure's Magazine*, March 1907, 492–97.

Collins, Carita. "How Walter Regained His Manhood." *Crusader*, May 1919, 10–12, 29–30, 32.

Daly, Victor R. "Private Walker Goes Patrolling." *Crisis*, June 1930, 199–201, 213.

Davis, Richard Harding. "The Man Who Had Everything." *Lost Road*, 308–30. New York: Charles Scribner's Sons, 1916.

Ferber, Edna. "One Hundred Per Cent." *Metropolitan*, Oct. 1918, 11–14, 57–60.

Fitzgerald, F. Scott. "May Day." *Tales of the Jazz Age*, 61–125. New York: Charles Scribner's Sons, 1922.

Hughes, Langston. "Poor Little Black Fellow." *The Ways of White Folks*, 129–55. New York: Knopf, 1934.

Hunting, Ema S. "The Soul That Sinneth." *Midland: A Magazine of the Middle West*, August 1920, 128–36.

Jacks, Leo V. "One Hundred Per Cent." *Scribner's Magazine*, November 1928, 569–73.

Johnson, Fanny Kemble. "The Strange-Looking Man." *The Best Short Stories of 1917*. Edited by Edward J. O'Brien, 361–64. Boston: Small, Maynard, 1918.

McKay, Claude. "The Soldier's Return." *Trial by Lynching: Stories about Negro Life in North America*. Translated by Robert Winter. Edited by A. L. McLeod, 35–41 Mysore, India: Centre for Commonwealth Literature and Research, 1977.

March, William. "To the Rear." *Midland: A Magazine of the Middle West*, April 1931, 134–47.

Nason, Leonard H. "Among the Trumpets." *Saturday Evening Post*, July 27, 1929, 10–11, 64, 66.

Porter, Katherine Anne. *Pale Horse, Pale Rider. Pale Horse, Pale Rider: Three Short Novels*, 179–264. New York: Harcourt, Brace, 1939.

Springs, Elliot White. "Big Eyes and Little Mouth." *Nocturne Militaire,* 13–63. New York: George H. Doran, 1927.
Stallings, Laurence. "The Big Parade." *New Republic,* September 17, 1924, 66–69.
Stout, George L. "Dust." *Midland: A Magazine of the Middle West,* May 1924, 211–23.
Wharton, Edith. "Writing a War Story." *Woman's Home Companion,* September 1919, 17–19.
Wiley, Hugh. "The Four-Leaved Wildcat." *Saturday Evening Post,* March 8, 1919, 9–11, 45–46, 49.

ANTHOLOGIES

Burns, Vincent Godfrey, ed. *The Red Harvest: A Cry for Peace.* New York: Macmillan, 1930.
Callaghan, Barry and Bruce Meyer, eds. *We Wasn't Pals: Canadian Poetry and Prose of the First World War.* Toronto: Exile Editions, 2001.
Cardinal, Agnes, Dorothy Goldman, and Judith Hattaway, eds. *Women's Writing on the First World War.* Oxford: Oxford University Press, 1999.
Glover, Jon, and Jon Silkin, eds. *The Penguin Book of First World War Prose.* New York: Viking, 1989.
Great Short Stories of the War: England, France, Germany, America. London: Eyre and Spottiswoode, 1930. Republished as *Great First World War Stories.* London: Chancellor Press, 1994.
Higonnet, Margaret R., ed. *Lines of Fire: Women Writers of World War I.* New York: Plume, 1999.
———. *Nurses at the Front: Writing the Wounds of the Great War.* Boston: Northeastern University Press, 2001.
Kerlin, Robert T., ed. *The Voice of the Negro 1919.* New York: Dutton, 1920.
Korte, Barbara, and Ann-Marie Einhaus, eds. *The Penguin Book of First World War Stories.* London: Penguin, 2007.
Mason, F. van Wyck, ed. *The Fighting American: A War-Chest of Stories of American Soldiers from the French and Indian Wars through the First World War.* New York: Reynal and Hitchcock, 1943.
Sanford A. P., and Robert Haven Schauffler, eds. *Armistice Day.* New York: Dodd, Mead, 1928.
Smith, Angela K., ed. *Women's Writing of the First World War: An Anthology.* Manchester: Manchester University Press, 2000.
Tate, Trudi, ed. *Women, Men, and the Great War: An Anthology of Stories.* Manchester: Manchester University Press, 1995.

MEMOIRS, BIOGRAPHIES, AND CRITICAL WORKS

Aichinger, Peter. *The American Soldier in Fiction, 1880–1963: A History of Attitudes towards Warfare and the Military Establishment.* Ames: Iowa State University Press, 1975.
Allen, Hervey. Introduction to *It Was Like This: Two Stories of the Great War,* 1–13. New York: Farrar & Rinehart, 1940.
———. *Toward the Flame.* 1926. Ed. Steven Trout. Lincoln: University of Nebraska Press, 2003.
Barloon, Jim. "Very Short Stories: The Miniaturization of War in Hemingway's *In Our Time.*" *Hemingway Review* 24, no. 2 (Spring 2005): 5–17.
Beegel, Susan. *Hemingway's Craft of Omission: Four Manuscript Examples.* Ann Arbor: UMI Research Press, 1988.
Borden, Mary. *Journey Down a Blind Alley.* New York: Harper & Brothers, 1946.
Boyd, Thomas. Foreword to *Points of Honor,* vii–ix. New York: Scribner's, 1925.

Brittain, Joan B. *Laurence Stallings.* New York: Twayne, 1975.

Bruce, Brian. *Thomas Boyd: Lost Author of the "Lost Generation."* Akron, Ohio: University of Akron Press, 2006.

Bruccoli, Matthew. *Some Sort of Epic Grandeur: The Life of F. Scott Fitzgerald.* New York: Harcourt Brace Jovanovich, 1981.

Cooperman, Stanley. *World War I and the American Novel.* Baltimore: Johns Hopkins University Press, 1967.

Conway, Jane. *Mary Borden: A Woman of Two Wars.* New York: Munday Books, 2010.

Davis, Burke. *War Bird: The Life and Times of Elliott White Springs.* Chapel Hill: University of North Carolina Press, 1987.

Davis, David A. Introduction to *Not Only War: A Story of Two Great Conflicts,* by Victor Daly. Charlottesville: University of Virginia Press, 2010.

Edsel, Robert M., with Bret Witter. *The Monuments Men: Allied Heroes, Nazi Thieves, and the Greatest Treasure Hunt in History.* New York: Center Street, 2009.

Fisher, Dorothy Canfield. *Keeping Fires Night and Day: Selected Letters of Dorothy Canfield Fisher.* Edited by Mark J. Madigan. Columbia: University of Missouri Press, 1993.

Foley, Barbara. *Spectres of 1919: Class and Nation in the Making of the New Negro.* Urbana: University of Illinois Press, 2003.

Fussell, Paul. *The Great War and Modern Memory.* New York: Oxford University Press, 1975.

Galloway, David. "Richard Brautigan, 'The World War I Los Angeles Airplane' (1971)." *Die amerikanische Short Story der Gegenwart: Interpretationen,* 333–39. Edited by Peter Freese. Berlin: Erich Schmidt Verlag, 1976.

Gandal, Keith. *The Gun and the Pen: Hemingway, Fitzgerald, Faulkner, and the Fiction of Mobilization.* New York: Oxford University Press, 2008.

Gilbert, Julie Goldsmith. *Ferber: A Biography of Edna Ferber and Her Circle.* New York: Doubleday, 1978.

Goldman, Dorothy, ed. *Women and World War I: The Written Response.* New York: St. Martin's, 1993.

Goldman, Dorothy, with Jane Gledhill and Judith Hattaway. *Women Writers and the Great War.* New York: Twayne, 1995.

Hager, Philip, and Desmond Taylor. *The Novel of World War I: An Annotated Bibliography.* New York: Garland, 1981.

Haytock, Jennifer. *At Home, at War: Domesticity and World War I in American Literature.* Columbus: Ohio State University Press, 2003.

———. *Edith Wharton and the Conversations of Literary Modernism.* New York: Palgrave Macmillan, 2008.

James, Jennifer C. *A Freedom Bought with Blood: African American War Literature from the Civil War to World War II.* Chapel Hill: University of North Carolina Press, 2007.

James, Pearl. *The New Death: American Modernism and World War I.* Charlottesville: University of Virginia Press, 2013.

Klein, Michael Holger, ed. *The First World War in Fiction: A Collection of Critical Essays.* New York: Barnes & Noble, 1977.

Matthews, John T. "American Writings of the Great War." In Vincent, *The Cambridge Companion to the Literature of the First World War,* 217–42.

Lamb, Robert Paul. *Art Matters: Hemingway, Craft, and the Creation of the Modern Short Story.* Baton Rouge: Louisiana State University Press, 2010.

———. "The Love Song of Harold Krebs: Form, Argument, and Meaning in Hemingway's 'Soldier's Home.'" *Hemingway Review* 14, no. 2 (Spring 1995): 18–36.

Lee, Hermione. *Edith Wharton*. New York: Knopf, 2007.

Lubow, Arthur. *The Reporter Who Would Be King: A Biography of Richard Harding Davis*. New York: Charles Scribner's Sons, 1992.

Matsen, William E. *The Great War and the American Novel: Versions of Reality and the Writer's Craft in Selected Fiction of the First World War*. New York: Peter Lang, 1993.

Mellen, Joan. *Kay Boyle: Author of Herself*. New York: Farrar, 1994.

Ouditt, Sharon. *Women Writers of the First World War: An Annotated Bibliography*. New York: Routledge, 2000.

Parfitt, George A. E. *Fiction of the First World War: A Study*. London: Faber, 1988.

Piep, Karsten H. *Embattled Home Fronts: Domestic Politics and the American Novel of World War I*. Amsterdam: Rodopi, 2009.

Polk, Noel, and Ann J. Abadie, eds. *Faulkner and War*. Oxford: University of Mississippi Press, 2004.

Price, Alan. *The End of Innocence: Edith Wharton and the First World War*. London: Palgrave Macmillan, 1997.

Reynolds, Michael S. *The Young Hemingway*. Oxford: Blackwell, 1986.

Quinn, Patrick J. *The Conning of America: The Great War and American Popular Literature*. Amsterdam: Rodopi, 2001.

Quinn, Patrick J., and Steven Trout, eds. *The Literature of the Great War Reconsidered: Beyond Modern Memory*. Houndmills, Basingstoke: Palgrave, 2001.

Raitt, Suzanne, and Trudi Tate, eds. *Women's Fiction and the Great War*. Oxford: Oxford University Press, 1997.

Ryder, Mary R. "Dear, Tender-Hearted, Uncomprehending America": Dorothy Canfield Fisher's and Edith Wharton's Fictional Responses to the First World War." In Quinn and Trout, *The Literature of the Great War Reconsidered*, 143–55.

Sherry, Vincent, ed. *The Cambridge Companion to the Literature of the First World War*. Cambridge: University of Cambridge Press, 2005.

Simmonds, Roy S. *The Two Worlds of William March*. Tuscaloosa: University of Alabama Press, 1984.

Smith, Angela K. *The Second Battlefield: Women, Modernism, and the First World War*. Manchester: Manchester University Press, 2000.

Springs, Elliot White. *Letters from a War Bird: The World War I Correspondence of Elliott White Springs*. Edited by David Kirk Vaughan. Columbia: University of South Carolina Press, 2012.

Stout, Janis P. *Katherine Anne Porter: A Sense of the Times*. Charlottesville: University of Virginia Press, 1995.

Tate, Trudi. *Modernism, History, and the First World War*. Manchester: Manchester University Press, 1998.

Trout, Steven, ed. *American Prose Writers of World War I: A Documentary Volume*. Vol. 316 of *Dictionary of Literary Biography*. Detroit: Thomson Gale, 2005.

———. "From 'The Namesake' to *One of Ours*: Willa Cather on War." *American Literary Realism* 37, no. 2 (Winter 2005): 117–39.

———. *Memorial Fictions: Willa Cather and the First World War*. Lincoln: University of Nebraska Press, 2002.

———. *On the Battlefield of Memory: The First World War and American Remembrance, 1919–1941*. Tuscaloosa: University of Alabama Press, 2010.

———. "'Where Do We Go From Here?': Ernest Hemingway's 'Soldier's Home' and American Veterans of World War I." *Hemingway Review* 20, no. 1 (Fall 2000): 5–21.

Wallis, R. Sanborn III. *The American Novel of War: A Critical Analysis and Classification System.* Jefferson, N.C.: McFarland, 2012.

Walsh, Jeffrey. *American War Literature: 1914 to Vietnam.* New York: St. Martin's, 1982.

Washington, Ida H. *Dorothy Canfield Fisher: A Biography.* Boston: New England Press, 1982.

Whalen, Mark. *The Great War and the Culture of the New Negro.* Gainesville: University Press of Florida, 2008.

Wharton, Edith. *A Backward Glance.* New York: Scribner, 1934.

Index of Topics